MY LIFE IN NEVADA POLITICS

My Life in
Nevada Politics

The Memoirs of Senator Richard H. Bryan

RICHARD H. BRYAN

WITH JOHN L. SMITH

UNIVERSITY OF NEVADA PRESS | *Reno & Las Vegas*

University of Nevada Press I Reno, Nevada 89557 USA
www.unpress.nevada.edu
Copyright © 2024 by University of Nevada Press
All rights reserved

Manufactured in the United States of America

FIRST PRINTING
Cover photographs courtesy of Richard H. Bryan.

Library of Congress Cataloging-in-Publication Data
Names: Bryan, Richard H., 1937- author. I Smith, John L., 1960- author.
Title: My life in Nevada politics : the memoirs of Senator Richard H. Bryan / Richard
    H. Bryan ; with John L. Smith.
Other titles: Memoirs of Senator Richard H. Bryan
Description: Reno, Nevada : University of Nevada Press, [2024] I Includes index. I
    Summary: "The political memoir *My Life in Nevada Politics* tells the entertaining,
    informative, and, at times, poignant story of Richard H. Bryan's humble beginnings
    in Las Vegas to the top of the rough-and-tumble world of Nevada politics at a time
    of great change in the state and the nation. The result is a story that gives keen insight
    into the mechanics of politics and serves as a must-read for anyone interested in the
    political history of the latter half of the twentieth century."—Provided by publisher.
Subjects: LCSH: Bryan, Richard H. I United States. Congress. Senate--Biography. I
    Legislators--United States--Biography. I Governors--Nevada--Biography. I Poli-
    ticians--Nevada--Biography. I United States--Politics and government--1989- I
    Nevada--Politics and government--20th century. I Las Vegas (Nev.)--Biography. I
    Nevada--Biography. I LCGFT: Autobiographies.
Classification: LCC E840.8.B786 A3 2024 I DDC 328.73/092 [B]—dc23/eng/20240314
LC record available at https://lccn.loc.gov/2024004455

ISBN 9781647792190 (paper)
ISBN 9781647791766 (ebook)
LCCN: 2024004455

The paper used in this book meets the requirements of American National Standard for
Information Sciences—Permanence of Paper for Printed Library Materials, ANSI/NISO
Z39.48-1992 (R2002).

To Bonnie Fairchild Bryan, Nevada's First Lady,
and mine. Without her, many of the chapters
in this book could not have been written.

"It is not the critic who counts; not the man who points out how the strong man stumbles, or where the doer of deeds could have done them better. The credit belongs to the man who is actually in the arena, whose face is marred by dust and sweat and blood; who strives valiantly; who errs, who comes short again and again, because there is no effort without error and shortcoming . . ."

—THEODORE ROOSEVELT

Contents

Illustrations follow page 246

MY LIFE IN NEVADA POLITICS

CHAPTER I

Early Years

I was born in Washington, DC, in 1937. It was a year that portended an ominous future in Europe and the Far East. Japan renewed its conquest of China and by the year's end the world would be horrified by the Rape of Nanking. The German Luftwaffe bombed Guernica as the Spanish Civil War raged on. Italian fascist strongman Mussolini launched an attack on Ethiopia in 1935, and the next year Germany reoccupied the Rhineland.

At home the Great Depression continued to cast a long shadow on the economic horizon. Although much had improved since Franklin D. Roosevelt declared, in his first inaugural address, "We have nothing to fear but fear itself," eight million Americans were unemployed, and the gross domestic product had not recovered from the pre-Depression level of 1928.

The fiery crash of the Hindenburg airship at Lakehurst, New Jersey, was a major news story that year. The disappearance of Amelia Earhart, America's favorite aviatrix, as she circumnavigated the globe captured the public's attention. In San Francisco, the Golden Gate Bridge was completed.

The New Deal was in full swing in the nation's capital. That is where my story begins as the son of Lillie and Oscar Bryan. My father's origin is shrouded in a family mystery. No one knew, or at least was willing to say, anything about his parentage. He was given the last name Bryan by the woman who raised him. Bryan was the name of her previous husband. The family always referred to her as "Grandmother Bryan." She maintained that she took him in as an infant, but there is some family speculation that perhaps she had him out of wedlock. His childhood was nomadic and lonely. He spent some time on a ranch in Pegram, Idaho, and later moved to Rock Springs, Wyoming, and Ogden, Utah. I recall him telling me of the winter of the Spanish Flu pandemic when he was a child of ten; he came home from school and read a note left by his caretaker that began, "Oscar, I am sorry I can't take it any longer. I am leaving." He was alone.

In 1926, he came to Las Vegas to live with his sister and enrolled as a senior at Las Vegas High School. After graduation and laying out a year, he enrolled in the University of Nevada in Reno to pursue his dream of becoming a lawyer. It was the Roaring '20s, the era of the speakeasy, and Reno was as dry as a rain forest. Fraternities and sororities dominated life on campus, and my father wanted to be a fraternity man. He became president of the Sigma Phi Sigma fraternity and debated on the team with Alan Bible, later a Nevada attorney general and US senator. His debate coach, and later mine, was Bob Griffin. In later years he would often recount stories from his college days. It was obvious he had many fond memories of fraternity life during his undergraduate years.

Graduating in 1932 in the depths of the Depression, he considered going to law school a distant dream. He campaigned for US Representative James Scrugham of Nevada that year, and later Scrugham opened the door of opportunity for him. In the meantime, he worked as a rodman on a highway survey crew near Ash Meadows, about one hundred miles from Las Vegas. Leonard Wilson, later a prominent Las Vegas attorney, was his tent mate.

For a poor young man eager to pursue the law in the '30s, going to Washington, DC, and getting a government job during the day while attending law school at night provided the most realistic opportunity to obtain a legal degree. Congressmen and senators through a system of patronage were allocated a number of appointments they could make to entry-level jobs in the burgeoning federal bureaucracy. My father's time came in 1936 when Scrugham's office informed him that a position as a purchasing agent was available in the Agriculture Adjustment Administration, a New Deal agency in the Department of Agriculture.

Leaving Las Vegas with a packed lunch and a few dollars from his sister, he arrived in DC in the winter of 1936. There he found hundreds of young people who were pouring into the city to fill new positions created by the Roosevelt administration. A picture of FDR always graced our home along with a number of Roosevelt biographies. Later that year, my dad met my mother at the Old Post Office building on Pennsylvania Avenue, recently the location of a Trump Hotel, and that fall they were married in Leesburg, Virginia. I was born the following year.

My mother was a granddaughter of a Confederate Civil War veteran and a daughter of a brakeman on the Southern Railway. Born in Alexandria, Virginia, one of four sisters, she was a product of the Old South. Educated in the Alexandria public school system, she was an excellent student and studied Latin in high school for four years. In the 1920s, young women from families of modest means never considered college, and that was certainly true in my mother's case.

In 1927, Liberty Bonds issued during World War I were maturing. My mother took an examination, passed, and was hired as a secretary in the Liberty Bond office in Washington, DC. She lived at home with her parents until she and my father were married. My mother was a devout Episcopalian, and I was baptized in Christ Church in Alexandria, where she had attended services since childhood. I was reminded often as a child that this was the church George Washington attended and where Robert E. Lee was confirmed. I attribute my lifelong passion for history to my mother and her pride in her Virginia heritage and all those Virginians who played such a prominent role in our nation's history. Among the first books I read was *The Life of George Washington* and *Robert E. Lee, Boy of Old Virginia*. I heard often from my mother about the noble character of both Virginians.

My earliest memory is attending nursery school at the Grasshopper Green, and the apartment where we lived in Presidential Gardens in the George Washington Building. I remember parking my little toy car in a closet surrounded by my father's law books. Many years later, in retracing the steps of my childhood, I learned that the portico of the George Washington Building was constructed from lumber that had been used for scaffolding at FDR's second inaugural.

My grandfather was a kind, soft-spoken man who would take me to the corner store for an ice cream cone. He shaved with a straight-edge razor, and I was fascinated by the razor strap that hung from the bathroom sink. He died in December 1941.

My father had graduated from law school in the preceding year, but we delayed our move to Las Vegas because of my grandfather's failing health. At that time, it was the custom for the deceased to be placed in an open casket at home where relatives and friends could come by and pay their respects. Such was the case with my grandfather, and I remember the family gathering to pay their respects.

On a crisp, foggy January morning, we were packed and ready for our trip to Las Vegas in our 1939 Plymouth. Before departing we visited my grandfather's grave site. I was too young to appreciate all the emotions my mother was feeling. She had just buried her father, and she was leaving her family and the only place that had been her home for an uncertain future in a dusty desert town of just 8,500 people on the eastern edge of the Mojave Desert. My mother was crying, and I was upset. My father explained that this was where my mother's father was buried.

My life in Nevada was about to begin. Our trip west was uneventful. My father drove, and my mother with map in hand was his navigator. I had a small suitcase filled with my books, and when my mother wasn't navigating, she read to me. En route to Las Vegas, we stopped in Ogden, Utah to visit my father's brother George and his wife. We slept in an enclosed sleeping porch. That night a powerful wind came up, and my mother steadied my cot with her hand. My father assured her, "Nothing to worry about. The wind always blows like this in Ogden." When we made our way out of town the next morning, downed trees blocked the highway in all directions. So much for the wind always blowing like this in Ogden.

We arrived in Las Vegas during the first month of our country's involvement in World War II. Housing was difficult to find, but my father's sister Elnora and her husband, Charlie, owned property on Main Street between Lewis and Clark Avenues, where the new Las Vegas City Hall now stands. Suffice to say it was not the Taj Mahal. My father, who was waiting to take the Nevada Bar Exam, worked a swing shift at the new magnesium plant in Henderson. My mother worked for the US Bureau of Reclamation and commuted daily to Boulder City, now as then the garden spot of Southern Nevada. I remember spending a day or two in Boulder City when my mother was at work. Even as a child I recognized there was something special about it. My mother dreaded the drive to Boulder City that first summer. Cars had no air conditioning then, and it must have been brutal. After that first summer my mother got a new job as a deputy county clerk in the Clark County Courthouse, which was just a couple of blocks from where we lived.

My mother and I were alone most evenings. It was all but impossible during the war years to get a new telephone hookup, and we had no phone. One night shortly after I went to bed in a small alcove that served as my bedroom, a stranger started tapping on my window. I was frightened, as was my mother. With no way to call for assistance, we huddled in the bathroom and locked the door, waiting for what seemed like an eternity. At last, she cautiously opened the door. The stranger had gone. In retrospect, living as we did across the street from the railroad tracks, it was probably some hungry fellow looking for a meal.

Although not yet five, I was interested in all things related to the military. The war effort had a pervasive influence on all aspects of community life. Today, we would call it recycling, but then it was assisting in the war effort by crushing tin cans and taking them to a collection point. Tin foil was saved and reused. I did my best. Every civilian had a ration book issued by the government. I remember I had one. Those items that were rationed required coupons, or a certain number of points before you could purchase them. I recall going to the grocery store on Saturdays at Sewell's Market on Third and Fremont, which is the present site of The D hotel-casino. My mother was an inveterate coffee drinker, and coffee was on the ration list. Several women with whom she worked at the courthouse were members of the Church of Jesus Christ of Latter-day Saints (LDS church) and didn't drink coffee, so she was able to trade her coupons on other commodities for all the coffee she needed.

The Las Vegas Army Air Corps base, later renamed Nellis Air Force Base, had an enormous impact on the small community. Uniforms, insignias, ranks, and the branches of the services fascinated me. My parents gave me a poster which identified by insignia all officer and enlisted ranks, and branches of the army and navy. I quickly memorized them. My parents bought me a little dress white navy uniform with the shoulder boards of a full lieutenant. It was my favorite outfit.

The army called up my father twice for what was described as a pre-induction physical. Its purpose was to determine fitness for military service. As a child, my father had fallen down a flight of stairs and suffered an injury to one of his eyes that impaired his vision. He was rejected for service on the first call-up. The second call-up came later in the war when the manpower pool was severely depleted. That made induction more likely. I remember discussing with him what branch of the army he would likely serve in, and he pointed to the poster on my wall and said, "Probably Quartermaster Corps." He was rejected for service once again.

My father was anxious to establish himself. In the first year of our new life in Las Vegas, my father filed to run for the Nevada Assembly. It was an ill-conceived venture. He had no money, and he had been away from Las Vegas for six years. He lost the election that fall. That was not the only family setback that year. He was unsuccessful in his first attempt to pass the Nevada Bar Exam.

At five years old, I did not appreciate the impact of both disappointments on my father. My mother later told me that he was so discouraged that he wanted to return to Washington, DC, to work for the government again. My mother, a steel magnolia, urged him to remain in Las Vegas.

One family that my parents socialized with quite frequently was the Horsey family, Chic and Laverne and their daughter Barbara Lee. Chic's father was politically active and later served on the Nevada Supreme Court. Chic would go on to establish the Horsey Insurance Agency and found Nevada Savings and Loan. Barbara Lee and I would play together while our parents visited, often past our bedtime. On those occasions, we would be tucked away in bed, side by side. On one occasion many years later as governor, I was asked to give a speech and saw her in the audience of several hundred people. I pointed her out and announced that she was the first woman I ever slept with—much to her mortification. The audience was aghast. Had the governor lost his mind publicly humiliating this woman? After a long pause, I indicated that we were both four and a half years old at the time.

The biggest event in my life that first year was starting kindergarten at Las Vegas Grammar School, which we all called Fifth Street School. The building now enjoys a historic designation and is still in use by the City of Las Vegas. As mothers have for generations, on the first day of school my mother took me to meet the teacher, the legendary Doris Hancock. After her long career as an educator, a school was named in her honor. She was a traditional kindergarten teacher: strict, structured, and proper. In the years before preschool became part of the American family experience, kindergarten was more of a socializing experience than an academic one. There were two half-day sessions, one in the morning and one in the afternoon. I was in the morning session. Stories were read to us, and we learned our colors and numbers. That was the outer reach of the academic challenge. Each day we took a nap on a little mat we brought from home. Frequently notes were pinned to my shirt advising my parents of my progress. One in particular I remember. The assignment was coloring a kite, which was outlined on a piece of paper. The note read, "Richard needs to learn how to stay within the lines." That may have been prophetic of the challenges I would face in life. Years later I was at a gathering with Miss Hancock in attendance, and I said, "You were right." That first year I met Phil Waldman, and we became good friends. It was one of many friendships that would play an important role in my childhood.

At the end of the year, I had a perfect attendance and I received a certificate. With those in my class gathered in a semicircle, I was asked to show it to each student. I was so proud.

That summer my father continued his job at BMI (Basic Magnesium Inc.) and studied for the bar exam. My only recollection of his work was a large yellow sticker on the windshield of our '39 Plymouth, which must have given him access to the plant.

My father took the bar exam again in Reno that fall. My mother and I joined him by bus. It seemed like an endless journey with wartime speed limits being imposed. My most memorable experience was stopping in Tonopah at the historic Mizpah Hotel. The Tonopah stop was a restroom break and an opportunity to get something to eat. It was also a mortifying experience. My ever-protective mother did not want me to go into the men's room alone, and she dragged me into the ladies' room. I was so embarrassed.

The fall of 1943 would be a turning point for our family. Gray Gubler, Clark County district attorney and a bar examiner, had offered my father a job as his only deputy if he passed the bar. Many years later my mother shared with me that a few weeks before the bar results came out, Gubler had asked her what my father's bar exam number was. She told him.

The bar results were announced in October. Only two applicants from Las Vegas were successful, my father and C. Norman Cornwall, who would become a family friend. Their bar numbers were seven and eleven. I have often wondered over the years about Gubler's question to my mother. However it happened, our family's luck had changed from the year before, and our future had changed along with it. My mother gave me the opportunity to miss school and attend my father's swearing-in as a newly admitted member of the Nevada Bar. I declined, fearful that it would compromise my perfect attendance record. It is a decision I later regretted when I was old enough to understand how important passing the bar was. There would be no perfect attendance for me that year. A few weeks later, I came down with the chicken pox and missed several days of school.

The Clark County District Attorney's office was in the Clark County Courthouse, not far from where we lived. In 1943, the work week was five-and-a-half days. The courthouse was open until noon on Saturday. One Saturday when I was visiting my father at the DA's office, he looked at me and said, "You need a haircut." He gave me a silver dollar and said, "Go over to Art Harris' Barber Shop. They know me there, and they'll take care of you. I'll meet you at the barber shop shortly." With a silver dollar clutched in my hand, I was on my way. Silver dollars were commonly given as change rather than paper dollars then. If paper dollars were preferred the expression was, "Could I get soft dollars for change?"

The barber shop was crowded, and I waited my turn. When it came, Harris asked me what my name was, and when I told him he responded, "I know your dad." That gave me a boost of confidence, which faded when he finished my haircut and said, "That'll be six bits." Six bits? I had no idea what he was talking about. I was afraid I wouldn't have enough money and would be embarrassed because my father had not yet arrived at the barbershop. Very tentatively, and with my hand trembling, I handed him the silver dollar and nervously awaited his response. He returned from the cash register with a quarter as my change. Later my dad explained two bits was a quarter, four bits was fifty cents, and six bits was seventy-five cents. Then he treated me to a milkshake at the Rancho Grande Creamery, which was a couple of blocks from our house. The cost: two bits. My anxiety had been worth it.

The Huntridge subdivision was under construction in 1943. Even by today's standards it was large. It was bordered on the north by Charleston Boulevard, not yet completed to Maryland Parkway; on the south by Oakey with no development beyond it; on the west by Tenth Street; and the east by Fifteenth Street, with vacant desert all the way to the Boulder Highway. The sales office was located at Tenth and Charleston. On one wall was a large map of the subdivision with pins indicating which lots were sold and which were available. After touring the subdivision, our family selected a corner lot at 1141 Maryland Parkway on the east side of the park. The price for our new home was $5,500. Family and friends questioned why we would want to live so far from town.

For me, the Huntridge years would be among the happiest in my life. Here I made friends that would last a lifetime and made memories that I would cherish forever. Our family's move to Huntridge was a defining event in my childhood. Our home, all nine hundred or so square feet of it, was a vast improvement over the old and very dilapidated house on Main Street. Built during the war, it consisted of two bedrooms, one bathroom, living room, dining area, and kitchen with a very small laundry area. The doorknobs on all the interior doors were made of cheap plastic that had a yellowish cast to them. By way of contrast, the floors were beautiful parquet that over the years I helped my mother polish on many occasions. The kitchen countertops were linoleum and probably a health hazard, capturing bacteria in all the cuts left from carving. An oil furnace provided heat, and a rooftop swamp cooler worked well in the dry climate, making the scorching summer bearable. Lighting the furnace always provided some excitement. The standard operating procedure: opening its door, priming the furnace, and finally lighting it by tossing in a flaming section of newspaper while praying you didn't blow up the house.

Almost no exterior amenities were provided. Each homeowner was responsible for all landscaping. We struggled with the lawn that first winter. Blow sand was laid down and topped with seed and fertilizer. The wind frequently blew sections of the yard away. Many of the shrubs we planted died because they were unsuited to the desert's harsh soil. Oleanders, a staple in the desert and virtually indestructible, flourished.

Las Vegas was growing, and Huntridge was the nicest new sub-division in the city. Tom Oakey was the developer, and the last street in the subdivision bears his name. He lived across the parkway from our house. As a child, I was told Hollywood stars Loretta Young and Irene Dunne had invested in the development. A year after we moved in, hundreds of bales of peat moss, to be used as fertilizer, were delivered to the park in anticipation of a lawn being planted. We kids stacked bales of peat moss and made forts to play in. It was a grand time.

The neighborhood had kids, lots of them, on every block. Their parents were doctors, lawyers, accountants, insurance agents, crafts-men, and employees of small businesses in the community. All the houses were the same size with the same amenities. Only the eleva-tion varied. The doctor's kids lived in the same sized house as the truck driver's kids. During the war years, you couldn't buy a new car or travel great distances because of gas rationing. Everyone seemed to have the same standard of living. In the immediate postwar years, more affluent families converted their carport into an extra room or made other improvements such as replacing old, rough asphalt with a concrete driveway.

The first week in Huntridge I made two new friends, Mickey Carrol, whose father was stationed at the air base, and Don Fen-nell, whose father worked at an electrical repair store. Although we moved into Huntridge in the fall, I remained at Fifth Street School until the end of the semester. My new school was John S. Park, where I reconnected with some of my kindergarten classmates, including Phil Waldman. Although I was behind the rest of the class, I caught up by the end of the school year. The school consisted of temporary buildings with about thirty students in each classroom.

Unlike today, where children have endless entertainment options, kids then were expected to provide their own entertainment. And we did. Hide and seek, kick the can, cowboys and Indians, and later when the park was completed, pickup baseball games during the summer months. We flew kites in the windy months of spring. During summer we would ride bicycles into the desert to the south of Oakey, making a stop at what today is the intersection of Sahara and Maryland Parkway, where an artesian well flowed to the sur-face, and we rested in the shade of the tall cottonwoods. The water was so cold it made your teeth hurt. How refreshing it was on a hot summer day.

From the artesian spring we would ride farther into the desert in what today would be Paradise Valley. The valley featured natural sand dunes. Many a day we made our way out to them, climbing to the top and jumping off. It was great fun.

In our family, my mother had two cardinal rules: be home for lunch, unless you had made other arrangements, and always be home for dinner. Within those parameters, the day was our own for the making. Parents today do not enjoy the luxury of this small-town, bygone era. Sadly, an unaccompanied walk to a neighbor's house generates anxiety for today's parents. It is a different time with real risks, but sometimes I wonder if we may be overprotective. All life has risks, and our children cannot be protected in a cocoon of safety forever.

The war dominated much of our activities in our first two years in Huntridge. We planted Victory Gardens to show our support for the war effort. Mickey's family planted their entire backyard. We planted a much smaller garden. I planted cucumbers, radishes, and carrots. My cucumbers were county fair quality. The radishes and carrots didn't fare as well. Boosting morale on the home front was important as the horrendous casualties from Europe and the Pacific mounted. One of my cousins was stationed in Europe, and he sent me a German bayonet, which I prized. Another cousin was in the China Burma India Theater. He sent me part of a parachute. My Uncle Keith was in the Philippines, and he sent me some of the local currency.

The army air base periodically held open houses for the community with a variety of planes on display. I could identify most of them from a little book that my parents had given me. The P-38 Lockheed Lightning with its twin tail was one of my favorites, and the Bell Airacobra was particularly sleek. The B-17 Flying Fortress, frequently seen in newsreels, generated considerable attention. Some planes on display had visible battle damage with the sheet metal repairs obvious. As part of a nationwide tour, at the old War Memorial Building, which later served as the Las Vegas City Hall, German aircraft that had been shot down were displayed. In the last year of the war, a B-29 was flown in for an open house. The B-29 had several advanced systems, including the first pressurized cabin. This enabled pilots and crew to move around without wearing oxygen masks. The entire plane, however, was not pressurized—only the compartments where the crewmembers were stationed. A long tunnel connected the two sections, and crawling through the tunnel was pretty exciting stuff for a seven-year-old boy.

The war had an impact on all of us, young and old alike. As kids we did not appreciate the enormous toll it took on families that had just lost loved ones or the anxiety families endured. The invasion of Normandy and the island-hopping campaign in the Pacific would bring a new wave of casualty reports. Many homes in Las Vegas, as throughout the nation, had small pennants hanging in the front window. The pennants were trimmed in red and blue with a white background with a blue star or stars in the center depicting the number of family members in the service. My aunt and uncle's home had a pennant with two blue stars indicating two sons in the service. Newsreels in movie theaters depicted the most recent military action in Europe or the Pacific.

Wartime shortages manifested themselves in unusual ways. Horse-drawn trucks delivered milk to our house for a time. Sliced bread was not available. War Department regulations eliminated bread-slicing machines. We did not have a bread knife, and slicing a loaf with a butcher knife to make a sandwich was a real chore.

I have no specific memory of the Normandy invasion on June 6, 1944. But in September, the Allies broke through at Saint-Lô. Mickey Carrol's mother taped to her living room wall a large map of France, Belgium, the Netherlands, and Germany. Each day she would listen to the radio and learn of the Allies' latest advances. Mickey and I would rush over to his house after school, and his mother would inform us of the battlefield progress that day. Our job was to locate the towns and cities that had been captured by the Allies and color in the advance with a red pencil. Berlin was depicted on the map, and even as children we understood that when we reached Berlin the war in Europe would be over.

My brother was born that June, and I faced my first moral dilemma. I was seven. The occasion was my brother's baptism at the old Episcopal Church at Second and Carson. The Rev. Kerstetter was the rector, and I was an acolyte. During the service the rector handed me a book of matches and asked me to light a candle. My mother had always told me to never strike a match. As family and friends looked on, I was paralyzed with uncertainty. What should I do? Follow the rector's instruction, or heed my mother's warning? I hesitated for what seemed like a lifetime, until my mother nodded that it was okay to proceed. As it turned out, I didn't know how to strike the match on the matchbook cover, and the rector had to light the candle himself.

In the fall of 1944, the Huntridge Theater opened a block from my house. I attended the first Saturday morning matinee. The admission for a child at other theaters in town was fourteen cents. I stood at the end of a long line that morning with fourteen cents in my pocket that my mother had given me. Standing in line, I learned the price of admission for the matinee was twenty-five cents. I hustled eleven cents, a penny at a time, before reaching the ticket booth. It was my first of many, many fundraising endeavors to come. Upon reflection, that may have been the genesis of my intense dislike for fundraising. The matinee itself consisted of a feature-length movie, typically a Western, a special feature, often the Three Stooges, a cartoon, and the all-important serial adventure. Each Saturday the serial ended with the hero facing real danger. This was designed to encourage your attendance next Saturday to learn how he escaped.

In the summer of 1945, my mother, little brother Paul, and I traveled to Harlan, Iowa, to be with my mother's sister during the final days of her pregnancy. We traveled by train. It was crowded with men in uniform being transported to their next assignment. We traveled by Pullman Car, which featured a self-enclosed compartment that enabled us to be seated during the day and converted into sleeping berths at night. It also had a sink and toilet. We were traveling in style. Cal Cory would become my father's law partner, and he was a favorite of Nevada's senior senator, Pat McCarran. It's possible that Cory's connection with McCarran made that possible. Shortly after Cory graduated from law school, the senator arranged for him to become the local counsel for the Union Pacific Railroad. McCarran made things happen for the young men who enjoyed his patronage, and they were intensely loyal to him. McCarran understood the role these young men would play in their communities once they returned to Nevada and began their legal careers—and how that would be beneficial to him politically. For years after his death these men joined for dinner periodically to salute their patron and proudly call themselves "McCarran's Boys."

My mother's sister was expected to have a complicated delivery because of a fall she had taken. My aunt's husband, my Uncle Keith, was in the Philippines, and my mother wanted to be with her sister. In the evening the neighbors would gather outside on the lawn and talk about various things, but the war was always discussed. Everyone understood that the war in the Pacific would not end until the Japanese homeland was invaded. Everyone knew the casualties would be enormous, and my uncle would likely be a part of the invasion. Unbeknown to the public, on July 16, coincidentally my eighth birthday, the atomic bomb was successfully tested in the New Mexico desert. Not long after, the bomb was dropped on Hiroshima. There was much excitement throughout the country and a sense that the war might be near its end. My aunt even considered naming the new baby Victoria if she were born on V-J Day (Victory over Japan Day).

The war ended in August, and back home school was ready to begin. After classes finished for the day, the race was on to get home and listen to the radio. Serials were very popular. Jack Armstrong, the Lone Ranger, Speedy, and the Green Arrow were among my favorites.

There were school carnivals, but the biggest event each year was Helldorado, sponsored by the Elks Lodge. There were several days of a rodeo. The Old Timers Parade featured stagecoaches, the Twenty-Mule Team, and all sorts of entries from around the West. The horses were beautifully groomed, and saddles and bridles were often trimmed in silver. Following the Old Timers Parade was a Saturday Children's Parade, and on Sunday came the Beauty Parade with floats sponsored by the Strip hotels. Some were large enough to accommodate a swimming pool, and all were adorned by showgirls from the hotels. I remember riding in one of those parades with veterans of the Spanish-American War, World War I, and World War II. It was heady stuff.

My father was an officer in the Elks Lodge, and all the officers rode in the Old Timers Parade. They were also introduced on horseback at the beginning of the rodeo each night. For my father this was not a problem. He had grown up on a ranch and was very comfortable on horseback. In the parade he would wave to the crowd and guide his horse through several moves. For other officers of the lodge who were not experienced riders, the parade was a challenging experience with no waving or horsing around. They gripped tightly onto the saddle horn and prayed that the parade would end without incident. Even more challenging was the introduction at the rodeo, attended by several thousand locals. After being introduced, each officer would ride out to the center of the arena, rein his horse to a stop, and align himself with the other officers who were previously introduced. This could be tricky, but my dad enjoyed it. He was a bit of a showoff and wanted everyone around the arena to know he could ride. He would charge out of the chute galloping at top speed, rein in his horse, spin around and doff his hat to the crowd. The last officer introduced was the exalted ruler, the highest officer in the hierarchy of the lodge, who was announced with considerable fanfare. Some years later as a Boy Scout selling soft drinks at the rodeo, I watched as the exalted ruler came out of the chute and reined his horse too hard. The animal stopped on a dime and the exalted ruler went flying off. To make matters worse, this was only the first night of the rodeo. He had several more nights to go. The next night I happened to be near the exalted ruler's family box, and one of his kids asked his mother, "Will daddy fall off the horse again tonight?"

Of all the Helldorado activities, none was more popular than the Helldorado Village at North Fifth and Bonanza. That's where each year a carnival with a Ferris wheel and a midway full of games and goodies came to town.

The stadium where the rodeo was held was called Cashman Field, in honor of one of the leading families in the community. Jim Cashman Sr. was an active Elk and served as a trustee of the lodge for many years. The stadium, which accommodated several thousand people, was a community effort built by volunteers from the Elks Lodge. On Saturdays, the lodge members would get together to assist in construction. The Elks auxiliary, the Emblem Club, prepared a noon meal. As an officer in the lodge, my father was there many Saturdays. He brought me along on several occasions. I was too young to be of any real help. But as the elevation sight lines for the stadium's steps were laid out, I was a rodman, and the surveyor would instruct me to move right or left, up or down, until he got the right elevation. The completion of the stadium was a big community event. My dad was the exalted ruler by then and presided over the dedication. A pageant called "Vegas in Calico" was part of the dedication ceremony, and I participated with many others appropriately attired in western wear.

I was blessed, as so many of my generation were, with wonderful teachers. In second grade, Miss Strand was stern but strict, and I benefited from that. The only downside that year was my pathological dislike of math, or as we called it, arithmetic. Math required intellectual discipline. History, already a favorite subject, was largely memory. I could have used more of the former. In third grade, I was unsuccessful with the only nonacademic classroom project during my years at John S. Park. At the beginning of the year, each of us was given a candle wick, and each week Miss Elifson, our teacher, would heat a huge vat of candle wax and we would dip our wick in the vat. In theory, each week we would add a new layer of wax to the wick, and by the end of the year we would have a large, homemade candle. Alas, I left my candle in the vat of wax too long and managed to reverse the process. By the end of the year I wound up with the scrawniest candle in the class.

It was around this time that I let my classmates know my career goal. When asked what I wanted to be when I grew up, my answer never varied: not a firefighter or a baseball star, but the governor of Nevada.

Miss Carmody, our fourth-grade teacher, was very athletic. She wore her hair in the style of "Babe" Didrikson Zaharias, a champion golfer and one of America's great women athletes of the era. Jack Binion, who later rose to prominence as a premier casino operator on Fremont Street at the Horseshoe Club, joined our class that year. His arrival in a Cadillac limousine caused quite a buzz. He lived some distance away on Bonanza Road, but we did not know that. Everybody else rode a bike or walked to school. That year, I had a brief thespian career with a nice role in the class production of *Peter Pan*. We performed before the other classes in preparation for a final performance before our parents, but I caught the measles before the crowning show and had to stay home.

In the fifth grade, Lucile Chandler was my teacher. She drove a Studebaker, and when she wanted a new one, she always drove back to South Bend, Indiana, where they were manufactured, to pick up the latest model. She was one of my favorites. We studied American history that year, and it was obvious to me she loved the subject as much as I did. She was from Minnesota, the Mesabi Range, and she would share with us the hardships endured by the early pioneers.

Every year there would be a school carnival, and each class was responsible for a booth. These were simpler times, but we always looked forward to the school carnival.

I'd like to say I was another DiMaggio in those summer pickup baseball games played almost daily at the park across the street from my house, but in truth I was not very good. If you were able to hit the ball out of the park into the street, it was called an "automatic," our version of a home run. One year, I was good enough to hit a few automatics. More often, I was tasked with retrieving the ball when it landed in Mr. Oakey's yard.

Later, organized teams were formed, and a regular schedule was played. I was on the Hudson Hornets, which was sponsored by Phil Waldman's father, the local Hudson dealer. The best team was the dreaded Ashworth Outlaws, which sported Dave Powell, Jerry Eggers, and the more gifted athletes in the area.

One summer I took swimming lessons at the Biltmore Hotel, at Main and Bonanza, some distance from our home. As I later came to understand, my father had a divorce client who was a swimming instructor and she was staying at the Biltmore Hotel to establish her six weeks of residency, a requirement before obtaining a divorce. An uncontested divorce fee was $150. I suspect my swimming lessons were in exchange for legal fees. The Biltmore was new then, and apparently investors believed they had found a promising location. Today, it is difficult to visualize the corner of Main and Bonanza as a prime site for a resort hotel. Like its contemporaries, the El Rancho Vegas and the Hotel Last Frontier on what came to be known as the Las Vegas Strip, it had a large dining room where floorshows were performed nightly and a pool in front that faced the street. The only person I remember meeting at the pool was Jack Dix, who lived in the nearby neighborhood. A few years later when I ran for sophomore class president, Jack cast the tiebreaking vote for me.

I liked swimming and was pretty good at it. No one in Huntridge had a swimming pool. In fact, I knew of no one in the whole community who did. The venues of choice were Twin Lakes and the Old Ranch. Twin Lakes was so far out of town that a parent had to take us. In my father's time, it not only had a swimming pool, but also featured a dance pavilion surrounded by a spring-fed lake. It was called Lorenzi's after the pioneer who built it.

By the '40s the dance pavilion was in ruins, but the enormous swimming pool remained a popular attraction. In its center was a tower with water flowing from the top. You could sit on a shelf at the base of the tower. In recent times the area has been renamed Lorenzi Park. The swimming pool has been replaced by a large city park that's enjoyed by a new generation of Las Vegans.

The Las Vegas Strip was growing in the 1940s. the El Rancho Vegas was followed by the Last Frontier, the Thunderbird, and the Flamingo. By the early 1950s, the Sands, Desert Inn, and Sahara joined the neon-lighted lineup.

Credit cards such as Visa and MasterCard did not exist in the '40s. As part of a marketing effort to the local professional and business community, the Strip hotels established city ledger accounts, which allowed locals to charge for lunches and dinners at casino properties. It was a great hook that encouraged local businesses to patronize the hotel and bring their families for special events.

An additional benefit of a city ledger card was that it included swimming privileges for family members at the hotels. With my father's city ledger account, I swam frequently at the El Rancho, Last Frontier, and Flamingo.

That era came to an end as the Strip grew, but it was a glorious time while it lasted. By the time I was in high school, we had to sneak into the pools at the Sands and other hotels and we were frequently spotted by the lifeguard and asked to leave.

Scouting was a big part of my youth, but my Cub Scout career was brief. I was a member of Pack 73 of the Boulder Dam Area Council, and my den mother was Mrs. Hanson, whose son was a classmate. I made it through the Bobcat and Wolf rank before our den fell apart.

By spring 1949 many of my friends had turned twelve and were eligible to join the Boy Scouts. Two of my friends, Phil Waldman and John Gibson, joined the B'Nai B'rith–sponsored Troop 70. That summer they attended camp for a week in the Spring Mountain Range. I was not yet twelve and I could not go, but I attended all the meetings. Later that summer I turned twelve and joined the troop.

The Elks Lodge–sponsored Troop 65 planned a trip to the Grand Canyon that September—an exciting venture in 1949. We left Troop 70 and joined Troop 65. Troop 63, one of the troops sponsored by the LDS church), traveled with us. The following year Jim Bilbray, a future US representative, joined the troop, as did Richard Sutton, who would later become a physician at the University of Utah where my son Richard Jr. served his medical residency.

Although my father was no longer the exalted ruler of the Elks Lodge, he remained an active member. Attending the first meeting as a member of Troop 65 and still a Tenderfoot, I was made the troop quartermaster. I would like to believe that my potential was immediately recognized, but that was not the case. Our scoutmaster, Jimmy Roberts, was an active Elk, and Francis Brown, who would soon rise to exalted ruler, was the lodge's liaison to the troop. Brown was so interested in my advancement that one of the Scouts asked me if Brown was my father.

The truth was less bizarre. Each exalted ruler selects his esquire. When my father held that position, he had chosen Brown to be his esquire, the first step in becoming the exalted ruler. In that era, the exalted ruler enjoyed a high profile in the community. It was a coveted office. Brown was profoundly grateful to my father, and he was always there for me.

The day after my appointment, my father and I went to the Fremont Drug store to meet owner Harvey Parvin, who was another friend of my father's. The quartermaster was responsible for maintaining a first-aid kit, and my father purchased $20 worth of supplies. I had enough medical supplies to operate a small Mobile Army Surgical Hospital (MASH) unit.

In the weeks that followed, I moved rapidly up the ranks attaining star rank by spring 1950, the year of a national jamboree at Valley Forge, Pennsylvania. I was selected to represent Troop 65.

About thirty-five of us representing Boulder Dam Area Council troops assembled in early summer at the Scout office downtown for a rehearsal of what was expected of us. A long list of equipment was required, all to be obtained through J. C. Penney's, the authorized Scout retailer. Among the items was a vinyl air mattress, which I had never seen before. The smell is one you never forget.

At the rehearsal, I came face to face with racial discrimination for the first time. The municipal pool was nearby, and we were given time off in the afternoon to go for a swim. All of us but one. The African American troop in Las Vegas was represented by one of the Hoggard brothers. The municipal pool was segregated: no Blacks allowed. As we all made our way to the pool, Hoggard leaned on his duffel bag watching us with a look of envy in his eyes.

In mid-June we departed Las Vegas by bus to Phoenix, where trains were preparing to take Scouts from Nevada, Arizona, and California to Valley Forge. We arrived late in the evening, and it was still brutally warm even for us Las Vegas desert rats. Hundreds of Scouts were arriving at the staging area. It reminded me of some of the World War II newsreels I had seen of troop trains heading for coastal cities on the way to Europe or the Pacific.

The golden age of passenger travel by train was over, at least for us. Our train was pulled over on a siding for freight trains, which enjoyed a priority over us. It took several days to travel through Texas. At a stop in Texarkana, the segregation of the Old South was evident. At the train station, drinking fountains and waiting rooms were identified as "Colored" and "Whites Only."

Our route would take us to Niagara Falls and then to New York City before our encampment at Valley Forge.

We had taken a burro with us as a mascot, and walking the streets of New York with our burro attracted a lot of attention. Curious passersby, barely believing their eyes, reached out and touched the animal. We stayed at the McAlpin Hotel, where most of us watched television for the first time, Arthur Godfrey and His Friends. We also went to Yankee Stadium and saw Joe DiMaggio play during the twilight of his career. Automat restaurants were all the rage, and we were fascinated by the rows of small, coin-operated boxes with glass windows, and the prospect of limitless slices of pie.

Next, we visited historical sites in Philadelphia, including the Liberty Bell and Betsy Ross's house, and Independence Hall, where the Declaration of Independence was signed. For a boy who loved history, it was a thrilling experience.

At Valley Forge, we departed the train with duffel bags on our shoulders and hiked to our campsite, where 47,000 Scouts were assembling. Each troop prepared its own meals. Cooking and other duties were rotated.

Shortly after we arrived, the Korean War broke out. That was big news; none of us could have anticipated how long it would last. After all, we had defeated two of the greatest military powers of the twentieth century just five years before.

General Eisenhower, World War II hero and soon to be named the supreme commander of the North Atlantic Treaty Organization (NATO), spoke to us the first night at Valley Forge. President Truman addressed us the next. We spent the next days meeting other Scouts from around the country.

We left Valley Forge for Washington, DC, and toured the historic sites of the city. My mother, brother, and sister were in DC visiting my mother's relatives who lived in nearby Annandale, Virginia. While we were in DC, my mother and I had lunch with Senator McCarran in the Senate Dining Room, where forty years later I would be the one playing host to my constituents. My father had lost the Democratic primary for district attorney that June to Roger Foley, who would later become state attorney general and a federal judge. Foley's four brothers would also hold public office.

McCarran was a powerful figure in Washington, and although he was cut out of the same bolt of cloth as rabid anti-Communist Joe McCarthy, he was a relentless advocate for Nevada's interests. A reform movement swept the country in the post–World War II era, and illegal gambling operations in Miami; Hot Springs, Arkansas; and elsewhere were shut down. Many viewed Nevada as a pariah state. Gambling debts were as a matter of law unenforceable because gambling was considered contrary to public morality. McCarran had many racial prejudices and character flaws, and his attempt to put his outspoken critic *Las Vegas Sun* publisher Hank Greenspun out of business was unconscionable. McCarran also fended off attacks on Nevada's gambling interests. For all his many faults, the Strip as we know it today might look quite different without his powerful influence.

Back home, I entered my eighth-grade year at John S. Park and continued to be involved in scouting with campouts at Red Rock Canyon, Death Valley, and icy Lee Canyon. My interest in scouting waned as I was about to enter high school. I had attained the rank of Life Scout, but I faltered on the trail to Eagle Scout, falling a few merit badges short.

When I was in the eighth grade, the Huntridge Theater once again assumed an important place in my life on Friday night in the form of the boy-meets-girl ritual. If you were lucky, you might even put your arm around your girlfriend. I had no such luck. Mrs. Hatfield, the stern-faced manager who patrolled the aisles with flashlight in hand, tapped you on the shoulder or gave you a withering stare that meant you had crossed the line of what she thought was appropriate.

My grade-school athletic career was undistinguished, to say the least. I played football in the seventh and eighth grades in what could charitably be described as the "B" League. I was a little better at basketball, but always found myself a seldom-used reserve. Track was the only sport I excelled in. I was fast and anchored the relay team to a first-place finish in the annual all-school meet.

As graduation approached, an election for class president was scheduled. Our two eighth-grade teachers were Miss Schultz and Miss Strand. Miss Schultz, an imperious and rail-slim six-footer, towered over most of us. She was not one of my favorites, and the feeling was mutual. When I was elected class president, she was not exactly rhapsodic. She was the only teacher I had before college who addressed me by my last name. When she was particularly exasperated, she would place her head on her arm and pound her fist on the desk, exclaiming loud enough for the class to hear, "That boy, little Mr. Bryan!"

She was a good teacher, demanding and committed to her students. She was the prototypical old schoolmarm who wore her hair up and drove an old 1928 Model A Coupe. Some of us tormented her, too, which does not speak well of us. One Halloween, we placed a potato in her exhaust pipe.

The night before we graduated, I presided over our class dinner at the Las Vegas Municipal Golf Course. The next morning, I presided over our graduation, which was outside on the concrete basketball court.

As summer began, to earn extra money I continued my practice of mowing and watering the neighbors' lawns while they were out of town. I did not have a power mower, and all the trimming was done by hand, but I earned enough money to pay for my indulgences.

Las Vegas was no longer a dusty railroad town, but not yet the Entertainment Capital of the World. It was an era before suburban malls. Most retail businesses were on Fremont Street, and Ronzone's was the community's answer to the big-city department store. It was a simpler time, to be sure.

Our family routine was simple as well. On Sunday we attended church, where I continued to serve as an acolyte. During the summer there were church picnics at Twin Lakes or at Edie Woodward's home on North Main Street with its large shade trees. On Sunday my father also bought the Los Angeles Examiner, whose color comics featured the adventures of Prince Valiant and his beautiful wife, Aleta. With the war over, one year we traveled to Yellowstone National Park and then on into Canada at Lake Louise and Banff.

Such was life in Las Vegas in the latter half of the 1940s. Simple and pretty uncomplicated. As September approached, I knew my life as a high school student would be very different from my idyllic years at John S. Park.

CHAPTER 2

The Jewel of the Desert

Although its population had almost tripled over the previous decade, Las Vegas was still a small town in the 1950s. Reno remained the largest city in the state, but Las Vegas was on the move. The Strip was expanding. The Nevada Test Site had opened about sixty-five miles to the northwest, and it was clear to most thoughtful observers that Las Vegas would not remain in second place much longer.

Las Vegas High School was the center of my universe. There was no University of Nevada, Las Vegas (UNLV), and LVHS was the only high school in town. Football and basketball games were community events. By the 1950s, several thousand people turned out to watch the Wildcats play for the state championship against Reno at Butcher Field, named for the high school's first football coach.

There were no middle schools or junior highs. Graduation from eighth grade was a rite of passage. No one was more excited than I to be a "Wildcat." On the first day of school in 1951, I reconnected with my old friend Don Fennell, who lived right around the corner. We walked to and from school each day, once in the morning and once at lunch.

Most of the freshman classes were in Frazier Hall, named for Maude Frazier, a prominent educator who had been the high school's principal before going on to serve as a state legislator and lieutenant governor. My first class was general science with Mr. Lee, and that was my homeroom. Each homeroom elected a representative to the student council. I ran for student council and was opposed by Bob Seno, who had graduated from the Fifth Street School. When it came time to cast our ballots, a false sense of modesty suggested it would be improper to vote for myself. So, I voted for Seno—and lost by one vote. I would not make that mistake again.

My classes were those of the typical freshman: algebra, English, physical education, and general science. I also had a speech course.

It was in speech that I was introduced to the work of Robert W. Service, the poet of the Yukon, and his classic, "The Cremation of Sam McGee." One of my classmates chose it for a required memorization. I reveled in the rhyme and seventy years later can still recite many of its stanzas from memory.

Like most schools, Las Vegas High had a pecking order based on class. The movers and shakers, primarily the upper classmen, gathered before class and after lunch on the front steps of the main building taking in the view. Those with cars would make a point of being seen driving by in front of the school. Much of the dating ritual occurred there. Couples "going steady" could be seen walking hand in hand up the front steps. But those steps were off limits to the freshman boys. Alas, we dwelled at the bottom of the social order.

Class officer elections were held in October. Undaunted by my homeroom loss, I ran for class president. My opponent was again the well-liked Seno. I abandoned my false sense of modesty and voted for myself. It was not enough. Noteworthy in that campaign was my use of printed cards. Thanks to local printer Mark Wilkinson, a good friend of my father, I distributed hundreds of "Bryan for Class President" hand cards. Alas, to no avail.

Another disappointment followed my defeat in the political arena. I tried out for the freshman basketball team, the Kittens, and made it to the last cut before my athletic ineptitude became too great to conceal. Getting named to the honor roll was little solace; I'd be watching the games from the bleachers.

A friend who'd fared poorly in his classes was forced by his parents to quit his after-school and Saturday morning job at Bond's Jewelers at Third and Fremont Streets. He introduced me to Stan Fayman, the store manager. Bond's was in the same building where my father had his law office upstairs. I got the job and worked there periodically for the next eight years, washing windows, sweeping the sidewalk, and cleaning up the store at closing time. I was also the mailing clerk. Every day I would go to the post office at Third Street and Stewart Avenue (now the site of the Mob Museum) and take packages that were sent to the home office in Los Angeles and pick up the mail that was in Bond's post office box. Some packages were sent by registered mail, return receipt requested. Others were insured or sent by parcel post. Each day before going to the post office, I filled out the paperwork at the store in a register that kept track of all packages sent. Initially it was challenging for a fourteen-year-old high school freshman. Mrs. Mateucci at the registered mail window was particularly helpful and understanding. She had two sons, Gene and Al, who were several classes ahead of me and had been outstanding athletes at LVHS. They later became attorneys.

After work I'd walk over to the Elks Lodge at Third and Carson and wait for dad to finish his card game, which took place in the basement that was off-limits to nonmembers. The game of choice was pan. I could hear the laughter and swearing as each hand was dealt. Even at a distance I could tell they were having lots of fun. The club's manager, O. K. Adcock, would sometimes treat me to a Coke while I waited for the final turn of the cards. From the lodge, we'd head home for dinner shortly after six o'clock. If the card game ran late, I was instructed to tell my mother that I had to work late at the jewelry store. To this day I still suspect she never believed me.

Bond's not only provided valuable work experience, but I was paid well: $12.50 a week. That was good money back in 1951. And I had plans for that money. Every Saturday I deposited $10 in my account at First National Bank with a goal of saving enough to buy a car when I turned sixteen. The remaining $2.50 was more than enough to cover my expenses. A movie ticket was fifty cents, a milkshake just a quarter.

Teenagers, then as now, had an interest in the latest fashions. I was no exception. Not everyone appreciated our fashion sense, or our obsession with getting the style just right. Potts and Christensen's, men's stores favored by my father, considered teenagers scourges to be avoided whenever possible. The body language of their salesmen sent the message, "Please don't touch the merchandise." Down the street, Allen & Hanson's offered a more enlightened attitude toward high school students and also recognized that teenagers spent a disproportionate amount of money on clothes. Felix Allen was a great salesman who would spend an hour, if necessary, just to sell you a pair of socks. Jack Hanson enjoyed the repartee with high school students, and I loved bantering with him. They were smart enough to hire some of the most popular boys in school as salesmen, and that atmosphere made it an inviting place to drop by. Add to that the store's "Wildcat Player of the Week" display and the pretty girls from school they hired as gift-wrappers at Christmastime, and in their way Allen & Hanson were entrepreneurial geniuses. Buy a new suit, and they'd throw in a tie for free. I was a regular. That first year in high school I bought a wool jersey short-sleeve shirt in my favorite color: Sherwood Forest green. Cost? $5.

As a freshman, my school routine was largely driven by the athletic schedule: Friday night football in the fall and basketball games in the winter. When no game was available, we gathered at the movies.

Christmas at Bond's Jewelers was very busy. In the 1950s, the credit world as we know it today did not exist. Most people had one credit card to purchase gas. My dad was a Standard Oil customer and patronized the gas station at Fifth and Fremont. The two biggest jewelry stores were M. W. Davis and Christensen's, which were very traditional. If they extended any credit, it was very limited. Bond's, on the other hand, recognized the potential of making credit widely available and established a weekly or bimonthly payment schedule for customers. Credit was a huge part of their business. Mr. Jacobs, the credit manager, had several people on his staff devoted to collections. There was a charge for purchases on credit. As I recall it, it was 10 percent and was designated on the sales invoice as a carrying charge.

Among Fayman's friends were two young businessmen, Jerry Mack and Irwin Molasky. Mack would team up with banker Parry Thomas to become major landowners in the valley. The Thomas & Mack Center at UNLV is named in their honor. Molasky, meanwhile, became one of the community's major developers. Sunrise Hospital and the Boulevard Mall are two of his early successes. Fayman, Mack, and Molasky met regularly for coffee across the street at the Melodie Lane Coffee Shop. One day, while I furiously swept the sidewalk and generated a cloud of dust, Irwin passed by me. I had not seen him. He was covered in dust. I was mortified, much aware that he was Fayman's good friend. I thought he'd be angry, but he graciously accepted my apology. "Forget it, kid," he said, "you didn't see me coming." Years later, when I was governor, I reminded him of that moment and told him, "You didn't treat me any differently back then than you do today."

At Christmas, Mr. Fayman added to my duties. After I'd washed the windows and cleaned up outside, I was elevated to salesman status. I kept a tie and a jacket in the backroom to wear when I was on the sales floor.

My time with Mr. Fayman was formative. Most of the sales staff were Jewish and frequently spoke to each other in Yiddish. The salesmen delighted in schooling me in some of the words, mostly the profane ones. I wasn't allowed to sell diamonds, watches, or other high-end merchandise, but cuff links and cigarette lighters were within my purview. At Christmastime, the store, small by today's standards, was every bit as crowded as the crush of "Black Friday" shoppers after Thanksgiving in today's retail world.

Mr. Fayman was very good to me. And he was generous. He gave me a $100 bill as a bonus at Christmas. It was the first time I'd ever seen one. We became friends, and several years later when I became a master mason, he accompanied me to the lodge.

As winter turned to spring, March was tournament time for the state high school basketball championship. It was always held in Reno at the University of Nevada gym, the only place in the state big enough to accommodate several thousand fans. Las Vegas High had a very competitive team, and my father agreed to drive a couple of my friends and I to Reno if the Wildcats reached the state championship finals. When they did, he kept his promise. We stayed downtown at the Riverside Hotel on the banks of the Truckee River. Reno had much more of a big-city feel and look to it than Las Vegas.

The championship game was between Las Vegas and Ely's White Pine High School. It was one of the most exciting I have ever attended. The gym was jam-packed with fans, most of whom were rooting against Vegas with its small contingent of supporters. It was my first exposure to the intense sectionalism that existed between Northern Nevada and Southern Nevada. In years to come I'd experience much more of it.

The Wildcats started slowly and trailed badly at the end of the first half. The second half was a different story. The momentum was all with Las Vegas. As the buzzer sounded, the Las Vegas team's stunning comeback appeared complete when Dick Pribble, a reserve guard, scored what we believed was the winning basket. The scoreboard read: Las Vegas 60, White Pine 59. It was a real shocker. The Vegas section went crazy. When things calmed down, however, we noticed a cluster of officials gathered around the scorer's table. A foul had been called against a Vegas player, and the question being debated was whether it occurred before or after the final buzzer. Gene Mastroianni, the university's graduate manager, was running the clock. When he held up his thumb and forefinger indicating the foul had occurred before the buzzer sounded, all hell broke loose. We thought we had been robbed, and that's still my view seventy years later. The Vegas fans rained pennies on the floor, and officials struggled to regain control. Finally, White Pine guard Frank Evans advanced to the free-throw line. Despite the pandemonium, he coolly sank the first free throw. Our hearts sank. Evans must have had ice water running through his veins. He calmly approached the line again and broke our hearts. All net, no rim. Vegas had lost, 61–60.

During the time we were in the gym, nearly a foot of snow had fallen on Reno. It felt colder inside. My dad was a friend of Las Vegas coach Pat Diskin, who let us ride back to the hotel on the quiet team bus. The loss was depressing, but I wanted to be able to ride with the team again. I knew that I didn't have the talent to make the roster as a player. Was there a way to contribute? Perhaps the next year would provide an answer.

I was not much of an athlete, but I was nothing if not persistent when it came to politics. When I decided to run for sophomore class president, I gave more thought to how I could reach out to more students than just my former John S. Park classmates. As fortune would have it, the Las Vegas High quarterback Johnny Demman also lived in Huntridge and graduated from St. Joseph's Elementary School. I had known him for several years. He had no interest in student politics, but I approached him with a proposition: we'd run for president as a ticket with Bryan for president and Demman for vice president. He agreed. My strategy was to broaden my base and hopefully pick up additional support from former St. Joseph's students. I took some of my supporters to lunch at the Hickory Wood Bar-B-Q on Fremont Street to plan our campaign strategy. My opponent was Clyde Turner, whose mother had been my sixth-grade teacher.

I was working at Bond's on election day when the news came

that the vote was tied 88–88. When Jack Dix, whom I'd met years before at the Biltmore Hotel pool, stepped up to break the tie, I learned an important political lesson: not only does every vote really count, but also that it pays to be nice to people. Although Dix was a friend of Clyde Turner's, he laid an X down by my name. I was a winner at last by a single vote. Clyde went on to become a certified public accountant and a very successful casino executive. During speaking engagements years later, after my political prospects had risen somewhat higher, I'd occasionally spot my friend in the audience and point him out, letting the crowd know that had the fateful vote gone the other way I might have been as successful as Clyde.

After celebrating my landslide win, I learned the basketball team's student manager had quit the position. This was opportunity knocking. If I could secure the position, I'd travel with the team and by year's end earn a coveted letterman's sweater identical to the one the athletes received. Good old dad came through for me again. He placed a call to Pat Diskin, the coach. A day or two later, I met with the coach and he informed me that I would be the student manager. It was another lesson learned along life's journey: sometimes it's not what you know, but whom you know that counts.

When I was a sophomore, most of my classes were in the main building. Many of my friends had taken Latin the previous year, and I was eager to enroll in Mrs. Shaver's Latin class. She was a gem. I found the origins of the English language, much of which is derived from Latin, very interesting. It wasn't all about vocabulary and the conjugation of irregular verbs. I joined the Latin Club. And later that year the class went to the El Portal Theatre to watch the newly released Hollywood classic *Quo Vadis*. Translating *Caesar's Commentaries* in the second year was more difficult, but a rewarding journey, one which found us reciting an old ditty which generations of Latin students know well: "Latin is a language as dead as it can be. It killed the ancient Romans and now it's killing me."

If Latin was a challenge, geometry was a positively obtuse experience. It was taught by Harvey Stanford, who had been the football coach at Las Vegas High School from 1936 to 1951 and whose wife taught me freshman English. Their daughter Jo Ann and I had shared classes since kindergarten. Mr. Stanford was decidedly old-school.

He wore a coat and tie every day, and his shined shoes would have passed muster by the toughest Marine drill sergeant. I disliked the class—it was math, after all—but I remember one thing about it. Every morning he wrote a "thought for the day" on the blackboard. I don't know my polygons, but a couple of those thoughts have never left me. One was, "If the elevator to success is not running, take the stairs." And my favorite: "Procrastination is the thief of time." Perhaps to atone for my academic shortcomings in his class, many years later I played a significant role in persuading the Clark County School Board to name a school for Mr. and Mrs. Stanford.

But it wasn't all Latin verbs and isosceles triangles. There was my job as the basketball team student manager. My hard-working assistant, Louie Reitz, was a big help. The basketball team traveled by bus. Early in the season we traveled to Panaca for a game, and it was easy to see we would be very competitive. In December we played at White Pine and at Reno at its beautiful new high school, and we won again. The Wildcats won game after game and were undefeated as the season progressed.

It was clear we'd challenge for the state title. On those long bus trips, I made friends with the players. There was Rod Reber, a neighbor and grade-school idol, at starting forward. Another neighbor Kent Huntsman played center. Chuck Handley, a John S. Park product, was our leading scorer and would later star with the University of Nevada Wolf Pack. George Ball and George Wilkinson were standouts as reserves.

Returning from a road trip to Reno, we stopped at Goldfield for a break. Across the street was a gas station and beyond that was the frame of an old airplane fuselage with a rusted engine still mounted on the front and a propeller attached. It was obvious the plane would never fly again, but within minutes curiosity got the better of a team member and in moments he was standing by the rusted hulk lifting the rear end of the frame. When he did, the plane tilted forward, and the prop cracked when it hit the ground. Worse yet, the gas station's owner saw it all happen and called the sheriff. After he arrived, the sheriff and the coaches discussed what penalty should apply and what damages should be collected. Somehow it was decided to pass the hat, and each of us was required to empty our pockets before being allowed to leave. It was not exactly due process, but the lesson was learned: don't mess with someone else's property; damage it, and you'll pay the price. Passing through Goldfield many times over the years, I've often thought about that old plane.

Our unbeaten streak was broken when White Pine and Reno came to play in Las Vegas. We lost one game to Reno and one to White Pine. Student assemblies were very spirited, even rowdy, and a big part of the high school routine. Our precision drill and dance team, the Rhythmettes, were so popular they would eventually appear on *The Ed Sullivan Show*. They performed at many of our assemblies. At the assembly preceding the Reno game, several students dressed as Old West undertakers carried a casket into the gym and chanted, "Reno, the Wildcats are after you today!" And the Reno team was in attendance. Those players had never seen anything quite like it. Nor had they likely witnessed members of the junior and senior classes extending middle fingers while chanting their class names. Lots of energy filled the old Wildcat gym.

When March rolled around and we headed for the state tournament, we were on a mission to be vindicated for the previous year's loss. The Wildcats won the state championship, and I received a letterman's sweater and a state championship jacket.

Strip entertainers were frequently willing to make appearances at our assemblies. As sophomore class president, I initiated the Sophomore Hop. As unbelievable as this may seem, as a fifteen-year-old high school student I managed to reach Mr. B himself, Billy Eckstine, and asked him to come to the dance and sing a few numbers. He agreed.

As the school year was coming to an end, I made yet another attempt to grab the brass ring on the athletic field, this time in track. Encouraged by a coach, I tried out and appeared on my way to making the team when the only illness of my high school years struck. I was diagnosed with glandular fever, whatever that is, and missed several weeks of school. My track career was over before it began.

But thanks to my dad, I didn't remain on the sidelines for long. When he took in a 1946 Dodge Coupe as a divorce fee, he made me an offer: pay half the car's value, which came to $375, and it was mine. I gladly complied with the terms. My thriftiness had paid off. I had my real first car. My automobile fixation, which may have begun as a toddler with a little toy car, was now a permanent part of my psyche. I have never been able to shake it. No high school kid was eager to have a '46 Dodge. I began looking for a '49 Ford and found one at the Ford dealership, owned by my father's good friend Archie Grant. The price was significantly less than other '49 Fords. This should have been a red flag for me, but I wanted the car. And when the dealer offered to paint it any color I chose, I took the bait. Later that year, I recognized that the dealer got the better end of the transaction when I had to replace the transmission.

One last chapter in the saga of my frustrated "Hope Springs Eternal" athletic pursuits needs to be told. Though slight of frame, I decided to go out for football. I still don't know what I was thinking. I weighed 135 pounds. I joined the grueling two-a-day practice sessions in the August heat. Between the summer sun and the humid monsoon effect, just being on the field was a demanding workout. Head football coach Angelo Collis knew from long experience that some would drop out. His only request was, "Be man enough to turn in your gear." And after four days of colliding with much bigger and more experienced players, some nearly twice my size and superbly conditioned, I'd had enough. Manning up, I walked into Collis's office, which was crowded with his assistants, dreading every second.

"Coach," I sputtered, "I don't think I'm cut out for football."

He could have made it a humiliating experience. He did not. He was all class and thanked me for trying out and for turning in my gear. In doing so, he taught me a life lesson. I never forgot how he handled the situation. Years later as Shriners, we became friends. As I left his office that day, a sense of relief swept over me. My athletic follies had, at last, come to an end. If I were to excel in life, it would be on other fields.

With the mobility of an automobile, I was now able to participate in another part of the '50s high school ritual: the drive-in restaurant. It was a place to see and be seen. Cars were parked in a semicircle two and three rows deep at Sill's Drive-in on Fifth (now Las Vegas Boulevard) and Charleston or the Round-Up over on Main and Fifth. A carhop, as they were called in the '50s, came to take your order. With your side window rolled down, or better yet in a convertible, a trip to the drive-in was a great way to flirt and visit with friends. If you were fortunate enough to have a date with one of the popular girls in school, these were places you really wanted to be seen.

Each generation of high school students has its own eccentricities, and we certainly had ours. For instance, for a reason I've never understood we also referred to the glove compartment as the jockey box. In our drive-in days, it was thought that your date would be impressed if she could open the jockey box and her own personal condiments—salt, pepper, mustard, and ketchup—were there. The condiments had to be purloined from a previous visit. Seems absurd, perhaps, but that's the way it was.

After a stop at Sills or the Round-Up, it was time to cruise Fremont Street, then open to traffic all the way to the train depot on Main. Cars were waxed and polished, and engines were revved and ready to make the crawl back and forth on Friday and Saturday nights. We burned a lot of fuel, but it was an important part of the ritual.

Another popular venue was the Wildcat Lair, which hosted several teenage activities, primarily dances after football or basketball games. It was governed by students and directed by Jeannie Roberts. And it was a happening place. Strip performers dropped in to play a set at the Lair. One I remember well was Rosemary Clooney, who stopped by between shows and performed for us. Her big hit that year was "Come On-A-My House" and when she arrived at the Lair she was greeted with a banner that read, "Welcome to Our House."

Although I trust that teenagers haven't changed, I'll wager their taste in senior ball and junior prom fashion has shifted a bit. For those who could swing the staggering rental fee, the appropriate attire called for a white dinner jacket and pants with all the accessories. Price? About $5. Exorbitant, I realize, but I was willing to go to such great lengths to get it right on prom night.

Buy a corsage for your date, and you were set to go. Dances were held either at the Wildcats gym or an LDS church, which had a recreation room large enough to accommodate the dance crowds. Class dues covered the price of the dance. The event itself was important, but the evening was still young.

About ten o'clock, the action heated up. Couples would head out to the Strip to take in the late-night show. There was no cover and no minimum. For the price of a Shirley Temple or a Coke, about a buck, a high school kid could see top-notch talent. During my high school years, I saw some of the great entertainers of the age for a few dollars. Following the late show, we'd spend another buck and go to the "smorgasbord" that today is better known as the buffet. Cost from dinner jacket to smorgasbord? About $20.

The ritual was not available to all students. The Strip's hotels were segregated—no African American patrons allowed. It was one of the harsh ironies of the time. Some of the great performers of the '50s, including Nat King Cole, Billy Eckstine, Sammy Davis Jr., Lena Horne, and the Mills Brothers, were headliners on the Strip, but weren't allowed to eat or sleep at the hotel. In some of my high school yearbook photos of those big dances, you can tell what time of the evening the photos were taken. If most of the couples were African American, then that photo was snapped after the exodus of the white students to the Strip properties.

Las Vegas was labeled "the Mississippi of the West" during the earliest days of the civil rights movement, and there was more than a little truth to the characterization. Although the only high school was fully integrated, movie theaters still had a section for African Americans, and neighborhoods were segregated. As already noted, the municipal swimming pool was off limits to African Americans. No Black families lived in Huntridge, and no Black students attended John S. Park. Whether this was the result of restrictive covenants or de facto practice, no matter. It was real. The sad truth was, most African Americans in Las Vegas lived in a ghetto, commonly referred to as the "Westside," where even into the late 1950s some of the roads weren't paved and streetlights were still years away.

Later, as a young lawyer, I served as counsel for the local chapter of the National Association for the Advancement of Colored People (NAACP). I was very proud that the organization presented me with the Justice Award at the annual banquet. As a state legislator and later as governor, I found myself in a position to make a statement on behalf of a community that had been either actively ill-treated or beleaguered by institutional neglect. My actions were guided not merely by conscience, but in no small part by memories of my comparatively idyllic youth in segregated Las Vegas.

Having lettered in basketball as a student manager, I was now eligible for membership in the Varsity Club. I joined. The initiation involved some hazing, certainly impermissible today.

As the basketball season approached, Louie Reitz and I began our second year as managers. On road trips I sat at the scorer's table and kept track of the statistics: shots, free throws, and fouls on each player just as I had the previous year.

The most interesting class my junior year was chemistry taught by Mr. Richert. Its lab component led to my most memorable mishap. I enjoyed memorizing the periodic table and working with the Bunsen burner. My lack of coordination surfaced once again when I accidentally spilled hydrofluoric acid on my finger, and it spread under my fingernail. I couldn't wash it off. The pain was intense. After all, hydrofluoric acid is used to etch glass. I left school and headed straight to Dr. Fightlin's office a few blocks from campus. He reminded me that a "base" solution counteracted an acid. And he instructed me to place my aching finger in a test tube filled with a base solution, which I dutifully did. Voila! Relief! The rest of the day I was a walking chemistry experiment with my finger jammed in a test tube. The sight caused another reaction, of sorts—plenty of comments from classmates.

After a Chemistry Club meeting and making the obligatory stop at Sill's, we were out past curfew. A police car spotted us, and we made the big mistake of taking evasive action. When the police located us and made the stop, we were asked to get out of the car. We were searched. When they discovered all the quarters we'd collected earlier that evening at the Chemistry Club meeting, which we intended to use for the Christmas party, they immediately concluded we must have been knocking off vending machines. Our explanation was to no avail. We were booked into custody at the juvenile home, then located on Shadow Lane a couple of miles from campus, and spent the night.

Our parents were notified. My mother was mortified. Although she never raised her voice, it was clear she believed she now had a son with a criminal record. My dad, who'd seen much worse when he was in high school, took it in stride and laughed it off. After all, our only offense was a curfew violation, not generally considered a gateway to a life of crime.

Late to class the next morning, we arrived on campus celebrities of sorts. We were peppered with curious questions. What was the juvenile home like? What did they do to you?

One of our classmates, not connected with our group, was in custody on another matter. His name was Clayton Sampson. Years later as a deputy district attorney, I would prosecute Sampson and go up against a young defense attorney named Harry Reid.

Another election season rolled around by spring, and I became a candidate for student body president. I knew plenty of athletes through my duties as student manager of the basketball team and membership in the Varsity Club. One of those early contacts was Kenny Gragson, whom as governor I later appointed to the Nevada Gaming Commission. Through those athletes and the popular girls who were attracted to them, I was acquainted with the "Front Steps Crowd."

Surely that would be enough to prevail against my opponent, Tony Rosenbaum, who was a member of the school band. He was not a mover and shaker and was not well known to the juniors and seniors. That was my base. He was better known in the freshman and sophomore classes, and that was his base.

Our showdown came at a school-wide assembly, where we gave our speeches. As an only-in-Las Vegas warm-up, a Strip act that worked with electric eels was scheduled to perform. After they had playfully touched the eels, they called for a volunteer. My athlete supporters began chanting, "We want Bryan! We want Bryan." I no more wanted to touch those eels than to have a frontal lobotomy performed. Touching those eels was the last thing I wanted to do. But if I had not agreed to do so, I would be humiliated before all the students assembled. So I touched the eels. The shock was really nothing painful.

It did give me the opening line in my speech.

"I hope in the few moments I have, I can electrify you just as those eels did to me." Not a bad line. If only it had won hearts and minds as well as laughs.

Rosenbaum won the election. It was another valuable lesson in politics that I would use to better effect as a candidate for president of the Associated Students of the University of Nevada (ASUN). The lesson: never neglect or ignore those who aren't part of the "in" crowd. There are many more of them than those sitting on the front steps.

That summer I was selected to attend Boys State as one of the representatives from Las Vegas High School. For reasons that defy explanation, a decision had been made that summer to hold Boys State at the LVHS gym. It was late June, the temperature was climbing over one hundred degrees, and the gym was not air-conditioned. I became acquainted with boys from all over the state, including some I'd later meet during my university days. I ran for attorney general and was defeated by Bob Lombardi. Although I was unsuccessful, I'd hold the office at the state level nearly three decades later. I also made my first television appearance, a panel discussion on Boys State broadcast on Channel 8.

My obsession with cars continued even if the '49 Ford left a trail of oil wherever it went. It had style, but it was a car only a mechanic could love. The engine was balky, and a dropped transmission necessitated a tow all the way from Mount Charleston. I looked to up my game, and at a used-car lot a '51 Chevy Coupe caught my eye. With pal Gerald Eggers riding shotgun, we took it out for a test drive on the Boulder Highway. The engine blew up almost immediately. At least it wasn't Mount Charleston. At the car lot, the salesman promised to repair or replace the engine, and I imagined my mechanical worries were over. So, I bought the car. It would prove another mistake on the road to the future. A few months later while returning from a football game in Reno, the Chevy blew its engine, and we were towed back to town past Sill's, an embarrassment in itself.

But I was a senior at last and loved it. My credentials included being vice president of the Chemistry Club, vice president of the Latin Club, sports editor of the yearbook, and an officer with the Varsity Club. I was on a roll. And it would get better. I was elected senior class president and represented my homeroom on the student council. I'd come a long way since losing to Bob Seno by a single vote back in Mr. Lee's general science class.

At the homecoming game that final year, halftime festivities included a parade of school club-sponsored floats that circled the football field on the cinder track. The Chemistry Club's entry was powered by an old convertible I'd persuaded a local used-car dealer to loan us. We built a wooden frame around it and wrapped it in chicken wire, stuffing the holes with paper napkins. It was a thing of beauty. As budding chemists, we added a smoke generator for that certain science lab touch. Midway around the track, however, our theory of relativity began to fail when the smoke generator malfunctioned, and the napkins caught on fire. Putting out the fire wasn't easy considering the float's wooden frame. Exiting the vehicle was even harder. By the time we were safe, the convertible was a total loss. Fortunately, the salesman who'd loaned us the old heap must have been seeking redemption for past sins because he never made a claim against us. My parents were in the stands, and my mother looked on in horror.

If I was supposed to take the parade float disaster as a sign that I wasn't really cut out for science, I ignored it. I next tried physics and struggled from the beginning. I managed to transfer into Mr. Viggo Victor's second-year journalism class with help from my friend Jim Joyce. The future Nevada political maven was even then a titan of the typewriter, banging out stories for the Las Vegas High School student newspaper, *The Desert Breeze*. I met Roger Bremner and Bob Peccole in the class. Roger would later become a college roommate, and Bob would be a classmate at law school, my chief deputy at the public defender's office and attorney general's office, and one of my trusted appointments to the Nevada Gaming Commission. It's funny how life works. It has its twists and turns. But I've often thought that had I not experienced an academic disaster in physics, our paths might not have crossed the way they did, and I might not have made two of my life's great friends.

I enjoyed my classes and most of my teachers. In my senior year, Sally Riggs taught a survey of English literature from *Beowulf* and *The Canterbury Tales* to the Elizabethan authors and the giants of the nineteenth century. I had no desire to major in English in college, but thanks to great teachers I became acquainted with the classics and was made a more rounded person. I recognize that school experiences are different for today's students—more complicated, to be sure. But I hope today's teachers still recognize how important this broad exposure to the language and great writing are to understanding our culture. It is a unifying bond no matter our ethnicity or nationality. From John Donne's "No Man Is an Island," to Alfred Lord Tennyson's "The Charge of the Light Brigade," the richness and elegance of the English language, when commanded by a master, is a wonderful thing to behold.

Don't get the wrong impression. I didn't spend my spare time in high school quoting Shakespeare. Although I was no longer the manager of the basketball team, we followed the teams on the road all the way to Reno and made more than a little mischief. One story can be shared in part because the statute of limitations has expired and many of my fellow culprits have gone to the Big Lair in the Sky. After Las Vegas lost to Reno in the state basketball tournament, we wanted to leave the victors with something to remember us by. So, we decided to burn a large "V" for Vegas on Reno High's front lawn. The following Monday, principal Walter Long made an announcement over the public address system requesting any student who knew anything about the incident to please come to his office. No one responded to the call.

It was on that trip to Reno that I was invited to the Alpha Tau Omega (ATO) fraternity house for lunch. George Ball and George Wilkinson, who had been on the Wildcats basketball championship team in 1953, were the only Las Vegas members of the fraternity. From that experience, I knew I would love university life. Although I had no close friends who were going to Reno, I was reminded by my father, always focused on my future, that students from all over Nevada would be there, a powerful attraction if I wanted to have a future in public life. These students were important contacts in the future. I decided to go to Reno and never regretted it.

As graduation approached, I was offered the chance to speak at commencement and jumped at the chance. Earlier that year, Las Vegas police officer Robert Dula was killed during a traffic stop. An award was created in his honor that would be given to the outstanding boy and girl graduate each year. I was selected as its first recipient and swelled with pride. I titled my speech, "The Avenue of Life."

CHAPTER 3

University Days in
"The Biggest Little City"

By late summer 1955 my thoughts turned to my fall enrollment at the University of Nevada in Reno. None of my close high school friends were going there, but several people I knew from school were enrolling and we decided to travel together.

I had made no arrangements for housing and still can't believe my parents allowed me to head off to school without a place to live. The first night I wound up on a sleeping porch at the ATO House. Later that week, I ran into Roger Bremner and Dave Harris, who informed me that they were renting two rooms, a block away from campus, and that there was space for me. At last, I had found my college home.

Registration began by signing up for classes. This meant waiting in line for each class. There was a long registration form that was called a "railroad ticket" with perforated sections. A section was left with registration officials as you signed up for each class. The only stressful part of the registration process was the English class placement exam. Passing the exam meant enrollment in a basic freshman English class; failure consigned you to a remedial English class for which no credit was given, pejoratively known by all as "Bonehead English." I escaped the "Bonehead" fate.

The Greek system of fraternity and sorority houses was a dominant part of campus life, and "rush week" ran concurrently with class registration. My father had been a fraternity man at the University of Nevada in his day, and since boyhood I'd heard him recount his exploits at the Sigma Phi Sigma House. I knew I wanted to be a fraternity man, too. George Wilkinson and George Ball, who played on the Las Vegas High School state basketball championship team two years earlier, were both in Alpha Tau Omega, a house known for its athletes. As the student manager of the team, I had gotten to know the two. I was predisposed to pledge the ATO House. Its members were from towns all over the state. Again, my father's counsel was wise. He made me aware of the importance of knowing people in every part of the state if I were to embark upon a political career.

On Sunday afternoon I had my first "rush week experience." With Bremner and Harris in tow, we went to Virginia Lake where the ATOs were hosting a beer bust. The first person who approached us with a beer in his hand and a smile on his face was Len Savage. Len's family had been in Nevada since the days of the Comstock Lode, and the family owned a plumbing company, Savage and Son. The logo was a Reno landmark: two cannibals standing around a boiling pot. It would unquestionably be politically incorrect today. It was another rite of passage; I was now a college man. Later that week, Bremner, Harris, and I visited several other fraternities. At the Sigma Nu House, I became reacquainted with Larry Brunetti, whom I had met at Boys State that summer. Brunetti urged me to join Sigma Nu. At the SAE (Sigma Alpha Epsilon) House, Bob Petroni, whom I had met at Lake Tahoe in a previous summer, was a member. He urged me to join SAE. By the end of the week, I had visited all the fraternities and was prepared to make my decision.

The next week after dinner at the ATO House, led by Wilkinson, with a pledge pin in hand, he urged me to join them. By then I knew this was the fraternity for me. I was now a fraternity man. Bremner and Harris followed.

The first semester I signed up for physical geology, French (one year of a foreign language was required in the College of Arts and Science), philosophy (logic), English, ROTC, and physical education. The latter three were required courses.

Shortly after I pledged, there was a meeting of all the pledges. I met Jim Santini, Mack Fry, and Jim Corica from Reno. They became close friends. A pledge class president was to be elected, and I threw my hat into the ring. In the discussion that followed, one of the pledges from a rural county got up and said, "We can't have someone from Vegas as our pledge class president." Those sentiments carried the day. I had a lot of work to do.

The ATO House made men out of boys. Among the role models I greatly admired were Roland Westergard, the house president, later the head of the Nevada Department of Conservation and Natural Resources, and Roger Trounday, who among other positions in state government became the chairman of the Nevada Gaming Control Board.

Life for the pledges at ATO House was the equivalent of marine boot camp. Hazing of pledges was part of the routine. It was intended to bring young men from different backgrounds and different parts of the state together as brothers. Some of it, in retrospect, was quite silly.

The house had a hierarchy: Juniors and seniors had the power of the paddle and the ability to impose fines at lunch and dinner for various infractions. Sophomores had no authority.

Swats were administered with a paddle that consisted of two leather straps bradded together at the handle. The artful use of the paddle was not how hard you could swing it, but whether you could snap your wrist so that only the edge of the leather straps would strike the rear of the offending pledge. Not every upper classman mastered its use, but as a pledge you knew with the first contact those who did. The paddle was always administered on a large section of carpet near the front door. The carpet was gray but was always referred to as the "green." "Bryan on the green for three," which I heard many times during my freshman year, commanded me to get on that section of carpet, bend over, and prepare for the swats.

The offenses for which the paddle could be used were highly subjective. For instance, pledges were required to answer the phone within three rings. Failure to do so meant a trip to the green. As part of the give-and-take, pledges were encouraged to be provocative—even though it guaranteed a trip to the green. Bremner and I frequently provoked a trip to the green. Except for the few upperclassmen who had mastered the art of the paddle, swats didn't bother us.

The pledges were encouraged to act together as a class. One such event I recall was when the pledge class stole the house's evening meal, a steak dinner with all the trimmings, which we enjoyed at our own picnic. On this evening, unbeknown to us, the house president had invited the dean of student affairs to the house for dinner. Bad timing, but that was the life of a pledge.

Pledges had work assignments, hashing for lunch and evening meals, housework on Saturdays, both inside and outside the house. One Saturday morning, while I was raking leaves on the front yard,

I was startled by several shotgun volleys coming from the roof of the house. Geese were flying over the house, and seconds later several came crashing to the ground around me. I ran for cover. The brothers who had fired on the geese came running out of the house and disappeared back into the house with their kill. Within minutes the wailing sound of sirens could be heard as several police vehicles roared up to the front of the house. Apparently, the neighbors sounded the alarm. The police officers moved quickly into the house, asking questions and searching everywhere for the geese. Not surprisingly, no one saw or heard anything. After an exhaustive search, the police left empty-handed. Later that afternoon I learned the geese were stuffed in empty commercial-size milk containers that were stored in a refrigeration unit in the basement.

Bremner, Harris, and I were the only Las Vegas pledges that first semester. George Wilkinson, a junior, was the only Las Vegan living in the house. There was considerable skepticism about us. Every Las Vegas pledge either dropped out or flunked out the previous year. There was a growing resentment of Las Vegas. In retrospect, some of the resentment was self-inflicted. We were always eager to proclaim the merits of how Vegas did things.

Freshmen from rural communities dominated the pledge class. Tiny Eureka, for instance, had more pledges than Las Vegas. Reno had the largest contingent, and I quickly developed several friendships with them.

I wanted to be active on campus. The freshmen and sophomore service organization was the Sagers, and I joined and began developing friendships with members from other fraternities. Homecoming was a big event.

At homecoming, all ATO pledges were required to run from the old Sparks High School to Mackay Stadium as part of the intramural competition. As perhaps the least athletic of the pledges, I saw this as an opportunity. If I could finish—not win, but finish—I might gain some credibility among the doubting Thomases in the house. It was a grueling three to four miles from start to finish. Along the way many dropped out. Rounding the turn from Fourth Street to University Avenue (Center Street), the grade became much steeper, and even more fell away. I was in a world of hurt, but I knew if I made it to the campus the rest of the way to the stadium was downhill, and I would finish. A few minutes later I crested the hill.

Entering Mackay Stadium, I could hear my fraternity brothers urging me on. My adrenaline kicked in, and I actually passed a few competitors in the final few hundred yards. For a fleeting moment, Roger Bannister had nothing on me. I crossed the finish line, and Bob Genasci, the house manager, was the first to embrace me. Others followed. I always thought I gained a little credibility that day because most of my pledge class didn't make it to the finish line.

At the university, the '50s were a time of costume dances, and each fraternity sponsored its own event. For the ATOs, in the fall the theme was "the Bowery," a boisterous affair and lots of fun. Sorority dances were invitation-only, and Carol Gardenswartz from my French class asked me to accompany her to the Tri Delts dance. Our paths would cross frequently over the next four years, and as a senior Carol was elected Associated Women Students president.

As the first semester was ending, it was increasingly clear to me that I would have to move into the house to get the most out of the fraternity experience. I had become good friends with Jim Santini, Mack Fry, Jim Corica, and others from Reno, but I was missing out with the brothers who lived in the house. At the semester break, I moved into the ATO House. My roommates were Ray Trease, Larry Fritz, and John Seeliger, all from Fallon. This was a good move for me because I had much more contact with the brothers from rural Nevada.

Almost everyone had a nickname at the ATO House. Harry Summerfield was called "Rhino." Bob Scott was "Nail." Gail Monk was "Stork." The nickname frequently referred to a physical characteristic of the brother.

I received mine that semester. Coming out of the shower one morning, Chuck Evans turned to the brothers, chuckling, and said, "Bryan looks like a white orchid" in a reference to my pale complexion. That morphed into "Whitey," and it stuck. Years later, if someone referred to me as Whitey it had to be someone who knew me from my college days.

When final exams week arrived, I was confident I would make my grades despite the fact I hadn't studied particularly hard. I did have a scare in physical geology. For the final exam, professor Larsen passed around a box of rocks to identify. Because I did not take the afternoon lab, which was optional, I hadn't seen the rocks and was completely unprepared. I was forced to guess, and I remember one of my answers was "phenocrysts of plagioclase feldspar." I think Larsen recognized that those who hadn't taken the lab couldn't be expected to be able to identify the strange rocks. I managed to receive a C grade in the course.

After final exams, I was initiated into the fraternity as an active member and became entitled to wear the ATO pin, shaped in the form of a Maltese cross and numbered on the back. I was number 68415. The number determined the order of your room assignment in the house and where you sat at meals. The evening banquet was held at the Santa Fe in downtown Reno and was a raucous affair with many toasts and more than a little ribaldry. We were embraced as brothers, an important milestone in the fraternal bonding process.

The sophomore class in the fraternity in the grand scheme of things had no power. They were neither upper classmen with the power of the paddle and the ability to impose fines, nor pledges. One of the sophomores from Fallon was Sam Beeghly, a good guy. Sam was one of the few in the house with any musical talent. He played the accordion, and on Saturday morning his music filled the house. Sam had been giving us a hard time, and we wanted to teach him a lesson. We sneaked into his room and took his accordion, then pawned it at a downtown shop. Sam was frantic. "Where's my accordion?" he thundered.

The following day at lunch, we displayed the pawn ticket. He went Vesuvian. He swore up and down that as long as he was a member of the house no one from Las Vegas would ever become active. In time, Sam cooled down. The accordion was redeemed at the pawn shop, and he never again gave us a hard time. Such was life at the ATO House.

The semester unfolded with traditional fraternity events, Winter Carnival, and more traditional fraternity and sorority dances. Mackay Day honored one of the "Big Four" of the Comstock, John Mackay. He made a fortune during the boom days in Virginia City as had the others. He was the only one who remembered Nevada. He provided the money for the Mackay School of Mines, Mackay Stadium, and later his son Clarence provided the money for the Mackay Science Building. That occurred when my father was a student, and the yearbook that year featured a photo of Clarence being carried across the Quad by my father and another student.

In the spring, elections were held for campus officers, including student body president. Our candidate was Chuck Coyle, an air force veteran ten years older than the rest of us. Campaigns for president were big events on campus. The rivalry between fraternities was keen. Chuck, who had long been involved in campus politics and all the intrigue that went with it, emerged victorious. Tradition dictated that the winning fraternity host a beer bust for the entire student body. We procured a flatbed wagon and arranged twenty kegs of beer on all sides in the back of the house. A grand time was had by all.

Chuck's election had important implications for my political future. As ASUN president, he appointed the chairmen for all campus activities. Bob Faiss, a former Las Vegas High classmate and future law partner at Lionel Sawyer & Collins, served as chairman of the Assembly Committee in my freshman year. He asked me to join the committee shortly after I arrived on campus. Chuck now appointed me chairman of the committee the following year. This made me eligible to attend the annual leadership conference at the beginning of the school year at Lake Tahoe. All the student leaders attended, and this was an important entrée for me in student government.

That summer I worked at Bond's Jewelers again. I decided that my car problems could only be resolved by buying a new car. I chose a 1956 Buick Special two-door hardtop, bare bones except for an automatic transmission. With my trade-in plus a little money I had saved, I had enough for the down payment. My father cosigned on the car loan. My payments were $92.02 a month for thirty-six months. It was a big mistake. The car was great, the color Tahitian Coral was a winner, but I was financially strapped for the remainder of my student days.

Returning to school I attended the student leadership conference at Lake Tahoe. Coyle presided over the conference, which served as a planning session for all student activities.

To make my car payment, I needed a job. Having worked at Safeway, I began my job search at supermarkets, finally landing work as a box boy and occasional checker at Hansen's Food Market. I was never very fast on the cash register and didn't know a cabbage from a head of iceberg lettuce when I started, but working at Hansen's taught me an important lesson: casual meetings early in life can take on greater importance with the passage of time. Working at Hansen's, I met grocery stockers Marv Rubin and Duane Laubach. We hit it off. Both eventually became active in the Las Vegas Board of Realtors and years later became important political supporters. Duane and I also connected in the Masonic fraternity after law school. High schooler Lynn Baker was another box boy at the store. The son of a future Reno mayor, Lynn would move to Las Vegas, join the Jaycees, and step up as a member of my campaign staff when I ran for governor in 1982. Always remember, it's a small world.

As a pre-legal major with history as my field of concentration, I was fortunate to take several classes from Russell Elliott, Wilbur Shepperson, and Don Driggs, who were among the best professors I had as an undergraduate. My grades in history classes were quite good, and I was elected to Phi Alpha Theta, an honorary history fraternity.

I continued my campus activities, getting elected to the student union board. The campus did not have a student union, but it did have a generous legacy donation from early transportation pioneer Jot Travis. Like so many government projects, the bids exceeded the amount of the gift. The building would have to be downsized, and that caused a delay in its construction. We interviewed candidates for the student union director, and Bob Kersey was selected. He became a part of the student life for many decades, and he and his wife became close friends.

I had been the sports editor for the Las Vegas High School yearbook, and I applied for the same job at the university and became the sports editor of its *Artemisia* publication. As sports editor, among my other duties, I was responsible for arranging team photos. I had selected one particularly skillful shutterbug named Don Dondero to take the team photos. On the day I scheduled photos of the football team in their game uniforms, Don forgot the film. The coach was very upset that we had interfered with his practice schedule. Don went on to become a legend in Reno for his celebrity photographs, and he was a man I'd get to know better during my years as attorney general and governor. I knew Don's darkest darkroom secret. I remembered the day on campus when he forgot to bring film for his camera. Whenever I would see him in later years I'd shout, "Don, did you bring film?" It was our inside joke. That college experience put me in a close working relationship with the entire yearbook staff. By far the most demanding extracurricular activity, and frequently the most frustrating, was lining up programs as chairman of the Assembly Committee.

In the second semester I moved out of the ATO House and rented a basement apartment with Paul Huffey, who had just gotten out of the army, and Butch Pepple. Huff, as I always called him, pledged ATO and immediately adapted to college life. The highlight of our time at the apartment was making beer using a Canadian recipe that produced a vile, sediment-clouded concoction. It won no prizes for taste but produced the desired effect. Capped in used 7UP bottles, it was named "Whitey's Black Forest" in my honor.

As the spring approached, it was once again election season. I decided to make my move and run for senator at-large. I felt good about my chances, but all of that changed when Don Travis, an ATO, was persuaded by the Aggies on campus to run as a write-in candidate for student body president. The SAEs had a candidate they were running for student body president. Although Travis was not the ATO candidate, the SAEs felt betrayed when he entered the race as a write-in candidate. The backlash was swift and devastating for my candidacy. The novelty of a write-in candidacy carried the day for Travis. I was defeated by LeRoy Arascada, a member of Lambda Chi Alpha.

Because the University of Nevada was established as a land-grant institution, two years of ROTC were required for every able-bodied male under the age of twenty-six without prior military experience. Senator Justin Morrill of Vermont authored the legislation, and the oldest building on campus bears his name. As my sophomore year ended, I applied for advanced ROTC, which would lead to a commission upon graduation. The draft was in effect, and we all expected to serve in the military after graduation. I found myself among familiar faces because Bremner, Fry, Santini, and Corica had also been accepted.

There was an academic surprise at the end of the school year. I managed to flunk bowling, the class I'd chosen as my physical education requirement. The class started at 8:00 a.m. at a local bowling alley, and I had missed several classes because of the bitterly cold, early-morning weather. With no automatic pin-setting machines in those days, as half of the class bowled, the other half would set pins. I was shocked to receive an F, the only academic failure in all my school years. I made an appointment with the instructor to try to persuade her to change my grade. My case was weak, and the instructor was unmoved by my argument. No ATO had ever failed a class requiring any measure of athletic ability, a fact my fraternity brothers rarely let me forget. With two years of PE required for graduation, I would have to take the class in my junior year.

Before school started, I again attended the student leadership conference at Lake Tahoe. On campus, I was an upperclassman at last. At ATO, the power of the paddle and the right to impose fines were at last mine at the fraternity. I could hardly contain myself. No one was more eager than I to exercise these new privileges. Travis, as the new student body president, had the power to appoint the chairman for each of the major campus events. Homecoming chairman was the big prize, and whether he felt guilty because his candidacy for ASUN president was a big factor in my defeat the previous spring or whether he thought I was the most qualified, I will never know. He appointed me. That would provide an effective vehicle to demonstrate any organizational abilities that I might have.

Santini and I decided it was time to be part of the debate team, which was coached by Bob Griffin. Unlike in my father's time when debates were formal events in the evening with debaters attired in a tuxedo, we debated in the afternoon in empty classrooms or wherever there was an empty room. One room in which we debated was just outside the restroom. Some of our most salient points were drowned out by the sound of a flushing toilet.

Santini and I did surprisingly well for first-year debaters. We debated at the University of Pacific in Stockton, California; Pepperdine in Malibu, California; and the University of Arizona in Tucson. It was a great experience. We traveled by car, and Griffin loved to describe the flora and fauna along the way. Tucson was particularly pleasant and warm when Reno was still in the grip of winter.

At the ATO House, I became assistant house manager. There was a small stipend that helped with my staggering $92.02 monthly car payment. As assistant house manager, I supervised the pledges' housework on Saturdays. I made them remove every piece of furniture in the living room—chairs, couches, and lamps. The pledges hated that almost as much as the paddle and fines. It was an outstanding pledge class, but trouble would lie ahead that I did not see coming.

I had to take a PE class, and that put me in the same class with several pledges. The graduate assistant, John Borda, taught the class and made my life uncomfortable. He knew my situation and reveled in it. I was fearful at one point I might get another F. The pledges delighted in my angst and gave me much grief.

As soon as I became eligible as an upper classman, I joined Blue Key, a service organization. I also continued my service on the student union board.

Homecoming was a success with a full house at Wolves Frolic. There were many entries for the parade, and the crowning of the queen went smoothly.

The ATOs won the parade entry, but the selection was controversial. Built in a garage, the float's most prominent feature was a volcano. The theme "Forge on Alums" featured a character, Vulcan, forging metal on an anvil. The brothers had been careless: as the float was being moved out of the garage to the parade route, the volcano failed to clear the doorway. At the last moment, the top part of the volcano had to be chopped off. This was quite apparent as the float moved onto North Virginia. Nevertheless, the ATO float won top honors. The following Monday I got a call from the Sigma Nu House asking for an explanation. The vote remains a mystery to this day.

I was enjoying my junior year. In addition to the Blue Key and student union memberships, I had a pin number that entitled me to select the only two-man room in the house. As a benefit of being in advanced ROTC, I received ninety cents a day for each day of the month. If I missed a class, I was docked $1.80.

At the house I frequently exercised all the perks of being an upperclassman, including the frequent use of the paddle and imposing fines at lunch and dinner. Alan Bible was our senior US senator, and he was scheduled to speak at the Wolf Den, a coffee shop across the street from campus. As I left the ATO House for the short walk to the Wolf Den, a group of pledges accosted me. I put up a fight, but I was easily overpowered. I knew where they were taking me, Manzanita, a lake on campus that was frozen. I was "laked," the term used when someone was thrown into the lake. Crashing through the ice, I got wet from head to toe. It was so cold that icicles began forming on my clothes on my walk back to the house.

When I entered the house, the pledges had gathered around and were enjoying themselves immensely and to my consternation the actives were much amused as well. "To the green," I roared for the customary swats. On the following night I was "laked" again and walked back to the house half-frozen. The pledges were not done with me. There would be a third night. Bill Witt, an upperclassman from Henderson, came to my aid. Both of us were tossed into the lake. A group that called themselves the "Steel Helmets" led the pledge class. This was all part of the ritual, and I was deserving of the attention I received.

The campus election season was approaching, and I was determined to make a run for student body president. I knew LeRoy Arrascada, who defeated me for senator at-large the previous year, would run. The Sigma Nus, the largest of the fraternities, had not elected a student body president since 1955. They had a very gifted candidate, Bob Morrill, who later would graduate from Harvard Law School and practice law in Silicon Valley. Bob had been very active on campus, participating in several of the same organizations that I did. I viewed him as the most formidable challenger. He was from Reno and part of a family that owned an office supply store.

If elected, I would be the third ATO in a row to serve as ASUN president. That prospect caused understandable resentment in the Greek world, as fraternities and sororities dominated campus politics. There was another problem. The ATOs and the Tri Delts were very close. Don Travis, the current student body president, had married a Tri Delt during the year. Jim Joyce, the current house president, was pinned to a Tri Delt he would ultimately marry.

That created a problem for me in the Theta House, archrivals of the Tri Delts. Joyce, ATO president and a classmate from Las Vegas High School, and later a preeminent political figure in state politics, joined me in crafting a strategy to address the "Theta Problem," as we called it.

Candidates for student body president were extended invitations to attend the spring dances of fraternities who did not have a candidate in the race. The Phi Sig's dance, "The Comstock Stomp," was an upcoming costume dance, and the fraternity had no candidate in the race.

As part of our strategy, Joyce suggested I take a Theta pledge to the dance. I agreed. It was a decision that would be a defining moment in my life. "Let's get a list of the Theta pledges," I replied. On that list was the name Bonnie Fairchild. I knew she was part of what we at the ATO House referred to as the "California Crop," attractive girls who arrived on campus each year from the Golden State. Bonanza Airlines, which served the Las Vegas to Reno route, was replacing its old DC3s with a new plane, the Fairchild F-27. She could be an airline heiress, I imagined. Let's see if I could get a date with her to the Phi Sig dance. Thankfully, she accepted. She wasn't an heiress but would become someone far more important in my life.

Thanks to Jim Santini's contacts at the Reno Little Theater, we were able to select our costumes from the theater's wardrobe department. I can still remember Bonnie's dress, a champagne color with a loop on the train that she could slip over her wrist when dancing. I am the original tangle foot on the dance floor and without the loop one of us would have been injured. I selected a Civil War officer's uniform as a reminder of Nevada's 1864 statehood during the Civil War. Our costumes were good. Bob Morill's was better. He was a mining engineering major and came as a Comstock miner complete with a nineteenth-century mining lamp, which he carried around all night.

Four years before, I lost a race for student body president at LVHS because I had neglected those who were not movers and shakers on campus. I had learned my lesson. I campaigned door to door at Lincoln Hall, a men's dormitory, where many independents lived. Hartman Hall was another men's dorm where a lot of older veterans lived. I went door to door there as well.

Morrill and I prevailed in the primary. Many hijinks ensued on campus. Campaign banners were spread out over its entrance. On election morning, armed with portable loudspeakers, campaign operatives in small boats on Manzanita Lake invited women living in Manzanita Hall to ride across the lake to class.

Keith Kellison, a fraternity brother from Hawthorne, was able to get his high school mascot's costume, a serpent. As a parody on the Sigma Nu nickname, the Snakes, several of my fraternity brothers wandered around campus much like a dragon on Chinese New Year. The serpent carried a sign reading, "Even the snakes are voting for Bryan." Santini was running for senior class president. The election would be close, and I awaited the outcome at the ATO House. Late in the afternoon, the sound of racing automobiles approached with horns blaring. Pledges and actives alike were cheering. I had won. Jim Santini had also been elected senior class president. It was quite a day for ATO. This time, even the "laking" Santini and I received was welcomed. In no time we were carried out to Manzanita Lake and tossed in. We emerged looking more like drowned rats than presidential, but the black-and-white photograph taken at that moment remains one of my life's prized possessions.

The traditional beer bust followed in the back of the house and brought people from across campus that night. I'd come a long way in three years from hearing, "We can't have someone from Las Vegas as our pledge president." Whatever can be said against the fraternity bonding process and all the rituals, some of them indeed strange, that went with it in the 1950s, we were truly a band of brothers that night.

I took office in May and by September had my own office in the new student union building. As the student body president-elect, I was invited to attend the Pacific Students Presidents Association annual conference in Eugene at the University of Oregon in 1958. PSPA included student body presidents and student body presidents-elect from all the western states. During that trip I met Oregon governor Mark Hatfield. Years later I'd greet him again as a colleague in the US Senate.

The conference's theme was "Oregon's Great in '58." I was determined to bring the annual meeting next year to Reno by using the theme, "Reno's Fine in '59." There was really no competing school, and Reno was selected. But some, having a little fun at my expense, entered a bogus school, Catalina University, that offered attractive enticements to win the conference. For a while they really had me going as I campaigned vigorously among my snickering colleagues.

By summer I was back working at Bond's Jewelers. In June I headed to Fort Lewis, Washington, for a six-week ROTC training exercise. With 1,200 ROTC members in attendance, it was the closest I'd ever come to experiencing marine boot camp. We were up and running at the crack of dawn from one location to another in the field. We learned to fire an array of army weapons, including the M1 rifle, with which I surprised myself by qualifying as a marksman.

I will never forget one exercise in particular. It was after lunch, and I was a bit drowsy. All the cadets were assembled in bleachers for a demonstration of the 105-milimeter artillery piece. Our instructors demonstrated the responsibility of each member of the firing team: one man inserted the shell, the second closed the breach lock, the third sighted the weapon, a fourth pulled the lanyard that fired the gun, and the fifth member of the team removed the spent shell. The instructor stressed that the shell needed to be removed immediately because the heat transferred from the barrel of the gun would make the shell casing extremely hot. Five of us were randomly called up to fire the artillery piece. I said to myself, "Oh, God. Any position other than the guy who has to remove the shell."

The instructor then assigned each one of us a role. "Bryan," he said, "you will remove the shell after the weapon is fired."

When the gun was fired and the breach lock was opened, smoke poured from the barrel. A surge of adrenaline flowed through my body. Frankly, I was scared to death. I reached into the barrel, grabbed the shell as quickly as I could, and flung it at least twenty-five yards. All 1,200 cadets began laughing. None of them would have wanted to trade places with me that day.

We spent time in the tear gas chamber, drove tanks, and studied army missions and tactics. Individual cadets were called out to lead the platoon or company during various exercises. When you heard your name, the pressure was on. You might be called upon to march the platoon to lunch or to put the outfit through a drill, but with all eyes of your fellow cadets on you no one wanted to be embarrassed by screwing up. Among the cadets attending was Arizona's Dennis DeConcini, whom I'd later join as a Senate colleague, and Dave Brandsness, who would become the chief executive officer of Sunrise Hospital.

That summer my father filed to run for justice of the peace in the Las Vegas Township. I obviously wanted to be able to register and vote for him. The problem, however, was that I left for Fort Lewis in June but didn't turn twenty-one until July 16, and by the time I returned from summer camp registration for the primary would be closed. My mother, ever the steel magnolia, sprang into action. She made a strong argument for me to be able to register early, arguing that by the time of the primary election in September I would be twenty-one. But the district attorney's office rejected her entreaties. Ultimately, I registered in Washoe County.

A word about the justice of the peace in Las Vegas in those days. There was only one for the entire township in 1958. The position from a legal standpoint was not challenging, but it was the most highly compensated elected office in the United States because of the large number of marriages the justice of the peace performed. My father would be frequently called out in the middle of the night to perform a marriage ceremony. The gratuities were often quite generous. He later appeared on the television show *What's My Line?*

He was the answer to the question, "Who is the most highly compensated elected official in America?"

Shortly after the primary, he complained of increasing hip pain and was referred to Cottage Hospital in Santa Barbara, California, where he was diagnosed with terminal prostate cancer and was given two years to live. He was just fifty years old, but he carried on about his work and his life despite the increasing hip pain he experienced as the disease metastasized.

As my senior year unfolded, as student body president I was in charge of the annual student leadership conference at Lake Tahoe and at Mackay Stadium welcomed new students to campus. I recalled the day just three years earlier when I listened to Jerry Mann, the student body president, welcome us as incoming freshmen. I'd looked around that day and had known, at most, a dozen students. Now I was in a leadership role. The new student union building opened that September, and I participated in its dedication.

The 1958 election year rained victories on the Democratic faithful. In the US Senate, Democrats picked up fifteen new members for a total of sixty-four seats. Howard Cannon, a close friend of my father, filed for the US Senate in the Democratic primary. Although he had lost in his bid to unseat Representative Walter Baring in a primary two years earlier, as Las Vegas city attorney Cannon enjoyed a high profile in Clark County and was known for clashing with the local power company. Cannon was challenged by Reno physician Fred Anderson, a former Rhodes Scholar, in the primary. Cannon managed to carry only Clark and Lincoln Counties, but prevailed thanks to a wide margin of victory in Clark.

Cannon faced two-term incumbent Republican George "Molly" Malone in the general election. Perhaps Malone should have been nicknamed Lucky. He won in 1946 because of a split in the Democratic Party. He was reelected in 1952 with the support of Senator Pat McCarran, a Democrat, after fellow Democrat Tom Mechling's primary defeat of McCarran protégé Alan Bible. The Malone-Cannon race shaped up to be a barn burner.

Charles Russell, the two-term Republican governor, was also seeking reelection. His Democratic opponents included Attorney General Harvey Dickerson, a favorite of the power structure; George Franklin, former Clark County commissioner; and Grant Sawyer, Elko County district attorney. Although not well known, Sawyer was a gifted speaker with a magnificent mellifluous voice. He was young and progressive and represented the future of Democratic Party politics. Sawyer prevailed in the primary.

At the university, the Little Wal (short for Little Waldorf) watering hole became the unofficial headquarters of the Cannon campaign. Supporters of Sawyer's campaign and many other Democratic Party candidates would stop by from time to time.

On election night, the scent of victory filled the November air. The election returns from the East began indicating a Democratic tidal wave sweeping across the nation. In an extraordinary year, Democrats enjoyed Senate victories in Wyoming, Utah, California, and Nevada. Not only did Cannon claim Malone's seat, but Sawyer defeated Russell, Roger Foley was elected attorney general, and Peter Echeverria defeated Forrest Lovelock in Washoe County's state senate race. If you were a Democrat, November 1958 was as good as it gets.

I had cast my ballot for all the winners. In Las Vegas, my father prevailed in the justice of the peace race and was a winner at last. Sawyer invited me to the Inaugural Ball in the Carson City High

School gym, a modest and understated event compared to the ones held a quarter century later when I was the one that was doing the inviting.

My term as student body president was not without controversy. In presiding over the student senate, I pressed hard for the establishment of a student court. The senate was very supportive. The weekly *Sagebrush* campus newspaper editor Warren Lerude was not. He railed against the idea and dubbed me "King Richard" in the *Sagebrush*. His broadsides put me in damage control each week and reminded me that Mark Twain was right when he remarked, "Never pick a fight with a man who buys ink by the barrel."

Warren wasn't vicious, and I never really took his comments personally. I'd buy him a beer when we'd run into each other at the Little Wal. Since he'd labeled me a British monarch, I thought I'd return the favor and call him John Peter Zenger after the free press defender in colonial America. Warren would go on to win the Pulitzer Prize, edit the *Reno Gazette-Journal* with great professionalism, and write acclaimed books. I'm glad to have helped him sharpen his editorial saber—even if it was at my expense.

Seniors in the advanced ROTC program assumed command of the platoons, companies, and battle groups. The brigade commander was a cadet colonel, the highest rank, and Bob Morrill was appointed to that position. The one position I did not want was to become the adjutant. Although it carried the rank of major and outranked company and platoon leaders, it meant using the so-called "adjutant's walk," a very short choppy step, from the sidelines to the center of the formation. The walk was very affected and was guaranteed to generate laughter. It certainly did in my case.

Early in the semester each of the senior ROTC students was required to make their request for branch assignments. Each cadet was required to include the three combat arms, infantry, artillery, and armor, and could make two additional choices. I was fortunate to get my first choice, Adjutant General Corps.

I wanted to go on active duty as soon as possible so I could enroll in law school in the fall of the following year. I applied for six months. When I received my orders, I was directed to report to the Adjutant General School at Fort Benjamin Harrison in Indianapolis, Indiana, on July 20, 1959, for six months.

I hosted the Pacific Students Presidents Association (PSPA) in Reno in the spring. When the convention convened, the student body-elects attended, as I had the year before. Tom Stone, the student body president at Brigham Young University (BYU), had been elected as the PSPA president the year before. Three years older than I, with an LDS mission in Tahiti under his belt, he was impressive. BYU's student body president-elect was Rex Lee, who became dean of the BYU Law School and later president of BYU. As attorney general, I engaged him to assist us in Nevada's Sagebrush Rebellion legislation, which was passed by the state legislature. I was flattered when he asked me to write a letter of recommendation for him in support of his application to be the solicitor general in the US Department of Justice.

The Riverside was the host hotel, and Reno really extended itself for the gathering. Bonnie Fairchild served as the PSPA committee hostess. I didn't know it then, but she was just beginning to help me get to where I wanted to go in life.

The year and my college days were coming to an end. June 1, graduation day, dawned on a perfect spring day in the Truckee Meadows. My mother and father came to Reno, and Bonnie attended as well.

In the morning, attired in my dress blue uniform, I was commissioned an "officer and a gentleman" by an act of Congress, as the old saying went. By tradition, the first enlisted man to salute a newly commissioned officer was given a dollar by the new officer.

The year 1959 was the sesquicentennial of the birth of Abraham Lincoln. It was also the 100-year anniversary of the discovery of the Comstock Lode, where Mackay made his fortune. Famed poet and Lincoln biographer Carl Sandburg was our commencement speaker. Who arranged it, I don't know, but it was impressive for a small school to attract a speaker of national acclaim.

My university days had come to a close. My journey now would continue on a more serious and challenging road.

CHAPTER 4

Army Life

I arrived at Fort Benjamin Harrison northeast of Indianapolis on July 19, 1959, and was assigned to a Bachelor Officer Quarters (BOQ). Our class of about thirty-five represented a cross section of the 1959 college graduates from throughout the country. Harvard, Stanford, Notre Dame, Syracuse, the University of Kentucky, and the University of Maine were among the universities represented. It was an impressive group. The draft was still in effect, and all of us faced the prospect of active military service. Each of us had chosen a four-year ROTC program, which led to a commission as a second lieutenant upon graduation.

My home for the next six months was a World War II barracks partitioned into individual rooms outfitted with a bed, desk, and chair. None of us was interested in pursuing a military career. We were satisfying our military obligation. Most of us, I would learn, were heading to law school or graduate school after our six months was up.

Our classes were conducted at the Adjutant General School. The curriculum consisted of learning the army's recordkeeping system and how to process personnel actions. We had only one outdoor exercise—a compass class that lasted one day. I remember it well because I failed it the first time and had to repeat it.

With our evenings and weekends free, I read nonfiction bestsellers and spent time at the officers' club getting to know the other bachelor officers and talking about our career plans. The weekends often found us socializing in downtown Indianapolis, still the heart of the business community and a great place to meet locals. I liked the people I met and was impressed with their Midwestern values. They weren't flashy, just solid folks.

One of our classmates was a graduate of Notre Dame, and he got us tickets to a Fighting Irish football game in South Bend, Indiana. Studebakers were still manufactured there in 1959, and every other car on the street was a sensible Lark, flashier Silver Hawk, or top-of-the-line Champion. Notre Dame was not yet coed, and the students never sat during the entire game. The priests, in black with their Roman collars, all sat in one section. From across the field, it looked like one of the halftime card sections that are part of college football games. The game was memorable, my first big-time college football game experience. The marching bands with their kettle drums on wheels paraded up and down the field at halftime. But the glory days of legendary Notre Dame coach Frank Leahy were over. We were treated, however, to a glimpse of the future. Northwestern, coached by Ara Parseghian, defeated Notre Dame that day. Parseghian was hired by the Fighting Irish in 1964 and returned the program to the pinnacle of college football.

Wright-Patterson is a large air base in Dayton, Ohio. The base was the home of the Military Air Transport Service. When space was available, it was possible for an officer to hitch a ride wherever the plane was going. One weekend, Marv Honig, whose room was next to mine at the BOQ, wanted to visit his girlfriend in New York City. We drove to Dayton on Friday evening, and the next morning caught a flight with a group of nurses heading to New York City. Others in our class used their leave time to travel to Europe via the transport service.

We completed the Officer Basic Course in September. The army was then confronted with a perplexing decision. With just a few months of active duty remaining, assigning us to a unit in the field left little time for on-the-job training. The decision was made to keep us at Fort Benjamin Harrison for additional courses. We were given an exam. Those who finished in the top half would go to a data processing class, the rest to an advanced personnel course. The test had a fair amount of math, a subject I had detested since second grade, but somehow I finished in the top half.

One of the officers who hadn't finished in the top half asked me if I'd be willing to approach the school commandant and try to persuade him to allow us to trade places. I was clueless about data processing, but my classmate was a business major from Kentucky who knew automated systems were the wave of the future and would be important to his civilian career. Then came the sweetener: if I were successful, he'd give me $300—a lot of money in 1959. My second lieutenant's base pay was just $222 a month. I would have made the inquiry for nothing since I had no interest in data processing, but for once I kept my mouth shut. I told him I'd give it a try.

The commandant was a bird colonel, a career man from head to toe. I requested an appointment with him, which he granted. I reported to his office and saluted. He asked me what was on my mind. Although I had been in the army for just a few weeks, I had already learned a key phrase: "For the good of the service." I framed my argument to the commandant around that principle. I explained that my plan after leaving active duty was to go to law school with an intention of later requesting a branch transfer to the Judge Advocate General Corps. My Kentucky classmate, on the other hand, was a business major whose service and civilian career paths would benefit from the data processing class that I'd been assigned to. The army, I argued, would greatly benefit from the synergy of his military training and his career plans if he, rather than I, was assigned to data processing. The colonel hesitated for a moment, then said, "Lieutenant Bryan, that makes a lot of sense to me. I'll have the order cut."

My classmate was ecstatic, and he promptly paid me what he promised in cash. I was pretty excited as well, and in the ensuing years have always regarded this as my first fee for professional advocacy. That week I went out to a suburban shopping center, the first mall I'd ever set foot in, and bought a blue blazer and my first three-piece suit. That would be my wardrobe for the next three years. It was a big improvement from my undergraduate attire. The rest of the money I saved. In later years I thought about how my Kentucky classmate might recall the change of classes. He probably became a high-flying business executive on the cutting edge of systems technology and told his friends about this guy from Vegas who was so unsophisticated he didn't know what he'd given up.

My last class was a postal class for the enlisted men, and over the years I have been much amused at the instruction we received. It was pretty basic: we were taught how to place a stamp on the upper right corner of an envelope and to care for the leather postal pouch by periodically applying Neatsfoot oil to keep the bag supple. I remembered as a youngster using Neatsfoot oil on my baseball glove. The enlisted men were mostly draftees serving just a few years after the end of the Korean War, and Korea was not considered a choice assignment. Our instructor would frequently chide them by saying, in a good-natured way, "I don't know where you guys are going, but they're serving a lot of rice at the Mess Hall. Looks like you're heading to Korea."

At Christmas that year, I returned to Las Vegas and attended several parties with my mother attired in my "dress blues." She beamed with pride.

I enjoyed my military experience at Fort Benjamin Harrison. None of us were super patriots, just guys trying to honor our military obligation. We were exposed to military life, and the military gained an understanding from a new generation of young men coming out of the nation's colleges and universities. Military service was an expected part of growing up for every able-bodied male in the 1950s. Today, I think the civilian and military ranks miss that perspective. I have always been proud to stand at events when those who have served in the military are recognized.

In retrospect, the thirty-five of us in that Officer Basic Course had little impact on the army. One thing occurred, however, that we were all very proud of, and that could have had an enormous impact on one of our classmates. During one of our examinations, our instructor, a captain, informed us that "Committee Work" would be accepted. We all took that to mean that we could share answers. The captain left the room, and another officer, a major, entered and saw what he thought was cheating going on. Charges were pressed against one of our classmates. The officer who gave the "Committee Work" approval did nothing to explain the situation. Fearing our classmate would receive a dishonorable discharge that would jeopardize his future, the manifest injustice of such a consequence galvanized us to take action. None of us were career types, so there was no reluctance to go directly to the commandant and challenge the major's actions. We made our case to the commandant, who rescinded all disciplinary action. We were civilians, in the military for only a short time. But I have often wondered if we'd been career officers, would we have so boldly lobbied the commandant? I'd like to think we would have. I believe that an army that includes a broad range of citizens is far less likely to be isolated from the rest of society, and it is far healthier for the rest of us to have a military that understands that. I think we are missing that today with the volunteer army. Relatively few citizens are exposed to military service, and I think all parties concerned miss out on something in the process.

It was a heady time for me, and I admit being a bit smitten with myself. I decided to return to Las Vegas by way of Reno and visit some of my fraternity brothers at the University of Nevada and preen a little. After all, at twenty-two I was a college graduate and an officer and a gentleman by act of Congress. I toured the campus in my snappy blue blazer and visited with some of my professors, then put in an obligatory stop at the Little Wal. The campus was abuzz about the approaching Winter Olympics to be held at Squaw Valley in a few days.

Returning to Las Vegas, I felt the world was my oyster. In short order, reality collided with my high opinion of myself. January was a tough month to find work in Las Vegas in 1960. I checked in at the usual places and came up empty. I made calls to friends and had no success. I tried to prevail upon some of my father's old pals and tapped out. With the air steadily leaking from my personal parade balloon, as a last resort I went down to the unemployment office and filled out an application. I stopped by the Reynolds Electrical and Engineering Co.'s office and put in another application. REECo, as it was known, was a major contractor at the Nevada Test Site that provided housing, food services, and recreation to thousands of workers. Maybe I'd get lucky with one of those jobs. No one seemed particularly impressed by my college diploma or my commission as an army second lieutenant. For the first time in my life, I struggled to find work.

When the unemployment office called a few days later to report an opening as a porter at the Hacienda Resort Hotel & Casino, I was appropriately humbled and said, "I'll take it." Before I was scheduled to report to work, I received a call from Jim Holcombe at REECo, who offered me a job on the graveyard shift in the housing office at Mercury, the base camp for the Nevada Test Site. I accepted the job immediately, and I thanked the good folks at the Hacienda and informed them that I'd found other employment.

Behind the wheel of my pink '56 Buick, I began making the nightly 65-mile commute to Mercury on the two-lane strip of asphalt notoriously known as "the Widowmaker." As the name implies, the Mercury highway was one of the most lethal stretches in the state.

Long hours at the test site, often working a double shift, followed by a stop on the way home to Las Vegas at the Dug Out Bar in Indian Springs, made for a deadly combination. Later that year, my friend Chuck Johnson would be one of the Widowmaker's fatalities. It was a lonely ride, but fortunately one I shared with Chuck Ferris, who also worked the night shift at Mercury. Chuck later went into the sheet metal business, and as a member of the local trade association he became an active supporter during my political career.

The test site had many contractors, and there was a well-established pecking order for housing assignments. Although a few of the workers lived at Mercury, generally those passing through the housing office were staying for only a few days. At the top of the contractor hierarchy were the national labs, Lawrence Livermore National Laboratory and Los Alamos Scientific National Laboratory. Their employees, along with Department of Defense officials, were assigned to small individual trailers, the best housing available. On the other end, the REECo employees slept in group housing reminiscent of my army barracks but without the partitioning for individual rooms. In the middle were Fenix & Scisson, Holmes & Narver, FSI, and other contractors.

I functioned as a glorified clerk, making housing assignments and collecting fees. With little traffic until five o'clock in the morning, the nights were long and lonely. I was the only person in the housing office. The lulls in activity left me time to read and visit with Joe Dauenhauer, who worked across the hall in what was derisively called the "Idiot Badge Office." Because of the top-secret work being done during the era of atomic bomb development and testing, everyone entering the test site was issued a badge that listed the areas to which the wearer had access. With thousands of people on the job, virtually every night someone arrived at Mercury who had forgotten his badge. Joe's job was to issue temporary badges, known by all as "idiot badges."

I soon learned the test site had its own culture. Employees who lived at Mercury participated in a range of activities offered by REECo. On those occasions when I pulled a double shift, I got to know the daytime crew. I was a short-timer in the housing office, but many of its employees had worked at the test site for years.

Everyone in the office knew I was headed to law school in a few weeks. But I regard my time in the housing office as another of my life's valuable experiences. Although the job skills I acquired were limited, some of the people I met became friends. And the fact that I had once been a test site employee put me in good stead with workers there during future campaigns for public office. I would never forget Jim Holcombe's kindness, not only in hiring me, but in lending support in future years. Tall as a basketball forward, Jim was a well-liked sports referee who also owned Pogo's bar on Decatur Boulevard not far from a test site bus stop. My campaign signs were always welcome at Pogo's.

With a mix of swing shift and nights on graveyard, my work schedule played havoc with my social life. The clerk's job paid little more than minimum wage. I missed out on some good times, and after a few months at the test site I started to look for work a little closer to home. Before leaving REECo, I was asked to rewrite my job description as a housing clerk. There was a fair amount of turnover in the position because of the low pay, and it was hoped that my rewritten job description might be used to justify a higher salary for future clerks. I left REECo with a philosophy that I'd follow for the rest of my life: never burn a bridge, for you never know what the future may portend.

In high school I was a member of the Order of DeMolay, sponsored by the Masonic Lodge, and I had become acquainted with Pete Rasmussen, the Las Vegas chapter's advisor. Pete worked at Ronzone's department store, which was owned by a local family who had opened its first store in the central Nevada boomtown of Manhattan. Mom Ronzone's son Dick managed the store, served on the school board when I was in high school, and would later join me in the Nevada Assembly in 1971. In the days before Las Vegas had shopping malls, Ronzone's on Fremont Street was as close as we came to a big-city department store. Ronzone's also had a small women's and men's shop in the Tropicana Resort & Casino. When the manager's position opened at the Tropicana store, Rasmussen arranged for me to get the job. Let's just say "store manager" was a somewhat inflated title. There were only two employees. I ran the men's shop, and a beautiful German girl named Inga Surles handled the women's apparel.

At the time, the Tropicana was one of the newest hotels on the burgeoning Las Vegas Strip. The clientele at the Ronzone's shop was upscale, and there was always a lot of action. I ate lunch in the coffee shop daily and was given a front-row seat to some of the Strip routine for the first time. I gained some insight into what it was like to work at a Strip property.

The Masonic bodies included some of the most prominent men in the Southern Nevada community in 1960. I wanted to be a part of that group. My father was very active in Democratic Party politics and community service. He had been blackballed for membership in the Masons, but knowing of my interest in pursuing a political career he recommended that I petition for membership. I followed his advice, was accepted, and in time became a 32nd-degree Scottish Rite mason, which broadened my community contacts. (Years later, Ed Pine, whom I had gotten to know when he was chapter advisor to the ATO House, was elected to the highest position in Scottish Rite Masonry in Nevada. In that capacity, he selected me to be a 33rd-degree mason.)

With law school looming, my thoughts turned to the challenges ahead. The Las Vegas Rotary met weekly at the Tropicana, and members of the organization passed by the men's store. One of the Rotarians was Jack Cherry, who had just been appointed district attorney following the midterm resignation of George Foley. Cherry was a young lawyer not yet thirty and the son of a prominent Southern Nevada family. Jack was the DA, and I hadn't started law school. My anxiety level rose. The road to the top, always challenging, had one more youthful contender that was far ahead of me. From that day, I always felt that others were ahead of me and I must quicken the pace. Every minute counted. Every day must be marked by progress. I was the quintessential young man in a hurry. In retrospect, those fears were exaggerated, but at the time I was strongly affected by them.

Those months after leaving the army and before starting law school were carefree and happy times spent drinking beer with great friends such as Dave Powell, Paul Huffey, and Gerald Eggers. Those days of leisure were about to end.

CHAPTER 5

The Paper Chase

Although I'd been a decent student in college and high school, I didn't exactly light up the world with my academic discipline. School came easily for me, and I'd never had to do much heavy lifting. If my grades could have been better, my record of attendance at social functions and sporting events was nearly perfect. I knew that casual approach would spell disaster in law school. It would have to change if I was going to be successful at the University of California Hastings College of Law in San Francisco, where daily studies left little room for distraction. Could I maintain the commitment? I was not sure if I could study six to seven hours every day after class.

My father had encouraged me to go to law school in Washington, DC, where he had gone, but for a political junkie like me such an electrified atmosphere would have been impossible to resist. And recent University of Nevada student body presidents who had gone to law school in DC had not graduated. Hastings in downtown San Francisco, with its nominal tuition of about $200 per semester with an additional $500 per semester for nonresidents thanks to the largesse of California's system of higher education, made better sense. Even as a nonresident, it was helluva bargain. It was an urban campus with few distractions and a class schedule that went six days a week. It would force me to stay home and study on Friday nights. Before the Silver State had a law school of its own, Hastings was often referred to as "Nevada's Law School" because it produced so many good Nevada lawyers. A few among many: Bill Raggio, future Washoe County district attorney and state senate giant; George Dickerson, Clark County district attorney; Bill Beko and Jim Brennan, district judges; and Michael Douglas, a Nevada Supreme Court justice.

I sold my '56 Buick. I wouldn't need a car in San Francisco, and the ready cash would come in handy. With a steamer trunk containing all my worldly possessions, I bought a bus ticket to San Francisco and left on the 7:00 p.m. Greyhound from the downtown station on a route that cut through Bakersfield and up through the heart of the verdant San Joaquin Valley, the remarkable American breadbasket. As the bus moved along, I saw sweeping and abundant fields filled with seasonal farm laborers from Mexico who were in California as part of the federal Bracero Program. As our journey progressed up the great valley, farm workers got on and off the bus. As they did, I began to better appreciate my own good fortune and came to greater respect their backbreaking and monotonous work.

By the time we finally rolled into San Francisco in the early morning, only a few non–Spanish speaking riders remained. In years to come, I would be reminded often of that long bus ride when the complex subject of immigration was broached, and I'd remember that the program didn't just happen, but was enacted by the Congress to provide workers for the seasonal harvest.

Once off the bus, I wrestled with the steamer trunk and walked up the street toward Hastings a bit apprehensive of what lay ahead. The environment was like nothing I'd experienced. It wasn't welcoming, but indifferent to my presence. I used to say, all it took to gain admission to Hastings was a pulse and a room-temperature IQ, and there was some truth to it. The real challenge wasn't getting into Hastings; the hard part was getting out with a law degree. The attrition rate was withering, and the atmosphere was intimidating. Dostoyevsky would have loved Hastings, but I was feeling the chill.

Just a block from the school, a car pulled up to the curb. I noticed it was a brand-new Ford Victoria. Out of the car popped Bob Peccole, my classmate from high school journalism, who somehow had recognized me as he was passing by. I had not seen Bob since our high school days. He got out and looked at me and said, "What are you doing here?"

"I'm going to law school," I replied.

"So am I," Peccole said. "Throw your trunk in the back, and let's register."

And so I did. That chance meeting would prove to be one of the most fortuitous events in my life. It began a lifelong friendship. Bob invited me to join him and his wife, Nancy, for dinner at their home. Later that evening, he dropped me off at the boarding house where I'd be living.

Less than twenty-four hours later, I found myself sitting with Bob in a group of three hundred first-year law students. A few of the notable names that were in the class ahead of me in 1960 included future state attorney general and governor Bob List, Bob Petroni, and my friend Jim Santini, who would enjoy a long legal and political career highlighted by eight years as Nevada's lone representative.

The class grew silent as David Snodgrass, Hastings' legendary dean, began to speak. He offered a variation of the old saw, "Look to the right and left of you. Only one of you belongs here." He added the chilling corollary, "Our job will be to find the one that does." There was no suggestion that hard work could ensure survival. It was the law school equivalent of academic Darwinism.

Although many greatly admired Snodgrass, a fixture at Hastings since 1928, I was never a fan. On a visit to Hastings during my last year at the University of Nevada, I sought an introduction. When I mentioned that my father was a lawyer, he replied, "Those are the students that often flunk out." I was taken aback by his brusqueness, but in retrospect it probably helped focus my mind on the daunting task at hand. Snodgrass was no charmer. When Santini's father died during finals week, Snodgrass was unsympathetic and made it clear that there would be no flexibility in the examination schedule for him. Cold as a piece of steel, I thought. My bias was set. His less-than-comforting welcome message didn't change my initial impression.

To give him his due, he assembled an impressive faculty known as the "65 Club." In 1960, the law still allowed universities to compel mandatory retirement at the age of 65. Snodgrass wisely recognized that many professors that age were still at the top of their game, and he recruited them to Hastings. Among my favorites that first year: Everett Fraser, who taught real property and for whom the University of Minnesota Law School was named; Rollin Perkins taught criminal law after years spent as the dean of law schools at Iowa and the University of California, Los Angeles (UCLA); and George W. Goble, who taught contracts, had a distinguished academic lineage reaching all the way back to Samuel Williston, a giant in the field.

The law school routine was fixed with all classes scheduled in the morning. We finished by noon. Bob Petroni organized the morning carpool to class and charged us for the ride. He and his wife managed a group of apartments and were so frugal they were the only couple I knew who left law school financially ahead. Most days I would walk back to the boarding house, stopping for a hamburger at a drugstore counter on the corner of Pacific and Van Hess and a package of Hostess cupcakes at a grocery store down the street. On some days I would join Bob and Nancy, who worked downtown, and we'd enjoy a fast-food lunch. They were special times.

The boarding house on Broadway Avenue was plain and shared a common management with one around the corner on Pacific Avenue, where we took our meals each morning and evening. The couple who ran the boarding house drank heavily every night, and it was my first experience with the debilitating effects of alcoholism. We all ate together in a melting pot of humanity. I took a long dinner break every evening and enjoyed visiting with the boarders. My roommate, Jim Corica, a fraternity brother, was in San Francisco enrolled in an insurance training program. He was the only boarder I knew. The rest were strangers from many walks of life. There was a student who attended San Francisco State, a secretary who worked in the financial district, and a native South African who called working class people "the vulgar herd." A construction worker, an old-age pensioner, even a freshly divorced high school assistant principal: the boarding house residency offered a little bit of everything.

After dinner and another four hours of hitting the books and that first year frequently conferring by phone with Bob, my studies ceased for the evening. The paper chase continued early the next morning. Saturday offered a lighter class schedule and an afternoon study group that included Bob and fellow Nevadans George Allison and Buzz Kwapil. Saturday night and much of Sunday was time off. With no meals served at the boarding house on weekends, Jim and I often grabbed a bite. Attending a University of Nevada–San Francisco State football game that fall comprised most of my social activity. It was a time of work, and that included Sunday until midnight.

I was busy with the books, but San Francisco was casting its spell on me in other ways. The great *San Francisco Chronicle* columnist Herb Caen was so right when he nicknamed the city Baghdad by the Bay. In the early 1960s, San Francisco was on the cutting edge of the social and political movements that would dominate the national debate for the rest of the decade. A year before my arrival, a protest was held at City Hall in opposition to a hearing held by the House of Un-American Activities Committee. One of the first non-clandestine gay bars in the country opened across the street from the apartment that Bonnie and her roommates later rented. It was also the home of the politically active Hallinan family—icons of the left. Vincent, the family patriarch, had run for president in 1952 on the Progressive Party ticket and collected the third-highest number of votes. His son, Terence "Kayo" Hallinan, was a Hastings law student and later became the district attorney of San Francisco. I was able to attend a lunch where Vincent was the speaker. I like to think of myself as a moderate, so suffice to say he was far to the left of my political views.

North Beach pulsed with entertainment. At the hungry i nightclub, the Kingston Trio performed. Down the street at the Condor Club, Carol Doda would proudly remind visitors of the wonders of silicone. It was a great time to live in San Francisco if you were young and single, but, alas, I participated in almost none of the nightlife. My goal was to graduate from law school, and in the first year I managed to stray from my study routine on just three occasions.

Bob and I joined a legal fraternity, Phi Alpha Delta, and I spent one delightful evening off the books at a fraternity event at the Pabst Blue Ribbon Brewery, which had a stunning view of the City by the Bay.

It was an election year at a time the US was on the precipice of social change. The sleepy 1950s were over. It was Nixon vs. Kennedy. I was a Kennedy supporter, but when Nixon visited for a campaign rally in September I wanted to be there to experience what one was like in a big city. I wasn't disappointed. The event was held at Union Square. A crowd estimated at 40,000 gathered to meet the vice president with the hometown *San Francisco Chronicle* declaring the next day, "How S.F. Crowd 'Revived' Nixon." Nixon assailed the Democrats for their "politics of despair" and promised to keep America's military the greatest in the world "whatever the cost of sacrifice." He wouldn't win the race, but his words would echo through history as the war in Vietnam began to take its toll.

On election night two months later, we gathered at the Crocodile Casbah near Van Ness and Pacific to watch the returns. In front of the bar was a small pond where a solitary swan paddled and preened. When the results came in, we toasted Kennedy's victory with every state he carried in one of the closest elections on record. Later that evening after victory was assured, we left the bar.

I'm not sure whose idea it was, and mercifully the statute of limitations has passed, but that night we managed to capture the swan and transport it back to the boarding house. As with all newsworthy events in San Francisco, the bird's disappearance was immediately tipped to Caen at the *Chronicle,* who duly reported it in his daily column. So you might say I once made Caen's column. For the record, the next day we went to the Palace of Fine Arts, on the site of the 1915 Panama-Pacific International Exhibition, surely a more fitting home for such an elegant bird, and we released the swan into the lagoon.

The fun and games were over. It was time to get back to the books. For the first time I was truly challenged academically, and I found it exciting. I had never studied so hard or learned so much. I was reminded of Justice Oliver Wendell Holmes, who observed, "The mind expanded by new knowledge, never returns to its original dimensions."

As the days passed, I developed my own study regimen. Each day, cases were assigned from the casebook, and I outlined them on paper with a gummed edge that could be placed on a page in my notebook. I took notes on the professors' class lectures and compiled an outline for each class that consisted of briefed cases, class notes, and outside reading. I made the practice of reviewing the outline, one class every night, beginning with our first assignment. By the end of the year, I could visually recall the contents of each page. It was an important exercise, for most classes were a year long and capped by a single exam. Personal property, the only semester class I had that first year, provided a test for my study technique. When I received an A on the final, I felt good that my study routine was working.

My father's death from prostate cancer came mercifully on January 29, 1961. He suffered greatly in the final months. He was just fifty-two years old. He left my brother, sister, and me no financial inheritance—only his good name—but it was a legacy that has been helpful many times in my life. Shortly after my father's funeral, his friend Archie Grant, a university regent and the local Ford dealer, called and asked me to come to his office. He asked me if I could use a little financial help. I told him I could. He wrote out a check for $500 and handed it to me. Although I repaid him the following summer, I've always felt guilty for not showing more gratitude and thanking him in a personal way.

At Hastings, criminal law was taught by professor Rollin Perkins, a dapper Stanford man attired in suit, vest, and tie. He wrote the book on the subject, *Perkins on Criminal Law.* Standing behind his chair, his shoulders shaking slightly, Perkins began each class with the same word with an unmistakable resonance I can hear to this day: "*Su-ppose* A strikes B with a crashing blow to the forehead. What crimes, if any, is A guilty of?"

He would glance at the seating chart then slowly scan the room like a sniper before calling out a student's name. The student would then stand. Over the next forty-five minutes, Perkins fired hypothetical questions at the victim of the day. The answers weren't always clear-cut.

Each day I was filled with anxiety. Would this be my day? With 150 people in the class, no one wanted to make a fool of himself.

On the day Perkins called my name, the question concerned the elements of an attempt to commit a crime. By coincidence, it was also one of the six questions on the final exam, and one that Bob Peccole and I had focused on. The professor lived to 103, and his obituary noted the signature word "Su-ppose" that filled law students with such trepidation.

When the time arrived for the final exams, my study schedule did not change. Having reviewed the material time and again in each of the previous weeks, I was as prepared as I would ever be. It was do or die, sink or swim. When I arrived for my first exam, it took several minutes to control my nerves. I paced a moment to calm myself, then went to work.

At the end of my first year of law school, I returned to Las Vegas for the summer. At Hastings, if you did not get an average of 70 each year, you flunked out—no probation. Such a misstep meant you had to sit out a year and reexamine for the failed course.

Grades wouldn't be released until mid-July at a time I was serving two weeks of reserve duty at Fort Ord on the Monterey Peninsula, one of the largest army posts in the West. Nights were cold even in July, and I remember shivering as I called my mother from a pay phone booth. When she told me that my grades had arrived in the mail, I found myself shaking so badly I was literally bouncing off the sides of the phone booth.

"How did I do in civil procedure?" It was the class I was most worried about.

"You got a 76," she said in her mellifluous Southern accent.

She continued reading and the news got even better. I'd finished No. 3 in the class.

Thanks to the father of my good friend Paul Huffey, that summer I got a job at DeLuca Importers. DeLuca was the largest wholesale liquor distributor in the state. I was hired as a boxcar swamper. It would be a hard job that meant lifting and moving hundreds of cases of beer, wine, and hard liquor a day. My assignment was to stack the cases coming down the conveyor rollers on wooden pallets. The summer temperature in Las Vegas soared above 110 degrees, but that was almost balmy compared to the heat inside the boxcars— up to 140 degrees.

On the morning when I first reported to work, the swampers chuckled when they saw me. Pale after a year in San Francisco, I resembled a ghost next to the husky, physical men. They wasted little time putting me through the paces by asking me to palletize the cases as they came off the conveyer rollers and stack them in a pattern that kept them from falling while they were being moved to the warehouse by a forklift.

You can guess what happened next. The guy unloading the boxcar sent cases down the line faster and faster. Several cases fell onto the loading dock. He sped up the usual routine, smiling as he went, and by noon I felt like I'd just survived the Bataan Death March. Exhausted and sore, I returned to work in the afternoon for more of the same and managed to finish the day.

I'm sure the group had bets on whether I'd return the next morning, but I did. By the end of the week, they began to lighten up. I had passed their initiation. They were regular guys who appreciated that despite being overmatched I never complained. I'd never match their efficiency, but I worked as hard as I could.

The work ethic is what we had in common. I soon learned the difference between cases of beer and cases of wine and liquor. Bottles of wine and quarts of liquor are packaged twelve to a case. Cans of beer and pints of liquor are twenty-four to a case, half-pints forty-eight to a case. The backbreakers were the half-pints, and opening a boxcar full of half-pints in the late afternoon was the definition of depressing.

But the job was not without its perks. Every Friday at the end of your shift, you could fill out a request for your weekend needs and pay wholesale for beer, wine, and liquor. Although cases of beer came in handy, when I was trying to impress a date a bottle or two of Mumm Extra Dry Champagne was a nice touch.

In short order, I managed to meet everyone in the warehouse from the people who filled orders for the hotels and bars to the drivers who made the deliveries. Once in a while I'd run into one of the big bosses. And when I learned the dockworkers were represented by the Teamsters Union, I joined and attended a few meetings, and met still more people. By the end of summer, the word got around that I was studying the law and would be returning to school soon. I was heading back to a world far away from the loading docks of DeLuca Importers, but the experience reminded me that this was a summer job for me. For many of them, it was a job they would have for the rest of their lives. I can't tell you how many times when I was in the DA's office that I saw those DeLuca drivers delivering to the downtown hotel-casinos while I was heading to or from the courthouse. I made a point of stopping and visiting with them. When I decided to run for the Nevada Legislature, I'm sure that many DeLuca employees supported me, and I later did some legal work for the company.

Back at school, we anxiously waited to see who had made the grade. Many did not. Most Nevadans fared well, including Bob Peccole, who applied the same competitive intensity to his law classes as he displayed as an athlete on the baseball field and basketball court. Both of us had done well enough to write for the law review. I was feeling a bit more confident.

There is an old law school expression: "The first year they scare you to death; the second year they work you to death." There was a new slate of challenging courses, but the excitement had worn off. A new marathon had begun. No one was safe. There would be a sizable attrition at the end of the year.

Seneca was right when he said, "Luck favors the prepared." Studying a case in our equity class, I read the excerpt in the casebook and couldn't understand it. So, I decided to go to the law library and read the entire case. It was something I rarely did in three years of law school. But after reading the whole case, *Ayer v. Philadelphia and Boston Face Brick Company,* I finally understood it.

And the very next day, by coincidence the professor called on me and put me on the spot about the case, questions that couldn't be answered from reading the abbreviated casebook alone. It was a tour de force. I parried his every advance. Afterward, classmates expressed utter amazement. How did I know the issues with such intimacy and ready recall? I demurred. I never told them that I'd just finished reading the entire case. At the end of the year, I laughed when a classmate, fond of horseracing, posted a tout sheet handicapping where some of us might finish in the class standings. "Could be a strong closer," he wrote next to my name, citing the *Ayer* case. I could only hope so.

But of all the moments that second year at Hastings, by far the most profound event—and the one that would forever change my life— was getting together with Bonnie again. We'd dated at the University of Nevada but hadn't seen each other for two years. Bonnie grew up in Lodi, California, and loved San Francisco. She graduated from the university in 1961 and that fall joined her college girlfriend Kathy Bailey and shared an apartment with two other young women. I'd met Kathy in college and knew her as a quintessential organizer of parties. Before school started, she invited all the Nevadans living in San Francisco to get together at their apartment. Bonnie and I became reacquainted and began dating regularly.

We became engaged on December 7, Pearl Harbor Day. If that wasn't exactly the most romantic day on the calendar, at least I was assured I'd never forget our special day. Earlier that evening, I bought Bonnie a sundae at Blum's, a special treat for a struggling law student but a bit pricey. Some ambiguity exists about the proposal. Perhaps it was the influence of my law school training, but I was laboring under the impression that we were just talking about getting married. Bonnie understood we were engaged. All ambiguity was clarified the next day when she informed me that she had told her parents we were engaged—and so we were. How my life changed, and for the better. I'm thankful every day that she chose to share her life with me.

Her apartment was within walking distance of the boarding house. I walked to the apartment many times. Sometimes she would join me for dinner at a little Chinese restaurant, where a hamburger steak and a wedge of apple pie cost a buck, including a dime tip. I ate the same meal every night. We decided on a mid-September date, but moved it back because Jim Santini, a member of the wedding party, was scheduled to take the Nevada Bar Exam that week in Reno.

That summer I clerked in Las Vegas for Jones, Wiener, and Jones, one of the most prominent firms in the state. Law firms in the 1960s had just a few partners and associates, nothing like the legal giants of today. At the law office, I was again reminded that I was lucky to be Oscar Bryan's son. Lou Wiener and my father had been friends, and Lou had loaned me money to help pay my rent the previous semester. During the clerkship that summer, I was able to repay him. The atmosphere was full of energy, the work interesting, and down the hall I met attorneys Bill Boyd and Jim Brennan. Jim went on to a political career that included justice of the peace, Clark County commissioner, and district court judge. Boyd, the son of casino gaming pioneer Sam Boyd, later joined his father to build one of the largest gaming companies in the country.

Wiener was convinced that the worst thing a young lawyer could do was to get married early in his career. Just before I was scheduled to leave Las Vegas for Lodi to get married, he hosted a dinner for me at which he announced, "You know, California has a three-day waiting period after your blood test, and you don't have enough time to get the results before your wedding."

I panicked. I left the dinner immediately and called Bonnie, who as you might imagine was beside herself. Her family called their lawyer, and I headed to the law library to research the California Civil Code. I located the provisions in California law that required a blood test but found nothing about a three-day waiting period. Many couples came to Las Vegas just to avoid what they believed was California's three-day waiting period. But, as Bonnie's family lawyer informed us the next day, there was no statutory three-day waiting period in California. That only referred to the approximate time it took to have a blood test processed. Arrangements were made for me to get the test as soon as I got off the bus the next morning. My future mother-in-law was waiting for me. The results would be available that afternoon, and Bonnie and I could get the license later that day.

Bonnie was part of a fourth-generation Lodi family, and her family and friends were in attendance. My mother, brother, and sister came up from Las Vegas. The rehearsal dinner was at a private home, poolside, and very nice. The wedding was at the Methodist church the family attended. We had so much fun with the ushers and bridesmaids at the rehearsal that the minister presumed we'd been drinking and gave us a stern admonishment. Innocent of the charge, we were intoxicated by the moment itself.

I had a wife, but no car. After borrowing her father's big Cadillac, we honeymooned in Carmel, one of Bonnie's favorite places. That first night in Carmel we stopped for a glass of wine at a lovely place overlooking the Pacific. When we returned to the car, we found its battery had died. I had neither the cash nor a credit card to pay for a new battery. Fortunately, Bonnie had her dad's credit card. I hadn't been married a day, and I'm sure Bonnie's dad thought this was a terrible beginning.

As she would so many times over the years, Nancy Peccole came through for us and located a small apartment in San Francisco. We bought groceries and other items that a newly married couple would need. But the grocery store wouldn't cash Bonnie's check, so I drove her back to her old neighborhood where she was known. She cashed her check and remained with her former roommates while I returned to the grocery store in Bonnie's father's Cadillac to pay the bill and pick up the goods.

On the way back to pick up Bonnie, with the car loaded with groceries, I was T-boned at an intersection. The force of the collision on the driver's side sprung open the passenger side door. The groceries went flying onto the pavement and rolling down the street. I was unhurt—Cadillacs were built like Sherman tanks in those days—and this time it was Bob Peccole to the rescue. I got to a pay phone and informed him of my dilemma, and initially he thought I was joking. I'd only been married two days, and I'd already totaled Bonnie's father's car. But as I explained, he realized I wasn't kidding and sprang into action. It must have been quite a sight watching two grown men picking up canned goods and the other groceries that had rolled down the street.

After finishing 13th in a class of 286, I felt more confident when school began. So few of us remained that we all fit into one classroom. An entire row from the previous year, save one fortunate soul, flunked out. His average was 70.0. He'd survived with the narrowest margin possible. He was the class anchorman. I would eventually finish third in the graduating class.

The specter of professor Judson Crane, who taught corporations, hung over the class like a storm cloud. He had a reputation for sinking students. If he didn't like your final exam, he slapped it with a 40, making it virtually impossible to cling to a 70 average. My own study habits remained steady. I wasn't about to deviate from something that worked for me. I was worried about the income tax course, but got an A, and was one step closer to my goal.

The Cuban Missile Crisis topped the news that October. The next-day attendance was noticeably down. The air force reservists in class were activated and deployed to Florida. Within twenty-four hours I received orders to report to a reserve unit at the Presidio in San Francisco. I asked Bob Peccole to drive me to the Presidio, which was the headquarters of the XV Corps. A military call-up might prevent my graduation. Once there, I explained my predicament to the captain, a decent guy who immediately reviewed my military record and concluded it wasn't very impressive. I could not disagree. He pored over the paperwork and pointed out that I was deficient in the number of points required to remain a reservist in good standing. With few options available, he mentioned one that I thought might work. I could take correspondence courses to make up the deficient points. I agreed despite the extra workload. He rescinded the order attaching me to a unit.

Within days the missile crisis passed. Life returned to normal. But a deal was a deal. For the remainder of the year my Saturday nights, my only free night of the week, I worked feverishly in our apartment on those damned correspondence courses while Bonnie joined the Peccoles at their apartment.

The year concluded in May with our final exams followed by graduation on the University of California, Berkeley, campus joined by all the other graduates. With thousands in attendance and all the pageantry of that great university on display, the faculty paraded like academic peacocks in caps and gowns representing their degrees from some of the most prestigious European universities with academic lineages dating to the Middle Ages. It was a happy day for all the Berkeley graduates.

Those of us from Hastings shared no such feeling. Although my mother and sister had come up for the ceremony, I wouldn't know if I had graduated for several weeks. There was no class dinner, nothing to indicate we'd made the grade after three long years. We weren't feted in the least. The shadow of Judson Crane hung over us. Sixty years later, I still feel embittered by that experience. What should have been a time of personal satisfaction and joy was not.

A week later we began our bar review class in San Francisco with hundreds of California law school graduates who were studying for the California Bar Exam. Our Nevada contingent was so small it didn't justify a separate class, but much of Nevada law is derived from California. The Nevada Bar Exam could cover twenty-six different courses, more than any student could take in three years.

We learned our grades in July, but not by the traditional method. One morning during the bar review, a classmate who performed janitorial services at Hastings to partially offset his tuition burst into the room shouting, "I've got 'em." In his hand he held a carbon copy of our grades that he'd retrieved from the trash. We gathered around him and strained for a peek, some of us on our hands and knees. Most of us made it, but sadly a handful did not.

The bar review ended in the dog days of August. In 1963, the Nevada Bar Exam was an annual test over three days and held only in Reno. Bob Peccole and I stayed with our classmate Buzz Kwapil at his Reno home.

We assembled at the Masonic Temple and were seated at large circular banquet tables and for three full days answered essay questions on different sections of the law. All of us were in the same room, including those who typed their answers. The questions contained a lengthy recitation of facts that we were required to analyze. It was exhausting, and the time allowed never seemed quite enough. On the first day, as I was still reading the first question, the sound of the typists clattering on their manual machines filled the room and left me irritated and feeling like I was already running behind. A bit paranoid, I thought this was one more obstacle that the bar examiners had created to make life more difficult. After another four hours, it was time to take a break for the day.

Drained of all energy, at the end of the day I joined Peccole and a few others at the bar in the old Mapes Hotel. The pianist was fond of Lerner and Loewe's "Camelot," then playing on Broadway. The strains of "If Ever I Would Leave You," made famous by Robert Goulet, was a personal favorite.

On the afternoon of the last day of the exam, the pressure remained high. We were physically and mentally exhausted and running short of time, and the last question was particularly lengthy. I was furious. I was convinced in my own mind that this was one more deliberate attempt by the bar examiners to add to the pressure we faced. But I channeled my anger and generated a surge of adrenaline that helped overcome my fatigue. It turned out to be an easy question.

That week I met several people who would play integral roles in the Nevada legal community for decades to come. There was Jim Rogers, a fellow Las Vegas High School graduate and later perhaps best known as a co-owner of several Nevada television stations. And there was David Hagen, who would rise to become a US District Court judge. Al Becker was one of the more colorful characters who took the bar that year. He had taken the bar on three prior occasions, failing each time. Shaped like a pear, he cut an unusual figure in a short-sleeved shirt cuffed to hold a pack of cigarettes. The fourth time was a charm for him. He'd later be elected justice of the peace after several attempts.

It was also at the bar exam in Reno that a young guy from Searchlight came up and introduced himself. We shook hands and began a friendship that has lasted through the decades. His name was Harry Reid.

CHAPTER 6

Getting Started

The Nevada State Bar results would not be available until late November. Until the results were released, my future was in a holding pattern. I had sold my car before entering law school. Now I would need a car to return to Las Vegas. I had no money and no job.

Fortunately for both of us, Bonnie was gainfully employed and had saved some money. When I expressed deep affection for a new 1963 Plymouth Valiant convertible with a sticker price of $3,300, she bought the car. It was titled in her name because I was unemployed. We were on the road—with a slight detour for two-week reserve duty at Fort Ord.

It was there I was assigned to work under 1st Lt. Dale Vennes, a capable officer and a real credit to the service. In his career he'd been stationed around the world from Germany to Taiwan, was fluent in Vietnamese, and earned a Purple Heart after being injured while rescuing a visiting dignitary during his tour there. He and his wife, Carol, were gracious and invited me into their home for dinner. He'd just completed a tour of duty in Saigon, a place he described as the "Paris of the Orient." He admired the people and the culture so much that he said he longed to return there. None of us knew in 1963 that within two years President Lyndon Johnson would commit hundreds of thousands of American troops to the country and comparisons to Saigon and Paris would be over. I have often thought about Vennes and whether he was again assigned to Vietnam, and how a man of such good character remembered the war.

My father's friendships and contacts would help me many times in my life. Long after he died, his relationships would open doors and bolster my prospects as I navigated the world. But back in 1960 he'd made a terrible mistake when he decided to run for reelection as justice of the peace. First, the "Marryin' Sam" position was so lucrative that it was considered poor form by local tradition to keep the office for more than a term. Moreover, he was terminally ill with prostate cancer and knew it. He had just a few months to live. Despite that, he decided to charge ahead. Ted Marshall and Myron Leavitt, who were both classmates at Las Vegas High, also filed.

Marshall ran a particularly nasty campaign against my father, questioning couples that my father had married about the size of the gratuity they'd given him. Then he raised the specter of whether my father had paid taxes on those tips he'd received. In 1960, that was considered hitting below the belt. My father lost in the primary and threw his support to Leavitt, who was elected that November.

Two years later, Leavitt and Marshall were facing off again, this time in the district attorney's race. Because of the hard feelings engendered in the 1960 campaign, I supported Leavitt, who promised me a position in the DA's office if he were elected. Although Leavitt was favored, Marshall ran a smart campaign. Leavitt was the JP in Las Vegas, but he wasn't well known outside Las Vegas. Marshall campaigned countywide and was aided by a local college student named Don Williams. Displaying the kind of tactics that would make him successful in politics for decades to come, Williams worked tirelessly on Marshall's behalf and pulled off an upset.

My father had always recommended that I go into the district attorney's office for trial experience, but the animosity generated during the 1960 JP's campaign made that impossible. With no hope of a job in the DA's office, I recalled a casual conversation with Joe Foley the summer before when I had worked for Lou Wiener. Joe had told me to stop by and see him after I graduated.

Joe was a member of the legendary Las Vegas legal family headed by District Judge Roger T. Foley. With Nevada roots in Goldfield, the Irish Catholic Foley brothers were prominent Democrats and big Kennedy supporters.

The five Foley brothers were all successful lawyers. Roger D. Foley, who had defeated my father in the primary for DA back in 1950, was now a federal judge. Joe and brothers John and Tom had a bustling law practice. Former DA George was a criminal defense attorney. Joe went on to serve as a university regent, John joined me as a state senator, and Tom became a district judge.

After I graduated, I took Joe up on his offer to clerk for the firm. Foley Brothers had just completed a three-story office on Fourth Street, and on that first day of work I walked into a brand-new building with a starting salary of $600 a month. That was big money in 1963. It was a comfortable fit for me.

It was less comfortable at home. We were living with my mother. Bonnie was pregnant, homesick, and pining for a place of our own. I told her we could not afford it yet. Enter Nancy Peccole—again—just when we needed her. Bob's grandfather had just finished an apartment building at 1905 Fairfield in an area later known as "The Naked City." And the building needed a manager. Bonnie was bored with her job at Holmes & Narver, and we jumped at the opportunity. We were now going to be apartment managers.

On the last Sunday morning when we were still living at my mother's house, I received an early-morning call from my fraternity brother Roger Bremner, who had just completed two years of active duty in the Quartermaster Corps and was assigned to the local army reserve unit, the 427th Civil Affairs Company. I had four years remaining on my reserve obligation.

"Bryan," he said, "I just told them where you are."

I hadn't been hiding. I notified the army of my change of address when we left San Francisco. Generally, it took the army bureaucracy a year or more to catch up with your new address. Within a week I received orders assigning me to the 427th.

Most of the downtown Las Vegas retail that I had patronized as a high school student remained on Fremont Street, but the winds of change were blowing. Las Vegas was a different community than it had been in the late '50s. By 1960 Las Vegas had surpassed Reno as the state's largest city. An explosive building boom had transformed the western part of the city and Paradise Valley from empty desert to major housing developments and commercial infrastructure to support the thousands of new residents who had moved into the community. Irwin Molasky, the friendly guy whose shoes I'd accidentally swept dust on while working at the jewelry store, had emerged as a prominent developer. After completing the construction of Sunrise Hospital, Molasky and his partners built the Boulevard Mall as part of their plan to transform Maryland Parkway.

It was an exciting time in the valley. The Fremont was the first high-rise hotel-casino in the downtown gaming corridor at a luck-defying thirteen stories when it opened in 1956. It was the tallest building in the state at the time. But now the Sahara-Nevada Corporation was planning a real skyscraper called the Mint, which would be twenty-six stories high upon completion. Change came at a cost, of course: the old courthouse where my father had been a deputy district attorney had been torn down despite the fact it was designed by Nevada's most celebrated and prolific public architect, Frederic DeLongchamps. Like so many figures in Nevada history, DeLongchamps was an autodidact who managed to succeed at a high level without much academic training. He designed the Heroes Memorial Building in Carson City, where I would one day have an office as attorney general, and the Nevada Supreme Court building. As a reminder that some changes aren't always for the better, when the time came to replace the old courthouse in Las Vegas, the design was a hideous example of the worst of the post-modern style.

I was anxious to get moving, but with the bar results still clouding my future I was forced to mark time along with five dozen other hopefuls anxiously standing by. On Friday, November 15, the Board of Bar Examiners held its final meeting in Reno and the results began to trickle out. At that time anyone who knew a bar examiner could call and get the results. Bob Peccole had such connections and learned that he had passed by the late afternoon.

I tried to find out my status. No one seemed to know. I feared for the worst. A sleepless night followed. In the morning, my increasingly frantic inquiries continued. To relieve the tension, I went over to my mother's house and began painting her fence. At midday, I learned I had passed. I was relieved and ecstatic. To this day I don't remember whether I ever finished that fence.

On the following Wednesday, I was sworn in as a member of the Nevada Bar. The formal part of my educational journey had ended. My real education was about to begin.

My legal career got off to less-than-auspicious start. Foley Brothers represented a client embroiled in a dispute involving a golf course in Boulder City. The proposed development polarized and divided the community. None of the partners wanted to drive out to the bucolic place affectionately called "the Best Town By a Dam Site" for what promised to be a contentious evening City Council meeting. So they decided to send me. With the ink on my oath of office barely dry, I was handed the file. No lawyer was ever less prepared than I. Behind the wheel of my new Valiant, with storm clouds boiling prophetically, I made the twenty-six-mile drive south and arrived as the City Council meeting was starting. The chamber was full of animated residents—standing room only—and equally divided. It was often said during my political career that I loved addressing a packed house, and that is true, but on that night, I dreaded the prospect at hand. Fortunately, opposing counsel Don Winne was a real gentleman. He sensed that I had drawn the short straw and had little background on the issues being debated. George Franklin Jr., the city attorney, had been a friend of my father and sized up the situation. He was equally charitable and made no attempt to embarrass me despite the fact I knew so little about the issue.

I survived that evening, but I never forgot how those two lawyers refrained from humiliating me despite ample opportunity. They were gentlemen, and I vowed I would always conduct myself in like manner. My maiden voyage wasn't noteworthy but reminded me to never allow myself to be put in that position again. I've forgotten what I said that night, and mercifully those in attendance have forgotten as well.

Two days later, on Friday, November 22, 1963, our world would change forever. By late morning, fragmentary news broadcasts from Dallas reported that the president's motorcade had been fired upon. As the news grew bleaker, we gathered in Tom Foley's office and hovered around his radio. Shortly before noon, the national tragedy was confirmed: Our president was dead. The office immediately closed. In the days ahead, the Las Vegas Strip would go dark and downtown's retail stores hung wreaths in their windows as the nation mourned.

Less than two months earlier, on September 28, President Kennedy had appeared at the Las Vegas Convention Center at the end of a five-day conservation-themed tour of the country. Nevada governor Grant Sawyer and Senators Alan Bible and Howard Cannon had greeted him, and the Foley brothers, who had helped him carry Nevada, attended. A photograph of Kennedy, bathed in light during his speech in the convention center rotunda, hung prominently in the law office.

Kennedy on that day talked about the importance of tempering our military strength abroad without losing sight of the greater goal of peace across the globe. He spoke of how "essential it is to conserve our natural resources and make the best use of them" and reminded those in attendance that "water is the key to growth and its wise use essential to the development of the western United States." He stressed education and expressed admiration for the state. "There is no state of the Union where these two twin concepts of conservation, to conserve and to develop, can be more clearly seen than here in the state of Nevada."

Now he was gone. The nation was riveted to its black-and-white television sets. We watched CBS News anchor Walter Cronkite report the grim news from Dallas and later tearfully pronounce the president was dead. In the days to come, we would watch the president's funeral cortege making its way down Pennsylvania Avenue to Arlington National Cemetery. The riderless horse with boots reversed in the stirrups symbolized a fallen warrior as it has since the time of Genghis Khan. It was followed by the president's casket draped in the American flag. The nation mourned.

In the weeks that followed, the country slowly moved forward. In Las Vegas, my life as a newly minted lawyer, husband, and soon-to-be father, not to mention apartment manager, began to follow a fairly predictable routine. At Foley Brothers, I performed legal research for the partners and represented the pro bono cases the firm accepted. And I made my first court appearance representing a client seeking a divorce. It was still the era of the uncontested divorce in Nevada, which for decades had provided an easy living for many of the state's lawyers. It was not a heavy lift, but I was learning the ropes.

The uncontested divorce in the Silver State has an interesting history. You might say it's rooted in Nevada's boom-and-bust mining history. The state's population boomed with the 1859 discovery of the Comstock Lode near present-day Virginia City, but those census figures declined just as rapidly when the silver ore began to play out. By the turn of the century, Nevada's population had dwindled to 43,000. A state government heavily dependent on mining revenues for its very existence was imperiled. When the boom-and-bust repeated itself in the early twentieth century at Tonopah and Goldfield, Nevada leaders cast about for a replacement industry, a challenge that had plagued Nevada since its statehood.

A change in the nation's social mores provided an opportunity with the rise of the uncontested divorce. As the '20s dawned and women gained the vote and a modicum of independence, divorce became more common across America. The law in most states, however, afforded very limited grounds for marital dissolution. In New York, for example, adultery was the only grounds for divorce well into the 1960s. Most state legislators were reluctant to loosen state law for fear of being labeled anti-family or even immoral.

Nevada saw other states' reluctance as an opportunity. The state made itself a more attractive venue for those seeking divorce by shortening the time to establish residency and broadening the grounds for dissolution. Those changes ushered in a new era for the state as America's divorce capital. And the revenues from a different kind of gold discovery poured in.

The celebrated divorce of "America's Sweetheart," silent-screen star Mary Pickford, focused national attention on Nevada's liberal laws. She arrived in Reno under the eye of the press, and was met by young Nevada lawyer Pat McCarran, the future Senate powerhouse. Pickford wanted to marry legendary silent film star Douglas Fairbanks Sr.

The headlines followed, and the nation buzzed with the news. If Nevada was good enough for America's Sweetheart, it was good enough for unhappy couples from across the nation, who flocked to Reno, and later Las Vegas.

During the depths of the Great Depression, with the state once again suffering, the residence requirement was again shortened. A generation of lawyers, my father among them, made good money by handling uncontested divorces. For some lawyers it was their only source of income. My admission to the bar coincided with the twilight of that era of Nevada's legal history.

In court, the rules of engagement were well established. To be granted a divorce, the party filing for divorce had to establish a six-week Nevada residency. The concept of "mental cruelty," conduct by one spouse that renders the other's life miserable and unendurable, was almost always used for this purpose. Mental cruelty as grounds for divorce covered the waterfront. Testimony offered in support followed this general line of questioning: "During the course of your marriage did you and your spouse drift apart? Were there frequent arguments? Did they cause you to become upset and under a great deal of mental stress?" That was sufficient.

Establishing residency required the plaintiff to testify that he or she had been physically present in Clark County each of the preceding forty-three days. An eyewitness was required to testify that he or she had seen the plaintiff in the county each one of those days. The final question: "Is it your intent to make Clark County, Nevada, your one and only permanent home and residence for at least an indefinite period of time?" That "indefinite period" left enough wiggle room for those who, figuratively speaking, had a suitcase packed in the hall outside the courtroom.

In the early 1960s, women increasingly wore fashionable pantsuits instead of skirts and dresses. As freethinking as Nevada law was about divorce, the court had not yet caught up with changing times and new fashions. The judges required women to wear a dress or skirt for court. On more than one occasion I had a client arrive at the courthouse to secure her divorce fashionably attired in a pantsuit. Not to worry. Hanging in a closet of the law library across the hall from the courtroom was a one-size-fits-all wraparound print skirt that was used in just such emergencies. It was a hideous and shapeless like a muumuu, but it technically met the dress code. It was quite a sight to see an attractive woman dressed to the nines draped in that makeshift skirt. But it was a different era.

Back at home, Bonnie and I were happily navigating our young marriage. Forced to share our one automobile, Bonnie felt somewhat stranded as she managed the apartments and made do without a television. That was another extravagance we could not yet afford. I'll never forget when my good friend Paul Huffey and I surprised Bonnie with a handsome twenty-one-inch black-and-white TV set on a rolling stand. Life was getting better all the time.

Foley Brothers had been kind enough to hire me fresh out of law school, but privately I hoped to find a way to join the DA's office. When Ray Jeffers left Foley Brothers for the prosecutor's office and my friend Bob Petroni established himself as a deputy DA, I was very envious.

Leaving court following an uncontested divorce hearing with Lloyd George, who later became a federal judge, he asked me how I was getting along at Foley Brothers. I told him I was faring well, but that I'd always hoped I'd be in the DA's office. I explained that the door remained closed following the bitter 1960 campaign with my father. George and Ted Marshall had been classmates at Las Vegas High School. He offered to speak on my behalf to Ted Marshall.

The next day I received a call from Marshall inviting me to come to his office for a conversation. Ted said he had not realized how sick my father was and told me that if I could put that behind me, he would like me to join his team. I accepted and was sworn in as a deputy DA almost twenty years after my father had become Gray Gubler's deputy.

CHAPTER 7

District Attorney Days

The Clark County District Attorney's Office was small in 1964 with just nine deputy DAs, six in the criminal division and three in the civil division. I joined the deputies in the criminal division, which included former Foley Brothers associate Ray Jeffers. Paul Parraguirre served as the chief deputy. Former university and law school classmate Bob Petroni was assigned to the civil division. In time, Jim Bilbray and Leonard Gang would join the criminal division.

Each new deputy in the criminal division was assigned to the Las Vegas Justice Court, where preliminary hearings on felonies and gross misdemeanors cases were conducted and misdemeanor cases were tried. In 1964, there was only one justice of the peace for the Las Vegas Township. Deputy DA Ray Little, who had previously been assigned to the justice court, accompanied me for the first couple of days. Then I was on my own. In the macho legal world in the DA's office of the '60s, the prevailing view was a baptism by fire. And I immediately felt the heat.

There was no time to waste and little time to think. My job included subpoenaing witnesses, interviewing witnesses—both law enforcement and private citizens—and presenting the state's case at a preliminary hearing. Because the hearings were stacked, at least two preliminary hearings were always scheduled at the same time, and there were many witnesses. The theory behind stacking was to make sure at least one preliminary hearing was ready to go in each of the scheduled time slots. I often met witnesses for the first time in the hall outside the courtroom just prior to a preliminary hearing. Cases had to be continued frequently because the arresting officer or key witness was unavailable. Confusion abounded outside the courtroom as I determined what witnesses were present and whether I had the necessary witnesses to put on the state's case.

Subpoenaed witnesses who had taken time off from work only

to find themselves bumped by a continuance often grumbled, and I couldn't blame them. It was not an ideal situation. This was particularly true in sexual assault cases in which the victim and the accused were forced to remain in proximity outside the courtroom waiting for their case to be called. One of the most enlightened recent reforms is to protect the victim from the trauma of standing next to their assailant before giving testimony.

Justice of the Peace Tom Pursel and his successor Jim Brennan knew the law and had good judgment. To bind a felony or gross misdemeanor over to the district court for trial, the prosecution only needs to establish probable cause of guilt. It's a lower standard than in district court, where the prosecution must prove a defendant's guilt beyond a reasonable doubt to secure a conviction. Both Pursel and Brennan from time to time would inform me whether there was enough evidence to bind over a case for trial, but not enough to establish guilt beyond a reasonable doubt.

One night each week misdemeanor traffic cases were scheduled. If the preliminary hearings were chaotic, traffic court was a proverbial Tower of Babel. Dozens of cases would be negotiated from a driving under the influence charge to reckless driving, or a speeding ticket from 25 miles per hour over the speed limit to 10. The courtroom was packed with citizens making an initial appearance and lawyers plea-bargaining on behalf of their clients.

In May, Richard Jr. was born. Bonnie's pregnancy was an easy one. Happily ensconced in a less sophisticated time, I was unaware of all the things that could have gone wrong. At the appropriate time, I drove Bonnie to Sunrise Hospital. My mother told me about her protracted labor, and I planned to settle in for a long wait. It was Sunday morning, Mother's Day. I bought the morning editions of the *Las Vegas Review-Journal* and *Las Vegas Sun,* then published separately. Fathers were not allowed in the delivery room. That was fine with me.

I had not yet finished reading the newspapers when curiosity got the better of me. Feeling a bit sheepish, I approached the nurse sitting at the desk in a room where other expectant fathers were waiting.

"It's probably pretty obvious to you that I am a first-time dad," I said. "Is there anything I should be doing right now?"

"Let me see where things stand," she replied.

She left the waiting room and returned a moment later.

"You can go back now," she said. "Your wife just had the baby."

As I entered the long corridor, I met a nurse walking down the hall holding Richard Jr. by his feet upside down. I was overwhelmed with emotion. There went my son!

Bonnie was awake and doing fine. We visited for a time, and then I let her get some rest. I left the hospital in a daze. I drove to church, went inside, and thanked the good Lord for my blessing—a healthy son. It was still Sunday. But our world had changed dramatically. I now had another title added to my name—father.

When court opened the next day, I went back to work. Two cases stand out in my mind in justice court. The first was a preliminary hearing for a defendant named Wagstaff represented by the leading defense attorney of his day, Harry Claiborne, who would later become a federal judge. Wagstaff was charged with robbery and was brought into court handcuffed by Deputy Sheriff Steve Whitaker, who was assigned to the jail. During a brief conversation with Wagstaff, he asked me my name, and when I told him he responded, "Must have been your father who prosecuted me twenty years ago." Sure enough, his rap sheet showed a prosecution in Las Vegas in that time frame. Claiborne was late, and I stepped out of the courtroom to call his office. Judge Pursel was performing a wedding in his chambers.

As I returned to the courtroom, I heard quite a commotion. Wagstaff had jumped Whitaker, who had been leaning back in his chair. Whitaker was on his back with Wagstaff on top of him, bearing down and holding a shiv fashioned out of a toothbrush handle. Whitaker was holding him back with one hand. With his other hand, Whitaker unholstered his pistol and got off one round into Wagstaff's stomach. In the small courtroom, it sounded like artillery fire. Whitaker was shaking so badly from his near-death experience I thought he might accidentally fire again.

Pursel came dashing out of his chambers and roared, "What's going on in my courtroom?"

He ordered Whitaker to put his gun back in his holster. In the seconds that had passed, word had traveled through the courthouse, and several sheriff's deputies led by Undersheriff Lloyd Bell raced into the courtroom. Wagstaff was fully conscious but uttered not a word. The incident generated quite a bit of press converge, but it could have been much more serious. The sheriff's office immediately instituted a new policy: all prisoners, in addition to being handcuffed, were to be shackled when taken into court.

The next day I was in district court handling a preliminary hearing. During a recess Judge Pursel's brother, Bill, who was an insurance agent, approached me.

"Dick," he said, "you're in a pretty dangerous business prosecuting all those criminals. You have a wife and a child. You need a disability insurance policy."

This could only happen in a small town. I bought one immediately. Good old Bill, great salesman that he was, saw an opportunity for a sale and was waiting for me when I walked out of the courtroom. I've laughed about that many times but maintained the policy for forty years.

The other memorable preliminary hearing that occurred in justice court involved the arrest of my boss, Ted Marshall, the district attorney. In preliminary hearings, the DA's office presents just enough evidence to get the case moved to the district court for trial. Defense counsel puts on no evidence. The standard to bind the defendant over for trial at the district court level is probable cause. A preliminary hearing affords defense counsel an opportunity for discovery—how strong is the state's case and how credible are its witnesses?

The defendant, Andrew Heikila, was charged with the murder of a Thunderbird Hotel employee. The fact pattern was somewhat complicated, and I needed to call several witnesses. Heikila's defense counsel was George Foley, a former district attorney who ranked with Harry Claiborne as one of the ablest trial lawyers in Nevada. For reasons never made clear to me, Foley subpoenaed Marshall as a defense witness. The subpoena commanded Marshall to appear in justice court on the day that the preliminary hearing began. I was unable to complete the state's case in one day, and the preliminary hearing was continued several times. In my years in justice court, I had never seen defense counsel call witnesses. I told Marshall I would alert him when I had finished presenting the prosecution's case so he could be in attendance to respond to the subpoena. When I rested the prosecution's case, I alerted Marshall and he came down to the justice court. Judge Pursel wanted to know why Marshall did not appear in court on the day directed in the subpoena. He responded that I had made him aware that the prosecution's case had not been concluded and that I would alert him when the defense was given an opportunity to present its case. Judge Pursel was not satisfied with Marshall's explanation and held him in contempt of court and remanded him to the custody of the sheriff's office. Getting your boss thrown in jail is not exactly a career-enhancing move.

A flurry of activity followed. The DA's office was conflicted in representing Marshall or the state. In the meantime, Marshall sat in custody. Counsel was soon secured for Marshall, and he was released from custody. Clearly there was some bad blood between the judge and the district attorney, and this was payback time.

My starting salary in the DA's office was $827 a month, more than first-year lawyers were paid in private law firms at that time. An increase to $877 in six months was automatic. I opened an account with the Clark County Credit Union and had each pay raise automatically deposited. This began a relationship with Nevada's credit unions that carried into the state legislature and the US Senate. I was very supportive of their legislative positions, and after I retired from the Senate represented them in Washington, DC. It all began because of my frugal nature. That $827 a month was good money in 1964. But that wasn't all. Deputy DAs were also allowed to have a private practice. There were time limitations, so nothing terribly complicated or protracted could be taken on. Uncontested divorces, adoptions, securing court orders for persons under the legally required age to marry, and the like were typical of the matters handled. Moreover, there was no rent to be paid and no secretarial overhead. The secretaries in the DA's office provided secretarial support. Later as public defender, I eliminated private practice for my deputies.

In September just before the World Series, I bought a color TV console that included a radio and record turntable beautifully styled in a Mediterranean finish. I paid $995 and used the money I had made in private practice that month. Not every month was that good.

The following year, Bonnie and I became homeowners. We purchased a three-bedroom, one-and-three-quarters baths house for $25,000. The house was two years old, fully landscaped with a sprinkler system and a garage. After growing up in Huntridge with no garage and watering the yard by hand, those features attracted my attention.

Leslie was added to our family that fall. Her eyes were as big as saucers and reminded me of the Keane paintings, which always depicted children with large eyes. It was always a wonderful feeling coming home in the evening because as soon as she heard the garage door opening, she started crawling at first, and later walking to greet me. What a thrill.

After the stint in justice court, I moved up to the district court, the trial court level. My first trial was a forgery case. I spent a lot of time in preparation, carefully interviewing each witness before trial. That would be my modus operandi for all trials. Law enforcement witnesses were appreciative of the time I spent with them in preparation. The case was investigated by the Las Vegas Police Department (before its consolidation with the Clark County Sheriff's Office.) Detectives Burgess and McCauley were old hands in the forgery unit, and I went to the police department to interview them.

I was about to prosecute a jury trial, and I had never actually witnessed one. I was nervous. I would handle the forgery case alone. Paul Parraguirre patiently mentored me through the process and answered my myriad questions. Paul would later become a successful private practitioner and district court judge.

On the morning of trial, I was prepared. Jury selection went smoothly. The victim had an unusual name, Phrizel Kleinpeter. The case fell nicely into place. After I rested the state's case, the defendant decided to change his plea to guilty. It was a victory of sorts, but not a jury verdict, which I believed was the ultimate test of one's success.

In the months that followed, I handled many jury trials for murder, rape, robbery, and child abuse—the gamut of criminal offenses. I should have declined one case that I was assigned since I did not have my heart in it. It was a burglary charge against former Las Vegas High classmate Clayton Sampson, who was at the juvenile home on a serious charge when I spent a night there for a curfew violation. Harry Reid represented the defendant, and he secured an acquittal.

Another case I tried in district court was later featured in the *State Bar Journal*. The jury included *Las Vegas Sun* executive editor Bryn Armstrong. Armstrong was a working member of the press, and by common practice either the prosecution or defense excused the "ink-stained wretches" who were summoned for jury duty. Not this time. He wound up one of twelve triers of fact. In fact, he was elected to serve as the jury's foreman and announced the verdict, "Guilty."

What followed was most unusual. He wrote a column for the *Sun* that was a paean to the American system of jurisprudence. His opening line: "Come on in, the water's fine." Armstrong related how conscientiously the jurors adhered to the presumption of innocence to which the accused was entitled—in contrast to Soviet-style courts.

After complimenting Judge Mowbray's demeanor, and the effective defense provided by Al Matteucci, the son of the lady at the post office who had helped me when I was a fourteen-year-old mail clerk at Bond's Jewelers, Armstrong turned his attention to me:

"They were impressed also by the obvious sincerity of the young prosecutor, Richard Bryan, whose late father graced the Bar of the State of Nevada for many years, and they appreciated his obvious concern with the rules of fairness while doing his bit to serve the society which he represented."

The column was republished in the July 1965 *State Bar Journal*.

The most unusual case I tried was a misdemeanor embezzlement charge for an alleged theft of casino chips valued at less than $100. The defendant was found guilty in justice court, but under the law at that time the defendant had the right to appeal to the district court for a new trial. The setting was the Riviera Hotel & Casino, and the defendant was a casino craps dealer charged with palming chips and slipping them into his pocket. It was not a strong case. The key witness's testimony in justice court was not compelling. To see what he claimed to have seen would have tested Superman's eyesight. At trial in justice court, the witness was asked to demonstrate how the defendant had palmed the chips. The chips slipped from his hand.

Because the offense was a misdemeanor not committed in the presence of a law enforcement officer, the hotel had to make a citizen's arrest. When the sheriff's deputies were called to the hotel to take the defendant into custody, they conducted a perfunctory search and found no chips. It was only after getting to the jail when the defendant was asked to remove his pants and change into jailhouse coveralls that the chips tumbled out of his pants pockets.

This would have been a fairly routine case, but the defendant had a civil suit against the hotel alleging that he had been roughed up, and he had secured a judgment against the hotel for $30,000. Once the case was set for trial, I received a phone call from defense counsel, Drake DeLanoy, who handled the civil case. DeLanoy was a prominent member of the bar who handled many insurance-defense claims, and he pledged his full cooperation.

I also received a call from the Riviera. I was asked to come out to the hotel and discuss the case and how they could help. It was a dinner meeting at the hotel's gourmet restaurant. I had never been to a gourmet restaurant. It was an epicurean experience. The chief executive at the Riviera was Ross Miller, the father of future Nevada governor Bob Miller.

I knew nothing about gaming. The workings of a craps table were a complete mystery to me. The positions of the players on the table were referred to as first, second, and third base. One dealer watched the player to make sure the dice were not changed after they were thrown. A second dealer watched the chips to make sure the player didn't change the bet. The third dealer observed the other two. In the ceiling a hotel employee watched from what was called the "eye in the sky," which provided an overhead view of the action.

Miller was very patient with me as I tried to understand how the game worked. He told me, "Whatever you need, I'll get it for you." I told him I wanted a craps table and someone who could explain to the jury how the game was played. Miller's response, "You got it."

On the morning of the trial, my key witness called and said he was not sure he could make it. What he sought was a comped room and meals while attending the trial. I agreed.

A misdemeanor trial in the district court on appeal from the justice court wouldn't ordinarily attract attention, but this was no ordinary case. On the morning of trial, I approached Judge Mowbray's Department 3 and saw Ross Miller, true to his word, walking down the hallway with several Riviera employees rolling a craps table on a dolly into the courtroom. On a casino floor, a craps table doesn't look particularly large. In the confines of Mowbray's small courtroom, it took on gigantic dimensions.

By now the courtroom was abuzz with excitement. "What's with the craps table?" The local press, ever curious, saw the potential for a good story. So did a *Los Angeles Times* reporter.

George Franklin, who had been the Boulder City attorney the

night of my inauspicious beginning as a newly admitted lawyer, represented the defendant.

The press clamored for an opportunity to photograph the craps table in the courtroom. At that time, photographers weren't allowed in the courtroom. Judge Mowbray was not averse to the heightened press coverage and indicated that he had no objection if counsel had none. No one enjoyed press coverage more than Franklin, who responded enthusiastically that he had no objection. I offered none.

The courtroom was full. Jury selection went smoothly. As I laid out my case, the witnesses did reasonably well, but some of their testimony was a bit of a stretch. Franklin's defense was there could be no embezzlement because there was no trust, an essential legal element of the crime. In cross-examining each of the craps dealers, he elicited an acknowledgment that everyone on the table and the "eye in the sky" above were watching each other because nobody trusted anyone.

In addition to some lukewarm witnesses, my case had a major weakness that was likely to cause a reasonable doubt in jurors' minds: why were no casino chips found in the defendant's pockets when he was searched at the Riviera by the sheriff's deputies, but chips flew from his pockets when he was booked into the county jail?

Final arguments were made to the jury. By now the *Los Angeles Times* was following the trial, and a photo of the craps table was featured in the newspaper. The case looked like a loser to me. The jury retired to deliberate. Late that night, I received a call from the bailiff informing me the jury had reached a verdict. Arriving at the courthouse, I was surprised to find Miller already waiting in the courtroom.

The judge convened court and asked the jury if it had reached a verdict. The foreman elected by the jurors was Ray Millisor, a local real estate agent I knew. I also knew his wife, Naomi, who was very active in Democratic Party politics. Ray responded, "We have, your honor." The jury form was handed to the judge, who read it silently and then returned it to Millisor and directed him to read the verdict aloud. He said, "We the jury find the defendant guilty of embezzlement."

I was the most shocked person in the courtroom. Miller was elated and shook my hand. Later I asked Millisor how they reached the guilty verdict. He told me the first vote was 11–1 for acquittal.

He was the only hold out. This is the reverse of the celebrated movie, *Twelve Angry Men*, starring Henry Fonda, in which the jury in a murder case initially voted 11–1 for conviction. Fonda ultimately persuaded the jury to acquit. As Millisor explained his position, he was ultimately able to sway more jurors to his way of thinking. There were a few holdouts concerned about the missing chips that suddenly turned up. Millisor said he advanced this proposition to the holdout jurors by asking them, "If I can demonstrate to you, wearing the defendant's pants, how by taking off his pants chips could fall out of those pockets onto the floor, would you change your verdict?" The reluctant jurors agreed. Millisor successfully demonstrated how this was possible, and the decision to convict was unanimous.

My evenings were as busy as my days. It was the end of an era when civic organizations played a greater role in community affairs. Las Vegas was a much different city than it was in the '50s. Tens of thousands of new residents had come to Las Vegas to make it their home. The challenge for me was to establish a presence in the rapidly growing community.

Before I left Foley Brothers, Joe Foley asked me to join the Elks Lodge. It was a sentimental journey for me. Many of the members had fond memories of my father. Helldorado was still a major community event, and I became a member of the Helldorado Committee and active in lodge functions.

My father had been a past president of the Las Vegas Host Lions Club, and Toy Gregory Jr., later a municipal court judge, invited me to become a member. I joined and was appointed chairman of the Lions Club Oratorical contest. In the late '40s, Ted Marshall, now my boss, participated in the contest and made it to the national finals.

The Jaycees were young men active in the community and sponsored the annual Clark County Fair. Many of its members were new to the community and were owners of small businesses. Al Levy, later a city commissioner, served as president one year and was followed by Ken Gragson. I served as parliamentarian and co-chairman of the State Fair and got to know many members who became highly successful business leaders.

In 1964, at the time of my admission to the Nevada State Bar, there were no African American attorneys in the state. Charlie Kellar was seeking admission, but the bar opposed his admission based on allegations of misconduct in the state where he was licensed. His application for admission to the Nevada State Bar was on appeal to the Supreme Court.

The growing American civil rights movement was exposing many of the prejudices the African American community faced. I joined the local chapter of the NAACP, and as ever Bonnie was on board. We hosted a meeting at our home for the local chapter. I became acquainted with the Rev. Marion Bennett, the local chapter president and later a state legislator. Other members included African American community leaders Bob Bailey, the first chairman of the State Equal Rights Commission; David and Mabel Hoggard; Dr. James McMillan; and Alice Key. These were exciting times. The 1964 Civil Rights Act and later the 1965 Voting Rights Act were enacted during my tenure as local NAACP legal counsel. President Lyndon Johnson's "Great Society" created, among many other programs, the Economic Opportunity Board. I was appointed to serve on the local board. At the annual NAACP dinner, I was proud to be presented with the Justice Award for my efforts on behalf of the chapter.

Former Las Vegas High classmates Terry Jones and Norman "Ty" Hilbrecht, with whom I'd later serve in the Nevada Legislature, encouraged me to join the Legal Aid Society, and I did. I eventually served as president. My participation in the Legal Aid program would have a profound impact on my career when the Legal Aid Society became an advocate for a public defender program.

The year 1964 would also be remembered in Nevada for two high-profile political races. One was the election of LBJ, the other the reelection campaign of Howard Cannon for US Senate. Harry Claiborne filed against Cannon in the Democratic primary. It was a spirited primary, but Cannon prevailed. Under the rubric politics makes strange bedfellows, Claiborne represented Cannon in his controversial general election win over Paul Laxalt, who lost after a recount by just forty-eight votes. In 1978, Cannon forwarded Claiborne's nomination to President Jimmy Carter for Claiborne to serve on the US District Court.

I joined the young Democrats along with Harry Reid and several other politically ambitious contemporaries, including Hilbrecht,

Jim Bilbray, Joe Pavlikowski, Jim Brennan, Darwin Lamb, and Mel Close. It was a time of great participation in politics. The Women's Democratic Club of Clark County held monthly luncheon meetings that attracted a couple hundred women and most of the Democratic Party officeholders. Bonnie and I became members.

Will Rogers was right when he observed, "I am not a member of any organized political party. I am a Democrat." I learned that when it came time for the election of precinct captains and delegates who would attend the Clark County Democratic Convention that year. The party always seemed to have rival factions seeking control of the county and later the state convention. The process began with the election of delegates to the county convention. Meetings were held in the evening in private homes and notices went out to Democrats in each precinct. Controlling the precinct delegate election process was essential to controlling the county convention. It was not unusual for one of the contending factions to have its supporters arrive before the meeting time. Once there, the doors were locked, the lights turned out, and they elected their delegates.

This often led to confrontations at the credentials committee, which is charged with certifying the delegate list. Altercations broke out from time to time on the floor of the convention. At one county convention, Hilbrecht was involved in a scuffle and one of the delegates broke his jaw. But the local convention also brought party activists together. Flora Dungan, Myrna Williams, Harriet Trudell, and Virginia Catt were constant presences.

I canvassed my precinct and was elected to the county convention. All these activities were very time-consuming. I attended meetings several evenings a week. This was retail politics of the old school. In the decade ahead as Las Vegas continued to grow, the role of media, particularly broadcast media, would assume a more dominant role in the political structure. One TV or radio ad, properly placed, could reach many more voters than I could in a month of organizational meetings.

In December 1965, a new opportunity surfaced. Clark County was considering the establishment of the first public defender's office in the state. I was prepared to make my move.

CHAPTER 8

Establishing the Public Defender's Office

In 1963, the US Supreme Court issued its landmark *Gideon v. Wainwright* decision, which held that a criminal defendant charged with a felony who was unable to afford a lawyer must be provided one at no cost. That represented a seismic change in the law for many states. Before the *Gideon* decision, in many states only those charged with capital offenses such as murder were entitled to such protection. For its part, Nevada was the first state in the Union to authorize the appointment of attorneys in criminal matters if the defendant was unable to pay for his own representation. The father of the right to counsel in Nevada was Thomas Wren, a former prosecutor from Austin at a time when it was the state's second largest city. As an assemblyman, Wren introduced legislation authorizing the appointment of attorneys in 1875. Two years later, he served a term as Nevada's lone representative.

The *Gideon* decision was the catalyst for a national debate on the criminal justice system. It caught the attention of Judge John Mowbray, who was intrigued by the Ford Foundation's decision to provide financial incentives to jurisdictions that established public defender programs. On point for the Ford Foundation was General Charles Decker, the retired judge advocate general for the US Army and a man who had had a long history of involvement with the criminal justice system. Mowbray contacted Decker and, no doubt aided in part by the Nevadan's experience as a teacher in the School of Military Government in Virginia, the two bonded immediately.

In 1965, the Nevada Legislature considered enabling legislation sponsored by the Clark County delegation that would allow counties to adopt a public defender system. After debating whether the public defender would be an elected or appointed position, the

Assembly Judiciary Committee voted unanimously to forward a bill that vested responsibility by appointment with the county commissioners. The Assembly and Senate concurred, and Governor Grant Sawyer signed the bill.

The legislation generated great controversy and a spirited debate in the Clark County Bar Association, whose older members opposed the new office. Their argument: the current system provided an opportunity for young lawyers to get trial experience and provided judges with flexibility in more serious cases to appoint more experienced counsel. The accused, those opposed reasoned, would be better served by attorneys appointed on an ad hoc basis.

The Clark County Legal Aid Society, founded in 1958, took the lead in countering the argument by noting the obvious: that the criminal justice system was undergoing rapid change thanks to the Warren Court. New ground was being broken that required additional safeguards for the accused. As such, those who developed expertise in this increasingly specialized field of law would be better able to represent the criminally accused. It was a stormy session, but in the end a divided bar endorsed the creation of the public defender's office.

Mowbray's relationship with Decker paid enormous dividends. The Ford Foundation offered to pay half of the county's three-year indigent defense budget of $395,089 if Clark County created the office. This was the ammunition Mowbray needed to persuade the commission to adopt the proposed ordinance.

At the commission meeting on December 7, 1965, Mowbray appeared and made his case. He advised the commissioners that the county and state bar associations and Nevada Supreme Court chief justice Frank McNamee also favored the adoption of the public defender system for Clark County.

The clincher was the Ford Foundation's generous offer. The tax savings to citizens of Clark County, he argued, would be $196,000. It was an offer the commissioners couldn't refuse. The ordinance was adopted unanimously. With the ordinance came the creation of a public defender's office advisory board consisting of members of the local judiciary and bar association. The board was charged with, among other responsibilities, screening applications for the office and recommending three candidates to the county commission.

The prospect of being the first public defender in Nevada excited me. It was an opportunity and a challenge. As public defender, I would choose my staff and establish the protocols for the operation of the office. Every decision made would set a precedent—pretty heady stuff for a twenty-eight-year-old lawyer out of law school less than three years. I was reminded of Seneca's observation that "luck is what happens when preparation meets opportunity." After two years as a deputy district attorney and myriad community activities on my side of the ledger, I was prepared. It was a carpe diem opportunity for me, and I would seize the day if I could.

Nine local lawyers submitted their applications to the public defender's office advisory board, which met on May 19, 1966, in Mowbray's chambers to cull the list to three finalists for the position. I was reasonably confident my name would be one of the three submitted to the commission.

Several advisory board members were strong supporters, including Mowbray, Justice of the Peace Jim Brennan, and Bar Association appointee Bob Gifford. I could identify no detractors among the district court judges. The other appointees from the Bar Association were Herb Jones and Bill Singleton. Once again, I had to tip my hat to my late father, who had known each member of the advisory board for many years. To what extent that might be helpful I couldn't quantify, but it surely couldn't hurt. My dad had been dead for five years, but he was still in my corner. A day after the meeting, by unanimous vote, I was recommended together with former justice of the peace Tom Pursel and Edward Weinstein.

Mowbray made it known to Decker that he strongly favored my appointment. But at the Ford Foundation's office, my youth and limited experience raised serious concerns. The national legal community was watching the public defender issue, and Clark County was being funded as a model project. A failure of the Clark County Public Defender's Office would reflect poorly on the foundation. Moreover, placing a young and relatively inexperienced lawyer in the position would raise questions about the foundation's judgment.

The foundation sent an emissary to Las Vegas to take my temperature and report back. The man they chose was Illinois attorney "Big Jim" Thompson, who had gained national publicity for his prosecution of the Danny Escobedo murder case. While in police custody, Escobedo asked to speak with his attorney, who was in an adjacent room. Detectives refused, and the suspect eventually gave them an incriminating statement. Escobedo's confession-based conviction was overturned by the US Supreme Court, which held that when an accused's request to speak with an attorney is denied, any confession taken thereafter is inadmissible. *Escobedo v. Illinois* would later be eclipsed by the Supreme Court's groundbreaking *Miranda* case, but in 1966 the legal community was keenly aware of the impact of *Escobedo* and the role of Big Jim Thompson.

Based on his prosecutorial background and the uneasy reaction of the Ford Foundation, I expected a thorough vetting of my experience and a grilling of my credentials and character. That did not occur. Instead, we had a pleasant lunch at the Riviera. I gave him the lay of the land and told him what I intended to do. Remarkably, our paths would cross again two decades later. That time we connected as equals as governors of our respective states.

Clark County Sheriff Ralph Lamb would be the key to my appointment. In the 1960s, he was the most powerful man in the county—and among the most popular. Born and raised in the ranching community of Alamo ninety miles north of Las Vegas, the Lamb brothers carved out a political dynasty in Southern Nevada that lasted the better part of two decades. Ralph's brother Darwin Lamb was a county commissioner, and I would need his vote. His older brother, Floyd Lamb, chaired the state Senate Finance Committee. His brother-in-law, Wes Howery, was a member of the Las Vegas City Commission. Ralph's sister was married into the prominent Peccole family.

During my tenure in the DA's office, the sheriff's office was down the hall from the DA's office on the third floor of the courthouse. I'd exchanged greetings in the hallway many times with him. My father had been a member of the sheriff's mounted posse and had come to know Ralph well. And so, when I requested a meeting with the sheriff, he was happy to do so.

The meeting was brief. After sharing a few memories of my father, Ralph cut straight to the point: "You've got my support. Tell Dard, I am with you." Dard was the nickname of his brother, Darwin, who as county commissioner held one of the votes that I'd need to win the appointment. In a follow-up with Darwin Lamb, he committed his support. Next came Lou LaPorta, a commissioner from Henderson who was in the insurance business. I drove to his Water Street office and was greeted by his executive assistant, Bea Campbell, another close friend of my father. During our meeting, Lou said, "I knew your dad, and Bea says you're all right. You'll have my vote."

Jim Bilbray had joined the district attorney's office earlier that year. His dad, James Bilbray, was the Clark County assessor and knew the political ropes. He and my dad had been active in the Elks Lodge. Jim's dad volunteered to weigh in on my behalf with the other commissioners, Bob Baskin, owner of a restaurant where local politicians gathered; Bill Briare, an insurance agent who later served as Las Vegas mayor; and James G. "Sailor" Ryan, a Southern Nevada labor leader.

On May 20, the Clark County Commission held its regular meeting with the public defender item on the agenda. Although the tapes of that meeting no longer exist, the minutes reflected a motion by Commissioner Lamb followed by a unanimous vote. Richard H. Bryan is appointed public defender.

I was at my desk in the DA's office trying to keep busy when Bilbray came busting through the door shouting, "You've got it!" I would be heading a newly created county department at age twenty-eight. A *Las Vegas Sun* newspaper columnist wished me good luck in print and added presciently, "Distinguished service in this post could pave the way to the Governor's Mansion." I hoped his observation would prove prophetic.

There was little time to waste and almost no one in Southern Nevada with whom I could discuss the nuances of running a public defender's office. The Clark County Commission advanced a small travel allowance that enabled me to visit and survey public defender operations in California. I went on the road, first to San Diego, then Fresno, and finally San Francisco. It was helpful and made the task ahead feel less intimidating. The Las Vegas office was scheduled to open on July 1, 1966.

First, I had to find an office to call home. I was responsible for securing sufficient space and purchasing the necessary furniture and office equipment. Boomtown Las Vegas was in the midst of one of its periodic overbuilding sprees that year. Plenty of commercial space was available downtown. The new Title Insurance and Trust Building at 309 Third Street caught my eye. The company's manager, Harold Wandesford, was eager to lease the space and offered an attractive price and included several tenant improvements. I continued my due diligence and reviewed other options, including the CH Baker Building at Third and Fremont, which is now the location of The D Las Vegas Casino & Hotel. The Baker building wasn't exactly old, but it was well past its prime.

I favored the Title Insurance building but began to feel mounting pressure to locate to the Baker building. Young and naïve, I had no idea the source of the pressure. I felt the Title Insurance building was the better choice, and that was my recommendation to the Clark County Commission. I was shocked when they rejected my proposal. What was I missing?

Admittedly a bit slow on the uptake, I learned after an inquiry that the Baker building's owners weren't just any group of investors. They were the Desert Inn hotel-casino group headed by Moe Dalitz, Allard Roen, and Ruby Kolod. You know, "the boys." They were major players on the Las Vegas Strip and obviously had the ear of the commissioners. Their mob connections dated back to the Prohibition-era Purple Gang and Mayfield Road Gang in Cleveland. They never called me—they probably didn't think that would be necessary. But by rejecting my proposal, the Clark County Commission had delayed the scheduled July 1 opening of the office. And that incurred the ire of District Judge Mowbray.

No one who ever set foot in Mowbray's courtroom forgot the experience. At ease, his manner was almost priestly. When agitated, he was a lion in a black robe. His command of the law and deep baritone voice left no doubt who was in charge. To borrow a phrase from a once-famous television commercial, "When Mowbray talked, people listened."

Well known in the Las Vegas community, he was a proud Irishman active in virtually anything that concerned the island of his ancestors. He attended Mass daily, was an active Catholic layman, and played a leading role in establishing Bishop Gorman High School. And when he offered his rendition of "Danny Boy" on St. Patrick's Day, he could bring even the Ulster Defence Association to tears.

More than a judge, Mowbray was a fierce advocate for justice in the broader sense, justice for all. Born in Bradford, Illinois, he served as a pilot in the US Army Air Corps, graduated with honors from Notre Dame Law School, and moved to Las Vegas after a chance meeting with another proud Irishman, Senator Pat McCarran. After a stint as a Clark County deputy district attorney and bankruptcy referee, he was appointed to the district court by Governor Grant Sawyer and rose to the Nevada Supreme Court eight years later with an appointment by Governor Paul Laxalt. In his time on the bench, he modernized the district court master calendar program and fought for laws to protect abused children. He also saw the inherent challenge to justice created when people accused of crime could not afford counsel.

On the morning of July 1, I sat in Judge Mowbray's courtroom. He was the master calendar judge, and his courtroom was full of attorneys waiting for their cases to be called and assigned. As court convened, he looked at me. His face was red, and it was easy to see he was pretty worked up about something.

"Today!" he thundered, pointing his finger at me. "Today is the day this young man was scheduled to open the public defender's office!"

The judge paused for a moment, then pointed upstairs toward the commissioners' offices. Edmund Kean couldn't have delivered a more dramatic pause.

"They are playing games with him. If they keep horsing around, they are going to blow a quarter of a million dollars. The Ford Foundation won't go for that."

My heart sank. Had I failed so soon? I didn't know what to say or do. Thoughts raced through my mind that I served at the pleasure of the Clark County Commission, which had approved my appointment and could just as easily revoke it. I might be done before I began.

But Mowbray was a political force to be reckoned with, and the commission had no stomach to pick a fight with him. At the following commission meeting, on a 3–1 vote with Bill Briare dissenting, my lease proposal was revisited and approved.

Mowbray would go on to serve twenty-five years on the Nevada Supreme Court. When he hung up his robe in 1993, he was more popular than ever with the voting public. He'd forever be known as a champion of the little guy.

He died on March 5, 1997. As former district attorney George Dickerson said of him, "As a person, he is a devout man, a humanitarian of compassionate understanding; as a lawyer, he was a voracious reader with an insatiable appetite for knowledge; as a judge, he evidenced an enlightened, incisive and well-disciplined mind that grasps and applies controlling legal principle."

There was considerable skepticism about the public defender program in certain quarters of the Clark County Bar Association. Many viewed it as a trial run that was destined to fail. I was keenly aware of that sentiment. We would be closely watched, and our critics would be sure to point out any of our shortcomings. My selection of the four deputy public defenders as authorized by the Clark County Commission would be the key to our success or failure. For chief deputy I chose Bob Peccole, whom I'd gotten to know well at Hastings Law School. Bob was very competitive, fearless, and tenacious. No one would intimidate him in the courtroom. Those were the qualities we would need to provide effective representation for our clients—and to silence our critics. Roy Woofter, who was at that time associated with former US attorney John Bonner, was looking for an opportunity for more courtroom experience. Although I didn't know Roy, Peccole did. They had played baseball together, and Bob assured me that Roy would be a good fit for the office.

The office was allocated an investigator, and Jim Bilbray recommended Stan Colton. Stan was a certified polygraph examiner, and I thought we would be able to make good use of that skill set.

In designing a case management system capable of tracking hundreds of clients and cases, I modified the system that District Attorney Ted Marshall, my former boss, used in his office. Because so many of our clients would be in custody, it would be necessary to establish a timely and convenient access to them. My friendship with Sheriff Lamb paved the way. And, finally, our appointment to represent an indigent defendant had to be made by a district court judge. Mowbray made sure that would occur without delay.

By the middle of July, Peccole, Woofter, and I were operating out of a temporary office at the Title Insurance Building. We were ready to roll. Our impact was immediate. In the first few weeks of operation, we challenged a long-standing practice of jailing those arrested for several days without charging them with a crime or bringing them before a judge for an initial appearance. We filed writs of habeas corpus on behalf of several inmates and secured their immediate release.

Law enforcement was not pleased. But a new day had dawned in Southern Nevada's justice system, and the public defender's office was beginning to make its mark.

As I'd expected, Peccole was a hard charger and set the standard for the office. His demeanor was always professional, and he managed to maintain close working relationships with the deputy district attorneys with whom he socialized after work. Once he stepped into the courtroom on behalf of a client, however, no quarter was given and none was asked. Bob was a proverbial handful. You might beat him at the preliminary hearing, but rest assured he'd double his effort at trial in district court. If he lost there and felt the presiding judge had committed reversible error, he fired off an appeal up to the Nevada Supreme Court.

In time, Tony Earl, George Frame, Bob Legakes, Earle White, Leonard Gang, Oscar Goodman, and Bob Archie would join the staff with Mike Sloan as an investigator.

Except for Woofter, we were all in our twenties. And we were a team. We discussed legal strategies, talked about our cases, and shared our experiences with the judges we appeared before. On Friday afternoons, we adjourned to the office law library, enjoyed adult beverages, and reviewed the cases we had handled that week. It was a bonding process leavened by a collegiality that made us a team, and although not highly experienced, made us formidable adversaries. When the US Supreme Court was in session, we eagerly awaited its opinions and read them voraciously. In the era of the Warren Court, each new term produced decisions that provided additional safeguards and protections for our clients. We played our part in attempting to level the playing field for indigent defendants in a system long stacked against them. Today, the public defender's office has 110 deputies, and the intimacy we enjoyed in the '60s is impossible to replicate. Looking back, we also felt the additional pressure of proving our worth and mettle.

We'd have to prove it often in the days ahead.

CHAPTER 9

Life as a Young Lawyer

The Clark County Bar Association was still small in 1966, and the lawyers in the Clark County District Attorney's Office and defense bar socialized together after work. A favorite watering hole was Lulu's Room at First and Carson. Walk through the door and you'd find George Foley, a prominent defense attorney and Nevada's greatest storyteller, holding court and regaling us. There was Justice of the Peace Jim Brennan, a great pool player, running the table. Other unforgettable members of the bar who were regulars included James "Bucky" Buchanan, future district judge John Mendoza, and Justice of the Peace Herman Fisher. Fisher had been a star athlete at Las Vegas High School and later at the University of Nevada. After a few rounds of his preferred beverage, Fisher wanted to challenge each of us to an arm-wrestling contest.

We spent long hours at Lulu's Room waiting for juries to return their verdicts and enjoyed the camaraderie of our fellow lawyers there. Those days are gone forever, but while they lasted, they produced a treasure trove of memories.

In my role of office administrator, I assigned cases to each deputy, worked with the county on budget issues and the district attorney's office on policy matters, and responded to media inquiries. Although my load in court was smaller than the deputies, I also took cases.

The public defender's office was a new concept in Nevada that generated considerable curiosity. I responded to dozens of speaking engagement requests from service clubs, the League of Women Voters, the American Association of University Women, and the Nevada Southern University (soon the University of Nevada, Las Vegas) political science department. After lecturing to a political science class, I was asked to establish an internship program at the public defender's office. There was no law school at Nevada Southern, but professors and students believed an internship would have academic value. I readily agreed. Several of our interns later distinguished themselves in the US Attorney's Office and as prominent defense counsel.

As public defender, I was frequently called by the press for comment. When newly elected Governor Paul Laxalt said he would appoint only conservative justices, I responded, "The governor should make excellence the standard." The line generated front-page coverage in the Reno newspapers. When reports of officer brutality surfaced at the maximum-security state penitentiary in Carson City, I called upon the governor to appoint a bipartisan commission to investigate the serious charges. That, too, made headlines. The governor declined my request. Despite my criticism, when the governor decided to call a special session of the Nevada Legislature, he called to inform me that he agreed to add an additional item involving the criminal justice system that I had proposed.

I also kept busy in the courtroom. One of the more noteworthy cases I tried involved the defense of a character who called himself "Crazy Bob" Woerner, charged with possessing the psychedelic drug LSD. The prosecution was the first in Nevada and came at a time when psychologist Timothy Leary was considered the high priest of the congregation that advocated the use of psychedelic drugs. Leary conducted experiments at Harvard University and believed that LSD showed therapeutic potential. He popularized the catchphrase, "Turn on, tune in, drop out." President Richard Nixon once described him as "the most dangerous man in America." Woodstock was less than three years away, and the hippie culture and increased drug use challenged America's social mores. To paraphrase the bard of the generation, Bob Dylan, "The times, they were 'a-changin'."

With his long hair and scruffy appearance, Crazy Bob looked like a hippy right out of central casting. He was a media sensation, and he enjoyed the press attention. During the trial, at one recess he posed next to a framed copy of the US Constitution displayed in the courthouse. The media loved it. My high school chemistry teacher Paul Richert was the state's expert witness and testified that the substance found on the defendant was in fact LSD. But even the expert testimony plowed new legal ground. A forensic process known as thin layer chromatography was used to identify LSD. It was new to the legal system, and it opened a new chapter in identifying the rapidly expanding world of recreational drugs.

Deputy District Attorney Bucky Buchanan, later a prominent defense lawyer, prosecuted the case for the state in District Judge Howard Babcock's courtroom. With the defendant found in possession of the drug in question, I started the defense with a couple of strikes against me. I raised every challenge in the arsenal available to defense counsel. Despite my best efforts, Crazy Bob was convicted. Buchanan told the press that Woerner had been given a world-class defense. Such comments helped dissipate the assertion that the public defender's office provided an assembly-line defense. Woerner received one year in the county jail.

The case of Terry Lynn Conger before District Judge John Mendoza was the biggest and most challenging case I personally handled as public defender. It was a grim affair. Conger was charged with the murder of three employees at the Bank of Las Vegas branch in Overton, a small Nevada town sixty-three miles northeast of Las Vegas. The victims' bodies were stacked like cordwood in the bank vault. The evidence against him was stacked even higher.

The circumstantial evidence was compelling. Conger's fingerprints were lifted from a metal stanchion that posted a notice that the bank would be closed for a holiday later that week. Shortly before the homicides occurred, an eyewitness spotted Conger entering the bank. Earlier that afternoon, he had discussed staging a phony robbery at Mac's Bait Shop to divert the attention of the Overton deputy sheriff while he robbed the bank. The witness was prepared to testify that Conger told him that he would have to kill the bank's employees to get out of town before being identified. The murder weapon was a military-issue .45 caliber Colt 1911, identical to the one brought back from the Pacific theater by a member of his family who had served in World War II. A Colt was found in Conger's father's car.

Nevada used the gas chamber to carry out the death penalty. The prosecutors could smell the gas. Initially, I was told that the state would seek the death penalty. Although no defendant in Clark County had received the death penalty in recent years, the Conger case with the alleged premeditated murders of three innocent bank workers was an obvious candidate.

Mounting a real defense in a capital murder case bears little resemblance to the legal cases commonly aired on television. In the real world, building a credible defense against substantive witness testimony and circumstantial evidence is extremely difficult. I spent many hours researching every possible issue and trying to develop a defense strategy that might put my client in a better light—all to no avail. I was also concerned that a conviction and the imposition of the death penalty would rekindle criticism of the office and give the skeptics the opportunity to crow that a case of such magnitude was precisely the reason why the judge would, under the previous system, appoint a more experienced counsel. I wasn't just fighting to provide Conger the strongest defense possible. I was also battling to preserve the public defender's program.

As the trial date approached, I pored over the list of prospective jurors. At that time, the Clark County jury commissioner would randomly draw several hundred names from the list of county residents who would be available for all jury trials, civil or criminal. They would serve for several months, after which a new panel would be drawn.

By law, certain occupations were excused from jury service. Under the system, some of the job categories still on the books were carryovers from the previous century. For example, telegraphers were exempt from service. Members of law enforcement were also excused from jury duty upon their request—and most did. As I studied the list, I discovered that the jury commissioner had already deleted them from the panel assuming that law enforcement officers would exercise their right of exemption. As I read the law, only the law enforcement officer, not the jury commissioner, could exercise the option to be excused. On the eve of trial, I filed a challenge to the array in effect to the entire jury panel on the grounds the jury commissioner had erred in preemptively excluding law enforcement from the pool. Judge John Mendoza granted my motion.

The implications of his ruling went far beyond the Conger case. By declaring the prospective jurors were improperly excused, the entire panel was voided. No jury trials could proceed. That included Conger's case. By generating a postponement, I was given additional time to pursue a strategy that might save the defendant's life. In short, I was making every effort to provide the best defense of my client.

Around the courthouse, the ruling threw a wrench in the works of the justice system. I found myself persona non grata because I had created the chaos. Scheduled jury trials had to be vacated. The jury commissioner and her staff were livid. It was a bold move, and members of the defense bar, though not effusive with praise, were forced to admit "those public defender guys are no pushovers."

The Conger trial date was rescheduled into the new year. I knew Ray Jeffers, one of the hard-charging deputy district attorneys assigned to the case, wanted to seek the death penalty. In a criminal prosecution, the district attorney and defense counsel are allotted a limited number of peremptory challenges during jury selection. A peremptory challenge, unlike a challenge for cause, requires no showing of bias. Once challenged, the potential juror is automatically excused.

In the 1960s, the tide of public opinion was running against the death penalty. By law, jurors must reach a unanimous verdict to render a conviction in a criminal case. They also must agree unanimously for the death penalty to be imposed. If I could persuade the district attorney's office that with the peremptory challenges available to me it would be virtually impossible for them to get twelve jurors who were prepared to impose the death penalty empaneled, the door might be open to a plea bargain that would enable me to save Conger's life.

The Gallup and Roper polling organizations were nationally recognized and highly respected. Both companies' polls validated my contention that it would be highly unlikely for the district attorney to prevail in a call for the death penalty. Armed with this data, I approached District Attorney George Franklin and made my argument. It would be in the public interest to avoid a lengthy and expensive trial, I said, and it would be virtually impossible to secure twelve jurors to vote in favor of the death penalty. With a jury unable to agree, the presiding judge would be compelled to declare a mistrial, and a new trial would be ordered at great expense to taxpayers.

Despite the potential for a hung jury, Ray Jeffers urged Franklin to seek the death penalty. Franklin was more receptive to my overture. Recognizing the opening, I pressed on, and suggested the possibility of a guilty plea to each of the three first-degree murder charges with a sentence of life in prison without the possibility of parole with the convictions to run consecutively. Franklin seemed interested. He told me to talk with Conger and report back if he was agreeable.

My meeting with Conger was brief. I explained the only option on the table that assured he would avoid being put to death by the state. It was as simple as that. He authorized me to make the offer to the district attorney. Franklin accepted. The last step in the process was winning approval of the deal from District Judge Mendoza. His concurrence was not a foregone conclusion. He had a reputation of being independent, and he would not hesitate to reject a plea negotiation if he disagreed with it.

With jury selection set to start in twenty-four hours, I met with the district attorney's staff in Mendoza's chambers. The judge stated he wanted to think about it overnight. On Monday morning in open court, Mendoza put the DA's office and me through the drill. After closely questioning Conger, the judge agreed to accept the plea bargain. Conger's life was spared in exchange for accepting three consecutive life sentences without the possibility of parole. I was relieved and felt that I had done well. No court-appointed attorney, even those with far more experience than I, could have achieved a better result, and the credibility of the public defender's office was bolstered.

Under the rubric that no good deed goes unpunished, some years later Conger filed a petition in federal court claiming that he had been represented by incompetent counsel. I was called to testify in federal court on more than one occasion to defend my legal representation of the triple murderer.

It was not always smooth sailing. With Bonnie working hard at home with our young family, I still had to satisfy my army reserve obligation of two weeks each summer. The 427th Civil Affairs Company that I was attached to trained in California, either at Fort MacArthur in San Pedro or Camp Roberts on the Monterey Peninsula. In my absence, Chief Deputy Bob Peccole was in charge.

While I was away at summer camp, Peccole received a call from the North Las Vegas Police Department. A police officer had been killed in the line of duty, and a suspect was in custody. The suspect informed arresting officers that she wanted to speak with an attorney. The police were anxious to take a statement from the suspect. They believed that once the call was made, they could proceed with their questioning. After calling Peccole, they put the suspect on the line. Bob gave solid legal advice: say nothing and sign nothing. To do otherwise would have been a dereliction of his duty to a client, but the directive enraged police officers as the suspect then refused to talk to them. Later in the day when Peccole informed me of the incident, I knew there would be trouble.

The police contacted Paul Price, the hard-hitting columnist at the *Las Vegas Sun* with a reputation for taking law enforcement's side on almost any issue. The deceased officer was well known and well liked in the community. Price produced a blistering column that excoriated the public defender's office and accused us of interfering with the murder investigation. The killing of a police officer in the line of duty generates a great deal of media attention, and understandably emotion in the law enforcement community was running high. Fortunately, we were able to remind the skeptics that ethics required us to advise our client to remain silent.

The fledgling Clark County Public Defender's Office was a model for the Ford Foundation. As such, I was invited to attend a meeting that included the president of the American Bar Association, foundation representatives, and other national leaders of the criminal justice reform movement. The meeting was held in Williamsburg, the capital of colonial Virginia, which thanks to the Rockefeller family had been restored to its historic splendor. It's also home to the College of William & Mary, where the Wren Building is the oldest academic building in continuous use in the country. It was designed by Sir Christopher Wren, the architect who designed St. Paul's Cathedral in London. As a lifelong lover of history, I was captivated by the setting.

At the meeting, I gave a report on the progress of the Clark County Public Defender's Office. I am sure many may have wondered why I was speaking to a roomful of leaders of the American Bar Association and senior members of the Criminal Justice Project. As much as I enjoyed the meetings, the frosting on the cake was experiencing the living history of colonial Williamsburg. One of the highlights was visiting the House of Burgesses and standing where Patrick Henry once spoke the immortal words, "I know not what course others may take, but as for me, give me liberty or give me death."

The following summer I was invited to join other public defenders at a national conference near Washington, DC, where our special guest was Supreme Court Justice Abe Fortas. Fortas had been a protégé of Lyndon Johnson and, as his lawyer, had devised a successful defense of Johnson's controversial election to the US Senate. When he rose to the highest office in the land, President Johnson returned the favor and nominated him to the Supreme Court. Fortas was well known as the successful litigator of *Gideon v. Wainwright,* which established the legal right of indigent defendants to counsel in state criminal cases. My experience as a public defender was coming full circle.

One side benefit of the meeting was the opportunity to be admitted to the US Supreme Court. At that time, a personal appearance before the court in Washington, DC, was required. The petition seeking admission had to be signed by a member of the Supreme Court Bar, and few Nevada lawyers were members. My sponsor was George Dickerson. A Certificate of Good Standing from the Nevada State Bar was also necessary to complete the application. I secured the certificate, completed the other required paperwork, and asked my secretary to send it in.

The week before I was scheduled to be admitted, I received a call from Washington from my fraternity brother Jim Joyce, who was a member of Senator Howard Cannon's staff. Jim informed me that the court hadn't yet received my application. I quickly asked my secretary about it, and she responded, "I sent it in the day you gave me the paperwork." In a prescient moment I asked, "Where did you send it?" She replied, "To the American Bar Association in Chicago." And the mystery was solved.

With time of the essence, I quickly secured a new Certificate of Good Standing from the Nevada State Bar, and together with my petition for admission hand-carried the paperwork to DC. I met Joyce outside the Supreme Court Building on the evening before my scheduled admission. He identified himself as a Cannon staffer to the guard, who to my surprise let us into the building. Unescorted, we wandered through the dimly lit hallways until we found the clerk's office and slipped the packet under the door. Joyce informed me he'd spoken to the clerk's office earlier in the day and had been assured that as long as my petition was in by the early morning my name would be on the list of those to be admitted to the court. I was doubtful, but hopeful.

The next morning, I joined several attorneys and their sponsors before the bar of the court. Celebrated American architect Cass Gilbert designed the Supreme Court Building, one of the capital's iconic structures.

When the ceremony convened, Chief Justice Earl Warren presided. Warren's storied career was instructive: He'd been in the public arena for most of his professional life. From serving as California's attorney general and governor to serving as Thomas E. Dewey's presidential running mate in 1948, he'd been on the front lines during changing times in the United States. He had skillfully orchestrated the court's landmark 1954 unanimous decision in *Brown v. Board of Education of Topeka*, which overturned the nineteenth-century *Plessy v. Ferguson* case that had upheld the segregation doctrine of "separate but equal." In the *Brown* decision, the court declared that "separate but equal is inherently unequal."

As the court opened, Warren intoned "the court recognizes the attorney general of the United States for the purpose of moving the admission of the son of one of our brethren." The attorney general was Ramsay Clark, whose father, Tom Clark, had been a Supreme Court justice. The son was the scion of Justice William J. Brennan Jr., considered by many legal scholars to be the most influential associate justice in the history of the court. Being admitted to the US Supreme Court is a memorable experience for any lawyer, but being admitted the same day as the attorney general of the United States was presenting the admission of the son of a justice, suffice to say, it doesn't get more impressive than that.

Many lawyers were admitted that day, and I anxiously awaited my turn. Could an institution such as the Supreme Court respond to a petition slipped under the clerk's door in the middle of the night? My doubts increased. Then my name was called. I was admitted. It was a moment to give silent thanks for my life's many blessings. I thought of my late father, my steadfast mother, loving wife, and young family. It was a proud moment.

Later I'd smile and reflect that Jim Joyce had been right when we submitted the application. It may have been the high-water mark for government efficiency in the nation's capital.

Another blessing for our family arrived in 1967 when "Little Blair" was born. Together with her brother and sister, they have been the great joy of my life. My greatest regret is that I did not spend more time with them. Bonnie was the perfect mother, and their success can be attributed to her patience and understanding. My wonderful wife displayed plenty of patience and understanding with me, too. If I made any significant contribution as a parent, it was to instill a strong work ethic. Richard Jr. is a cardiologist, Leslie is a lawyer and partner at Fennemore Craig, and Blair is a schoolteacher with a master's degree. They have given us six grandchildren, which have brought us much happiness. Grandchildren are the greatest.

In early 1968, an election year, I received a call from Senator Alan Bible, then Nevada's senior senator. He asked me to stop by his office at the federal building. Bible was well known to our family. He and my father had been on the debate team at the University of Nevada in the late '20s. As I entered his office he greeted me with his trademark, "Good to see you," and briefly reminisced about my father and a few of their experiences together back in their university days.

Then he turned to the business at hand, his reelection to the Senate. He told me he expected to be challenged by Ed Fike, who had been elected lieutenant governor in the Republican sweep in 1966. It wouldn't be an easy campaign, he said, and he needed to shore up his base in rapidly growing Clark County. Bible said, "I need that young fellow in your office, Mike Sloan, to join my campaign staff." Sloan was one of my investigators.

I immediately replied, "You've got him."

The personal request was a class act on Bible's part. As a senator, he could have simply instructed Sloan to "tell Bryan you're leaving." Bible was from the old school, where a certain political etiquette was observed. And it proved a good move for Bible. Although Sloan was still in his early twenties, he knew the players in the Democratic Party and had been active in party politics since his days as a student at Las Vegas High School when he attended the 1960 National Convention in Los Angeles that nominated John F. Kennedy. It was also a good move for Sloan. When Bible won the election, he asked Sloan to come to DC and join his staff. Sloan went to law school, and upon graduation returned to Las Vegas and has enjoyed an illustrious career.

And 1968 was a year of decision for me as I contemplated a question never far from my mind: was this the time for me to resign and seek election to public office? In the previous two years, the public defender's office had made its mark. It had shaken up the criminal justice system by providing effective representation of hundreds of poor defendants from justice court to the Nevada Supreme Court, made more than five thousand court appearances, and saved the tax-payers many thousands of dollars—a trifecta of public policy successes. Moreover, I returned to the county each year thousands of dollars from our budget. The Ford Foundation was pleased, and the remainder of the grant money promised to the county was assured. None of this could have been achieved without a talented and dedicated staff.

No public office in the history of Nevada had assembled a more remarkable staff. Jim Santini would go on to become a justice of the peace, district court judge, and Nevada congressman. Roy Woofter served as a justice of the peace, Clark County district attorney, and the city attorney for Las Vegas and North Las Vegas. Leonard Gang, Robert Legakes, and Earle White would become district court judges. After a high-flying career representing associates of organized crime, Oscar Goodman would serve three terms as Las Vegas mayor. Mike Sloan was appointed city attorney for Las Vegas and was twice appointed as a state senator before becoming a highly successful gaming lawyer. Bob Archie returned from Vietnam to be appointed by Governor Mike O'Callaghan as the state director of the Employment Security Agency. Stan Colton was appointed Clark County registrar of voters and later elected state treasurer.

Finally, there's Bob Peccole, without whom I wouldn't have succeeded. He became my chief deputy for Southern Nevada in the attorney general's office, and later I appointed him to the Nevada Gaming Commission.

Although our early critics had been silenced, I did not want to resign until I was confident my successor would be the right person to continue the progress we had made. I wanted a seamless transition. My replacement would have to have the qualifications for the job and the political savvy to win the appointment. The obvious choice was Santini, who was a fraternity brother and a close friend, but also a man I trusted. He had been a JAG officer in the army and was a member of George Franklin's staff in the district attorney's office. In two short years he had established himself in the Southern Nevada community through membership in the Italian American Club and participation in a plethora of other community organizations.

Coincidentally, Woofter wanted to join the staff of the district attorney's office. Could a trade of sorts be made: Woofter for Santini? For that to happen, Franklin would have to agree. In short order he gave his blessing. I half expected the deal to make news in the sports section. Tongue in cheek, I reported back to the office that "We got Santini, but Franklin had to give up two draft choices on the next bar exam." I was kidding, but with the limited number of new members admitted to the bar each year, our offices did compete for fresh talent. I believe we got the best of the deal.

With Santini's appointment virtually assured, I was closer to plunging into the political waters. But what office would I seek? As a University of Nevada graduate with an interest in higher education, a seat on the Board of Regents sounded appealing. Another option was to run for Nevada Assembly. I debated the options at length with Sloan and Joyce. After thoughtful consideration, I concluded the Assembly would provide greater statewide exposure and an opportunity to work on a broader range of issues.

At the right time, I submitted my letter of resignation to the Clark County Commission. After thanking them for the opportunity to serve, I wrote, "I leave the office of Public Defender confident that establishing this position was in the best interest of all citizens in the county, from the poor who could not afford the legal representation they constitutionally must receive, to the tens of thousands of taxpayers who must pay for the prosecution and defense of criminal actions."

I was proud of my effort, but leaving the office also meant I was leaving behind a regular paycheck with a young family at home. I'd need to join a law firm. I had known Ian Ross since high school when he went by the name Ross Rosenbaum. Ian had formed a law practice with Oscar Goodman and Jerry Snyder. I knew Oscar, but not well, and had never met Snyder.

When I was approached to join the firm, I came away impressed. They were young and ambitious. Oscar, then as now, had an engaging personality. Jerry, previously an associate with Lionel Sawyer & Collins, was always looking for business deals that would enhance the partners' bottom line. Ian was a steady hand. I knew I could learn a lot from them. I had never been in private practice, and they had already developed a successful clientele. I accepted their invitation and became an equal partner.

Now all I had to do was juggle the new job, the family, and my goal of winning a seat in the Nevada Assembly.

CHAPTER 10

The First Campaign

In April, joined by Bonnie, the children, and my good friend Lloyd George, I filed as a candidate for Assembly District 4. Lloyd, who was called "Duco," had intervened on my behalf to encourage Ted Marshall to hire me as a deputy district attorney. His name would add credibility to my campaign, especially in the LDS community. When I asked him if I could use his name as the chairman of my campaign committee, he readily agreed.

Now it was my turn to call on US Senator Alan Bible to ask for his support for my candidacy. He had an underappreciated sense of humor. When I asked for his support, his response was classic. He replied, "Dick, I'll tell you what I'll do. I'll speak for you or against you, whatever you think would be most helpful." Over the years, I gave the Bible response to dozens of candidates who asked for my political support.

In 1968, Assembly District 4 encompassed the entire Las Vegas Township, which included most of the populated area of the county except North Las Vegas, Henderson, Boulder City, Moapa Valley, and Mesquite. Nine would be elected at-large to represent the district. Eight incumbents filed for reelection. Harry Reid and I were among the new kids on the block. Reid, the Searchlight native whom I'd met during the Nevada Bar Exam, had established his election bona fides by having been elected to the Southern Nevada Memorial Hospital Board of Trustees two years earlier. This would be my maiden voyage.

I was confident about my prospect for success. Surely, I thought, I could be one of nine. After all, I had a lot going for me. I had grown up in Las Vegas. My father had been active in the community, particularly with the Elks Lodge, and had many friends. I thought I had positioned myself nicely. I had been active in Democratic politics. I had joined the Elks and Lions Club and many other community organizations. My tenure in the district attorney's office had put me in close contact with the law enforcement agencies, and I had received a fair amount of publicity as a prosecutor and even more as the county's first public defender.

I began my campaign assuming I was well known. Out on the trail, I was quickly disabused of that notion. Las Vegas had experienced enormous growth since my days as a student at Las Vegas High School. In the 1960 census, Las Vegas for the first time had eclipsed Reno as Nevada's largest city. To the tens of thousands of newcomers, I was unknown.

My second major surprise was fundraising. The numbers would pale in comparison with the staggering costs of today's campaigns, but money talked as loudly then as it does today. Friends and supporters assured me there was no reason for concern. They would raise the money, they said, and once I announced my candidacy the contributions would be there for me. Wrong! Wrong! Raising money is the primary responsibility of the candidate. I disliked asking for money and was not good at it. I would be underfunded in my first campaign, and I paid a price for the shortfall. Fundraising was my Achilles' heel, and it would haunt me throughout my political career.

The dynamics of a campaign for one of nine seats at-large is much different than a race in which two or more candidates face off against each other and only one can win. When meeting a voter who was strongly committed to one of the other candidates, it was easy for me to say I know you are committed to, for example, Keith Ashworth, an incumbent seeking reelection in my race, but I hope you would consider me for one of your other eight votes in District 4. There was never a need to criticize an opponent or make the argument that I was the better choice. When talking to my supporters, I asked for a "single shot," one vote for only me. The rationale behind this: a vote cast for an additional candidate might have the unintended consequences of adding enough to his or her tally to eliminate me as one of the nine.

The voters of today would find many similarities to the campaigns of the '60s: paid media on TV and radio, newspapers, political endorsements from key interest groups, yard signs, road signs, door-to-door voter outreach, and candidates attending large events. The major differences: no cell phones, internet, social media, and no cable TV. In that day, only birds tweeted, Amazon was a river in South America, and your "in box" was probably hanging outside the front door of your house. In 1968, television consisted of the ABC, CBS, and NBC network affiliates. Because the Las Vegas Township was so large, I knew I would need TV and that would be my biggest expense.

With fundraising not my forte, whenever possible I opted for personal voter contact rather than begging for campaign contributions. By contrast, I loved the personal interaction with the voters—retail politics—and I was getting a positive response along the campaign trail. If only I could make personal contact with enough voters, I thought I'd be okay.

In 1968 there were no requirements to report how much money candidates raised or from whom they received contributions. And there were no fundraising limits. Moreover, candidates did not have to report any details of their personal financial holdings. A candidate could have major financial interests in a utility or other business entity and vote for legislation that directly benefited him or her financially. The public would never be the wiser.

Contributions were often made in cash. One personal fundraising experience I had is illustrative. An old classmate at LVHS was an executive in one of the local casinos. I went to him to request a campaign contribution.

"Sure," he responded easily. "I'll be happy to help you. You'd make a good legislator. Follow me."

He beckoned me to follow him over to the casino cage, where he reached into a box and returned with a roll of $100 bills totaling $2,000. He handed the money to me. All of this occurred on the casino floor, in plain view of anyone who might happen to be watching. I tried to act nonchalant, as if this was an everyday experience for me on the campaign trail. It was anything but that. On the contrary, it was the largest amount of cash I'd ever held in my hand. I thanked my friend and contributor and awkwardly crammed the large roll of hundred-dollar bills in my pocket. With no reporting requirement, I could have spent the money on something personal unrelated to my campaign and no one would have ever known. But I put the cash to good use.

Endorsements, then as now, were an important part of every campaign. A group's endorsement goes out to all its members, and those members are encouraged to vote for the chosen candidate. Racking up a series of endorsements could add real momentum to a campaign.

My first encounter with the endorsement process was an interview with organized labor and completing their questionnaire. Labor's endorsement was very important to me as a Democrat. The first question was, "If elected, would you support the repeal of Nevada's Right to Work Law?" I stirred with trepidation.

I knew from organized labor's point of view that the correct answer was "Yes." I also recognized that Nevada voters had expressed strong support for the Right to Work Law on a statewide ballot. After a pause, I indicated I would not be able to support repeal and gave my reason, primarily that Nevada voters had voiced their strong support for Right to Work legislation. I thought this might cost me the endorsement. I also knew that if I supported labor's position and it became public, I could lose the election. Fortunately, other questions gave me an opportunity to illustrate my support for labor's position, and I got the endorsement.

Today, virtually every interest group has a questionnaire that candidates are required to answer before getting the group's endorsement. That can be dicey for a candidate. Once the officeholder has a legislative track record of support for the endorsing group, it is much easier for the candidate to express his or her lack of support for a particular issue. But when you're a rookie, there's no track record.

For a candidate such as me, yard signs and road signs would be essential to get my name out before the public. Volunteers would assemble the signs. Yard signs were easy. The printed message "Bryan for Assembly" was professionally printed on poster board, stapled to a piece of plywood, and mounted on a wooden stake. Hundreds of signs were made, and campaign volunteers placed them in the yards of my supporters after getting the okay. We had a particularly clever yard sign that read, "This Home Sold on Bryan." A child of one of my supporters, upon coming home from school and seeing the sign, burst into tears believing his parents had sold their house.

The road signs were made of plywood, four-feet by four-feet, and required enormous amounts of time to assemble. When completed, the stakes on which they were mounted required a gas-powered auger to drill the holes necessary for placement, often through caliche.

The campaign message "Vote Bryan" printed on thin sheets of paper was professionally done. The assembly process required several days. The printed sheets would be soaked in water overnight in a shallow plastic pool much like kids wade in. The next day, glue was applied to the plywood with a long-handled brush. The printed sheets, now thoroughly saturated, were placed on the plywood and a squeegee was used to make sure the thin sheets of paper were firmly attached to the plywood. The next step required stapling the edges and letting everything dry overnight. The sign had now permanently bonded to the plywood. The final step came the following day with the trimming of the edges.

It was an enormously time-consuming process requiring hundreds of volunteer hours. Beer and wine flowed easily to ease the tedium. Returning from a night of campaigning, I would frequently join the volunteers at eleven o'clock and have a couple of beers with them. During a campaign, hundreds of signs were made this way.

In later campaigns, road signs were made of plastic with the campaign message imprinted on the plastic. All that was required was to load the signs onto a truck and at the desired location drive two pieces of rebar into the ground and wire the sign to the rebar.

By far the most enjoyable part of the campaign was the personal interaction with the voters. I thrived on it and was energized by it. I searched for activities where large numbers of voters were gathered and where my attendance would be appropriate. I attended school carnivals and organized picnics, always passing out hand cards that gave a brief biography and outlined my priority issues.

Candidates were allowed to visit county and city offices and pass out hand cards. The power company and gas company opened their facilities for candidates as well. Hundreds of voters could be reached in a relatively short time. I didn't want to miss one of them.

In the evening, one of my favorite locations was the bowling alley. There were many leagues, and on any given night hundreds of bowlers. Accompanied by a volunteer who would carry extra hand cards, I spent many hours at the Showboat Lanes and other bowling venues distributing hundreds of hand cards.

I always stayed back, waiting for the bowler to release the ball and then handed a card to each member of the team, frequently engaging them in small talk or complimenting them on a strike or spare. Visiting bowling alleys was a big part of every campaign for me from 1968 to my last run in 1994. In later years, many voters would recognize me and comment, "It must be election time. Here he comes again."

Candidate nights sponsored by various organizations were big, and I often participated in more than one per night. Candidates would make their way to each candidate night, waiting their turn to say a few words. In later campaigns, the number of candidate nights proliferated to the point there were frequently as many candidates as uncommitted voters in attendance. The best attended candidate night by far was at Temple Beth Shalom with virtually everyone a registered voter.

I did a lot of door-to-door campaigning. It's a part of the marathon of a campaign that tests a candidate's stamina and determination. Sometimes Richard Jr. would join me. He was always a hit. During the summer months, homeowners would look at his cute pink face and offer him a glass of water or a soft drink.

I selected precincts to walk with heavy Democratic registration. By today's standards it was not very sophisticated. Targeting is now a highly specialized field that relies on in-depth data collection, strategic targeting, analyzing voter turnout and precinct participation, among many criteria.

On election night, I placed third behind Harry Reid and Keith Ashworth. My hard work had paid off. I was encouraged, but I knew the general election would be more challenging. Republicans Zel Lowman, Woodrow Wilson, and Frank Young were incumbents with a base of support. They were likely to finish in the top nine.

As the general election loomed, I continued with my primary strategy with one notable addition, morning coffees held in my supporters' homes. In 1968 a large percentage of women were still homemakers not employed outside the home. But they were an important voting bloc, and holding coffee klatches was a way to reach them. It was fall, summer vacations were over, and the kids were back at school. Bonnie had made many friends with her membership in the Service League, later Junior League, and Junior Mesquite. Many of her friends agreed to host a coffee for me and invited their neighbors and friends. This provided me with an opportunity to meet and talk about my candidacy with women I did not know. It was a very enjoyable experience, and I owed it all to Bonnie. The groups were generally about fifteen to twenty people and made for a very personal connection with prospective voters.

In two years, Howard Cannon, running for reelection to the US Senate, would perfect and enlarge the morning coffees. With full-time staffers making all the arrangements, including the coffee and refreshments, and a van with a hundred or more chairs arriving shortly before the scheduled time, the hostess's only responsibility was to make her home available. After the coffee, staff would collect the chairs, clean up, and move onto the next coffee. This removed all the pressures on the hostess and made it easier to persuade more women to make their homes available and to invite many more guests.

On election night, I placed a disappointing seventh—not an auspicious beginning. What I had gained was the opportunity to serve in the state Assembly. How I made use of that opportunity would be up to me. That seventh-place finish reminded me, once again, to never take a single vote for granted.

The weeks following the election were exciting times for me. The newly elected Clark County delegation, with Republicans and Democrats gathering together, held meetings with various constituent groups and listened to their agendas for the upcoming session. Harry and I were the newcomers, but we were no shrinking violets. We actively participated in the discussions. That engendered resentment among some of the veteran legislators. We were young, obviously ambitious, and as lawyers were viewed as obnoxious. Maybe we were a little, but we were young men in a hurry.

When the Democrats met to decide committee assignments, I was assigned to the Judiciary Committee with Harry as well as the Fish and Game Committee. The Democrats were in the minority. We elected Mel Close as our leader.

Next, on to Carson City and the start of the legislative session. I couldn't wait to get there.

CHAPTER 11

The Gold Dust Twins

No one goes to Carson City in January for the weather. The notorious Washoe Zephyr's winds blow from the snowy Eastern Sierra, and Nevada's state capital at times seems better suited for a luge run than a meeting of the legislature. The fifty-fifth session was an especially snowy one. I couldn't wait to get there.

Nevada's earliest legislative sessions were held on land that later became the state prison. Read nothing into that about the character of public servants of the day. Then as now, they served on a part-time basis in biennial sessions.

The great Mark Twain, whom Nevada claims as its own because he got his start as a writer in Virginia City as a reporter for the *Territorial Enterprise* newspaper, was less than impressed with Carson City's capitol site the first time he saw it. He later recalled the experience in his great travel yarn *Roughing It*.

"The sidewalk was of boards that were more or less loose and inclined to rattle when walked upon," he wrote. "In the middle of the town, opposite the stores, was the 'plaza' . . . a large, unfenced, level vacancy, with a liberty pole in it, and very useful as a place for public auctions, horse trades, and mass meetings, and likewise for teamsters to camp in."

By 1969, it was among the prettiest state capitals in the country.

On the morning of January 20, accompanied by Bonnie and Richard Jr. and with the girls secure at home, I entered the Capitol Building. It was a bit intimidating entering the front door of the silver-domed structure with its Neoclassical Italianate design that gave visitors a sense that it was built to stand the test of time. Originally designed by architect Joseph Gosling, it was finished in 1871 and underwent a later expansion guided by Nevada's prolific public architect Frederic DeLongchamps. I'd been there before, but I saw it with new eyes as a newly elected member of the state Assembly.

It was the last year the legislature would meet in the old Capitol Building. The Senate and Assembly were scheduled to convene in the 1971 session in the new Legislative Building a short distance away. It was the end of an era.

During my years at the University of Nevada I had visited the building a couple of times as student body president with fraternity brother Jim Joyce, who knew it well because of his work on the *Sagebrush* student newspaper and as a stringer for one of the Reno papers. As Clark County public defender, I had testified before the legislature, but that still qualified me as a newcomer.

I made my way to the Assembly chambers without any real idea of the protocol. What was the procedure? Where would I sit? There had been no orientation for new members, no seminar in *Mason's Manual,* the heavy tome that laid out the rules of order. I would later learn that the 1969 legislative session was the first time since Herbert Hoover was president in 1929 that the Republicans held the majority in the Nevada Assembly. Republicans had chosen their leadership and committee chairs. Democrats had handed out their committee assignments.

At that moment, Assembly Speaker Howard McKissick stepped forward and extended his hand. McKissick represented Reno and the north Tahoe area. He was a Fleischmann Scholar, and, like me, a graduate of the University of Nevada and Hastings Law.

"Dick," he said, "I'm glad to have you here, and you'll be sitting over there."

The desks for the forty members of the Assembly were arranged in a semicircle, and mine was in the second to the last row. Harry Reid sat just ahead and to the left was Mack Fry, my fraternity brother at the University of Nevada. Behind me in the last row consisting of two seats sat Elko legislators Norm Glaser, a third-generation rancher, and Roy Young. Norm was a Democrat, Roy a Republican, and both were fiercely loyal to their rural constituents. The fact I was perceived to be a liberal young lawyer from Las Vegas, a place many Northern Nevadans perceived as a foreign country, was unlikely to impress them. Nevertheless, they were very cordial.

Governor Paul Laxalt gave his State of the State address the next day. He recalled his early years roaming the legislature's halls and listening to the speakers of the day before he laid out an ambitious legislative agenda buoyed by Nevada's booming economy. Laxalt knew those halls well from his Carson City youth when, as he put it, he was "knee-high to a small grasshopper."

The son of a Basque sheepherder, Laxalt was a conservative Republican with a love of the state. In those days, Nevada's live-and-let-live Republicans were often to the left of many Democrats on social issues. In later years when he was well known as President Ronald Reagan's "best friend," his politics tacked further to the right to fit the party's own increasingly staunch right-wing leanings. But in 1969 his concern for Nevada's well-being was evidenced in his calls to bolster public education spending, create a fledgling community college system, consider the growing call to allow public employees to negotiate for benefits, address the burgeoning illegal narcotic use among the young, and lower the voting age.

My own brief experience with Laxalt before the session had been instructive. As Clark County public defender, I had challenged him in the media on several occasions. I had called upon him to appoint a bipartisan commission to investigate the penitentiary system. Although he declined that request, when he called a special session of the Nevada Legislature, he phoned to tell me that he agreed with me on an issue I'd raised and was adding it to his criminal justice proposals. That left an impression on me that I carried into the '69 session. He was always gracious. And when he had a question about a piece of legislation I had sponsored, he wasn't too important to call and ask me to come to his office to discuss it. And he signed the bill.

Just days into the session, in my first official act, McKissick and I cosponsored a resolution that called on the secretaries of the Departments of the Interior and Agriculture to reconsider their plans to raise cattle grazing fees in the West. When I introduced the resolution, the Elko legislators were shocked that a Southern Nevada lawmaker would be concerned about grazing fees. When it passed, they looked at me less as a stranger from a strange land. It was apparent that I had made a favorable impression, and it was the beginning of my effort to develop a close relationship with rural legislators.

At the end of a long day, I'd frequently join many of the rural legislators for a beer at the Greeno Bar near the Capitol. The time I spent with them was invaluable. I got to know them, and they got to know me. In addition to Roy and Norm, I got to know other rural legislators, Bode Howard, Virgil Getto, and Joe Dini. Gradually, it became clear our differences weren't as great as our desire to do right by Nevada.

Dini would prove an extremely important contact as my political horizons broadened. He owned the Lucky Club in Yerington and was the man to know in Lyon County. I often traveled to Reno in the evening when requested to speak to local organizations and to civic groups throughout Northern Nevada. I saw that as an opportunity to become better known.

As strange as it sounds given the highly partisan times we live in today, there was virtually no partisanship in the 1969 Nevada Legislature. There were constituency differences, philosophical differences, and sectional differences, but the party lines weren't etched in stone.

Part of the general collegiality, I believe, was derived from the building itself. It was crowded, and we had no offices to retreat to. Only the leaders of each house had them. Legislators did not have a personal staff. You brought your work with you to your desk on the floor and shared from a pool of secretaries after the morning business was concluded. Everyone had to work around everyone else's schedule. There was no cafeteria. That meant there was mingling on the floor during breaks.

Many committee hearings took place in a room about ten-feet-wide by twenty-feet-long with a window that faced Carson Street and what was then the Supreme Court Building. There was a long table, but little room for reporters, observers, or witnesses to sit. The room would frequently be jammed beyond capacity with everything from citizens groups to the Clark County Ministerial Society. It was standing-room-only for many. The lack of comfortable accommodations may have accounted for the brevity of the testimony and the committee meetings.

That doesn't mean we always agreed. That first session I clashed often with Majority Floor Leader Zel Lowman, who stood to the right of his own party. As an example, when the state's low-paid teachers finally took to the streets and marched down the Las Vegas Strip in the name of better working conditions, Lowman from the

Assembly floor called for them to be terminated. I was only too happy to fire back.

Near the end of April, when we found ourselves on the same side of an issue, one legislator took the floor and said, "I believe this is the first time in the entire session that Bryan and Lowman have ever agreed on anything." Lowman wasn't a radical; he was an Eagle Scout and Silver Beaver recipient. But in my estimation his politics would not take the state in the right direction.

And Nevada's ever-present north-south sectionalism occasionally got contentious. One heated issue was the establishment of a two-year medical school in Reno. The bill passed largely on a sectional vote. The impetus was Howard Hughes, who had offered to provide millions to create a medical school. Little did we know, although Hughes's gift was generous, it covered only a fraction of the funding required to establish a medical school. Northern Nevadans were eager to embrace that donation and have the medical school in Reno. They realized that after the 1970 reapportionment, it would be highly unlikely with the Clark County legislative delegation in the majority in both the Assembly and Senate that Reno would be the site of the medical school.

At the height of the Vietnam War, with the counterculture hippie movement in full swing and Woodstock and the "Summer of Love" just a few months away, the Judiciary Committee considered a hefty slate of legislation aimed at penalizing illegal narcotics possession, use, and sales. The rising use of recreational drugs, especially among the young, alarmed the nation, and Nevada struggled to get a handle on it by, for the most part, placing tough sentencing laws on the books.

It was a reminder of how much the issue had changed in the public perception. When I was a boy, the arrest of actor Robert Mitchum for smoking marijuana had stirred a national scandal about the evils of "reefer" smoking. And now there were so many kinds of drugs being experimented with that it was hard to keep track.

I had considerable experience with drug-related cases as a deputy district attorney and as the public defender. I saw the issue from the prosecution and the defense side as well. I was also interested in showing my support for the law enforcement community. The legislation wasn't controversial. The Judiciary Committee approved legislation that enhanced penalties for drug offenses, for possession and sales.

The rising human cost of the Vietnam War would also have an effect when it came to the voting age, which in 1969 was twenty-one years old. Teenagers drafted into battle at age eighteen could fight and die for their country, but they couldn't vote for dogcatcher, much less the president. I was one of many on both sides of the aisle—including Governor Laxalt—who believed the law should be changed, but the issue needed to be decided by voters.

The issue wasn't as simple as passing a law. Section 1 of Article 2 of the Nevada Constitution had to be changed to reflect the will of the people. That meant approval in two consecutive sessions of the legislature and then a statewide vote. We jockeyed about whether to lower the age to nineteen, which Harry and I favored because we thought it had a better chance of passing, or eighteen, which reflected the actions of other states. The 1969 legislative session approved a bill that would lower the voting age to 18, and in 1971 we approved it for a second time. In a special election in June 1971, Nevadans by a narrow margin of 1,565 votes ratified the legislature's actions. It passed into law.

For the second consecutive session, legislation that would slightly liberalize Nevada's abortion law was introduced in the Assembly. In fact, many Republicans from both ends of the state voted in favor of the bill. The differences were philosophical, but that didn't make it any less contentious. It brought out faith leaders, predominantly from the Catholic and LDS churches, from across the state. One Catholic physician even came to my house over the weekend while I was mowing the lawn to voice his opposition to the bill being forwarded.

At the time, Nevada's law prohibited abortion unless the life of the mother was at stake. The change would have expanded legal abortion to include cases of incest and if a physician determined the child would be born gravely mentally or physically disabled—but only after a district court order based on the affidavits of a panel of three licensed physicians. The US Supreme Court's landmark *Roe v. Wade* decision was still four years away. Zel Lowman was among those who spoke passionately against the bill, but many others believed it was a compassionate improvement in the law. The bill was narrowly defeated in the Assembly when Virgil Getto changed his vote.

That first session, I made a point of raising an issue that made me few friends in the legislature's chummy lobbying ranks, who enjoyed essentially free and unfettered access. I sponsored legislation that would compel them to register and provide financial disclosures, which did not exist when I came to the legislature in 1969. Some took offense at my action. Frankly, in my experience, I never recall any of the lobbyists crossing the line, but I believed strongly that legislative reform that increased disclosure was important to maintaining the credibility of the process. The lobbying and campaign finance reform efforts would be a thread throughout my career in public service.

I also joined the unsuccessful effort in the Assembly to change the state's legislative schedule from biennial to annual sessions. The reasoning was simple: the legislature obviously was unable to complete its work in a fast-growing state and had held special sessions with one exception every year since 1954. The plan was shelved on a 19–15 vote with six lawmakers conveniently absent. Later, as governor, I reconsidered my position. A governor is the happiest person in town when the legislature adjourns and goes home.

The most important person I got to know better that first session was Harry Reid, whom I first met six years earlier. Speaker McKissick dubbed us "the Gold Dust Twins," recalling that years before he and Harry Swanson had shared that same nickname. Reid was indefatigable, constantly looking one step ahead and dreaming big.

Reid's close friend and political mentor was his former Basic High School government teacher Mike O'Callaghan. I'll never forget the first time I met Mike. He was visiting the state capital during the 1969 session and touched base with his friend Harry, who introduced us.

"Here's a guy that you want to keep your eye on," Harry said. "Once you meet him, you never forget him." Mike was charismatic. With a chipped tooth and a limp from the loss of a leg in battle, he was unforgettable. I realized immediately that Harry and Mike had a special relationship. Mike had been Harry's boxing coach at the Henderson Boys Club and had supported his efforts to rise from his Searchlight upbringing to graduate from law school.

Although seemingly mild-mannered, Harry burned with a passion for politics. He'd come up poor in Searchlight and was hungry to rise from those humble beginnings. He had been the Henderson city attorney, and I had been Clark County public defender when we ran for the State Assembly in District 4 at-large and were elected. Harry and I likely sponsored or cosponsored more bills than any legislators in Nevada history. Assemblyman Bill Swackhamer, a Democrat from Battle Mountain who was a former Speaker of the Assembly and was just a lovely guy, came up to both of us in the middle of the session and said, "You know, this is not the last session that the Nevada Legislature will ever convene." Today, the number of bills a legislator may introduce is limited.

Harry and I worked well together—perhaps a little too well in one instance. It was called Assembly Bill 499.

The previous year, Martin Luther King Jr. and Robert Kennedy were assassinated. The streets in America were ablaze with protests. Radical political factions on either end of the spectrum increasingly used firebombs to make their statements, often to tragic ends for civilians and firefighters alike.

When Harry was still Henderson's city attorney, the town's chief of police had asked him to introduce a bill to provide for enhanced penalties for firebombing. Harry asked me if I'd like to cosponsor the bill, and I said of course I would. Having been public defender, I was interested in positioning myself in the political center. This was a law enforcement issue that was legitimate, and I was happy to endorse. It was a bill that not only made sense to us, but also was sure to garner attention and improve our bona fides with the law enforcement and firefighting fraternities.

As members of the Assembly Judiciary Committee, we had no difficulty getting the bill approved in committee. Parenthetically, the committee was an impressive group that included a future US senator, governor, secretary of state, US attorney, and state district court judge. It went to the floor of the Assembly, and it passed without incident. Then it was time to move to the other side.

The Senate Judiciary Committee was chaired by Warren "Snowy" Monroe, an Elko County Democrat who had a journalist's background. We knew he was not terribly fond of lawyers—and young lawyers in particular. We knew we needed some horsepower. So we went to Deputy Legislative Counsel Frank Daykin, who was highly regarded by lawmakers.

When Frank spoke, people listened—in part because he spoke very slowly and deliberately in polysyllabic utterances. He agreed to help us get that bill through committee, and he was at his best. The bill moved smoothly through the Senate committee.

When it came time for the third reading, the final vote in the process before being sent to the governor for his signature, the suspense was palpable for Harry and me. We went up to the visitors' balcony in the Senate chambers to watch the action. With no controversial legislation on the agenda that day, we were the only two in the gallery.

At that time, there was seldom debate in the Senate on a bill once it was favorably reported out of committee onto the floor. The thinking was, and it would change a few years later, that it was disrespectful to question the judgment of the committee members who had processed the bill. Harry and I were waiting for our moment of triumph.

Then Senator Bill Farr, the fire chief of Sparks, rose to his feet. When he spoke, he was absolutely rhapsodic about the bill. Harry and I, proud legislative parents that we were, were practically giddy. Had the high-five been around in 1969, we would have been slapping one. We could hardly contain ourselves.

And then Farr lowered the boom. "You know," he said, "it's such a wonderful piece of legislation. I introduced the identical legislation two years ago, and it's been the law ever since."

We couldn't believe our ears. Talk about a letdown. We felt like slipping out of our chairs in the balcony, crawling out of the room, and slithering down the stairs.

The pace of the legislature left little time to sulk. We moved on quickly, chastened by the experience and a little wiser for it.

Another issue that session was a proposal for a dog racing track in Henderson, Harry's backyard. Henderson had a very tight business community led by banker Selma Bartlett. They came to believe as an article of faith that a dog track would be the catalyst for new economic opportunities. Their sense was that somehow this small community, built as a factory town during World War II, could be more than just a blue-collar community of workers at the old Basic Magnesium Incorporated plant.

Howard Hughes, eccentric that he was, for some reason had a pathological dislike for dog racing. His influence was powerful throughout the state, including the legislature and Governor Laxalt's office. Laxalt had controversially allowed Hughes to receive a gaming license without ever being compelled to appear at a legally required public hearing.

Harry and I recognized the challenge. Equestrian groups aided the dog-racing advocates. The debate raged in the press and behind the scenes, where lobbyists from both sides often met after hours at Lancer, a restaurant that overlooked Reno. Sometimes on the same night there would be dog-racing lobbyists hosting one set of legislators and the Hughes side hosting another set. Back and forth it went.

The bill was referred to the Assembly Commerce Committee, which was chaired that session by Jim Wood, a Reno Republican who opposed the bill. For the bill to be acted upon, the chairman had to have the bill in his physical possession. As a stalling tactic, week after week Wood intentionally forgot to bring the bill from home. The committee was evenly divided, but the prevailing view was that the bill would die in committee because of the intense lobbying effort.

Fully believing the bill was stillborn, some legislators made commitments to both sides of the issue. Suddenly, a newly elected assemblyman from North Las Vegas, Dave Branch, changed his vote. He then left Carson City, supposedly on an urgent family matter. The bill came galloping out of committee, and Harry found himself between a rock and a hard place.

Although he was born in Searchlight, Harry considered Henderson his real hometown and where his chief supporters were. But Hughes could make or break a career. Harry had to think quickly, and he did. Overnight, Harry developed a "conflict of interest" because his father-in-law owned property near the proposed racetrack, and Harry's wife, Landra, was the sole heir. On the roll call, he requested to be recorded as Not Voting because of his conflict of interest.

In the end, the dog racing bill passed and was signed into law. Las Vegas Downs was built in Henderson and opened to much fanfare, but it had a short lifespan.

But no one caught more flak when trying to avoid an uncomfortable vote that session than Assemblyman Bryan Hafen, a Republican from Mesquite. He avoided casting a vote by slipping out a side door in the chamber leading onto a metal fire escape. In a front-page story in the *Las Vegas Sun*, columnist Bryn Armstrong skewered him in an article headlined, "The 'Mesquite Mosquito' 'Bugs-Out' From Voting," recounting how he "flew out the Nevada Assembly window chambers," and noting that he went "zipping down a fire escape on the east side of the ancient vestibule." And that was just to avoid a vote to approve a one-half cent sales tax increase for the cities. Speaker McKissick roared, "Come back here," but Hafen had already taken flight.

It wasn't a simple impromptu exit. "A call of the house" had been invoked. Since the days of the Comstock Lode, the legislature had adopted a procedure that empowered the sergeant-at-arms to round up absent lawmakers and detain them—if necessary, by force—to compel their participation. Hafen did not return to the 1971 legislative session.

Harry and I worked hard, but there also was time for some light-hearted moments. It was a different era. There were some hijinks.

Harry and I were having dinner together one evening at the Carson Nugget. While waiting for the waitress, I read a copy of the *Nevada Appeal* and came across an article that caught my attention. In the newspaper was a small article headlined, "Las Vegas lobbyist loses wallet." I won't mention the name of the lobbyist, but he was a fine guy who I'd known since college. I said, "Harry, we can have some fun with this."

After dinner, we went to the Western Union office and sent a telegram to his home. It read, "Dear———, Left your wallet at my place. See you next time you're up. Barbra." It created quite a stir at his house, but he knew who had sent the telegram and it didn't interrupt our friendship. He knew we were just pulling his leg.

On another occasion, we were invited by Assemblyman Swackhamer to address his constituents with the Battle Mountain Rod and Gun Club, a Northern Nevada outdoorsmen's organization, on our legislation that would create a three-day waiting period before the purchase of a concealable weapon. Failure to wait the three days would be a misdemeanor. It was an attempt to counter rising handgun crime in Clark County and was by no reasonable measure "gun control" legislation.

During my days at the ATO House at the University of Nevada, I had several fraternity brothers from Battle Mountain, and I understood the importance of guns to them. And I knew that this would not be a pleasant encounter. I declined the invitation. That left Harry to represent the bill in front of a very tough crowd.

Harry had boxed in college, so he knew what it was like to be on the ropes. Although the crowd failed to land a knockout blow, Harry was pelted with jeers. The greeting was so angry that *Sun* columnist Armstrong got wind of it and produced a humorous piece on it, quoting Harry saying, "It's kind of funny today, but it wasn't funny last night."

It was a bygone era, where the art of compromise was recognized as the way to process controversial legislation. It just made good sense, and learning the art of principled compromise has almost always been a key to the political process. The Great Compromise crafted during the Constitutional Convention of 1787 gave us a legislative branch of government with two senators representing each state and members of the House of Representatives being elected based on population.

Although the Judiciary Committee teemed with legislation, some of it controversial, the Fish and Game Committee on which I served was another matter. It was not a major committee, but it frequently generated a lot of controversy among Nevada sportsmen. I developed a close friendship with state Senator Cliff Young, who served on the Senate Natural Resources Committee. Cliff was a former Nevada representative who lost a close election to Alan Bible for US Senate in 1956 and would later serve as a Nevada Supreme Court justice. He was an avid outdoorsman and conservationist who rose to the presidency of the National Wildlife Federation. I was no outdoorsman, but through Cliff I learned to better appreciate conservation issues and the importance of protecting the environment. I would benefit from his insight and cherish his friendship. We spent several days together with our sons on horseback on a fishing trip into the majestic Ruby Mountains that I'll never forget.

The following year, I was named the Conservation Legislator of the Year by the local chapter of the National Wildlife Federation and received a small brass statuette of a bear that I still keep on my desk.

That session we passed legislation that would have consolidated City of North Las Vegas and City of Las Vegas into a single governmental entity. This had been a major objective of the business community in its effort to seek more efficiency in local government. I voted for it. When it reached the governor's desk, Laxalt vetoed it. His reasoning: It was unfair to North Las Vegas. The legislation did not contain a veto for the smaller community.

The session was memorable because it created the Interim Finance Committee, which although constitutionally dubious, avoided the necessity of calling a special session of the legislature to adjust the state budget when the legislature was not in session.

It also approved a constitutional amendment limiting the governor to two terms. I voted against it.

We also did battle with the state's powerful insurance industry. That year the industry was pushing for comprehensive changes in the state's insurance code. It was complicated and not clear what the impact would be on consumers. Bill Swackhamer and I became concerned those changes might disadvantage consumers. We held up the legislation and secured support for an interim study. Herb Denenberg, the former Pennsylvania insurance commissioner and renowned consumer advocate, was designated to conduct the interim review.

Another significant piece of legislation was a bill introduced by Senator Carl Dodge, a Republican from Fallon, that gave local public employees and schoolteachers the right to bargain collectively with their employer. Change came slowly to Nevada, but it was coming.

The taxicab wars were raging in Clark County that year. Some cabs were overturned and burned, and at least one homicide was associated with the conflict. In response, we created the Taxicab Authority, which gave officials the ability to better regulate the industry in Southern Nevada.

But no bill in my decade as a state legislator created more problems for me than Assembly Bill 70 in the 1969 session. I believed it was a constitutionally flawed piece of legislation that presumed to shield children from exposure to obscene materials in an era of rapid social change. The bill included provisions that would have had an impact on movie theaters and public libraries. Librarians, civil libertarians, and theater operators testified against the bill. Theater owner Lloyd Katz reminded legislators that just a year earlier the Motion Picture

Industry Association had created its own movie rating system. Katz noted that movies once considered too risqué for innocent eyes were regularly being aired on prime-time television.

But on February 28 when the Assembly voted, it easily passed. I was one of seven Assembly members who voted against it.

I moved on to other business, spent ten years in both houses, and forgot all about Assembly Bill 70. But when I ran for governor in 1982 against incumbent Bob List, it became a major campaign issue.

Spring was finally breaking in Carson City when the session ended in the last week of April. It was a welcome sight. I'd been fortunate enough to be named Freshman Assemblyman of the Session. It was a nice acknowledgment for a lot of hard work that softened the embarrassment Harry and I endured for trying to push a bill already in law. We've laughed about it often since then.

On the drive back south, the spring runoff was plentiful, and the sage-scented desert was in bloom. I would soon return to work at the law office, but after a single session in Carson City as a freshman legislator, it was clear to me that where policy was being made was where I wanted to be.

CHAPTER 12

Expanding the Base

The 1969 legislative session had been a good one for me, but I was eager to expand my political base. For reasons that I never understood, the legislature created Assembly District 5, called a floterial district. It included all the old Assembly District 4, which I had represented in the 1969 session, and all North Las Vegas. Mel Close was one of two assemblymen who represented District 5. In 1970, Mel filed for the Nevada Senate, creating a vacancy in District 5.

I filed for the open seat.

My race was unlikely to be difficult. Newcomers seeking an Assembly seat would likely file in my old district, where nine candidates were to be elected at-large. It was a cautious move, and many of my supporters pointed that out and reminded me that several of my political contemporaries and potential rivals had made bolder moves. Harry Reid filed for lieutenant governor after Lieutenant Governor Ed Fike announced his candidacy for governor. Roy Woofter challenged District Attorney George Franklin in Clark County. But the boldest move was made by Bob List, who filed for attorney general against three-term incumbent Harvey Dickerson, a member of a prominent Nevada political family. Bill Raggio challenged two-term incumbent Howard Cannon in the US Senate race.

The marquee event that autumn was the governor's race. Fike was heavily favored at the outset. Mike O'Callaghan faced well-known television news anchor Hank Thornley in the Democratic primary. Thornley had the support of many of the establishment in the Clark County Democratic Party. But the Irishman with the chipped tooth and wooden leg had the charisma that Thornley lacked and breezed to a primary victory.

Facing Fike in the general election, O'Callaghan was badly underfunded. Early on many of his campaign signs were hand-painted. But a new political force was about to take center stage: Nevada educators. The '69 session established a new salary ratio, which had the effect of imposing a more restrictive salary cap for career educators. The sleeping giant had been awakened. They created a new organization, Teachers in Politics, known as TIP. Teachers were assigned by TIP to work with each of the endorsed candidates. As a teacher himself, O'Callaghan had a natural affinity for educators. And they rallied to his cause. I had opposed the cap in the '69 session, and I received their endorsement.

As O'Callaghan closed the gap with Fike in the final weeks of the campaign, Fike made two fatal mistakes. At a time when he was favored to win, Fike's campaign took a withering hit when he was accused of a conflict of interest in connection with the purchase of 1,090 acres of public land near Laughlin by the Colorado River Properties Inc., a company in which he was listed as a vice president and director. The title company he owned was also implicated, and to make matters worse the scandal was broken by nationally syndicated newspaper columnist Jack Anderson. He denied wrongdoing, but he was staggered by the allegations. Reeling and on the ropes, Fike was pummeled by the O'Callaghan campaign after Fike floated a campaign ad promising to repeal the state sales tax on groceries, something beyond the governor's individual power. The state sales tax had been approved by a referendum of the voters and could only be modified or repealed by the same process. No governor or state legislature could repeal it. Las Vegas attorneys signed an advertisement calling him either "deceitful or misinformed." On election night, O'Callaghan and the kid from Searchlight carried the day. List defeated Dickerson in the attorney general's race, and Woofter upended Franklin in the race for district attorney.

I was the undercard to the political main events with my election to Assembly District 5. Three contemporaries were now better positioned than I. Reid and List were statewide officeholders, and Woofter was the district attorney in Nevada's most populated county. The climb to the top would be steeper now.

With an expected easy race in Assembly District 5 and a partnership in a successful law firm, Bonnie and I decided to put a down payment on a new home in Paradise Crest, a Collins Brothers development. The cost was $47,000, and our mortgage payment would double to $360 a month. We were scheduled to move in September.

Suddenly in July, my professional world imploded when the Ross, Snyder, Goodman & Bryan law firm broke up. The firm's attorneys went their separate ways. I was suddenly a solo practitioner, and I was very worried.

My campaign lay ahead, and if elected I would be in Carson City from January until April. I had a family to support and very little time to build my own legal practice. I was between the proverbial rock and a hard place. What to do? Should I withdraw from the Assembly race and back out of the purchase of the new home? Or should I soldier on?

As always Bonnie, a rock of support, said let's make the best of a very challenging situation. And with her support and encouragement, we did. We closed on the house in September. New clients came to my office. And our financial situation, not good by any means, at least had stabilized, and we could meet our financial obligations.

When the session began, we were in the new legislative building. Republicans were still in the majority, and they chose Lawrence Jacobsen from Douglas County as their Speaker. With Mel Close, the minority leader from the '69 session, now in the state Senate, I decided to run for Assembly minority leader. Norman "Ty" Hilbrecht, who had been elected to the Assembly in 1966, also announced his intention to run, and he edged me out.

The 1971 session would be very different for me. As a sole practitioner, I was running my law office during the week by making daily calls to my secretary. On Friday, I would make a mad dash to the airport and catch the 11 a.m. flight to Las Vegas. This would enable me to spend a couple of hours in the office and conduct business. I spent Saturdays in the office. My financial situation was a constant worry. I would be out of the office most of the time from January through April. John McGroarty, who had been an associate at Ross, Snyder, Goodman & Bryan, was appointed by Governor O'Callaghan to a senior position on his staff, and he and his wife had moved to Carson City. John was aware of my financial plight and offered to let me stay at his home. That was a big help.

The first order of business in the 1971 session was resolving an election challenge by Assemblyman Hal Smith, a well-liked and respected Republican from Henderson. Hal had been eliminated in the counting on election night by incumbent Democrat Art Espinoza, but the tally as recorded by the voting machine didn't make sense. I was appointed as a member of a bipartisan group of legislators chosen to fly to Las Vegas and examine the voting machine. In 1970, voting machines were only slightly smaller than a Buick and filled with gears and levers. The one we looked at must have weighed a ton. As soon as the election official opened the back, I spotted the problem immediately. One of the gears was jammed. You could easily see it. When we demonstrated by pulling the lever for Smith, it failed to add to his vote total. We reported our findings to the Assembly and by a unanimous vote returned a good man to the legislature. But talk about how times have changed. To complete our task, we also had to make the difficult decision of refusing to seat the incumbent Democrat. Our decision was not partisan, but I'm not sure such bipartisanship exists in the state legislature today.

As the 1971 session unfolded, we made sure Laxalt's teacher pay ratio rollback was reversed. O'Callaghan's broad-based plan to upgrade and revisit some long-neglected government departments was ambitious. For a time, an issue that was not on his agenda became a focus of the session: the status of Nevada's brothels.

Brothels predate Nevada's statehood, and by the time I reached the state legislature legalized prostitution was generally considered a rural issue. In sparsely populated counties, they were at least tolerated, and sometimes embraced, as taxpaying businesses and members of the community. It's fair to say that rural residents, by and large, were supportive then. Even a half-century later, an effort to outlaw them in Lyon County in 2018 failed.

By the dawn of the 1970s, they had become more controversial with the bare-knuckle war between Bill Raggio, Washoe County district attorney, and Mustang Ranch brothel baron Joe Conforte. Raggio used the "public nuisance" law to close Conforte's operation. It was reported that Raggio burned down Conforte's house of ill repute.

At the legislature, it was no secret that Conforte's political interests were being well served by longtime Republican lawmaker James "Slats" Slattery, who represented Storey County in the Senate from 1954 to 1970. That led to some strange lobbying efforts.

In 1971, Conforte's gifts of persuasion charmed Storey County officials into passing an ordinance that licensed brothels and prostitutes, effectively sidestepping the nuisance law. Seeing that, and realizing Conforte's fast friendships throughout the state, officials in Clark County successfully lobbied the legislature into passing a bill that limited legalized prostitution to counties with populations of 50,000 or fewer. The legislation received tepid support from District Attorney Roy Woofter, who was on friendly terms with Conforte. As I say, the issue transcended political party.

Insurance legislation introduced in the '69 session was so comprehensive that we wanted it to be reviewed from a consumer perspective. After receiving the interim study headed by renowned consumer advocate Herb Denenberg, which made some modifications, we quickly approved the legislation.

We often worked across party lines on a variety of issues that session. As much as I admired Governor O'Callaghan, a man whose temper was fast becoming legendary, I was part of a small group of Democratic legislators who disagreed with his decision to veto a bill that provided protection against defamation lawsuits by lawmakers when the legislature was in session. Members of Congress enjoy that protection, and we thought state legislators deserved it, too, but we were unsuccessful in overriding O'Callaghan's veto.

I was the prime sponsor that session of legislation that mandated consumers be paid the prime interest plus 1 percent by utilities that compelled them to put down a security deposit. And I was also the prime sponsor of legislation that added an additional consumer to the dairy commission. I introduced legislation that would establish unfair practices and other consumer protection measures to be administered by the Department of Commerce, but the bill died in committee. It was part of a consumer protection agenda that would define my decade of service in the state legislature.

I cosponsored legislation adding an ombudsman to the state workers compensation office, pushed to create the Division of Aging Services, and supported legislation that authorized reduced fares for seniors on public transportation.

In rapidly changing times, the threat of pollution in the environment became an increasing topic of debate. In the 1971 session, just a year after the first Earth Day, we enacted legislation establishing a state commission on environmental protection, which was authorized to reduce and abate air pollution. That session I supported a bill that would enable private citizens to sue companies and governments that were polluting, and I called out a Panaca legislator for watering down its language. A weaker version of the bill eventually passed.

Then there were the kinds of legislation that didn't attract much attention in the press. I sponsored legislation that would enable young people to seek a physician's care for drug addiction without parental consent. I fought against an attempt to force families of a juvenile in the justice system to post a $500 bond. I also joined with my colleagues in eliminating the stigmatization of the word "illegitimate" from birth certificates. Let me be clear: I wasn't alone in these fights. With apologies to John Donne, at the legislature, "No man is an island entire of itself; every man is a piece of the continent, a part of the main."

Although I didn't know it at the time, another piece of legislation we passed would have an impact on my own political life as governor. The legislation required certain state boards to have a balanced political representation. The law prevented party changes made for political expediency to avoid the charade of someone changing their affiliation just to satisfy the political balance. It prohibited the selection of anyone who had changed political party within two years of the appointment. In other words, no switching uniforms just to play for the winning team.

For me, maintaining the public's trust in government was paramount, and in 1971 Nevada had no ethics laws for public officials on the books. I cosponsored legislation with Assemblywoman Margie Foote that would limit campaign expenses and require a declaration of all expenses. We were unsuccessful, but it was an issue we would revisit in later legislative sessions.

Among the more significant pieces of legislation that we passed was the enactment of a Fair Housing Act and the creation of the Division of Aging Services within the Department of Health, Welfare, and Rehabilitation.

The most far-reaching issue of the 1971 session was reapportionment following the 1970 decennial census. Reapportionment in 1971 was every bit as controversial as it had been in the previous decade and was always a difficult political issue. In 1962, the US Supreme Court's landmark *Baker v. Carr* decision, followed by

Reynolds v. Sims, held that both houses of state legislatures had to be represented based on population. "One person, one vote" was the law of the land.

Before the *Baker* and *Reynolds* decisions, half of the Nevada Senate represented less than 8 percent of the state's population. In the Assembly, Clark and Washoe accounted for 75 percent of the state's population but received just 57 percent of the seats. Nevada's rural counties, which had dominated the legislature since statehood, would lose more representation when the 1971 legislature convened. There would be fierce resistance to the change.

The *Baker* and *Reynolds* decisions opened the way for a federal lawsuit filed by intrepid Assemblywoman Flora Dungan, a Democrat, and Dr. Clare Woodbury that would force the legislature to comply. When the 1965 legislature failed to act, the federal court ordered Governor Grant Sawyer to call for a special session.

There were fireworks from the opening gavel of the special session. At least twenty plans were discussed. Battle lines were drawn and redrawn. The Supreme Court was slandered. In the end, enough of a compromise was reached that pleased no one and in 1966 barely passed muster with a federal three-judge panel, which noted it was "not the fairest and best plan that the Nevada Legislature could possibly enact."

It was clear in the '71 session that the rural counties would lose even more representation to booming Clark County. The state legislature at the time was largely a collegial body with little political partisanship. Veteran Assemblyman Frank Young, a Republican from Clark County, worked across party lines and deserves the lion's share of credit for building a coalition through meticulous preparation and an emphasis on inclusion. Young's reapportionment plan created single-seat Assembly districts. It has stood the test of time, and fifty years later it remains the basis for all Assembly elections in Nevada.

CHAPTER 13

The First State Senate Race

The 1971 Nevada Legislature created forty Assembly districts to be represented by a single legislator, but the Senate retained several at-large districts. The enormous growth of Clark County in the previous decade enabled Clark County to gain three additional Senate seats and for the first time a majority in both houses. Senate District 3 in Clark County would have seven senators to be elected at-large—four in the 1972 election cycle and three in 1974.

A new legislative district was created in Clark County that encompassed the predominantly African American community, and Joe Neal would claim that seat in November and become the first African can American to serve in the state Senate. Three incumbents would be on the ballot in Senate District 3 in the fall—all political heavyweights. Mahlon Brown had represented Clark County since 1951, when each county had only one senator. Floyd Lamb chaired the Senate Finance Committee and was a member of the powerful Lamb family, which included Sheriff Ralph Lamb, who played a key role in my appointment as public defender, and County Commissioner Darwin Lamb. And there was Helen Herr, a longtime Democratic Party member and the first woman elected to the state Senate.

Then there was the fourth seat, the newly created one with no incumbent. That was the seat I had my eye on. *Tempus fugit.* It was time to make my move. The downside risk was minimal. I was reasonably confident that I could finish in the top four in the general election. But if—and this was a big if—if I would lead the ticket in a field dominated by Southern Nevada political heavyweights, it would send a powerful message that the new kid on the block may have a political future.

I was trying to enter a big tent in Southern Nevada politics. This would be a quantum leap from my prior Assembly races. I would need to raise more money, something that I always hated, open a campaign office with full-time staff, and assemble a ground game. Because I was running at-large seeking one of four seats, I did not have to run against any of the incumbents head-to-head. As I did in my first Assembly race, I would ask the voters to make me one of their four choices. For my supporters, I would ask them to vote only for me, the so-called single shot.

One advantage I enjoyed was that I was younger than the three incumbents. I had boundless energy, was laser focused on my objective and was prepared to work 24/7 to achieve my goal.

The first step was to find a campaign office for my staff to work out of. My friend Norm Jenkins had an auto-leasing business at the corner of Fifteenth and Charleston. He had a building that was unoccupied in the rear of the property. It would be large enough to accommodate my staff. Another advantage was its proximity to my law office, which enabled me to easily move back and forth as circumstances required.

Joan Kovacs had been a longtime activist in the Democratic Party. She knew all the players. She became a full-time, compensated employee. One additional advantage that Joan brought to the campaign was to bring her friend Jan Nitz to the office to volunteer almost daily.

Bob Peccole and Dave Powell would play key roles in our ground game. Together they would assemble campaign signs and place them in key locations around the valley as they had done in my previous campaigns.

With the headquarters up and running, we were ready for the launch. A campaign opening was a major event in the '70s. Political insiders viewed the size of the crowd as an indicator of success. As the days to the opening approached, one campaign supporter was able to secure two searchlights of the kind commonly used to light up the sky for movie premieres and the Academy Awards. My days as a boxcar swamper for DeLuca paid dividends when the company provided the beer. Hot dogs were also donated.

Dave Powell and I met at the headquarters at noon. Powell said to me, "You know, we could use some flowers." But bouquets weren't in the campaign's budget.

That gave me an idea. I knew the manager at one of the local mortuaries. I called and asked, "What do you do with the flowers once the services are over?" His response: "We just toss them out."

I said, "Would you mind if we came by and picked up some of the flowers?"

"Help yourself," he replied.

We did that. That night we had more flowers at the campaign headquarters than Marilyn Monroe had at her funeral. Those in attendance could only conclude that the candidate had many well-wishers. We were a little careless, however, because on one of the wreaths we had failed to cut off a ribbon with the heart-felt sentiment, "Mother."

That night was a huge success with spotlights dancing in the sky, beer flowing, and an enthusiastic crowd. It augured well for my election in the fall. My Senate campaign followed the pattern begun in my first Assembly campaign: distributing hand cards at bowling alleys, attending school carnivals, walking door-to-door through neighborhoods. In short, I went any place there was a crowd. In fact, it was said tongue-in-cheek, but became a point of pride, that "If two or more are gathered, Bryan will be there." I pursued every endorsement opportunity and was fortunate to receive the endorsement of both the *Las Vegas Sun* and *Las Vegas Review-Journal,* two newspapers that rarely agreed on anything. And once again I was proud to receive the endorsement of Teachers in Politics then led by future campaign strategist Gary Gray.

By the time I filed for office in the summer of 1972, I was already known in the press as the first candidate to volunteer to fully disclose his financial worth to the public. I did so once again at the outset of the Senate race. I'd fought for strong conflict of interest laws and increased rules for legislative lobbyists.

In 1968, our lawn sign reading "This Home Sold on Bryan" attracted a lot of attention. In 1972, it was our billboard that turned heads. Blair was an adorable five-year-old with a ponytail, and our billboard featured her whispering in my ear, with the words, "A man must listen to lead." Blair was obviously the star.

When primary election night arrived, my headquarters was jammed to the gunwales. Covering one wall were sheets of paper denoting all of Senate District 3's polling locations. County election department staff went to each polling location at the close of the polls. The voting machines were opened, and an election official read the total from each machine. I arranged to have volunteers at every polling place, and as the numbers were read out loud, a member of Team Bryan would copy the numbers and race back to headquarters. Clyde Turner, my old opponent in my race for sophomore class president, was now a CPA, and he and his brother were at headquarters to tally the votes. As each of the volunteers returned with the results, the numbers looked good and cheers went up as I carried one precinct after another. Within ninety minutes of the polls closing, we knew the results: I would lead the ticket in the primary.

The race to the general election was a sprint, and I had an energetic staff behind me. One of my opponents in the general election was Republican Ira Hecht, who was running at a time that state Senator Chic Hecht enjoyed a high name recognition. I was concerned that voters might confuse one Hecht for another. With that in mind I crafted an ad reminding voters that "Not all Hechts are the same."

I continued to campaign in every waking moment and once again benefited from Bonnie's many contacts through her membership in Junior League and other groups. Her friends agreed to host coffee klatches for me. As many of them were registered Republicans, meeting them enabled me to build support across party lines.

It all paid off in November in a campaign season that was a challenging one for Nevada Democrats in a year that saw incumbent Richard Nixon trounce George McGovern in the presidential race. In a field of some of the most powerful political figures in Southern Nevada, experienced senators who had been in the game for decades, I was able to top the ticket. This helped to further establish my political bona fides.

I was headed to the Nevada Senate.

CHAPTER 14

The 1973 Session

Joining me as a new member of the Nevada Senate in the 1973 session of the legislature was Bill Raggio, the former district attorney of Washoe County who later became the Senate majority leader and was a political force in the Senate for decades. History was also made with the addition of Joe Neal, the first African American elected to the Nevada Senate. And rounding out the new members were former North Las Vegas mayor Gene Echols and Rick Blakemore of Tonopah. The Democrats had regained the majority in the Assembly, and Keith Ashworth became the Speaker.

President Richard Nixon was inaugurated for his second term. Over the next three months, key Nixon administration insiders would resign in connection with what was becoming known as the Watergate scandal.

This would be my third legislative session. The Democrats were in the majority in the Senate and chaired all the legislative committees. In the arcane world of legislative seniority, I had seniority over the newly elected Democrats, and Mahlon Brown, the majority leader, asked me to chair the Education Committee.

The committee dealt with a broad range of legislative issues from special education to mandatory vaccinations of public school children. Interestingly, I don't recall any of the backlash to the required vaccinations at that time that schools faced during the COVID-19 pandemic.

The issues before the Education Committee brought the entire educational establishment to Carson City: teachers, school board trustees, superintendents, the State Board of Education—all were present with their representatives. Not everyone was on the same page. But in 1973, unlike today, there was a recognition that compromise was necessary to pass legislation dealing with contentious issues.

Kenny Guinn was the superintendent of the Clark County School

District, the state's largest, and assumed a leadership role in bringing the education groups together. He was a skilled negotiator and was frequently able to forge compromises on some of the major issues before the bills were scheduled for a hearing before my committee.

I also served on the Senate Judiciary Committee in 1973 at a time it was chaired by Mel Close, perhaps the best chairman with whom I've ever served either at the state level or in the US Senate. Among those serving on the committee were John Foley, Carl Dodge, and Spike Wilson. In a foreshadowing of a future race, Chic Hecht was also a member of the committee.

As the session began, I was proud to join Wilson in introducing the resolution calling for the passage of the Equal Rights Amendment. It was the epitome of simplicity: "Equality of rights under the law shall not be denied or abridged by the United States or any state on account of sex." The ERA was an effort to end discrimination based on sex that was embedded throughout our legal system.

Judging by the lopsided votes to approve the ERA in the House of Representatives in 1971 and the US Senate in 1972, it didn't appear controversial. (More than 90 percent of the members of the House and Senate voted for it.) With most of the 1970s to achieve ratification by three-fourths of the states, initially it appeared the constitutional amendment would be more of a celebration than a slog. In the first year alone twenty-two of the thirty-eight states needed climbed on board.

Then far-right conservative activist Phyllis Schlafly began her campaign to stop the ERA. She effectively sowed seeds of distortion. Momentum slowed to a crawl, some states that had approved it voted to rescind it, and the march toward equality stalled at thirty-five states.

Nevada had an opportunity to lead in the '73 session, but the measure failed by a lopsided vote in the Senate and died in committee in the Assembly. I was one of only four votes to approve it in the Senate. It was the start of a long decade of frustration for the measure.

While we couldn't gather momentum for the ERA in the 1973 session, we managed to make incremental progress for women by passing an act that increased and equalized the statutory minimum hourly wages for men and women. Another bill I cosponsored mandated for the first time that both spouses' signatures were required when executing conveyances and mortgages of community property. Before that, only the signature of the husband was required. We removed the "male preference" for the appointment of estate administrators. We equalized the "age of majority" at age eighteen, where before it had been twenty-one for men and eighteen for women. Those laws alone provided reminders of the unbalanced playing field that existed for women, and how much we needed to pass the ERA.

We crafted the enabling legislation that led to the negotiation of an interstate compact with California to help protect the Truckee River watershed, whose water quality and availability were essential to thousands of people in a rapidly growing region and in particular protecting the pristine waters of Lake Tahoe.

We also established the Bureau of Consumer Protection within the Department of Commerce and passed a bill that allowed customers to rescind purchases from door-to-door salesmen under certain circumstances.

We wanted to enact legislation that would provide property tax relief for seniors who owned their own home or rented their residence. The challenge for us was the Nevada Constitution that required a uniform rate of taxation. We would be unable to establish a different tax rate for seniors. The solution was to establish a senior citizen property tax assistance fund. Seniors could file a claim for reimbursement from the fund for the property taxes that they had paid.

I managed to join in with other successful fights that session. One was an act that required lobbyists to register and disclose vital information to the legislature. Another limited campaign spending for state legislative candidates and required them to file financial expenditure forms. This was an important first step and would prove a controversial one. In future sessions, we'd pass even more sweeping laws designed to improve ethics and transparency.

It was also the session that the business community was successful in its efforts to consolidate two of the largest Southern Nevada law enforcement agencies. We hammered out the details of the consolidation of the Clark County Sheriff's Office and Las Vegas Police Department into one law enforcement agency known as the Las Vegas Metropolitan Police Department.

We debated the consolidation issue regularly in the Senate Judiciary Committee. Sheriff Ralph Lamb's older brother Floyd Lamb chaired the Senate Finance Committee, and as soon as he finished with the morning's Finance Committee agenda, he'd pop his head into the Judiciary Committee meeting and ask, "How's it going?"

The Lamb family had a lot riding on the consolidation issue, and Ralph left little to chance. As originally drafted, the legislation all but guaranteed Lamb would remain sheriff. In an American population of 210 million people, there may have been half a dozen who possessed all the enumerated qualifications.

City officials favored an appointed person to head up the consolidated departments. The county favored retaining the sheriff as an elected position. To ease anxieties among the rank-and-file, the legislation assured that no officer would suffer a reduction in pay. Top positions in the new, larger department would be divided evenly between the former police and sheriff's departments. But there would be only one sheriff to emerge from the fray, Ralph Lamb. The sheriff would consolidate his political power along with the Southern Nevada's law enforcement.

Consolidation of local government services continued to be a priority for the business community. One of our last legislative enactments of the '73 session was the passage of a bill that provided for the appointment of a committee to work with local government entities. Implicitly, a consolidation of services was the motivation. The legislation also provided for a moratorium on any new incorporated cities in Clark County.

The early 1970s saw a national resurgence of Eastern and alternative medicine for everything from the relief of pain to the treatment of cancer. Some were glorified snake oil, and Nevada was no stranger to them, but others showed promise. And few that had enjoyed a long tradition of use in other cultures began wider use in the United States.

The Chinese medical treatment known as acupuncture fell into the latter category. It had begun to gain a new generation of patients who increasingly swore by its application of needles for a variety of treatments including pain relief. The practice dates back more than two thousand years, but its use wasn't legal in Nevada—and the state's medical association was working hard at the 1973 legislature to make sure it remained that way.

On the other side of the ledger, however, was a remarkable trio that included Arthur Steinberg, Yee-Kung Lok, and my longtime friend and fraternity brother Jim Joyce, who by the early 1970s had begun to carve out a legendary reputation for lobbying effectiveness in Carson City.

Steinberg was a semiretired attorney who was infatuated with traditional Chinese medicine and saw a place for it in America's medical future. Yee-Kung Lok was a doctor and the president of Hong Kong College of Acupuncture. He also had a successful acupuncture practice. And Jim Joyce was, well, Jim Joyce.

Thanks to Lok's many demonstrations, including treatments of curious legislators, in a matter of weeks the acupuncture bill went from foreign-sounding underdog to household name around the legislature. Joyce's calming influence and information sharing were an integral part of the process. It was a remarkable effort that resulted in the State Medical Association capitulating and the legislation being enacted. Nevada became the first state in the country to legalize the professionally licensed practice of acupuncture.

The history of the presidential primary process in Nevada had been one of fits and starts. The 1953 legislature passed it only to have it repealed by the 1955 legislature before the '56 presidential election in favor of a "closed caucus" format.

Lawmakers were ready to try again by 1973, and we passed new presidential primary legislation. The first Democratic primary after the bill became law was in 1976, when California governor Jerry Brown prevailed over Jimmy Carter. I met Brown that year and found him to be intelligent and engaging, if a little to the left of me politically. Of course, in those days Jerry was a little to the left of most people.

By 1981, repeal was in the air in Carson City and the presidential primary was again eliminated and replaced with the caucus format. The legislature changed once more in 1995 to allow the major political parties to choose between a primary and a caucus. Since then, the Democrats have engaged in a presidential caucus, but after a chaotic 2016 race it once again considered another change—back to the presidential primary. All of which reminds me of the lyrics, "Don't throw the past away/You might need it some rainy day/Dreams can come true again/When everything old is new again."

CHAPTER 15

The First Attorney General Race

In the fall of 1973, Democrat Alan Bible, Nevada's senior US senator, sent shockwaves through the political establishment. He announced he would not be a candidate for reelection. Bible, a protégé of the late senator Pat McCarran, had been a prominent figure in Nevada's political landscape for almost forty years. First as the district attorney of Storey County, later as state attorney general, and since 1954 as a United States senator. No Nevada senator in the twentieth century had ever left office of his own volition. Others left in the ashes of defeat or in a pine box. The political checkerboard was about to be reset, and the politically ambitious were eyeing their next move.

Democrat Mike O'Callaghan was in the catbird seat. After becoming governor in a close race against Ed Fike in 1970, he had become the most popular elected public official in the state. It was his call: run for the vacated US Senate seat or seek reelection. Because of his work at the federal level, conventional political wisdom was that he would seek the Senate seat.

A chain reaction was about to occur. Lieutenant Governor Harry Reid launched a campaign for governor. Equally ambitious Attorney General Bob List, a Republican, also announced his candidacy for governor. With List announcing he was not running for reelection, I made my move and announced my candidacy for attorney general.

I called List and told him that I did not intend to take any political shots at him because we were not going to be running against each other. It was a different time and a different era. List and I were opponents, but we continued to enjoy a civil relationship.

Weeks dragged on, and O'Callaghan had still not made his intentions known. Harry even opened a campaign office next to the historic Huntridge Theater that did not identify the office he was seeking.

And then in April, O'Callaghan dropped a political bombshell:

he would seek reelection as governor. A mad scramble ensued. Harry then pivoted to a campaign for the US Senate. His change was complicated by the fact that when he was running for governor he had raised money under a state law in which corporate contributions could be accepted. Running for US Senate, he could not. He had to return all that money and begin anew.

With O'Callaghan seeking reelection, List trimmed his sails and sought reelection to the attorney general's seat. Suddenly, a race that was never intended was about to occur.

I had two choices: withdraw my candidacy and return to the state Senate for the 1975 session and complete my term, or stay in the race. I did not relish the prospect of taking on List. But if I withdrew, the message sent would be that if Bryan faces a tough race, we can always get him to back out. That was not the message that I wanted to send.

Over my political career, I saw several quality candidates who were fully capable of serving in the highest offices of our state, but when faced with the reality of a tough race they were never able to pull the trigger. I decided to stay in.

List would be a formidable opponent for attorney general. He was part of a new generation of attorneys general who were transforming the role of the office.

As attorney general he traveled frequently throughout the state, cultivating personal relationships in every community. Republican candidates for statewide office could not ignore the burgeoning growth of Clark County and its importance in a statewide race. But for many, it was an obligatory stop: they had to go there. List not only recognized the political importance of Clark County, but he enjoyed the people he met there and spent time developing personal relationships with business leaders and other prominent citizens in Southern Nevada. He increased the number of deputy attorneys general in the Clark County AG's office and gave it a much higher profile than it had previously enjoyed. In selecting his staff, no partisan Republican pedigree was required. He was looking for young, energetic, and talented lawyers, many of whom were Democrats, and he hired them.

He was an effective campaigner on the stump. He liked people, and that was apparent. He would frequently appear on horseback in the traditional community parades in rural Nevada. As a private pilot, he could fly his own plane around the state. Many Republicans saw him as O'Callaghan's heir apparent.

By way of contrast, I was not comfortable riding a horse in a parade. Nor could I fly myself around the state. As a sole practitioner, I was still tethered to my Las Vegas law office for substantial periods of time. And fundraising was not my cup of tea, so I knew I would be underfunded.

But I had a few things going for me. I was reasonably well known in Clark County. The Democratic Party in Clark County enjoyed a wide registration margin, and I would have the full support of the state party. Following my father's advice of almost two decades ago, I had joined the ATO fraternity at the University of Nevada and had many fraternity brothers in every part of the state. When the legislature was in session, I frequently traveled to Reno in the evening to speak before various groups. This brought me into contact with people who were active in the Reno community. Those contacts would help. Joe Dini, who had become a close friend, would be helpful in Lyon County. I also had a tested Southern Nevada campaign office staff dating back to my '72 state Senate campaign.

And, of course, I had Bonnie. Wherever she went, she made friends. She represented me throughout the state. I know I am biased, but no candidate ever had a spouse who was more politically helpful than Bonnie. People loved her, and many were willing to overlook my flaws and put an X by my name on Election Day because of her.

Before battling List, I faced a primary challenge from Robert Van Wagoner, Reno city attorney. He was an impressive challenger. I prevailed in the primary with 60 percent of the vote, and he called and gave a gracious concession.

Bonnie and I spent most of our time in rural Nevada attending the traditional events that summer. She was a big hit wherever she went. Her warm and friendly personality helped to eliminate the impression that many in rural Nevada had that somehow people from Las Vegas were not real Nevadans. With all due respect to my hometown, Las Vegas has produced its fair share of phonies. Together we covered the state from Carson Valley Days in Douglas County to the Damboree Days in Boulder City, from Jim Butler Days in Tonopah to the pancake breakfasts in Elko and Fallon.

List was heavily favored, but the Democratic statewide slate in 1974 was very impressive: O'Callaghan at the top of the ticket for governor; Reid running for the US Senate; Washoe County district attorney Bob Rose for lieutenant governor; Bill Swackhamer for secretary of state, Mike Mirabelli for state treasurer, and Jim Santini for Nevada's sole congressional seat. I was the weak link in the chain. Everyone recognized that I had the toughest race.

The campaign pace picked up after Labor Day. Former governor Paul Laxalt, who had filed for the US Senate seat, emerged on the campaign trail. With charisma oozing out of every pore, he was a big hit—particularly in rural Nevada.

The opening of our Reno campaign office was well attended. In fairness to those who were staffing the office, I could not spend enough time with them to provide the necessary direction and guidance they needed.

Gerald Ford had become president after Richard Nixon resigned from office on August 9 in the wake of the Watergate scandal. I was hearing that Ford would make an appearance in Nevada on List's behalf. I thought to myself, "I've got enough of a problem without having the president of the United States come and endorse my opponent." But then on September 8, Ford pardoned Nixon, and the blowback was enormous. In retrospect, it was the right thing for the country. But the short-term impact was very unfavorable. Ford was suddenly uninvited, and Watergate loomed like a political cloud over the Republican candidates that year.

There were bumps along the road as well. I had a solid legislative record with the state employees' association, and I thought that I might get their endorsement or a co-endorsement. Instead, List received the sole endorsement. There were many memorable events on the campaign trail. One night in Ely stands out—a statewide candidates night in the high school gym. In all my political career, I can't remember a better-attended candidates night than the one in Ely. Laxalt was there. Cool, calm, and relaxed, he was ushered into a private area until the event began. Reid and List, for some reason, did not appear. When Santini, Rose, and I arrived, we furiously began putting up our campaign signs around the gymnasium. That night, I made a campaign speech that resonated well with the audience. Afterward, strangers came up and said, "You know, you spoke well," and I felt encouraged.

The next morning, I was once again reminded of the reality of the haves and the have-nots in American politics. I can visualize it to this very day. The sky was overcast, and the plane in which Santini, Rose, and I had arrived had minimal instrument flight avionics, and our departure was delayed. Not far away, spread out before a handsome jet aircraft was a red carpet, on which Laxalt walked gracefully, exchanging pleasantries with his entourage and the press. The shimmering jet took off, parting the clouded skies toward the blue above, and I said to Santini, "Damn it, it just ain't fair."

As with every campaign, I met people who had an impact on my later political life. Dale Lockard was employed by the state Department of Wildlife, and I had met him a few years earlier when the department was lobbying for a fishery at Lake Mead. He was now assigned to the department's Reno office and agreed to work with our campaign. Keith Lee was active in all my statewide campaigns and called Marlene Ramos and others to attend the opening of our campaign office. As Marlene relates it, on the way to the campaign office Keith told her, "Whatever you do, do not sign anything. You will never get off the campaign's list." Marlene being Marlene promptly went in and signed up for everything. She never did get off the list. At one point she was paired up with Dale Lockard, and the rest as they say is history. She would become Dale's wife and would become one of my closest political advisors. She went on to be office manager when I was elected attorney general, chief of staff when I became governor, and state director when I was in the US Senate.

When I declared my candidacy in early February, I believed I had a solid track record of fighting for the issues that mattered to Nevadans. In explaining my belief that the attorney general needed to be willing to advocate for the citizens, not just provide legal advice to elected officials, I could point to my own personal financial disclosure, conflict-of-interest legislation, expansion of the open meeting law in the state, and efforts at consumer protection as areas where I'd backed up my rhetoric with action. I wanted to toughen the state's notoriously weak securities laws and go after those who defrauded investors. Citizens regularly lost their life savings in Nevada-based stock swindles, pyramid schemes, and other too-good-to-be-true investment hustles.

I also had strong feelings about the scourge of increasing narcotics use in society and advocated for increase penalties for drug dealers. And I expressed a willingness to return to the legislature as attorney general to ensure the message was sent that victims of crime deserved to be compensated by those who had wronged them.

Although I'd been campaigning for weeks, I officially filed at the secretary of state's office in Carson City in early July with Bonnie and the kids by my side. After multiple terms in the legislature, where special interests grew more sophisticated with each session, I believed the people needed essential new laws that only an assertive attorney general could deliver. In essence, taxpayers needed their own lobbyist in their corner. I reminded reporters of my legislative focus on campaign ethics and consumer protection and said the incumbent "has compiled a track record which illustrates little or no concern for Nevadans." In the coming weeks, I'd do my best to hammer home the theme.

After the primary, List and I had a spirited debate on a range of topics, including the still-controversial use of court-authorized wiretaps in Nevada, capital punishment, and "stop-and-frisk" laws.

Although the Associated Press in mid-October was right when it concluded, "Dick Bryan facing an uphill battle," I felt I was gradually closing on List as Nevada Day approached. I jabbed him by calling him the best-financed Republican candidate to come down the pike. For his part, List claimed that somehow his office had saved the public millions in rate increases from Nevada Power. I scoffed at the suggestion.

Bonnie loved campaigning, and I had never seen her discouraged. We were running behind, but she stayed upbeat. Then in late October, just a couple of weeks before Election Day, at the end of a Veterans Day parade in Overton, List's wife, Kathy's, cookbook appeared. It included the List family's favorite dishes and recipes. List campaign staffers were distributing them along the parade route, and people were clamoring for a copy. It was a clever campaign handout. Unlike most campaign materials that are quickly scanned and discarded, this one people took home. On the way back from Overton, Bonnie was really down.

Notwithstanding the cookbook, things were beginning to fall into place for me. But I was still running behind. I reached out to Nevada's senators, Alan Bible and Howard Cannon, both Democrats, and I asked them if they would pen a letter endorsing my candidacy for attorney general to be sent to every Democrat in Nevada. They readily agreed, and I used their ringing endorsement as an advertisement in the *Las Vegas Sun* in early November. A plan was also made to quickly duplicate the endorsement and make sure it was mailed to every registered Democrat.

Early on election night, I was ahead. I'm sure many were quite surprised to find I was leading, and it looked like I might win. But I knew that the votes in rural Nevada, and Elko County in particular, had not come in. And List would run solidly there. In the final tally, I fell 701 votes short. Unlike Reid, who lost narrowly to Laxalt, I did not seek a recount.

Although disappointed by my loss, I was not discouraged. I had been a decided underdog in the race. I'd gone toe-to-toe with one of the most impressive and promising candidates on the Nevada political horizon and held my own, losing by just a handful of votes. I felt that the issues I raised in the campaign struck a responsive chord with Nevadans. I'd continue to try to accomplish my goals in the 1975 session of the legislature.

But the story does not end there.

The Saturday after the election, my phone rang nonstop. Caller after caller wanted to know why I sent the campaign endorsement letter from Bible and Cannon after the election. I was astonished. After the election? I believed it had been mailed before the election. I made an appointment with the Reno postmaster and discussed it in some detail. But after talking to him I was convinced there was no mischief afoot. The letter that should have reached thousands of Democratic voters wasn't delivered to the post office on time.

And so I was headed back to the state Senate.

CHAPTER 16

The 1975 Session

At the start of his second term as Nevada governor, Mike O'Callaghan put his plan to restructure state government into high gear, and it began in earnest with the 1975 legislature. Creating a Nevada Housing Division was high on his legislative agenda that session.

It was a shared objective of mine as well. He called me personally and asked me to handle the bill, and I was happy to do so. In 1975, fast-growing Nevada faced a major housing crisis that hit low- and middle-income individuals and families the hardest. O'Callaghan's goal was to create a state agency capable of helping to provide affordable housing that would not only put a roof over the heads of those who most needed one, but in doing so would result in revitalized neighborhoods and stronger communities.

The bill's passage opened the door for thousands of Nevadans of modest means to own their own homes. It was a life-changer for many, and I was proud to play my part.

The session again put us right back in the middle of the fight to ratify the Equal Rights Amendment, and just as before it was an uphill struggle. By 1975, Nevada, Utah, and Arizona were the only three states west of Kansas that had failed to ratify the amendment, and suddenly the 1979 deadline was beginning to loom. That session showed plenty of promise when the Democrat-majority Assembly passed the resolution, 27–13, but it failed once again in the Senate with just eight members including myself voting in favor with twelve opposed. Even the ERA's unabashed optimists were beginning to express concern.

We continued to review sexist statutes, one of which was the repeal of the sole trader act that required a husband to consent before his wife went into business on her own. We also eliminated the provision that gave husbands "management control" of community property.

We were making incremental progress, but all of that would have been unnecessary if we had ratified the ERA.

As a former prosecutor and public defender who handled a number of rape cases, one of the things that always appalled me was the vicious way rape victims were cross-examined by defense attorneys. The victim was interrogated about her prior sexual activities and suffered a horrifying level of humiliation and embarrassment. Following a precedent set in California, I was determined to limit that onerous practice in Nevada. I introduced legislation that forbid such questions to be asked at trial if the defendant claimed he was wrongfully identified. The rules were different if the defendant said the sex was consensual, but if he said he wasn't there, then his attorney couldn't ask anything about the victim's sexual history. Period. The bill became law.

In determining the admissibility of such evidence, the defendant's attorney, outside the presence of the jury, would be required to make an offer of proof summarizing the evidence that the defendant intended to introduce at trial. The presiding judge would then make the determination of whether such evidence would be admitted.

In 1975 we also created Nevada's Good Samaritan law, which gives legal immunity to a person who acts in good faith to assist in an emergency. A person who stopped to lend a hand at an auto accident couldn't be held liable if his best efforts fell short.

As chairman of the Education Committee, I worked to pass legislation that permitted parents with mentally challenged children to enroll them in special education programs as early as age three. We also worked with the Assembly to set parameters on the minimum age mainstream children could enter kindergarten—no matter how smart their parents imagined them to be!

As we had the previous session with the Truckee River watershed, we authorized a negotiation with Arizona and Utah on the allocation of the precious water resources of the Virgin River. If there's one war that never ends in Nevada, it's the water war.

Driving through Southern Nevada, home to rooftop solar units and industrial-scale solar fields that generate thousands of megawatts of electricity, I am reminded that the push to establish that renewable energy source took root back in the 1975 session, when we authorized the Desert Research Institute to establish a solar energy research lab. It seems like yesterday, but that was more than forty-five years ago. Although we couldn't see the future and there were critics of the whole idea, it was the right thing to do then, and the state's solar industry continues to expand well into the new century. In a similar theme, we also passed the first legislation aimed at requiring new construction of public buildings to adhere to the latest standards for energy efficiency.

My own long-term interests in protecting consumers and investors from rogue operators and outright con artists continued with legislation that raised the mandatory bonding required by mortgage lenders and securities dealers. That session we created a consumer division within the Public Service Commission, and we established a credit union division within the Department of Commerce.

As ever, the session found us with an eclectic array of subjects to pursue. We passed a law that allowed for a judge to approve alimony payments for ex-husbands under certain circumstances. As a real non sequitur, we also cracked down on the use of injected silicone for breast augmentation, a practice popular at the time but one that also was showing dangerous and debilitating long-term effects.

I led the effort to move Veterans Day from the last weekend of October back to its original place on November 11. If that sounds like a small thing, you need to ask a veteran. Many who served told me they felt slighted by the shuffling of the day in their honor to a three-day weekend holiday, and I promised I'd try to do something about it.

With so many veterans moving to Nevada, we amended the state law that authorized a tax exemption for those who served. Where once veterans received the exemption only if they were Nevada residents at the time of service, the new amendment enabled all veterans to enjoy the tax break.

Nevada also faced a crisis that year when it came to medical malpractice litigation. Malpractice insurance premiums were soaring, and physicians were threatening to leave a state that already had a doctor shortage. To prevent frivolous litigation and hold down legal and insurance costs, we crafted a law that created a malpractice screening panel, which consisted of three medical professionals and an attorney chairperson. Before filing a lawsuit, a litigant had to submit the malpractice claim to the screening panel for review with the goal of separating frivolous claims from those with merit. It didn't prevent a lawsuit from being filed, but it made it more difficult for a claimant to prevail if the panel found there was no malpractice.

Amid what it called "a crisis of confidence in government and in the established institutions of our land," in 1971 the Nevada Legislature resolved to study the issue of conflict of interest throughout government and make recommendations in the following legislative session. For a state without a single ethics law, even the discussion was controversial and not a single proposal passed. In 1975, Assembly Bill 610 created the state's first ethics commission and a statewide code of ethics. It set conflict-of-interest standards, spelled out disclosure rules, and enabled counties and municipalities to create their own ethics codes. We expanded the spending limits law first passed in the 1973 session. It wasn't a sea change; it was a tsunami.

We shouldn't have been surprised when the consolidated ethics bill was almost immediately challenged as unconstitutional, and a district court judge agreed and threw out the law in its entirety. Another lawsuit asserted the law was constitutionally vague and overbroad, and in 1976 the Nevada Supreme Court agreed in its *Dunphy v. Sheehan* decision.

In essence we were sent back to square one with respect to the conflict-of-interest law. The limitation on legislative campaign expenditures, modified in the 1975 legislation, remained in effect.

That session we were approached by Reno banker Sid Stern, who had conceived a plan to establish several thrift savings banks in rural communities to encourage savings and investment in areas where larger institutions were unavailable and generally unwilling to lend. Nevada had a long history of fly-by-night investment schemers, but Stern was solid. He'd graduated magna cum laude from the University of San Francisco and had grown Fireside Thrift of Redwood City, California, from a $25,000 startup into a seventy-branch, $100 million success story. He engaged Jim Joyce as his lobbyist.

We ultimately passed the Thrift Act after requiring a significant bond to help protect depositors. When we adjourned in 1975, we thought we had protected the public. Eight years later, as governor, I would realize how wrong we had been.

CHAPTER 17

Changing Times in the State Senate

I set a high bar for myself back in 1972 when I led the field against more established and well-known opponents in Senate District 3. The challenge in 1976 was simple: could I repeat that performance? I'd improved my name recognition with a competitive run for attorney general and had my share of success at the legislature, but this race was complicated by new entrants in the Democratic primary who promised to greatly increase the competition. Former Assembly Speaker Keith Ashworth and wealthy Henderson television station owner and real estate investor Bill Hernstadt entered the fray. Senate veterans Floyd Lamb and Helen Herr were running again, and when the general election rolled around Republicans Jean Ford and Zel Lowman would also be formidable opponents. Mahlon Brown, a 25-year veteran in the legislature first elected in 1950 at a time each county had only one state senator, did not file for reelection.

I ran first in the primary, but Ashworth ran a competitive second ahead of Lamb, and Hernstadt beat out Herr for the fourth slot. The real wild card was Hernstadt, who immediately tested the state's legislative spending limit law we'd worked hard to pass in 1973 and improve in the 1975 session. In the general, I led the pack followed by Ashworth and Lamb. Hernstadt beat out longtime political activist Ford for the fourth seat.

Hernstadt's win complicated matters in Senate District 3 after he revealed he'd intentionally violated the legislative campaign spending law on the grounds that he believed it was an unconstitutional violation of his free speech rights. He spent $41,578 in a race with an expenditure limit of $29,400.

Citing the US Supreme Court's 1976 *Buckley v. Valeo* decision, in which a majority held that expenditure limits in the Federal Election Campaign Act of 1971 were unconstitutional, Hernstadt sued to block Attorney General List and District Attorney George Holt of Clark County from enforcing the expenditure law. Holt returned the favor by filing a criminal complaint against Hernstadt, but the Supreme Court's decision was clear.

A month after the election, Hernstadt's attorney, George Franklin, obtained a preliminary injunction that blocked List from prosecuting him until his lawsuit was resolved. By mid-January, the district attorney's office folded its hand when it failed to respond to the lawsuit. Hernstadt was headed to the legislature.

Gerald Ford defeated Jimmy Carter in Nevada in the race for president, but nationally couldn't outrun the long shadow of Watergate against the peanut farmer and former Georgia governor who promised he'd never lie to the American people.

More important for Nevadans, on that same night New Jersey legalized casino gambling in Atlantic City with a plan to remake the dilapidated Boardwalk into the "Las Vegas of the East." With sixty million people living within a reasonable drive of Atlantic City, the news sent a shockwave through Nevada. The Silver State had lost its monopoly. Many pundits predicted Las Vegas's best days were behind it.

With New Jersey voters overwhelmingly endorsing legal casinos for Atlantic City, a new era of gaming regulation had dawned. The challenge was balancing the state's interest in maintaining its reputation for casino regulation with the reality that some Nevada licensees were anxious to test the potentially lucrative new market in the East. Protecting the integrity of Nevada's gaming was the guiding principle.

The answer was the Foreign Gaming Act. The act mandated that a Nevada licensee who wanted to seek a license in New Jersey must first file an application with the Nevada Gaming Commission. As an additional safeguard, the applicant also had to agree to operate under Nevada's standard of honesty and integrity. Any Nevada licensee operating in New Jersey who violated its regulatory standards was subject to investigation and sanction in Nevada.

With the passage of time, legalized casinos have become so accepted in many states that it may be difficult to appreciate just how large the approval of gambling in Atlantic City was to an industry

still evolving into the corporate era. When it came to casino regulation, Nevada was the gold standard, but now that two states were
in the game many questions remained unanswered. How would the
two states' regulatory agencies interact? As professionals, or competitors? What if New Jersey's licensees were held to a lower standard than licensees in Nevada? What if a Nevada licensee became
embroiled in a regulatory controversy in New Jersey?

The legislation was referred to the Judiciary Committee. I played
an active role in securing its passage. Like so many other lessons I'd
learned in my time as a lawmaker, working on the Foreign Gaming
Act would prove valuable in the future.

Undaunted by the Nevada Supreme Court's decision in 1976 to
declare our sweeping ethics and transparency legislation as uncon-
stitutionally vague, we returned to square one and found a new way
forward in the 1977 session. We managed to establish an ethics commission that provided procedures and rules to govern the conduct
of elected public officials. In 1983, as a newly elected governor, I
requested the legislature to provide funding for the Ethics Commission, which had been inactive for the preceding four years. You might
call it an overnight success fifteen years in the making.

When the 1976 election's dust finally settled, the balance of power
in the legislature had shifted even more in favor of the Democrats. The
ratio was so lopsided, in fact, that *Review-Journal* reporter Charles
Zobell quipped that Republicans at the legislature "may find themselves added to the list of endangered species in Nevada" with just
eight of sixty seats in the lawmaking body. With a popular Democrat in the Governor's Mansion, the 1977 session of the legislature
held real promise for substantive change.

But the session wasn't all laurels. The failure of the legislature to
come together to ratify the Equal Rights Amendment at a time the
Democrats enjoyed substantial majorities and a governor nearing the
end of a successful second term was a stunning setback.

With just a simple majority in both houses needed, the resolution
moved forward with hours of testimony and floor speeches, pick-
ets outside the building, and letters for and against piling up in lawmakers' mailboxes. It was crunch time.

This time, the Senate managed to eke out a victory with a controversial, late-night tie-breaking vote cast by Lieutenant Governor

Bob Rose as president of the Senate. The vote was 11–10 with just a simple majority needed. Immediately after Rose broke the tie, Senators Jim Gibson and Floyd Lamb, both of whom opposed the ERA, made a beeline to legislative counsel Frank Daykin's office to question the legality of the vote.

The Senate vote was the hard part, or so proponents believed. Suddenly the Assembly, which had voted to pass the measure in 1975, went off the rails. The vote was a lopsided 24–15 against ratification. A decision was made to submit the ratification of the ERA for voter approval at the next general election.

That gave opponents the time they needed to mount a counter-campaign that eroded support for the Equal Rights Amendment. The vote the next year on the ballot advisory question would not be close. It was defeated by a two-to-one margin.

Years after the deadline for ratification passed, Nevada Democrats attempted to reignite interest in passing the ERA in the state, even in the form of a resolution. The attempts usually failed along party lines, but in 2017—thirty-five years after the congressional deadline had expired—the legislature finally prevailed in passing an ERA resolution. It's only fitting, then, that Nevada in 2019 became the first state to seat a female-majority legislature.

In the 1977 session, we did manage more incremental steps toward equality of the sexes. We cut sexist language from the laws, changing "working men" to "employees" and eliminated the Nevada Highway Patrol's male-only requirement, enabling women to serve as troopers for the first time. We also eliminated a provision in the law which established a male preference for the administration of estates.

History was my favorite subject in school, and I enthusiastically welcomed the opportunity to sponsor legislation creating a division of historical preservation within the Department of Conservation and Natural Resources.

As the chairman of the Senate Taxation Committee, I dealt with myriad issues, including one that led to the construction of UNLV's Thomas & Mack Center and UNR's Lawlor Events Center. Both of the state's universities needed new places for their rising-star basketball teams to play. The land would be generously donated, but the construction funding had to come from somewhere.

A source was found with an assist from the legislature. It's probably little known that Nevada slot operators paid a $250 federal tax on each slot machine with most of the dollars generated returning to the state. We were determined to tap into more. Secretary of State Bill Swackhamer played a key role on this issue. If Congress decided, as anticipated, to increase its annual $250 slot machine tax rebate to the state from 80 to 95 percent, the additional money would provide the funding mechanism for the new arena construction at UNLV and UNR.

The Senate Taxation Committee kept busy. We eliminated the inventory tax. In recognition of my role as chairman, the Las Vegas Chamber of Commerce presented me with a plaque called the Whack-a-Tax Award.

Environmental issues continued to surface. We voted to require smog tests on automobiles to get polluting vehicles off the road. We authorized the State Board of Health to establish drinking water standards and enacted water conservation measures.

As a father of three and a former prosecutor, cosponsoring a bill that increased penalties for child abuse was a way to attempt to defend vulnerable youngsters. My prime sponsorship of a bill that created the Office of Public Guardian would help protect the rights of the elderly and infirm. We also enacted a requirement that school districts begin giving proficiency examinations in certain basic subjects. And we clarified the law regarding the power of the district attorney and Nevada Consumer Affairs Division to recover civil penalties for violations of Nevada's consumer protection provisions. That session, I also sponsored a bill that banned probation for a person convicted of robbery with the use of a deadly weapon. The thrust of the bill was to make probation impossible.

When a federal push for states to join most other countries in the world adopting the metric system was launched, many of the nation's business leaders agreed. A phased-in approach required highway signs to display both miles and kilometers, but the move wasn't popular in Nevada. The imperial system worked just fine and was favored by the building trades unions that had no interest in seeing their members forced to purchase new sets of metric tools.

The most controversial issue of the 1977 session wasn't battle over the ERA, but the legislature's decision to legalize the medical use of the "fountain of youth" drug Gerovital and the even more controversial cancer treatment drug Laetrile (Amygdalin.) Neither drug was approved by the US Food and Drug Administration. Discussing the issue publicly put us on the cutting edge—critics would counter over the edge—of alternative medicine in the country.

Gerovital was promoted by a colorful fellow named Marvin Kratter of the publicly traded Rom Amer Pharmaceuticals. He also was represented at the legislature by the ubiquitous lobbyist Jim Joyce. After much discussion lawmakers passed the first enabling legislation for the drugs with substantial restrictions.

Derived in part from ingredients found in apricot pits, Laetrile was promoted as a cancer cure. Some medical experts considered it the height of quackery, and the American Cancer Society called the promises of its promoters "the cruelest of all frauds." In Nevada, it would be legal for desperate cancer patients to receive Laetrile but illegal for the substance considered ineffective and even dangerous by some medical critics to be shipped across state lines to Nevada. The efficacy and legality of the drugs would be debated again in two years.

Among the major policy debates were some lighthearted moments.

Since 1866 state constitutional officers had been required to make their residences in Carson City. When Governor Grant Sawyer appointed District Judge David Zenoff from Las Vegas to the Nevada Supreme Court in 1966, Zenoff wanted to live at Lake Tahoe in Douglas County. The legislature accommodated his request by eliminating the Carson City residency requirement for Nevada Supreme Court justices.

In the 1977 session, a bill was introduced eliminating the Carson City residency requirement for secretary of state, state controller, and attorney general. This caught my attention because I planned to run for attorney general the following year. I do not know the origin of the bill and never found out. When the bill reached the floor of the Senate and the roll call began, I voted "not voting." That engendered much laughter from my Senate colleagues, all of whom recognized that next year I would likely be a candidate for attorney general.

Fully appreciating Nevada's north-south sensitivities, I believed there would be the perception that if I voted yes it somehow indicated that my family and I did not want to live in Carson City. I did not want that impression, and in fact Bonnie and I and the family moved to Carson City shortly after my election as attorney general.

As the 1977 session ended, the political chatter was all about who would step up and attempt to fill Mike O'Callaghan's formidable shoes in the Governor's Mansion. Many names were mentioned, mine among them.

I enjoyed the speculation, but I had my sights set on another office, the one that had eluded me in 1974.

CHAPTER 18

Nevada's Twenty-Seventh Attorney General

In a sense the die was cast in the 1978 attorney general's race by my strong showing against Bob List in the '74 race. When the filing period closed in July, the list of candidates running for attorney general may have been the most bizarre in Nevada history. In the primary I faced a spiritual mystic and exotic fish breeder by the name of Matia Melchizedek and Joe Kadans, a graduate of the University of Baltimore Law School, parenthetically, former vice president Spiro Agnew's alma mater. Because the law school was unaccredited, Joe could not practice law in Nevada.

No Republican attorney filed for attorney general. The Republican standard-bearer was Don Robb, who had been greatly exorcised by the handling of an estate in which the lawyers were alleged to have received more money than the heirs. He may have been right.

Joining the list of attorney general candidates was Merritt Ike "Pappy" Yochum, a tax protester from Carson City who filed as an Independent American. The Libertarian candidate was Harry Joe Mangrum, whom I had known from my days at Las Vegas High School. He was an attorney, but his campaign attire to say the least was strange. He was easy to spot on the stump. Everywhere he went he wore a porkpie hat to stand out in the crowd.

Unlike four years earlier when List was heavily favored, this was my race to lose.

That summer the Chinese government extended an invitation to the National Conference of State Legislators (NCL) to select a delegation of state lawmakers to visit China as guests of the Chinese government. State Senator Jim Gibson was active in the NCL leadership and was able to choose several Nevadans. Mel Close, Bill Raggio, and I were invited to join the delegation. As the old saying goes, it was an offer I could not refuse, and I readily accepted.

Only six years earlier President Nixon had stunned the nation and the world by traveling to China to open the way for a more normalized relationship between the two countries. This was quite a move by Nixon because he was one of the original Cold War warriors. At the time of our trip, we had not formally recognized the People's Republic of China, but it was clear that diplomatic recognition would occur in the not-too-distant future.

About thirty-five state legislators made the trip. We flew to Hong Kong, then a British Crown colony, and crossed over to the mainland and traveled through the New Territories to Lo Wu, the crossover point into the People's Republic of China. We were greeted by dignitaries, all of whom wore Mao suits, the typical attire during that time. Unusual as it appeared later in the trip, the men wore shoes. On only two other occasions in our travels in China did I see men wearing shoes: the honor guard at Mao's Tomb in Tiananmen Square, and in a meeting we had in Shanghai with the Vice Revolutionary Council. Everyone else wore sandals.

The first site we would visit was the fabled Great Wall of China. Its origins date back to the seventh century BC, and during the period of the Ming dynasty in the seventeenth century it was reinforced and took on its modern appearance. Its purpose was to prevent invaders from entering China. The wall, it is said, is the only manmade object on Earth that's visible from outer space. On the day we arrived at the Great Wall, it was very hot and humid. Ascending the wall we noted observation towers, so spaced that from one tower to the next a bonfire signal or the waving of a flag could warn of an approaching enemy force.

On top of the wall and making my way to the first tower, I did not notice that my Nevada colleagues had moved ahead of me. Passing through the first tower, I glanced to my left and was stunned. Taped to the wall was one of my own campaign posters—four feet by four feet—that in bright Day-Glo green proudly proclaimed: BRYAN ATTORNEY GENERAL DEMOCRAT.

Moments later, guards came charging in my direction with rifles at the ready. I did not know what to do. The perpetrators had retreated from the scene and enjoyed themselves greatly at my expense. My first thought was to tear the poster off the wall, and I crumpled it in my hands. Then I remembered the ancient Chinese act of subservience, kowtow, which involved a very deep bow. I could only hope they'd buy it. I bowed deeply and handed over the crumpled poster. The guards let me go. I'm not so sure that if a similar act had been performed by a Chinese visitor who had placed some kind of political work on the Washington Monument or the Lincoln Memorial that the National Park Service would be quite so charitable.

Our next stop was in Shanghai. It was immediately obvious when we arrived at our hotel that the difference in dialects made it very hard for Chinese from different regions to converse. Mandarin is the official language of the country. But the Cantonese dialect is spoken in Shanghai, and it was clear to us as unsophisticated observers that they were having great trouble communicating.

I went up to my room, and there was a message for me. I was alarmed. Why would I be getting a phone call? Had something happened to Bonnie or the kids? I returned the call, and a male voice answered in badly fractured Chinese-accented English. I asked to have him repeat himself several times as I struggled to understand. Finally, I made out three words, "secretary of state." I've never had a heart attack, but at that moment I was pretty close to it. My thoughts ran wild. Had I failed to complete some aspect of my declaration of candidacy? Had I forgotten to sign the paperwork? Am I about to be disqualified and lose to Melchizedek the mystic or the guy from Spiro Agnew's alma mater? Filing was closed. There was nothing I could do from almost six thousand miles away.

There was a long pause on the line for what seemed like an hour. Then I heard laughter on the other end of the line. It was Bill Raggio. His performance rated an Academy Award. I was convinced that it was a Chinese speaker trying to communicate in English. But that's Bill Raggio.

China had not yet emerged from its disastrous Cultural Revolution that sent some of its most sophisticated and highly educated people to work in the farming communes so that they could be infused with the revolutionary spirit that Mao demanded. Japan was our major competition in Asia at that time. But as we traveled through China, I witnessed a strong work ethic and a high energy level among the people. With a population exceeding one billion, it was clear to me that China would be formidable competition in the future.

I was also impressed with their programs for the academically talented. We went to observe an academically talented program for children on one Saturday. They are referred to as "Children's Palaces" in China. We were all impressed at the level of academic sophistication. Some of the youngsters were already performing acupuncture, a traditional Chinese medicine only recently approved by the Nevada Legislature. We all had a sense that we would hear much more from the Chinese in the years to come.

Foreign travelers to China were still uncommon, and we attracted a lot of attention—particularly when we took pictures with our Polaroid cameras. Dozens of children and adults gathered around us and looked on in amazement as they watched the photographs develop before their eyes. We also saw a glimpse of the future. Everyone on the street that day was attired in a Mao tunic, but in department store windows in Shanghai we saw for the first time Western apparel featured.

Returning home, I faced the same problem that arose in 1974. My Reno campaign office was challenging. Arriving in Reno from Las Vegas, I was often met by several campaign workers, each vying for my attention. I needed someone to take charge. I had been impressed with Marlene Lockard, who had walked precincts with me in the first AG's campaign. She was employed by the Boy Scouts of America. I approached her and asked if she'd be willing to head up my Northern Nevada campaign office. She was always open for a challenge, and she responded, "On one condition. If I do a good job for you, will you find a position for me in the attorney general's office?" My response was immediate and in the affirmative.

Within a few days, what had been a political Tower of Babel was organized and restructured. Marlene was in her element.

The state's Democratic slate that year was impressive. The featured race was the governor's contest between Lieutenant Governor Bob Rose, the Democrat, and Attorney General Bob List. Democrat Myron Leavitt filed for lieutenant governor and Stan Colton for state treasurer. Jim Santini was once again on the ballot for Nevada's lone congressional seat.

Although I participated in all the Democratic events, including a statewide caravan, I had more latitude about which events I would attend. In the past such decisions had been driven by an opportunity to become better known. Now I was more strategically focused. What events might present an opportunity to make important new contacts throughout the state? As in my previous statewide campaign, Bonnie and I attended all the traditional events in rural Nevada, a practice that I followed without exception for the next twenty-two years.

Although my competition for attorney general wasn't keeping me up at night, I knew the creation of an East Coast gambling capital in Atlantic City would complicate the job of the next Nevada attorney general, whose office serves as legal counsel to the gaming commission, gaming control board, and gaming policy committee. With that in mind, I reached out to New Jersey governor Brendan Byrne. He had become well known as the "governor who couldn't be bought" after some mobsters were overheard on a wiretap bitterly complaining that he was an honest man. I flew to New Jersey and met with him at the governor's official residence, where I was warmly received. The result of our meeting not only was the start of a professional working relationship, but I used it in an effective campaign commercial to help illustrate the stark difference between my experience with that of the other candidates.

It was clear from the start that Nevada licensees were intrigued by the possibilities on the Boardwalk. In the 1977 legislative session, we crafted and passed the Foreign Gaming Act that made that possible. There would be much for the next Nevada attorney general to discuss with New Jersey officials.

On primary night my margin of victory was more than 57,000 votes. Coming in second place was none of the candidates that I faced. A unique feature of the Nevada election ballot gives voters the opportunity to say, "None of the Above."

In the general election, the main attraction was the governor's race, where List defeated Rose. For me, the general election was a repeat of the primary. I won with 139,095 votes to runner-up Don Robb's 32,351, a 106,000-vote margin.

With that I was on to Carson City as an elected statewide officeholder. My family would join me, and we'd spend the next decade of our lives in Carson City.

CHAPTER 19

Defending Nevada

The days following my victory in the attorney general's race were exciting personally and professionally. I would be heading one of the largest legal offices in the state and representing all state agencies. In addition, I would serve as a member of the State Board of Examiners, the State Board of Prison Commissioners, and the State Board of Transportation. The Board of Examiners approves contracts between the various state agencies and vendors. The Board of Prison Commissioners sets policy for the state's penitentiary system. And the Board of Transportation determines construction priorities and the schedule for repairs on state highways. On a personal level, Bonnie and I had to find a home in Carson City and prepare for our move to Northern Nevada.

I anticipated that my working relationship with the governor would be a good one. List, the outgoing attorney general and governor-elect, had been very gracious in calling to congratulate me on my election as attorney general. We had known each other since our days at Hastings Law School. We wore different political jerseys, but there was never any personal animosity between us. In the aftermath of my 1974 loss to him in the AG's race, List had asked my help on a gaming issue that required legislative action. As a member on the Senate Judiciary Committee, I readily agreed.

To immediately establish a Northern Nevada presence, I wanted to reconnect with friends from my undergraduate days. Ever mindful of the north-south divisions in the state, one of my first moves was to get new license plates for my personal vehicle. In retrospect, that seems unbelievably unimportant, but in the 1970s license plates were identified by the county that issued them. I had a Clark County plate. I didn't want to be driving around Northern Nevada with a Clark County license plate. My new plates began with "OR" for

Ormsby County, indicating that I had been issued a license plate in Carson City.

My priority in the weeks ahead was to get my team in place and hit the ground running by the time I was sworn into office. List's generous offer to allow Marlene Lockard to work in the AG's office immediately after my election was very helpful. It gave her the opportunity to become familiar with the state's personnel and purchasing systems that would govern the attorney general's office. She was a quick study and was ready on day one as my office administrator.

I chose Larry Struve as my chief deputy. I'd become acquainted with Larry during my first race for attorney general. Keith Lee and others whose opinions I valued told me I couldn't do better. They were right. He was a lawyer's lawyer. He was able, careful, and had a passion for public service. His ethics were beyond reproach.

In Southern Nevada I asked Bob Peccole to serve as my chief deputy. He was an able lawyer and had served as my chief deputy in the Clark County Public Defender's Office. We worked well together. He knew what my expectations were. He provided an additional dimension that was important to me. I would be spending much of my time in the Carson City office. Southern Nevada was my political base, and I needed someone who knew the key players in Clark County and what was happening in Southern Nevada. He was essentially my eyes and ears, and we talked frequently by phone.

I wanted Jenny DesVaux to serve as my Southern Nevada office manager. In my absence I would need someone to represent me at the various community and political functions. I had known Jenny for some years and had observed her in leadership positions in Junior Mesquite and Junior League. More recently, she had been a staffer in my attorney general's campaign office, and I could see that she had organizational skills and the ability to work with people. She was poised, articulate, made a favorable impression, and she would be a fine representative wherever she appeared.

There was a hitch, however. List's counterpart in the Southern Nevada office was a legal secretary, a classified position in the state personnel system. Because the employee was classified, there were specific criteria and a cumbersome hiring process. By contrast, the deputy attorneys general were not part of the classified system and served at my pleasure. I would need to get approval from the state personnel office to change Jenny's position to an unclassified one. I requested a résumé from her, and when I received it I was a bit shocked. Her only entry under work experience was as a dancer at the Sahara Hotel & Casino.

I made an appointment with the state personnel office and explained what I was trying to accomplish. When I provided a copy of her résumé to the person waiting on me at the counter, I received a look of incredulity. The official retreated to the back office, where several employees were gathered. I could hear laughter. I overheard one employee say, "You won't believe it, but the new attorney general from Las Vegas wants to hire a dancer for his office manager." Over the years, Jenny and I had a lot of fun reminiscing about that experience.

I interviewed each of the deputy AGs and kept most. List had a talented team of attorneys. The big challenge was in the gaming division, the most high-profile area in the AG's office. The gaming division was frequently in the middle of the most contentious legal battles in the state. Bud Hicks, the chief deputy in the gaming division under List, enjoyed universal respect from the industry, regulators, and attorneys appearing before the board and commission. I offered to reappoint him. He declined and indicated he had accepted an offer from a prominent law firm in Northern Nevada. I'd known Bill Curran for some time. He was a fine lawyer, thoughtful and experienced. I tried to hire him, but the clock was ticking and he was unavailable in Mexico learning Spanish.

By chance I had a meeting with Harry Reid, chairman of the Nevada Gaming Commission, who recommended that I consider Ray Pike, who had been with the US Attorney's Office in Nevada. Small world. Ray's name sounded familiar to me. I later found out that his father was Doug Pike, with whom I had taken the Nevada Bar Exam. I'd even been a judge at one of Ray's Las Vegas High School debates. A check with his colleagues at the US Attorney's Office gave me even more confidence that he was the right person for the job. I offered him the position, and he quickly accepted.

With Ray on board, I charged him with assembling his own team, and he immediately chose Phil Pro, his former colleague at the US Attorney's Office, as his top deputy. Phil brought a first-rate intellect and a strong sense of ethics to the job, attributes that would serve him well years later when he was appointed to the US District Court bench. Bill Hammer, an experienced prosecutor, was added to the team. In short order, my team was ready to go.

In late November, Bob Brown, publisher and owner of the *Valley Times*, a North Las Vegas newspaper, reported that List had accepted comps from the Stardust Resort and Casino on the Las Vegas Strip at a time his office was investigating the scandalized casino. It was an inauspicious beginning for the newly elected governor. His political honeymoon was over before it began.

When his opponent in the governor's race, Bob Rose, was asked if he knew about the comp issue, he acknowledged that he learned about it in the final days of the campaign. Rose said he declined to use it because the information might be viewed as a last-minute cheap shot.

The press began hounding me as the attorney general–elect. What was my reaction to this? What did I intend to do about it? Getting into a conflict with the governor was not my intention. I was delighted with my new position. The accusation, however, was damaging. I did sense that there was some apprehension and uneasiness about me and how I would respond. I was careful not to directly criticize List. I even called Sig Rogich, whom I'd known since my brother was a classmate of his at Las Vegas High School. Sig had been a key member of List's gubernatorial campaign. I assured Sig I did not intend to make this an issue that would make life difficult for the governor.

But there was a dynamic playing out. The issue did have an impact on my relationship with the List administration and particularly with the Nevada Gaming Control Board.

A new issue arose during the 1979 legislative session that added more uneasiness between the governor's team and me. A bill was introduced that List had supported and included in his State of the State message. The bill would provide additional property rights for lakefront property owners at Lake Tahoe. Harry Swainston, one of my deputies who had been a holdover from the List AG's office, testified against the bill. Although he identified himself as testifying as an individual, his testimony was explosive. Swainston asserted that List's support for the bill was based upon a meeting that he held with Lake Tahoe property owners who would benefit from the bill. He then traced political contributions that List had received during his gubernatorial campaign from those lakefront property owners. The inference was clear that List supported the property owners who had contributed to his campaign.

Swainston argued that the property at issue was held in trust by the state for all Nevadans. Swainston had not informed me that he was going to testify on a bill that the governor included in his State of the State message to the legislature. I first heard about his testimony when I received a call from Governor List. He was highly agitated, and understandably so. List raged on, telling me that I needed to get control of my deputies. Although I was blameless, it was one more incident that caused List's staff to view me with increased suspicion.

The West was in rebellion in 1979. The Sagebrush Rebellion. The battle cry was the equal footing doctrine. In 1787, the framers of the US Constitution had debated, but eventually rejected, a provision that would provide that each new state would be admitted with the same rights and privileges as the original thirteen. However, with the admission of Tennessee in 1796, each state thereafter was admitted to the Union on an "equal footing."

In Nevada, the opening volley in the battle was fired when Assemblyman Dean Rhoads, a cattle rancher from Elko County, introduced a bill cosponsored by thirty-six of his Assembly colleagues that laid claim on behalf of the State of Nevada to all the unappropriated lands within the state. The legal predicate underpinning the state's claim was the equal footing doctrine. Rhoads's legislation asserted that Nevada had been denied admission to the Union on an equal footing. The legislation pointed out that 86 percent of the state's land mass was controlled by seventeen federal agencies. Federal control was even more intrusive in Esmeralda, Lincoln, Mineral, Nye, and White Pine Counties, where the federal government controlled between 97 and 99 percent of the land. The Sagebrush Rebels cited it as an egregious violation of state sovereignty, and it bolstered the state's case.

Indeed, Nevada as a condition to its admission to the Union in 1864 was forced to "forever disclaim all right and title to the unappropriated land within its boundaries." In making its legal argument, Nevada relied upon several Supreme Court decisions that sided with the states in interpreting the equal footing doctrine. Struve and I decided that we needed to engage someone who had the gravitas of a constitutional scholar and who had argued cases before the US Supreme Court. Rex Lee had been first in his class at the University of Chicago Law School, had clerked for Supreme Court Justice Byron "Whizzer" White, and had argued several cases before the nation's high court. Most recently he had served as the founding dean of the J. Reuben Clark Law School at Brigham Young University.

I wondered, could this man be the same Rex Lee I had met in 1959 when I was student body president at the University of Nevada and was hosting a conference of student body presidents in the West? It was. He was the student body president-elect from BYU. When we reconnected, we spent a few minutes reminiscing about our days as student body presidents.

Our first challenge was getting a case before a federal court in a timely manner. There was one case pending that appeared promising. The State of Nevada had sued the federal government after it declared a moratorium on new applications under the 1862 Homestead Act. As the case was moving toward trial, the US attorney representing the federal government made a clever move. He agreed to end the moratorium and allow new applications to be processed. That made, as the lawyers say, the case moot.

Before the case was dismissed, we sought to amend the complaint to include the claim of state ownership as contained in the Rhoads bill. The court rejected our attempt to amend the complaint and declined to render an advisory opinion on the constitutionality of the Rhoads legislation.

That was the posture of the Sagebrush Rebellion as I left the attorney's general's office and became governor.

In 1977 the O'Callaghan administration entered a twenty-year lease with US Ecology for the operation of a low-level nuclear dumpsite outside Beatty. In the late spring of 1979, a truck carrying low-level nuclear waste caught fire en route to the US Ecology dumpsite. At the time, the site was one of just three low-level nuclear waste dumps operating in the country. The alarm bell was sounded, and the Southern Nevada media began aggressively questioning the potential impact on public health. Can the public be harmed?

Governor List was between the proverbial rock and a hard place, and by October he called for the closure of the dumpsite. He directed the Department of Human Resources, which had issued the company's original license, to put a halt to future shipments. US Ecology appealed the decision, claiming that it was denied due process because it was not given sufficient opportunity to make its case. In addition, the company argued that the waste transported was not a threat to public health and safety.

The attorney general's office represents the Department of Human Resources. I asked Struve to review the record of the proceedings. After reviewing the record, he advised me that the department's case was tenuous at best. The department had provided no evidence that the waste posed a danger to public health and safety. Struve's first challenge was to find experts to bolster the department's argument that public health and safety were endangered. He canvassed the country for experts who would support the state's contention and traveled to several cities to take depositions from those experts. After the State Board of Health heard evidence from the state and the company, it overturned the department's directive. The department immediately appealed to the district court in Carson City for judicial review of the board's decision. Judge Mike Fondi concluded that the State Board of Health failed to make appropriate "findings of fact" with respect to the evidence presented at the hearing and ordered the case to be returned to the board for the appropriate findings consistent with the evidence presented at the hearings.

I didn't know it at the time, but the legal entanglement over the Beatty dump issue provided an invaluable introduction to an issue that would consume much of the rest of my public career. It was a prelude to an even bigger issue involving the transport and storage of high-level nuclear waste. The Congress in 1982 enacted the Nuclear Waste Policy Act, which required the study of a number of possible sites for a high-level nuclear waste dump. Three would be submitted to the president, who would then make the final selection. Suddenly the stakes were raised.

The attorney general's staff was still relatively small in 1979. I had the luxury of reviewing many of the formal written opinions issued by my office before their release. A controversy arose concerning a Lyon County school that was under construction. The law required that before a school construction contract could be awarded, the State Health Division had to certify that the construction complied with all the health and safety requirements. The law further provided that any contract awarded before the health and safety requirements had been certified was "void." The Lyon County School Board trustees had awarded the construction contract before the certification was received.

The school generated some controversy when under construction, and our office was asked by the Lyon County School Board to render an opinion on the legality of the construction contract. The draft opinion, prepared by one of my most experienced deputies, concluded that the construction contract was void. That conclusion would certainly thrust the county and the contractor into litigation. In fact, the state had certified that the construction did fully comply with all health and safety requirements, but the certification occurred after the contract was awarded. A strict construction of the word "void" would invalidate the construction contract.

It was clear to me that the legal requirement to provide the certification was grounded upon a public policy that schools needed to be safe. In this instance the certification had been made, but not in the proper sequence.

I called Struve into my office and shared with him the draft opinion. I told him that if the opinion were released, we would certainly create a costly litigation nightmare for Lyon County and the contractor. I then suggested to him that there were cases in which the courts had interpreted "void" as being "voidable." I asked Struve to research the case law, and in a couple of days he returned with several cases in which the courts had construed void to mean voidable.

The opinion was now changed. We opined that the contract was legally entered into. All public policy considerations were fully safeguarded, and protracted litigation was avoided. It's an example of how an attorney general's office can provide practical solutions to a potentially contentious legal problem.

In October, I faced another major issue that was literally a matter of life and death: the impending execution of admitted killer Jesse Bishop. Convicted in the 1977 murder of Las Vegas tourist David Ballard during a botched robbery on the Strip, Bishop was a hardened criminal who had no interest in fighting the death sentence he received. Bishop, who had spent more than half his life in prison, would tell an interviewer, "They want to force me to appeal, to wait just so lawyers can play their games. I feel that's cruel and unusual punishment. I never asked for the death penalty. They gave it to me. I'm only asking that they either give it to me or commute it."

Commutation was out of the question for the habitual criminal. Bishop refused to appeal his case and forbade his defense counsel from doing so. It certainly wasn't out of a sense of guilt or contrition. Bishop expressed not the least bit of remorse for shooting Ballard, a twenty-two-year-old newlywed and resident of Baltimore.

Despite Bishop's ambivalence about his death sentence, the American Civil Liberties Union on behalf of eleven Nevada taxpayers filed a last-minute petition to delay his execution. Its lawyers argued that spending taxpayer money on the execution violated their constitutional rights. Bishop's execution was scheduled for Monday, October 22. On the preceding Saturday, the Nevada Supreme Court scheduled a hearing on the ACLU's petition.

I was in Reno at a Saturday football game when I was informed that the Supreme Court had scheduled an emergency hearing on the petition for the stay of execution for later that afternoon. I raced to Carson City and successfully argued against the petition. On October 22, 1979, Bishop became just the third person to be executed in the United States following the 1976 reinstatement of the death penalty and the first to die in a gas chamber.

Just months into 1979, the Strip erupted with the news of the convictions of Aladdin Hotel Corp. principals James Abraham, James Tamer, Charles Goldfarb, and Edward Monazym on racketeering conspiracy charges in Detroit. The case involved hidden ownership with connections to organized crime. For Las Vegas specifically and Nevada gaming generally, it was the worst kind of news and threatened a gaming industry trying to emerge from the shadow of its historic mob associations.

The case was ably prosecuted by Organized Crime Strike Force prosecutor Stan Hunterton, who transferred from Detroit to Las Vegas and later served as a member of the President's Commission on Organized Crime before entering private practice. The board and commission ordered the casino closed.

If that sounds like a simple matter, it was anything but that. Closing the casino also threatened to put hundreds of Aladdin employees out of work—something none of us wanted to do. Although there was no statutory authority, Pike, Pro, and Hammer devised a plan to appoint a state supervisor so that the casino could stay open. Management was removed from operational control, and the commission designated Leo Lewis, a gaming industry veteran, as supervisor. US District judge Harry Claiborne, the storied former Las Vegas defense attorney, granted injunctive relief to the previous management, effectively reopening the casino under their control.

The attorney general's office appealed Claiborne's ruling. I personally argued the appeal before the US Ninth Circuit Court of Appeals, and the court reversed Claiborne's decision and affirmed the action taken by the commission. The supervisor took control of the casino operation and helped ease the troubled Aladdin into a new era of ownership by Wayne Newton and Ed Torres.

The tumultuous times for the casino industry continued at the Tropicana Resort & Casino, which struggled to turn a profit throughout much of the 1970s despite large cash infusions from several investors. Stauffer Chemical heiress Mitzi Stauffer Briggs knew little about the gaming business, but she believed it was an excellent place to put her fortune after learning of the potential for high returns. She was unsophisticated, naive, and somewhat eccentric. Her decision turned out to be disastrous after a federal investigation revealed hidden ownership at the Tropicana by Nicholas and Carl Civella, brothers who led the Kansas City mob. The Civella brothers were two of the original eleven members of Nevada's List of Excluded Persons, better known as the Black Book. As such, they were persona non grata and banned from setting foot in a Nevada gaming establishment.

That had not deterred the Civellas from managing to skim untaxed casino profits from the Tropicana with the assistance of inside man Joe Agosto, the erstwhile producer of the *Folies Bergère*, and Carl Thomas, at that time a highly respected gaming industry veteran. The skim continued as millions of dollars were diverted to the mob.

The facade of legitimacy at the Tropicana was shattered after the FBI recorded a secret meeting that took place in the basement of a home in a Kansas City suburb between Thomas and the Civella outfit. The recordings were known as the "Marlo Tapes" because the home where the meeting took place belonged to a Civella family relative Josephine Marlo. The recording revealed Thomas as a trusted associate of the mobsters. Thomas bragged about his role in the skim at the Tropicana, Stardust Resort and Casino, and Bingo Palace, but expressed concern that his criminal association would be revealed. Agosto's inside role was also recorded. They were caught cold, and when the wiretap was unsealed and the news hit the press, they were finished.

All that saved the Tropicana from closure was its forced sale to publicly traded Ramada Inns. If memory serves me well, it was the first entry of an outside publicly traded company to enter a major gaming market. It was a significant development, as it brought tighter regulation at the federal level from the Securities and Exchange Commission and at the state level from the board's fledgling securities division.

Thanks to the 1995 Martin Scorsese blockbuster *Casino*, the mob trouble at the Stardust is etched in the American moviegoing psyche as the greatest scandal in Las Vegas gaming history. I won't litigate the legend. The Stardust scandal was a terrible embarrassment for the state that came at a time of renewed scrutiny as legalized gaming expanded to Atlantic City. Suffice it to say that the Argent Corporation, led by Allen Glick, concealed the identities of the true owners and influencers of the Stardust and other casinos. The notorious men in the shadows comprised a rogue's gallery of organized crime, mostly from Chicago. The fall of the Stardust's mob betting expert Frank Rosenthal, combined with the law enforcement investigation of the Chicago mob's Las Vegas enforcer Tony Spilotro and his criminal "Hole in the Wall Gang," was another blow to organized crime in Las Vegas.

We scrutinized the Stardust's new owners, Herb Tobman and Al Sachs. The more we looked, the more we found. Tobman had been a longtime associate of Moe Dalitz, the former Cleveland bootlegger who had largely reinvented himself in Las Vegas. Sachs had straight-line connections to the Chicago hotel business through the Jockey Club and gaming industry figure Johnny Drew, who also had been associated with Chicago's Tony Accardo. With the Stardust's future already in serious doubt, and the Rosenthal-Spilotro era still playing out in court and on the street, Pike and Pro recommended a one-year license for Tobman and Sachs. A one-year gaming license would compel Tobman and Sachs to apply for a renewal after twelve months. The burden would be on them to get approval for a new license, and who knew what the next year would bring? We had our suspicions.

By contrast, if they were issued an unconditional license and questions of their suitability surfaced, the burden would be on the Nevada Gaming Control Board to prove their unsuitability. What the public didn't know was, the FBI had provided Pike and Pro with information that it had uncovered during its ongoing and wide-ranging casino skimming investigation. The information couldn't be made public until the investigation was completed.

What came next speaks to the political intrigue of the times. The Nevada Gaming Control Board, with Roger Trounday as chairman and Richard Bunker and Jack Stratton as members, voted unanimously to approve a one-year license for Tobman and Sachs. But just two weeks after the recommended approval, the Nevada Gaming Commission reversed the board on a 5–0 vote. Trounday believed he had been stabbed in the back after he discovered Bunker had met privately with several commissioners. Trounday resigned in protest. Bunker would serve as chairman of the board before leaving to accept the first of several jobs in the casino industry and eventually heading the Nevada Resort Association.

The relationship with Bunker and my staff grew increasingly tense. Pike and Pro were frequently excluded from meetings when the gaming control board staff was discussing strategy. When Pike and Pro provided legal advice that Bunker did not like, he said he would follow it, but if there was a backlash he made it clear that "this is on your boss's head."

As chief deputy of the gaming division, Pike enjoyed a high-profile position, and as with Bud Hicks before him it was only a matter of time before the industry came courting. Pike left the attorney general's office in 1981 for a position with International Game Technology but not before he assembled a seasoned team of attorneys who brought considerable experience to the AG's office at a critical time in the state's history. The previous year, Pro was appointed a US magistrate judge in Las Vegas and left the attorney general's office. Although legal acumen was paramount, whomever I chose as Pike's successor would also need the political skills it took to work with the board and commission on sensitive matters and give them the best legal advice possible—even if it wasn't something they wanted to hear.

Enter Patty Becker, a deputy attorney general raised in Las Vegas, educated in the public schools, and whose parents owned a shoe store there. She was smart, hard-working, and tough. After coming to the gaming division as a part-time deputy, she proved indispensable to Pike and Pro and soon was on their team full time.

There was no question about Becker's capabilities in my mind. Not only would she be the first woman appointed to the attorney general's gaming division, but she also would be the chief of the division. And it was hardly a secret that the gaming industry was largely a men's club. She was the youngest deputy in the division, but I knew she could hold her own on any legal issue or strategy being considered. I recall talking to Becker about some of the challenges she might face. She acknowledged them, but said she was ready for whatever came her way. I came away convinced that she was the right choice, and I was prepared to deal with any fallout.

In the next two years, she would successfully argue three of the most important cases that went before the Nevada Supreme Court during my term as attorney general. She more than justified my faith in her ability.

The first case she tackled was *Summa Corp. v. State Gaming Control Board*. The case arose from a four-year audit of the Desert Inn Resort & Casino that found numerous instances in which the casino issued gaming credit instruments, known in the business as "markers," that went uncollected. The unpaid markers were deducted from the casino's gross revenues, which reduced the amount of gaming tax collected by the state. Markers have a legitimate business purpose—to extend casino play—but a good-faith effort must be made to collect them. Failing to make that effort to collect them makes them "irregular" and therefore not deductible. Since the enactment of the gross gaming tax by the 1945 Nevada Legislature, casinos have been taxed on their gross earnings minus payouts to customers. The mob, however, had effectively used uncollected markers to funnel large sums of money to hidden owners and organized crime.

Over the years the state had adopted countermeasures in the form of gaming regulations that made markers deemed irregular and not deductible unless a good-faith effort to collect on them was made. Summa challenged those regulations. The district court upheld the regulations, and it found the regulations provided an accounting mechanism that determined gross revenue, and action by the regulators was consistent with the well-established Gaming Control Act. Summa appealed the trial court's decision, but the Nevada Supreme Court affirmed the district court ruling upholding the regulations.

In *State of Nevada v. Glusman,* the Nevada Supreme Court affirmed the Nevada Gaming Control Board and Nevada Gaming Commission's power to investigate the suitability not only of gaming licensees, but of business operators associated with the casino. In this case, Freddie Glusman owned dress shops inside the Las Vegas Hilton and Stardust. When his associations attracted regulatory scrutiny, the commission directed Glusman to appear before it for a suitability hearing. The district court granted Glusman's request for a preliminary injunction. At the Supreme Court, Becker successfully argued for the constitutionality of the gaming control board's power. The Nevada Supreme Court concluded, "Gaming control would be intolerably burdened if selective investigation were disallowed." Glusman landed on his feet, however, and established Piero's Italian Cuisine near the Strip as a Las Vegas culinary legend.

Becker's third and most high-profile victory before the Nevada Supreme Court came shortly after I left the attorney general's office in *Spilotro v. State of Nevada, Nevada Gaming Commission.* A team of attorneys led by Oscar Goodman attempted to have Tony Spilotro removed from the Black Book on constitutional grounds. Spilotro was a suspected hitman who had beat a murder rap in Chicago and was sent to Las Vegas to assume control of the mob's street crime activities. He had been placed in the Black Book in 1978. He didn't like it and immediately began to challenge his inclusion. The Nevada

Supreme Court ruled that the commission was within its constitutional and statutory authority to place the lifetime ban on Spilotro.

In 1977, California attorney general Evelle Younger was laying the groundwork for his gubernatorial campaign the following year. He saw a political opportunity in reviving the old boundary dispute between California and Nevada, by asserting the boundary between the two states was inaccurate and the correct line was farther to the east. If his argument prevailed, most if not all of Lake Tahoe would become part of California.

He filed a lawsuit against Nevada laying out his claim in April. Not surprisingly, Nevada responded by claiming that another survey line, which would move the boundary farther to the west, was the accurate one. The US Constitution provides that litigation between states must be filed with the US Supreme Court. The Supreme Court appointed a special master to review the voluminous record. The special master studied thousands of pages of historical documents and legal briefs to resolve an age-old dispute.

Students of Nevada history know that this war between the states has been fought before. Since California's 1850 statehood, surveyors and cartographers had differed about the precise boundary. Before Younger's litigation, the boundary issue had been resolved for eighty years with both states acquiescing to the existing line. In the twentieth century, the famous pool at the Cal-Neva Lodge & Casino on the North Shore of Lake Tahoe featured a stripe through it purporting to be the state line. It was a bit of playful marketing, but it also served as a metaphor for the long-standing issue.

Although the lawsuit was filed by California before I took office, oral arguments occurred during my tenure as attorney general. As fate would have it, the decision in the case was announced during the National Association of Attorneys General convention at Lake Tahoe's North Shore Cal-Neva. As Nevada's attorney general, I had the honor of hosting the event. To add to the intrigue of the moment, the legendary casino was in escrow. The buyer was purchasing a casino, and gaming wasn't legal in California. If the court adopted the boundary advocated by Younger, it would have forced the closure of the Cal-Neva's casino.

California's litigation had a high hurdle to overcome. The passage of time had largely settled the issue in most minds. The special master noted that counsel for the State of California had to admit he knew of no time in the twentieth century when both states claimed the same parcel of land. That passage of time led the special master to conclude that both states had accepted the existing boundary line, and he invoked the doctrine of acquiescence to resolve the dispute.

When the decision by the US Supreme Court was announced, a wire service report erroneously stated that California had prevailed in the legal dispute. The buyer of the Cal-Neva nearly went into cardiac arrest because he was purchasing a casino. In fact, the Supreme Court adopted the special master's findings and concluded that the boundary between the two states should remain the same as it had for decades.

The war between the states was averted without a shot fired. I met at the Cal-Neva with California attorney general and future governor George Deukmejian for a handshake and a photo commemorating the moment. We stood by the pool on either side of the painted stripe that marked the Nevada-California state boundary.

Utility rates were soaring in Nevada in the 1970s. In the previous decade Nevada Power had increased its rates by 160 percent, Southwest Gas by 100 percent. Ratepayers were frustrated and furious.

In 1975 as a state senator, I introduced legislation to create a state consumer advocate who would represent ratepayers before the Public Service Commission. The concept was new. Only a few states had created a consumer advocate's office. My proposal generated little support. I remained convinced that Nevada ratepayers needed a consumer advocate in their corner.

Randolph Townsend, a Reno businessman, took up the cause in 1980. He engaged two energy experts, David Schwartz and Jon Wellinghoff, and charged them with drafting an initiative petition that would create a state consumer advocate in the attorney general's office. They were later joined by Andy Barbano, a local political strategist and labor union activist. They put together the Coalition for Affordable Energy and launched a statewide campaign to collect the required signatures necessary to present the initiative petition to the 1981 state legislature.

When Governor Bob List was asked to support the petition, he declined to do so, declaring he didn't think it was necessary. List's opposition to creating a state consumer advocate would have a significant impact on his reelection bid in 1982. The coalition collected 38,000 signatures, more than enough to submit to the state legislature when it convened in January. Under state law governing initiative petitions, if the petition qualifies it is submitted to the legislature, which would then be given forty days to act. Failing to act automatically placed the initiative petition on the next general election ballot for voter approval.

When the legislature convened, there were two additional proposals to establish a state consumer advocate. Perhaps realizing the error of his ways in declaring the position unnecessary, Governor List suddenly proposed the creation of a state consumer advocate's office under the governor's control. Assemblywoman Peggy Westall also submitted a proposal.

The proposed legislation was referred to the Assembly Government Relations Committee and assigned to the Subcommittee on Consumer Advocacy chaired by Don Mello. It was clear to me that the legislature had crossed the Rubicon, and a state consumer advocate's office would be established before adjournment. Several issues were unclear, however. Where would the office be placed, in the AG's office or subject to the governor's control? What would the qualifications of the consumer advocate be? How would the office be financed? And if the office were placed within the attorney general's office, how would conflicts be avoided? The attorney general also represented the Public Service Commission.

These were legitimate legislative issues. The subcommittee reviewed the operation of consumer advocate offices in other states and the various organizational structures that they adopted.

Between February and April, the subcommittee scheduled several hearings on the legislative proposals. The hearings explored at great length the experiences of other states that had established such offices. Testimony was also taken from energy experts. The Townsend group, the driving force behind the consumer advocate initiative petition, testified as well. I asked Larry Struve to represent the attorney general's office at the hearings. His calm demeanor and thoughtful responses to the committee's questions was well received.

The subcommittee decided to request a new legislative bill draft that would incorporate the best features of each of the three proposals. The Senate would have to pass any bill that cleared the Assembly. State Senator "Spike" Wilson was on point representing the Senate in the negotiations on the bill draft. He was an able and highly respected lawmaker and was instrumental in fashioning compromises that moved the bill forward.

The bill, as drafted, placed the consumer advocate within the attorney general's office and organizationally followed the original legislative initiative by the Townsend group. When it reached the floor of the Assembly, there were thirty-four ayes and seven nays. After minor changes, the Senate passed it unanimously.

On June 14, Governor List signed the bill creating the office of consumer advocate. A journey that began in 1975 when I first introduced a bill to establish the consumer advocate position had at last ended.

I had known for some time that I wanted Jon Wellinghoff to be the consumer advocate. Jon had been present at the creation and had assisted in drafting the legislation that created the position. I offered him the position. He quickly accepted and just as quickly went to work.

By mid-September, Wellinghoff was in court challenging Nevada Power's $14.9 million requested rate increase. The rest is history. Wellinghoff later went on to a distinguished career as chairman of the Federal Energy Regulatory Commission.

List had spent a good deal of time out of state. In the absence of the governor, the lieutenant governor, in this case Myron Leavitt, a Democrat, argued that he was entitled to receive additional compensation for serving as the acting governor. The budget allocated for such additional compensation was small. It would be very embarrassing for List, who would be forced to appear before the Interim Finance Committee to request a supplemental appropriation to pay the lieutenant governor for his absence from the state. Leavitt in particular, and Democrats in general, were salivating at the prospect that List would have to request a supplemental appropriation. It would be politically damaging to him because it would highlight his absence from the state.

I was requested to provide an opinion about whether Leavitt as lieutenant governor was entitled to the additional compensation. As a Democrat, it was thought that I would welcome the opportunity to create a political embarrassment for List. Politics presents many ironies, and this was a delicious one. In 1965, Governor Grant Sawyer, a Democrat, and Lieutenant Governor Paul Laxalt, a Republican, crossed swords over an issue that arose at the state prison. Laxalt had urged Sawyer to convene a state grand jury to investigate. Sawyer had refused.

In late November 1965, Sawyer left Nevada to make a previously scheduled dinner speech in Sacramento, California. The governor departed Carson City at 5:20 p.m. and returned at 10 p.m. that same evening. In his short absence, Laxalt as lieutenant governor purported to assume the role of acting governor and empaneled a state grand jury. It was a blatant politically motivated act. The governor was outside the state for only a few hours, and those were on a Sunday with the courts closed. As the Nevada Supreme Court later wrote, there was no immediate need to act because no action could be taken until Monday morning, by which time the governor had returned. Upon his return to the state, Sawyer immediately revoked Laxalt's actions.

When the case was ultimately appealed to the Nevada Supreme Court, the legal issue hinged upon the interpretation of "absence." In a carefully reasoned opinion, the court construed the word absence as meaning more than mere absence. The questions: Was the governor unable to act? Was it necessary to act?

Representing Laxalt's appeal were several prominent Republican lawyers, including a young Bob List. The court in 1966 concluded that Sawyer's absence did not enable Laxalt to act as governor and convene a grand jury. I reviewed the court's earlier decision and responded. Adopting the earlier court's rationale, I concluded that Leavitt was not entitled to additional compensation as acting governor because there was no showing that List was unable to act, or that it was necessary for the lieutenant governor to act. Leavitt was furious, and many Democrats were angry with me because I had let List off the hook. The court's decision of two decades earlier had saved List some political embarrassment. I guess you can say, sometimes you can win by losing.

List's ascendency to the ranks of a major political player in the state had been mercurial. He was elected district attorney of Ormsby County just a few years out of law school, and his 1970 defeat of Attorney General Harvey Dickerson, a three-term incumbent, was impressive. The Dickerson family had enjoyed political prominence in the state for more than a half century. Harvey Dickerson's father served as acting governor. A brother, Denver Dickerson, was Speaker of the Nevada Assembly. Harvey's youngest brother, George, had been elected Clark County district attorney, defeating my father in the 1954 Democratic primary. List enjoyed the distinction of being Nevada's first Republican attorney general in the twentieth century. He was elected governor at just forty-two. He was formidable, sure-footed in navigating the political currents. I can attest firsthand, having observed him in action in the 1974 AG's race.

As governor, however, he developed a reputation of not returning phone calls from some of his most prominent supporters. If it was an issue involving the Nevada Department of Transportation, on which I served on the governing board, I made it clear that if List wasn't available to return their calls, I would be pleased to do so.

One of the biggest traditional events each summer in the backyard of the Governor's Mansion is the Wolf Pack Dinner, which helped fund athletic programs at the University of Nevada, Reno. Hundreds of the most active and influential business leaders and sports luminaries attended the dinner. There was always a nationally prominent person from the sports world to deliver the keynote. The governor served as the official host of the event, which dated back to the days when Laxalt was governor.

List failed to attend one year, opting instead to attend an event in California at the exclusive Bohemian Grove, the club where an invitee might meet a former US secretary of state, four-star general, or a Wall Street baron. It was, metaphorically speaking, a long way from the Nevada governor's backyard and the Wolf Pack Dinner. List's absence was noted and generated quite a buzz among the attendees. The message was unmistakable: List preferred to be at the Bohemian Grove rather than mingle with his fellow Nevadans. During my tenure as attorney general, and later as governor, I never missed the barbecue. It gave me an opportunity to get better acquainted with the business community and others in Northern Nevada.

List's initial refusal to support the legislative initiative to establish the consumer advocate was another uncharacteristic misstep.

As the 1981 legislative session loomed, List and his political advisors drafted a legislative proposal that would slash the state property tax but increase the state's portion of the sales tax. Some of his closest advisors were gleefully proclaiming that this was List's ticket to reelection the following year.

In his 1981 State of the State, List confidently declared, "I call for a dramatic slash in property taxes and a massive program of tax reform. . . . Let us shift the tax burden to all the people who utilize state services through the sales tax." The proposed shift was dramatic, reducing the property tax by 65 percent while increasing the sales tax from 3.5 percent to 5.75 percent, an increase of 64 percent. His critics argued that increasing the sales tax would affect those who could least afford to pay it and was a reversal of his previous campaign promise to reduce it from 3.5 to 3 percent. He steered a course that put him at odds with Nevada history.

As it had been in the nineteenth century, Nevada's dependency on a single industry to power its economy had been its economic Achilles heel and continues to the present day. In the nineteenth century, it had been mining. When the enormous riches of the Comstock Lode played out, Nevada's population precipitously declined from sixty-two thousand in 1880 to forty-two thousand in the 1900 census.

As Yogi Berra would say, it was déjà vu all over again. Nevada's post–World War II economy had become heavily dependent on gaming/tourism. Sales tax revenues are much more volatile than taxes imposed on real estate. When the national economy cratered, the impact on the state's revenue was immediate and devastating.

Cutting taxes sounds prudent when the coffers are flush, but what List couldn't predict was an impending national recession tied to the energy crisis. Nevada booming economy sputtered to a near-standstill, and unemployment climbed toward a peak of 10.8 percent in the worst economic downturn in the US since the Great Depression.

Sales taxes collected by the state plummeted. No governor likes to cut education and other important government services, but with revenues falling List was forced to make unpopular cuts to programs. Those moves added to his political problems.

The perception from the political cognoscenti was that List was politically vulnerable. There were growing pressures on me to enter the fray. I was told by some that I was the only one who could defeat List. As in life, timing is everything in politics. If I chose not to run, and a Democrat was elected, in all probability the next opportunity to run for governor might be in eight years.

Jim Santini, my good friend and old debate partner from our days at the University of Nevada, had decided to challenge US Senator Howard Cannon in the Democratic primary. It was a controversial decision that later led to him switching parties. As Nevada's lone representative, Santini had run statewide in four different elections and had the pulse of the voting public. He was very popular, particularly in the rurals. When he encouraged me to get in the race, I listened closely. He said, "In my opinion, you can win, and that's based on people I've talked to all over the state."

Apparently, my possible entry into the governor's race was also on the minds of some List insiders. One approached me and confided, "If you run for reelection as attorney general, we'll raise the necessary money to fund the campaign."

The political winds seemed increasingly favorable. If not now, when? That was a question I had to answer. I thought long and hard about it through the summer of 1981. By fall, almost like an inexorable force of nature, I was in. I knew it would be the toughest race of my life. This was the big leagues in the political world. On February 2, 1982, I was in the batter's box.

CHAPTER 20

A Dream Comes True

In some ways, February 2, 1982, was a typical midwinter day in Las Vegas. The sun was bright. The sky was clear and blue, and there was a chill in the air. But for me this was no ordinary day.

I was about to embark upon the greatest political challenge of my career, announcing my candidacy for governor. I would be running against a well-funded incumbent who had never lost a race and in recent weeks had regained his political footing that had made him such a formidable adversary. The family and I were heading to the Showboat Hotel and Casino in Las Vegas, where I would make my formal announcement.

As we drove to the hotel, we listened to the radio as the daily weather report came on with the announcement that today was Groundhog Day. That was news to me. I was concerned that the press might have a field day asking me why I had chosen Groundhog Day to make my announcement. I didn't want to get caught off-guard like Punxsutawney Phil. Worse, I feared that it might make the evening news and the subject of political columnists speculating that Bryan may be afraid of his own shadow.

A large crowd of enthusiastic supporters gathered at the Showboat to cheer me on. Governor Grant Sawyer had agreed to introduce me, and his mellifluous voice made the case for my candidacy and pointed out the sharp difference between Bob List and me. After my remarks, it was the press's turn to ask questions. The first question came out of left field. Earlier that morning in Washington, DC, Vice President George H. W. Bush's motorcade had narrowly avoided a piece of masonry that had fallen from a building. I was asked whether I thought someone had intentionally dislodged the piece of masonry to harm the vice president or was it simply a matter of happenstance. Of course, I had no idea. But I'd listened to the morning news report and was at least familiar with the story. I managed not to have a blank look on my face, gave an answer, and moved on. It was an auspicious beginning with no obvious missteps, and thankfully no one thought to ask about Groundhog Day.

That would come a few hours later when I flew to Reno to make my official announcement in Northern Nevada. Dennis Myers, a veteran newsman who could always be counted on to ask an off-the-wall question, did not disappoint. He asked about the Groundhog Day coincidence, and the question led to a playful exchange before the press moved on to other questions. Nothing ever appeared either in print or in the broadcast media.

In my previous campaigns, Dave Powell had been a constant presence. He helped to raise money. He traveled all over the state with me, and he helped recruit volunteers to place signs and perform other campaign duties. Along with Bob Peccole, Dave had been a mainstay of my previous campaigns. Powell and Peccole had little interest in politics. Their tireless effort on my behalf was purely and simply an act of friendship.

It was clear to me that the campaign team would have to be enlarged by adding professionals with the expertise I'd need in the coming weeks against List. My first addition was Peter Hart, a nationally recognized pollster. His polling would establish a baseline for me, identifying my strengths and weaknesses with a cross-section of voters.

Matt Reese & Associates was a nationally recognized political consulting firm. Reese first gained national attention by playing a significant role in John F. Kennedy's 1960 presidential campaign. Kennedy, a Catholic, faced questions about his religion. No Democratic presidential candidate after Reconstruction had ever lost a state that had been part of the old Confederacy. In 1928, Catholic Al Smith lost three Southern states Florida, North Carolina, and Virginia. Anti-Catholic prejudice was given as a reason for his defeat in those key states.

Could a Catholic candidate carry a heavily Protestant state such as West Virginia? Kennedy prevailed thanks in large part to Reese's efforts. He was a top strategist, famously known for registering and mobilizing voters, including Lyndon Johnson's massive get-out-the-vote effort in 1964. "If you want to pick cherries," he'd say in his West Virginia drawl, "go where the cherries is." Reese assigned

John Ashford to handle my race. It was a good choice, as John and I bonded and worked together on my campaigns thereafter.

Don Williams, a local political strategist, had been helpful in several previous campaigns. Williams had come to Nevada as a student at what was then known as Nevada Southern University (now UNLV). He was creative and thought "outside the box." Not every idea he proposed was a winner, but when he caught lightning in a jug it could be a game changer.

A major plank in my campaign was enlarging the Public Service Commission with two additional consumer-friendly appointees. Nevada Power was an obvious target with its rate increases. And it had just built a sparkling office building on undeveloped West Sahara Avenue in Las Vegas, which in 1982 seemed like the middle of nowhere. The utility building looked like a sultan's palace in the middle of the desert.

Williams' television ad was one of the best I had seen. After reciting the recent rate increases that hit consumers so hard, the tag line delivered the telling blow: "If it makes you mad, just honk your horn when you drive by." It captured the public's attention, and passing motorists would lean on their horns with some punctuating their protest with an extended middle finger. It became more than just a political ad. It made the evening news.

Running for governor, I would need to raise a great deal more money than I had in previous campaigns. Governor List appointed members of the gaming control board and gaming commission, and the casino industry was understandably cautious about contributing to me as a challenger. Frankly, they didn't want to get crossways with the governor. In 1982, money collected before the year of the campaign did not need to be reported. In the final months of 1981, I kept busy collecting as many contributions as I could from the casino industry. Their contributions would not appear on my campaign disclosure report.

Peccole was from a prominent Southern Nevada family. His father had been active in gaming for many years. He was extremely helpful in connecting me with some of the smaller casino operators, who made contributions to my campaign. Frank Schreck, who I'd known since he was admitted to practice law, was an O'Callaghan protégé. Frank was raised in Henderson at a time O'Callaghan taught government at Basic High School. Following his upset election as governor in 1970, O'Callaghan appointed Schreck to the gaming commission. Upon leaving the commission, Schreck developed a flourishing gaming law practice. I asked him to head up my fundraising efforts. His contacts in gaming opened many doors and significantly boosted my fundraising. Jim Nave, a veterinarian, joined the campaign fundraising effort. He opened a new world of opportunities for me with his many contacts.

In Northern Nevada, Keith Lee was again a major player in my statewide campaign. Paul Bible, a son of US Senator Alan Bible, was an important part of the team. His prominence in Northern Nevada added credibility to my candidacy. Paul's younger brother Bill served as the fiscal analyst for the Legislative Counsel Bureau. He knew the state budget inside and out. Bill was immensely helpful in formulating my economic agenda.

In my four years as attorney general, Marlene Lockard was my office administrator. But I quickly learned she could play a much larger role. She was smart, tough, and had a finely tuned ear for politics—particularly in Northern Nevada. She knew I trusted and respected her opinion, and she didn't hesitate to offer a dissenting view when group-speak took over our campaign discussions. In that role she was invaluable in helping me to rethink a course of action that could have been problematic.

Staffing campaign offices in Reno and Las Vegas proved another challenge. Bonnie had worked with Shari Compton on Junior League projects in Las Vegas. She suggested that Compton might be a good choice to head up the Southern Nevada office. I made an appointment with her, and after explaining the nature of the job, although she had no prior experience, I asked her to run the Southern Nevada campaign office. In Northern Nevada, I'd need someone to replace Marlene, who was busy keeping the AG's office running smoothly during my campaign. She recommended her good friend, Linda Lee. Although Linda Lee also had no previous political experience, I followed Marlene's recommendation.

Compton brought in her good friend, Lou Gamage, into the campaign. Like Compton, Gamage had no prior political experience, but she had a fine eye for organizational detail. She also had a flair for presentation. The campaign fundraising events she organized were flawlessly executed and the class of the field. For the next eighteen years she would be responsible for organizing most of my major fundraising events.

Schreck opened his political Rolodex and brought Sara Besser onto the team. A career educator, she had been a founding member of Teachers in Politics (TIP) that played a major role in galvanizing teachers in support of the 1970 O'Callaghan campaign. She became our scheduler. She knew the players and was a critical part of our team for the next eighteen years. Jenny DesVaux continued to manage the attorney general's Southern Nevada's office. She also represented me at various nonpolitical events during the campaign.

In a symbolic coup, Chris Schaller, who had been a top aide to Governor O'Callaghan, signed onto our campaign. Rumors continued to swirl around the state that O'Callaghan was considering running for a third term. Schaller's presence on our team sent a clear, if unspoken, message: he wouldn't have signed on with us if O'Callaghan was seriously considering running.

In a campaign for governor, there are hundreds of volunteers without whom no candidate could be successful. The hours are long, and the work is difficult, and the daily grind is often chaotic. Butch Snider is a great example of the kind of effort volunteers made on my behalf. A Clark County firefighter forced to take a medical retirement, Butch worked tirelessly as my driver, taking me at any hour wherever I needed to go.

The team was assembled, but there was still a troublesome cloud hanging over the campaign. O'Callaghan continued to hint that he might run for a third term. There was a substantial legal question as to whether he could run for a third term. The Nevada Constitution had been amended by a vote of the people in 1970, limiting governors to two terms. That was the year O'Callaghan was first elected governor, and there was some question whether he was bound by the constitutional limitation.

Weeks passed, and O'Callaghan played coy as I soldiered on. He was a successful newspaper publisher and columnist with a mile-high public profile. I had long since announced my candidacy, but as late as the state party convention in May in Las Vegas, a sign placed outside the convention center proclaimed, "We like Mike."

With a possible O'Callaghan candidacy on the horizon, it was difficult to get traction. In June, he finally announced that he would not be a candidate for governor. Other Democratic candidates were suddenly emboldened to jump into the race with both feet. State Treasurer Stan Colton, whom I'd appointed as an investigator when I was Clark County public defender, began campaigning vigorously after O'Callaghan's announcement.

And then Lieutenant Governor Myron Leavitt suddenly decided he wanted to run for governor. Leavitt brought an impressive political resume to the table. He was from a prominent LDS family, had served as a Las Vegas justice of the peace, Las Vegas city commissioner, and Clark County commissioner. I now had two statewide officeholders with whom to contend in the Democratic primary.

List had his own troubles within the Republican Party. Bob Broadbent, Bob Weiss, and Mike Moody talked about entering the race. When Moody decided to announce his candidacy at a Clark County Republican Men's Club meeting, excoriating List in the process, a motion to endorse List's candidacy for reelection was postponed to a later date.

In May, the List machine fired up. Vice President Bush spoke at a $5,000-a-plate fundraiser at Caesars Palace hosted by Clifford Perlman, whose old friendships with organized crime figures had placed him in hot water with New Jersey gaming regulators. By contrast I was holding a $17.50-a-plate fundraiser.

Then List made an unforced error. The Clark County School District had proposed a $69 million bond issue, which was on the ballot in March. The funding was badly needed for eighteen new schools and other capital improvements. List waded in on the issue, claiming it would result in raising the property tax, which was untrue. Many believed that his opposition was an attempt to deflect growing criticism of his tax shift, which his critics dubbed "the tax shaft."

The Clark County School District Board of Trustees was furious. Even Lucille Lusk, a lifelong conservative Republican, accused List of sabotaging the bond issue. The bond issue was defeated, and List was blamed for its failure. The bond may have failed even without List's opposition, but he was the villain in the educational community.

My support for the bond issue helped me secure the endorsement of the Nevada Education Association. It was a real plus for our campaign.

I convened a top-level strategy meeting in July. John Ashford came out from DC. Dave Powell, Keith Lee, Frank Schreck, Jean Ford, and Marlene Lockard joined the meeting. It was decided that the campaign needed a statewide coordinator, and I asked Keith Lee to assume that role.

I released my economic agenda for the 1980s late that month. Nevada's economy was in a free fall. With the state's population in 1980 at 800,000, approximately 45,000 Nevadans were out of work. There was double-digit inflation, and housing starts had plummeted by 60 percent. I proposed a reorganization of the state's economic development and tourism efforts. Under the List administration in 1979, the state's Industrial Development Advisory Board had but two meetings. Neither gathering was able to muster a quorum. In the following year, the director of the department had been unable to organize a meeting by phone. There was no record of a meeting in 1981. Not until the campaign heated up in 1982 was the advisory commission active.

The state's tourism development efforts were equally dismal. The state spent $40,000 in advertising—less than the Territory of Guam. In August, I issued another position paper titled, "Gaming and So Much More." The private sector was clamoring for the state to play a bigger role in promoting tourism. Burton Cohen, the president of the Desert Inn Resort & Casino in Las Vegas, expressed his concern and observed, "It's time for the state to create an advertising budget and help to sell [Nevada] tourism to the world." "Gaming and So Much More" made the case that although Nevada was the casino capital of the world, there was much more to the state than met the eye. Nevada's colorful history and rural attractions needed only to be discovered by tourists to be appreciated. At the Las Vegas Convention and Visitors Authority, Rossi Ralenkotter also weighed in and asserted that the state's presence was urgently needed. He implored state officials to be more concerned with tourism issues before the Congress. As with the Industrial Development Advisory Board, meetings of the Tourism Advisory Board had been infrequent and accomplished little: no quorum in 1979, no meeting record in 1980, and another zero in 1981. It wasn't until 1982 that the advisory board stirred to life.

Extensive cable television and social media platforms did not exist in the early '80s. Nevada was still relatively small. Politics was more personal, and I thrived on that personal interaction. As we had done each summer since my election as attorney general, Bonnie and I participated in all the traditional events in rural Nevada. Now with the campaign in full swing, and with an RV loaned from one of my supporters, dozens of volunteers converged on each community, covering parade routes and events with signs, stickers, and balloons proclaiming my candidacy. In effect these communities were blitzed with Bryan literature and volunteers.

It was a long day for my volunteers, but it was also fun. It was old-time Nevada campaigning. Those days are gone forever. Today, campaigns don't have time to make all the traditional small-town affairs. The demands of the new media world, and the staggering sums of money required to be competitive, have changed the nature of campaigns.

Although Southern Nevada would continue to be my base, the friendships I made at the ATO House during my undergraduate days paid major dividends. In virtually every community in Nevada I had a fraternity brother contact who was helpful.

Heading into the primary's homestretch, I felt my campaign was functioning on all cylinders. Although at the time I didn't appreciate it, in retrospect the entry of Leavitt and Colton into the race was probably a good thing. It gave the campaign team the opportunity to make the necessary adjustments so that it would be a finely tuned machine when we faced the List juggernaut.

The election returns in the Democratic primary exceeded my expectations. Running against Leavitt and State Treasurer Stan Colton, "None of the Above," and three unknown candidates, I won with 55,261votes—a clear majority of all ballots cast in the primary. Leavitt, the runner-up, fell short by more than 20,000 votes.

I survived the primary largely unscathed, but the campaign ahead would be a difficult one. When I look back, O'Callaghan's indecision was helpful in that it had the effect of holding Leavitt and Colton at bay and gave them very little time to make their case to the voters.

With the primary over, I sought Leavitt's endorsement. He declined to give it. When I reached out to Colton, he tried to negotiate a quid pro quo. He said he would endorse me if I would promise to appoint him as chairman of the Public Service Commission, or another high-profile appointment in state government. I was greatly offended. No dice, was my reply.

List's first campaign commercial was a blockbuster. He resurrected my 1969 vote in the Assembly when I voted against what I believed was an unconstitutional child pornography bill. I agreed with the strong objection to the legislation raised by civil liberties groups and the state library association, but my vote was in a distinct minority. The television ad was technically factual and definitely effective. The ad depicted two women talking to each other as they pushed their children on a playground swing. At one point, one mother turned to the other and said, "You know, I was going to vote for Dick Bryan, but do you know as a state legislator he voted against a child pornography bill to protect our girls?"

The commercial was damaging. My poll numbers dropped. Schreck enlisted former governor Grant Sawyer to rebut the commercial. "Dick Bryan," Sawyer said, "has two daughters of his own. He would never do anything to hurt children." It helped, but the impact of the ad still lingered.

List had his own sagging poll numbers, but he made skillful use of his incumbency and political contacts. President Ronald Reagan came to the state to appear at the University of Nevada, Reno, on behalf of List and US Senate challenger Chic Hecht. Popular throughout the West, Reagan won Nevada comfortably with 62.5 percent of the vote. The president's appearance was front-page news.

But List had also flip-flopped on several major issues, including the creation of the consumer advocate's office. To illustrate List's shifting positions, we produced a television commercial that featured a weathervane that spun faster with each of List's flip-flops. By the time the ad ended, the weathervane was spinning full force. It was an effective image that voters remembered.

The integrity of gaming control became a major campaign issue. I had received a $10,000 contribution from Herb Tobman and Al Sachs of the Stardust Resort and Casino. After FBI reports raised the issue of a possible connection between them and organized crime figures, I immediately returned the contribution. List kept his. His insistence on keeping the contribution highlighted our different approaches to gaming regulation.

Another issue surfaced when it was learned that Alma Bromley, secretary of Nevada Gaming Control Board chairman Richard Bunker, had personally picked up a $3,500 campaign contribution from the Sahara Hotel & Casino, which was then delivered to a tax group that opposed my candidacy. Bromley was suddenly unavailable for comment. The story by Las Vegas–based United Press International reporter Myram Borders caused some observers to shout, "Where's Alma?" Bunker declined to apologize for the questionable ethics.

State Senator Spike Wilson, a Democrat from Reno who represented the gold standard when it came to personal integrity, called out Bunker for the clumsy and ethically shoddy move. It was highly inappropriate for a gaming regulator, even through his secretary, to collect a campaign contribution from a licensee.

It was also revealed that List had made a late-night phone call to Nevada Gaming Control Board member Glen Mauldin on the eve of a board meeting at a time it was considering the licensing of Wayne Newton and Ed Torres as owners of the Aladdin. List urged Mauldin to make it a unanimous vote. The call threatened to compromise the independence of a gaming regulator.

List and Bunker also held a private meeting with Frank Sinatra on the eve of his licensing hearing before the board. In a state that depends on the sanctity of gaming regulation, it raised ethical questions.

It wasn't all drama. In each of my campaigns I had fun on the trail. On Columbus Day, the Eldorado Hotel Casino in Reno had an Italian food festival with various booths filled with delicacies. On one platform was a grape-stomping competition in which competitors stood in half barrels piled with bunches of grapes cut fresh from the vine. The object of the contest was simple: Stomp the grapes and collect the juice in a bottle. The one with the most juice collected wins. As always, Bonnie was game. And her legs were much better than mine.

This was not my first rodeo, so to speak. I immediately sought the expert opinion of a couple of old Italians in charge of the event. They shared a little secret. The key was to keep the screen at the bottom of the barrel from being clogged with leaves and twigs that prevented the juice from draining into the bottle. I was instructed to use one arm to keep the screen clear while Bonnie stomped. It was a winner. Bob Cashell was also entered in the competition and must have weighed 150 pounds more than Bonnie. But the girl from Lodi came through, and we won. They were so surprised that a woman had entered the contest that first prize, a sterling silver money clip, would not be appropriate for a lady. Eldorado founder Don Carano had Bonnie's award made in the form of a necklace.

Additional endorsements from law enforcement, labor organizations, and others followed and reflected the broad support I was receiving. Going many extra miles for years to meet and speak face-to-face with voters was paying off.

And it didn't hurt that List had made his share of missteps. He had alienated some Hispanic leaders who were inclined to support his candidacy. Cesar Martinez, the president of Hispanics in Politics and a Republican, bitingly commented about List's relationship with the growing Latino community: "We get a quicker response from the Guadalajara Chamber of Commerce than we do from the governor's office."

List also angered state and local government employees when he opposed the reappointment of Bob Archie, an African American lawyer in Las Vegas, as a hearing officer, and demoted Pat Dolan, another hearing officer. Bob Gagnier, the head of the state employees association, accused List of applying political pressure to punish both men. Eight years earlier in our 1974 AG's race, List had received the endorsement of the state employees association. In a reversal of my political fortunes, the state employees endorsed me in 1982.

Although he had declined to enter the governor's race, O'Callaghan remained a presence in the campaign as publisher of the *Henderson Home News* and *Boulder City News*. In endorsing my candidacy, he wrote that my "record in public service shows he's a man of integrity. And although we might disagree with him in the coming years, we will know that he is acting honestly in the best interests of the state."

Meanwhile, the *Las Vegas Sun* endorsed List, commenting, "We believe that trading Bryan for List would accomplish nothing, except to require Bryan go through the same learning period and make the same mistakes that List had made." The *Las Vegas Review-Journal*'s endorsement of my candidacy countered, "But considering the problems Nevadans will face in the next four years, the choice must go to Richard Bryan. He is thoughtful, reasonable, intelligent, stable, and has a firm grasp on Nevada and its problems. He is the better person in our view to sit in the state's most important office."

Newspaper endorsements played a much greater role in the era before cable TV and social media platforms. The knockout blow for our campaign came from the *Reno Gazette-Journal* editorial endorsement. Santini had given me a heads up following his endorsement interview before the editorial board.

"Be prepared," he said. "This is the most intensive newspaper endorsement interview I've ever had." Then he added a footnote: "I think you have a shot at the endorsement."

Ev Landers, the managing editor known for his own biting commentary, took the lead and was the most aggressive questioner. Santini had been right. It was tough with no punches pulled. But I was prepared.

On Sunday, October 24, the headline above the editorial said it all: "Bryan for Governor: A Matter of Integrity." The endorsement focused on ethics and character and its view of the List administration's ethical failures on gaming issues. It cited the private meeting that List and gaming control board chairman Bunker had with Sinatra a day before the board's hearing and the late-night call to control board member Mauldin urging him in a unanimous vote in the licensing of Newton and Torres at the Aladdin.

The editorial concluded, "From all of this, one can draw only one conclusion. List must go. . . . For the good of Nevada, Richard Bryan must be elected governor."

It was a carpe diem moment for the campaign. The campaign produced hundreds of copies of the editorial and distributed them widely throughout Northern Nevada. We were ecstatic. We could feel the momentum growing.

The campaign's October surprise came in the form of a full-page advertisement proclaiming, "List for Governor. Cashell for Lieutenant Governor." Democrat Bob Cashell was very popular in Northern Nevada. Our campaign was stunned, surprised, and angered. Cashell never repudiated the ad. It was the beginning of a very rocky relationship that would continue into my governorship.

On Nevada Day, October 31, we were just forty-eight hours

from the election. Nevada Day is the largest celebration of the year in Carson City. Its parade attracts hundreds of entries from all over the state. The leaves have turned, and the weather is usually quite cold.

The Carson Nugget Casino had just expanded to include a convention center on the second floor with windows facing the parade route. Someone in the campaign had a connection to the Carson Nugget and requested that the campaign be allowed to use the convention space during the parade. The manager readily agreed. We decided to hold a chili cook-off and welcomed everyone—no political litmus test required. My volunteers provided gallons of chili.

The weather was on our side. Hundreds of people came in from the frigid parade route to warm up and enjoy a cup of chili. Tom Baker, one of my key volunteers, organized a little band, and other volunteers placed campaign materials around the room.

The event was so spectacularly successful that for the next eighteen years until I left Washington, DC, as a United States senator, I sponsored the event each year. It became part of the Nevada Day schedule.

The timing was perfect. The wind was at our back, and I felt the brass ring of the Nevada's highest office was within my grasp.

Election Day began in Carson City. Bonnie and I voted early that morning, then I headed to the office. I had an appointment with Bill Bible, the Legislative Counsel Bureau's fiscal analyst. With his knowledge of the state budget, he'd been a key member of my campaign team. Bill was much more than a numbers guy. He had political savvy and had formed close relationships with important state legislators. I told him that if I prevailed that evening, I wanted him to be my state budget director. He was my first appointment, and over my six years as governor he would be in the huddle every time a play was called.

That evening, Bonnie and I and daughters Leslie and Blair drove to Reno, where my supporters had gathered at the Pioneer Inn Casino hoping to celebrate a victory. We entered the casino just as the television reported that I was the projected winner. Cheers rang out. It was an electrifying and unforgettable moment for me. Also projected as a winner that night was Democrat Tom Bradley, the Los Angeles mayor making a run for governor of California. Bradley was facing off against Attorney General George Deukmejian.

After a brief stop at the Pioneer Inn, Bonnie and I with our daughters and Marlene Lockard left for the Reno airport for a flight to Las Vegas to celebrate with our Southern Nevada supporters. En route to the airport, we listened to the radio to catch up on the latest returns. My euphoria was shattered by a bulletin announcing that Bradley no longer led in the California governor's race. In fact, the Republican Deukmejian was now projected to win. After hearing the news, my anxiety level rose: would I face the same fate as Tom Bradley?

We got on the plane. I've flown many times from Reno to Las Vegas, but I can say without qualification that was the longest flight I ever made. When I landed in Las Vegas, supporters gathered to meet me. As soon as I got off the plane, I knew that the news continued to be good.

My Las Vegas campaign headquarters was in the Huntridge subdivision across the park from my boyhood home at 1141 Maryland Parkway. Arriving at the campaign headquarters, a floodgate of memories opened and overwhelmed me. It was there in the park that I played pickup baseball games with my friends on those seemingly endless summer afternoons. In the spring we flew our kites and dreamed our dreams. It was here that I first dreamed of becoming Nevada's governor.

That night, my dream came true.

Pandemonium reigned at the headquarters. The Nevada press corps crowded in. All the Bryan clan, Bonnie's sister, her mother, and family were there. My brother and sister and their families were there. And, of course, Leslie and Blair.

I have thought many times about that joyous occasion. Richard Jr. wasn't present. He had just started as a freshman at the College of Idaho, and I didn't want to take him out of the classroom. Much like my boyhood decision not to attend my father's swearing in as a new member of the bar, it was a mistake. Richard Jr. should have been there as well.

Early the next morning I met with Marlene, Keith Lee, and other key advisors at the Sands Hotel Casino's coffee shop, the Garden Room. The campaign was over, and a new administration was about to be born.

CHAPTER 21

The Real Work Begins

In the weeks following my election, my priority was appointing the department heads who would be responsible for implementing my policies. As with any new administration, I was inundated with requests for appointments to positions in state government. Many of those requests came from people who had worked hard for me in my campaign. Expectations were high but sometimes unrealistic. Good people applied for positions for which they lacked the necessary skills to do the job. One of my most unpleasant duties during this period was to meet with those supporters and tell them that I could not appoint them to the positions they sought. There was understandable disappointment and some grumbling. I was hearing feedback: "We've worked hard for him, and he has already forgotten us."

Difficult as it was, I knew the success of my tenure as governor would depend on the people I appointed to head up the major departments of state government. I had to have the right people in the right spots. Bill Bible as budget director was my first appointment, made the day of my election. I spent many hours with Bill as he explained in detail the dire straits of the state's financial position, a $60 million shortfall in the current fiscal year. Among his many recommendations was to accelerate the gross quarterly payment of the state gaming tax to a monthly payment, which would have the effect of adding $25 million to the state's coffers in the first quarter. From his many years in state government, he had become well acquainted with the leaders of the gaming industry, and he recommended that we meet with those leaders before making an announcement of our intentions. Bill and I flew to Las Vegas, met with the leaders, explained the predicament, and they signed off on our proposal. Of course, they were not unmindful that I could have recommended an increase in the gaming tax. In fact, there had been considerable discussion with Bible and other advisors about imposing an additional tax on the state's seven largest casinos. In our conversations, they were referred to as "The Magnificent Seven." Ultimately, we chose not to pursue that course of action.

From my AG staff I appointed Larry Struve as director of the Department of Commerce. As my chief deputy in the attorney general's office, he had been invaluable. Wayne Teglia, my chief investigator in the AG's office, was a good fit to be the director of the Department of Motor Vehicles.

As attorney general, I worked closely with Marlene Lockard. I trusted her judgment and I appreciated the fact that she wouldn't hesitate to express an opinion contrary to my own and others'. I believe one of the major failings of political leaders and leaders in the private sector is to surround themselves with people who are unwilling or afraid to offer an opinion contrary to the prevailing view of other advisors. I have often reflected that I was fortunate to have advisors willing to challenge a proposed course of action I was about to pursue. The unwritten story of my tenure as governor is the press conference I did not hold, the press release I did not issue, the speech I did not give. I included Marlene in my inner circle.

Tim Hay was my legal counsel. He had done an outstanding job for me as a deputy AG. I needed someone with his legal background on my staff. I selected Crystal Reynolds as my personal secretary. She'd come to the AG's office right out of high school. I was impressed with her. She was a quick study, could multitask, and was unflappable. Those were the qualities I would need from someone who was handling my calendar. She managed to juggle all the requests for my time as well as all the requests for appearances at various community events throughout the state. In six years, she never made a mistake in scheduling me.

Jenny DesVaux had done an excellent job for me in the attorney general's Southern Nevada office. She was the natural choice to head up the governor's operations there. Lou Gamage, who had joined my gubernatorial campaign, had impressed me with her organizational talents and would be a solid addition to the governor's team in Southern Nevada.

Sara Besser had done my campaign scheduling. She had been active in Democratic Party politics from the days when Mike O'Callaghan first ran for governor. I appointed her as the executive secretary for the Employee Management Relations Board (EMRB). Her office in Las Vegas was in the same suite of offices as the governor's, and she was always available to help when things got hectic.

Having spent ten years in the state legislature and four years as attorney general had given me the opportunity to observe state officials who ably served many administrations, Republican and Democrat. Roland Westergard was included in that category. He had been president of the ATO fraternity at the University of Nevada when I was a pledge, and I was impressed with his maturity. After college, he spent his career in state government and currently served as director of the Department of Conservation and Natural Resources. I reappointed Westergard to that position. I had met Andy Grose, who was the director of research for the Legislative Counsel Bureau, when I was in the legislature. His experience as an air force reserve officer in coordinating many assignments made him a good pick to serve as my first chief of staff. He would be responsible for coordinating with all department heads in government. Following the 1983 legislative session, when the legislature approved my request to establish two new commissions to reorganize our economic and tourism policies, I asked Grose to be responsible for those programs.

Many talented individuals who served in local government could make a great contribution in similar capacities in state government, I believed. A major obstacle, however, was that salaries in local government were much higher than state government for comparable positions. I successfully recruited two: Pat Pine from Clark County, who would head up the Department of Taxation for me, and Myla Florence, who would head up the Division of Aging Services.

Before completing the rest of my appointments, I was urged to take a few days off and take the family on vacation. I did not want to, but I relented. The argument that carried the day was that Bonnie and the kids deserved it, and they did. They had been part of my political career for virtually their entire lives.

And, so, we went to Hawaii. I wanted to go to the Bishop Museum in Honolulu. The kids wanted to go to Waikiki Beach. They won, I lost. I was wound up pretty tightly and spent most of my time on the phone talking to Marlene, Andy, and Bill.

I didn't last long in paradise and caught a flight back to the mainland after a few days. Returning to the office without a tan, I found the transition going smoothly. List and his staff were very professional. It had to be a difficult time for him. He would be the first incumbent to lose reelection in sixteen years. His daughter Suzanne and my daughter Leslie had become good friends at Carson City High School, and during the campaign the two girls decided that the election was between "our dads." Suzanne indicated to Leslie that she hoped Leslie would get her bedroom at the mansion if I won. It was an act of maturity and friendship between two teenage girls. Their friendship continued, and they later became roommates at Santa Clara University School of Law. Recognizing their dads might be calling to check on their progress at law school, each recorded a separate message, one for Leslie and one for Suzanne. It went something like this: "Hello, this is Leslie. If this is one of our dads calling, we're at the law library." Recalling those times brings a smile to my face.

The integrity of gaming regulation was a major issue in my campaign. I believed that my reputation for integrity played an important role in my election. Paul Bible was the obvious choice to be chairman of the Nevada Gaming Commission. Paul and I had been friends for many years. A highly respected member in the Northern Nevada legal community, Paul was a straight shooter and had played a key role in advising me on gaming issues in the campaign. Before accepting my appointment, Paul made it clear that if I were ever to call him to try to influence his vote that he would immediately tender his resignation. I told Paul he'd never receive such a call from me, and he knew it.

Preserving my reputation for integrity was paramount. In my six years as governor, I never placed a call to a member of the gaming commission or the gaming control board requesting them to vote a certain way on any matter pending before them.

For the chairmanship of the Nevada Gaming Control Board, I appointed Jim Avance, the North Las Vegas chief of police. The third member I selected was Dick Hyte, a certified public accountant with a solid reputation.

History was made with my appointment of Patty Becker as the first woman to serve as a member of the gaming control board. I wanted those in the industry to know that she was not a token appointment, but someone who enjoyed my complete confidence. I scheduled several appointments with leaders of the gaming industry and made a personal introduction. Then I took her to the place I knew everyone would see her—a UNLV Runnin' Rebels home game at the Thomas & Mack Center. The Rebels were the toast of the town and played to capacity crowds. At home games, the movers and shakers of the community sat courtside in what was known as "Gucci Row." Becker was a groundbreaker.

My first crisis occurred on Sunday, the day before I was scheduled to be sworn in as governor. While I was still putting the finishing touches on my inaugural address, Struve called to inform me that he'd just gotten off the phone with Jim Wadhams, a former Department of Commerce director and a prominent lawyer who represented banking and other financial clients. The crisis was with a state-chartered bank in Las Vegas, Mineral State Bank. Wadhams was meeting with several directors of Wells Fargo Bank, then a correspondent bank for Mineral State Bank. Wadhams learned in the meeting that Mineral State Bank had been the victim of a multimillion-dollar check-kiting scheme. Kiting is a form of fraud for the purpose of obtaining credit by issuing or altering a check for which there are insufficient funds. Wells Fargo was no longer going to honor checks drawn on Mineral State Bank accounts and intended to report the scheme to the US Federal Reserve in San Francisco.

A major banking scandal was about to erupt. I knew this was trouble with potentially hundreds of depositors put at risk. I immediately directed Struve to fly to Las Vegas, meet with the bank's board of directors and federal and state regulators to get the lay of the land. Struve learned at that meeting that the federal reserve regulators had additional bad news. Because Mineral State Bank was a state-chartered bank, the federal regulators informed Struve that it was the state's responsibility to work through the crisis. They effectively dropped it in our laps.

No one could recall whether a state-chartered bank in Nevada had ever failed. Struve's research turned up a statute that authorized the state superintendent of banks to take control of a bank that was operating in an unsafe manner. But before Struve could issue a directive to the state superintendent, he had to make sure I had been sworn in as governor. He had no authority to act as director of the Department of Commerce until I was sworn in. A few anxious hours later, after I'd been sworn in, Struve issued the directive and the state superintendent took over control of Mineral State Bank.

In the days that followed, the bank's affairs were wound up. Chaos was avoided, and the depositors were protected. In time, the FBI learned that a half-dozen banks were victimized in the scheme, which had links to organized crime figure Joe Agosto. The investigation led to a fifty-two-count indictment in 1985 and the prosecution of six defendants. Agosto died of a heart attack in 1983.

Struve's decisive action made the difference. Upon returning to Carson City, I told him that he needn't feel guilty about collecting his paycheck that day. It was my way of saying, job well done.

The experience taught me that a governor's job can be a bit like that of an emergency room physician. You're on call 24/7, and you never know when a crisis may arise.

On a freezing January 3 in Carson City on the front steps of the Capitol, Bonnie and I joined other newly elected state officers who were to be sworn in. By tradition, former governors are invited, and Governor List and his wife, Kathy, were present among them. It could not have been easy for them.

I had been on that platform before when I was sworn in as attorney general. But this day was different. The crowd that had gathered wanted to hear from me and learn what I had to say and in what direction I would propose to take the state.

With Bonnie by my side and my hand on a Bible that my parents had given me when I was confirmed, Noel Manoukian, chief justice of the Nevada Supreme Court, administered the oath of office that would make me Nevada's twenty-fifth governor. As I looked out at the crowd estimated at one thousand, I was momentarily emotionally overwhelmed.

There was little time to celebrate. The state was in financial crisis and still reeling from the effects of the recession that had begun two years before. My inaugural address focused on a theme of unity and better days ahead.

Nevada had been in difficult straits before. A severe mining depression in 1890 virtually crippled the state. Mining and agriculture were in depression in the 1920s and 1930s. We would brave these head winds, too.

I reminded my fellow Nevadans, "Triumph over adversity has produced people who do not expect life to be easy. We are not strangers to hardship, rather we have been tempered and strengthened by it. At such times, the best comes forth.

"I am optimistic and confident because I know Nevada's people and the vast reservoir of good will and support which a Nevada governor can call upon."

Two weeks after I'd taken my oath of office as governor, I delivered my first State of the State biennial message to the legislature. The state's budget crisis dominated my address. I did not mince words. I outlined the gravity of the financial crisis: that the state faced a shortfall of $64 million in the current fiscal year. In addition to the year-end revenue shortfall, the state was experiencing a severe cash-flow problem. The state could not make the quarterly payments to local school districts in November. Checks had to be written on a month-to-month basis. A check written for the quarterly amount due would not have cleared the bank.

The legislature had already been helpful in easing the short-term financial crisis by approving my recommendation for the return of a $20 million loaned by the state to the state's retirement system in 1979. I thanked them but informed them that more was required to achieve an adequate cash reserve. Acting on budget director Bill Bible's suggestion, I requested the legislature change the payment of the gross gaming tax, currently paid on a quarterly basis, to a monthly basis, adding $25 million in the current fiscal year. The legislature approved my recommendation.

The difficult part came next. To balance the budget, additional revenues would be needed to protect the needs of our citizens. Then I shared with the legislature my view of the role that state government was required to play in this crisis.

"We have heard that in hard times, business tightens its belt. Government, we are told, should do the same. It is an appealing argument, and indeed when times are tough, government should cut expenses. Government cannot, however, avoid its responsibilities. When times are tough, businesses lose customers. When times are hard, government gains customers, and they are customers who cannot take their business elsewhere! More people are in need of assistance. Medical aid to the indigent increases. Social service agencies in mental health, child abuse and alcohol treatment experience greater demand. . . . When times are tough, government is more in the grip of uncontrollable expenses than is the private sector."

Unpleasant as I knew it would be, I proposed a variety of increased taxes on insurance premiums, liquor and wine, and corporate filing fees. I further requested extending the 5¾ percent tax on gross gaming revenues that was scheduled to sunset on July 1. The most controversial was my proposal of an additional seventy-five-cent increase in the property tax with all revenue earmarked to benefit local schools. I knew these measures would not be greeted with a standing ovation. I had structured my budget both to be balanced and to scale back the sales tax increases imposed in the 1981 session by the tax shift, which I believed were too high.

In my opinion, the key to Nevada's future was ending the state's historical dependency on a single industry. I proposed to harness the synergy that I believed possible by forming a public-private sector partnership. The private sector would bring its entrepreneurial energy to the table. The public sector would provide potential sources of funding and the ability to clear away bureaucratic obstacles. I proposed a reorganized Department of Economic Development and a reorganized "Tourism Department."

Fulfilling a campaign pledge, my first executive order was to make Martin Luther King Jr's birthday a state holiday, and I called upon the legislature to make it a holiday by statute. It was the start of a lengthy process. That year Bonnie and I rode in the King parade through downtown Las Vegas, the excitement in the crowd was emotional and celebratory.

I also proposed bolstering state ethics laws, creating cooling-off periods for members of top regulatory boards and commissions, and reactivating the state's executive ethics commission.

I was unduly optimistic about the 1982 passage of the Nuclear Waste Policy Act. Its provisions included, among other things, a governor's veto and a requirement for a two-thirds vote of the Congress to override a state's veto. I believed Nevada would be treated fairly. I was mistaken. The ink on President Reagan's signature on the bill had hardly dried when states began maneuvering to make sure they were not included in the national search. The nuclear dagger was pointed only in Nevada's direction. I would spend the next seventeen years of my political life fighting against the placement of a high-level nuclear waste dump in Nevada. Even after I retired from the US Senate, I served as chairman of the Nevada Commission on Nuclear Projects.

I also referenced Nevada's hospital costs—41 percent higher than the national average. Current billing practices made it impossible for the patient to understand what cost he or she is being billed for. I proposed legislation to require more easily understood billing practices. It would not be the last time I had occasion to address the legislature on this issue.

For seniors, I urged the establishment of a Nevada commission on aging and promised to convene a governor's conference on aging. The most recent one dated back to 1978.

I concluded on a personal note. I reminded them it had been a quarter of a century since the last governor with prior legislative experience, Charles Russell, had addressed them. I told them that I understood the enormous pressure upon them. I asked them for their help in assisting me in my new role. "Together we can build a stronger Nevada. You have my commitment to work in the spirit of cooperation. I now seek yours."

The challenge ahead was to get the legislature to approve my proposals. Having served in the legislature, I knew how important it was to always have my representative in the legislative building during the session. I knew Marlene Lockard was the right person for the assignment, but no woman had ever represented a governor in that role. When I first broached the idea with some of my key supporters, they cautioned me that some senior members of the legislature who would be important for the success of our legislative program might take offense to a woman lobbying on my behalf and may not accept her.

I considered their counsel but disagreed with their assessment. With Marlene, there was no hidden agenda. Misguided as my legislative agenda may be in the opinion of legislators, I wanted there to be no doubt that this was my agenda. In previous sessions, I had observed those lobbying on the governor's behalf often had a personal agenda as well.

As my supporters had predicted, there was a reluctance to accept her. Some initially refused to meet with her when she requested an appointment, but I felt confident that Marlene would overcome their initial reaction and accept her. And they did. She proved her worth, and by the end of the session it was clear she could hold her own in any discussion with senior members of the legislature.

Bill Bible would play a major role in persuading the legislature to enact my agenda. As my budget director, he was on point in defending my budget proposals. No one on my staff had a better understanding of the legislative process, and no one enjoyed a closer relationship with the legislative leaders of both parties.

Governors before me had sought to bring new business to Nevada. Grant Sawyer had traveled extensively during his administration in the early 1960s, ranging as far away as Europe. Sawyer's contingent sang Nevada's praises in white Stetsons, and the press took notice. For his efforts his critics called him "Gallivanting Grant."

I firmly believed that the state needed to assume a more active role in diversifying Nevada's economy and promoting its tourism industry. During the campaign, I outlined a plan to reorganize the state's economic development effort and tourism promotion. I proposed creating two new commissions: one dedicated to bringing in new industry, and the other to partner with local convention authorities and business groups to enhance a collective effort to promote tourism. The Economic Development Commission would be funded by an additional one-cent-a-gallon tax on jet fuel. An additional 1 percent increase in the room tax would be used to fund tourism statewide, with 5/8ths going to local governments and the rest going to the newly created state Tourism Commission.

As governor, I would appoint six members to each of the two commissions and fill the panels with people experienced in economic development or tourism.

The legislature was supportive of my proposal—with one exception. Bob Cashell, a Democrat and my newly elected lieutenant governor, wanted to be the chairman of both commissions. I did not favor that, in part because I did not trust Cashell, but it was more important to me to get the commission approved.

During my recent election, he talked a good game about supporting me, but was largely unhelpful and even appeared in that full-page newspaper ad urging the reelection of Bob List as governor and Bob Cashell as lieutenant governor. Marlene kept a framed copy of the advertisement in her office for many years. The relationship became even more strained in the early months of my administration when rumors began to circulate that he might be interested in challenging me in four years. Cashell did little to tamp down such talk. In short, he was not a team player.

Cashell launched a charm offensive with senior members of the legislature, flying them in his private plane to Runnin' Rebels basketball games out of state. I had good reason for being uneasy with Cashell being the chairman of the commission.

But I didn't need a crystal ball to know that the legislature was likely to support Cashell. Setting aside personal feelings, my priority was getting the commissions and making sure they were adequately funded. I relented. The legislature enacted my proposals with the Cashell amendment that designates the lieutenant governor to be the chair of the tourism commission. It was an apt reminder, and one not always remembered in modern politics, to paraphrase Voltaire, "Let not the perfect be the enemy of the possible." My personal preferences on the legislation were not more important than the state's greater interest in the good the legislation would accomplish.

Nevada has never been in the vanguard of ethics legislation, and I had long championed ethics issues as a state legislator. As late as 1975, Nevada had no ethical code of conduct or conflict of interest laws. The 1971 legislature passed a resolution to study the issue of conflict of interest and make recommendations to the 1973 legislature. But the 1973 legislature failed to take any action.

The 1975 legislature passed a consolidated ethics bill, but it was so vague that the Nevada Supreme Court declared it unconstitutional the following year. It fell to the 1977 legislature to create a state executive ethics commission that focused on the executive branch of government. As a member of the Nevada Senate, I strongly supported the legislation. During the List administration, no funding was requested for the commission, and it was inactive.

Ethical issues played a significant role in my 1982 gubernatorial campaign, especially in gaming regulation, and I pledged that if elected I would reactivate the state executive ethics commission and request appropriate funding for its operation. In my first State of the State message, I requested appropriate funding to reactivate the commission, and the legislature approved my request.

I also urged the legislature to approve a one-year cooling off period for members of the Nevada Gaming Commission, Nevada Gaming Control Board, and Nevada Public Service Commission before any of its appointees could participate in the industries they had regulated. The legislation ultimately passed in the 1987 session. The legislature also failed to act on several other of my proposals to strengthen campaign contribution reporting and financial disclosures.

Not all my proposals addressing ethical questions were adopted, but the winds of change were blowing. In my tenure as governor, several legislative proposals were enacted, including expanded campaign financial reports, lobbyist registration requirements, and a prohibition on legislators having financial interests in state contracts.

Within state government I made it clear I expected my appointees to adhere to high ethical standards. During my administration, I had to replace a few appointees who failed to live up to that standard.

Shortly after I took office, Larry Struve called me to report a very troubling incident. The housing division is within the Department of Commerce and issues tax-exempt bonds to help fund low-income housing construction. Struve explained that he'd been approached by the lobbyist who represented the securities firm that had been chosen by the previous administration to handle bond transactions for the housing division. The lobbyist handed Struve an envelope containing a substantial check that was characterized as "a belated campaign contribution" for me. Apparently, this had been a long-standing practice in the past. The belated contribution was clearly designed to secure favorable treatment. Struve rejected the overture.

The same lobbyist later approached the head of the housing division with the same attempt to deliver a "belated contribution." That prompted Struve to write a stern letter to the head of the securities firm whose representative had attempted to pass along those contributions and made it clear that such action was improper and would not be tolerated. A new sheriff was in town.

Sometime later I received a call from an attorney who had been active in my gubernatorial campaign bitterly complaining that his client, who was competing for a state contract, had been denied an interview by the Department of Commerce. I called Struve and told him to give the attorney's client an interview, but I also told him he should choose the most qualified applicant. Struve did, and the attorney's client did not get the contract.

During my campaign for governor, I indicated I would propose that the Public Service Commission be expanded by two additional members. The legislature approved my request. I believed the expansion would make it more sensitive to consumer issues. I held a press conference in June announcing my three appointments to the newly expanded commission: Scott Craigie, who had long been active as a senior citizen advocate; Fred Schmidt, who as a deputy in my attorney general's office had handled matters before the Public Service Commission; and Renee Haman-Guild, who had a background in utility issues. The commission had to be balanced by political party with no party having more than three appointees on the five-member board. Haman-Guild was a Republican appointee. She would become the most controversial appointment in my six years as governor.

Shortly after I announced my appointments, Jon Wellinghoff, whom I had appointed as the state's first consumer advocate when I was attorney general, lit the fuse that ignited the controversy. Wellinghoff contended that Haman-Guild had a conflict of interest and could not serve because her father-in-law was a member of the board of directors of Southwest Gas. I was aware that Clark Guild was a director of Southwest Gas, but believed she could recuse herself from voting on all matters related to the utility that came before the commission.

Wellinghoff's criticism spread like a prairie fire, generating public protests and reams of negative newsprint, and I realized she could not continue to serve as a member of the Public Service Commission. It was clearly my mistake. I requested an appointment with her. When she came in to see me, I asked for her resignation, apologizing for my mistake, and assured her that I would find her a new senior-level position in state government. I was somewhat taken aback by her categorical refusal. Public Service Commission members do not serve at the pleasure of the governor who appoints them. They serve for a fixed term. I was stuck between the proverbial rock and a hard place.

The controversy dragged on for weeks and was a distraction from the administration's important agenda. Wellinghoff, who had fired the opening salvo, retreated from the field of battle. I was alone.

I strategized with Bill Bible, Marlene Lockard, and Tim Hay to discuss options that might be available to force her removal. In the meantime, Haman-Guild began waging a campaign to defend her appointment, telling a newspaper reporter that Clark Guild had decided not to appear on behalf of Southwest Gas on any matters before the Public Service Commission. "I don't believe there's a conflict," she said.

More embarrassing news followed. It was reported that her husband had also represented Southwest Gas before the commission. The pressure mounted. One of my team members suggested that because she had lived in California, her party affiliation in that state might prove valuable. That could be significant because under the law there was a limitation on the number of appointees from one political party. Three members were Democrats, and Haman-Guild filled a Republican position. If she had changed her party affiliation to Republican in the previous two years, under the statute she would be ineligible to fill a Republican seat on the commission.

George Crown was dispatched to Sacramento, and in a Eureka moment he discovered that Haman-Guild less than two years earlier had been a registered Democrat. That would provide the basis for our asserting that she could not serve on the Public Service Commission as a Republican.

Hay approached Attorney General Brian McKay, a Republican, to request that he take action to force Haman-Guild's ouster. McKay was ambivalent, and Hay prepared the necessary paperwork, a *writ of quo warranto*, to secure her removal.

Undaunted, in January she requested an opinion from the State Executive Ethics Commission about whether she had a conflict of interest. There was an irony in her request: The commission had been inactive for many years, and I had called on the 1983 legislature to reactivate and properly fund it. They had honored my request, and now it was being tested. The commission concluded that she had an appearance of a conflict of interest because of her family's connections.

Meanwhile, she changed her strategy and went on offense accusing me of treating her unfairly because she was a woman. She asserted that my efforts to have her removed from the commission were made "more acute" because of her gender. In an appearance before a women's group, Haman-Guild contended that as a woman in her position she had to be "virginal." "You have to be perfect, and this is the magnified version of that," she said.

Things came to a head in March. McKay agreed to file a motion to remove her from the Public Service Commission. Tenacious as ever, Haman-Guild in May filed a motion before the court requesting a jury trial. It was a game effort, but District Judge Mike Fondi denied her motion, and two days later it was all over when on May 23 Fondi ruled that she was ineligible to serve. My nightmare was over. I quickly filled the vacancy with Tom Stephens, a Reno Republican, who had been an engineer working with the Nevada National Guard.

Nevada experienced several challenges during my time as governor, but most were teapot tempests compared to the Stardust skimming scandal, which threatened the reputation of the gaming industry and the state's ability to regulate it. During my tenure as attorney general, the Las Vegas casino made national headlines for skimming and its connections to organized crime figures. The casino had new owners, Al Sachs and Herb Tobman, but the same old troubles.

A few weeks before Christmas 1983, I received a call from Paul Bible, my newly appointed chairman of the Nevada Gaming Commission. I could tell by the tone of his voice that it was something urgent that he wanted to talk to me about. He requested a meeting in his Reno office. By coincidence, that evening Bonnie and I were going to Reno to attend a formal Christmas party at the Prospectors' Club. I met with Paul at 5:30 that afternoon. Bonnie, attired in her formal gown, waited in the reception area.

Paul informed me that he had just received a fifty-five-page affi-davit signed by each member of the Nevada Gaming Control Board describing in great detail a skimming operation at the Stardust. The board conducted an investigative hearing and had the licensees sworn and outlined the step-by-step process of the skim. Six weeks later, a board investigator returned to the Stardust and found the skimming operation was continuing. Paul was successful in securing a court order suspending the gaming licenses of Sachs and Tobman. That would effectively close the casino and displace more than two thou-sand Stardust workers a few weeks before Christmas. Fortuitously, when I was attorney general, my chief deputies in the gaming divi-sion, Ray Pike and Phil Pro, had crafted a supervisor regulation, which authorized the gaming commission to suspend a license and appoint a supervisor to run the operation of a casino pending the adjudication of the charges against a licensee. The 1979 legislature confirmed the regulation by statute.

I can't say I was completely taken aback when Paul told me about the skimming operation. During my gubernatorial campaign, there had been all kinds of rumors about the Stardust and its ties to orga-nized crime, and indeed I had returned a $10,000 contribution from the casino company during the campaign.

Paul asked me what I thought. My response: "Paul, I have com-plete confidence in your judgment. If you're satisfied with the evi-dence that you have before you, take the action that needs to be taken." With that, Bonnie and I proceeded to the Prospectors' Club Christmas party.

Paul secured a court order from a judge terminating the license of Sachs and Tobman. The following day, I landed at McCarran International Airport where fixed-base operators were serviced. As I was getting off the plane, Sachs and Tobman were boarding a pri-vate plane heading to Carson City. If looks could kill, I would have been a dead man walking.

Many legal maneuvers followed with an appeal to the Nevada Supreme Court and a filing in US District Court challenging the reg-ulatory efforts. The commission's actions in terminating the license and appointing of the supervisor were upheld. Ultimately, the Boyd Group, a longtime gaming family in Southern Nevada, acquired ownership of the property. Indicative of how small Las Vegas was in those years, I had met Bill Boyd when he was a young attorney starting out in 1962 when I was clerking for Jones, Wiener, and Jones. Now he and his dad, Sam, were major players in the gaming arena in Southern Nevada.

Many legal pitfalls confronted the Nevada Gaming Commission. Bible skillfully navigated through each of the challenges, and the state's position was ultimately validated. How fortunate I was to have Bible as the chairman of the gaming commission handling the Stardust case. It was a textbook example of how a Nevada regulator should handle gaming licensees whose conduct made them unacceptable to operate a casino in the state. Paul Bible is a wonderful example of the dedicated public servants who served the state so well during my term as governor.

Here's another instance in which Paul's insight and quick thinking paid dividends for the state. It involves none other than Donald J. Trump. During my six years as governor, I maintained an open-door policy. I had hundreds of meetings in my Carson City and Las Vegas offices. My meeting with Trump—later the chaos-making forty-fifth president of the United States—was among the most interesting. Strange, but interesting.

The issue that precipitated the meeting was "greenmailing," which was much in the business news then. It worked like this: The greenmailer would target a corporation and proceed to acquire a significant number of shares in the company. The greenmailer would then contact the corporate executives and advise them of his intent to acquire additional shares that would give him control of the company and replace the current management team. The goal was to acquire enough stock in the targeted company to make the threat credible. The greenmailer then would advise the corporate management team that the company could eliminate the threat if it purchased the greenmailer's shares at a premium much higher than the stock's current value.

Rumors had circulated for months that Trump, a darling of the New York tabloids who regularly made the cover of major business magazines, had targeted Bally's hotel-casino and was planning to greenmail the company. He retained a lawyer friend of mine to set up an appointment with me. Trump was not widely known outside of New York financial circles but was an up-and-coming player in Atlantic City, New Jersey, after receiving his gaming license in 1982. By 1986 Trump would acquire the Holiday Inn on the Boardwalk from Harrah's and soon rename it Trump Plaza Hotel and Casino. He loved to see his name in lights and was letting it be known that he planned to enter the Las Vegas gaming market.

On the morning of the appointment, Trump came into my office with his attorney and began at length to explain how he had read a great deal about me and how he had looked forward to meeting me. I may not be the sharpest knife in the drawer, but I can spot a phony a mile away. Trump's introductory comments were so over the top that I was offended. Did he really think I was so stupid that I would believe his effusive praise?

The purpose of the meeting was for him to deny that he had any interest in greenmailing Bally's. Its management knew a lot more than I about Trump's business dealings to be reassured by Trump's denial of any interest in targeting Bally's. Bally's retained Bob McDonald and Don Carano, who headed up one of the largest law firms in Nevada. They were both prominent Reno lawyers and highly respected in the community.

McDonald and Carano contacted Paul Bible, chairman of the Nevada Gaming Commission, and asked if there was anything in the state's casino regulatory structure that would prevent Trump from making a move against Bally's. Bible's answer was no.

Bible suggested there may be a way to stop Trump. New Jersey limited gaming licensees to no more than two gaming properties. Trump's move came at a time Steve Wynn had informed New Jersey officials that he was unhappy with the state's gaming regulatory climate and intended to sell his casino there. If Bally's bought Wynn's New Jersey property, it would own two casinos in that state and Trump would be precluded from acquiring Bally's. When Wynn sold in Atlantic City, he had a bankroll.

The doctrine of unintended consequences was about to come into play. With money from the sale of his New Jersey property, Wynn was able to design, finance, and build the Mirage hotel-casino and in doing so usher in the transformational mega-resort era on the Las Vegas Strip.

Could it be argued that Donald Trump's greenmailing folly is in part responsible for the Strip's modern skyline? I'll leave it to readers to reach their own conclusions.

Early in my first term, I honored a commitment I had made during my gubernatorial campaign to Bob Griffin, my debate coach at the University of Nevada who had also been my father's debate coach back in the 1920s and '30s. I promised him I would go to see Northern Nevada's Black Rock Desert's High Rock Canyon country.

Over the years, Griffin had assembled an impressive group of young debaters who would go on to play major roles in shaping Nevada's future: Alan Bible, a future attorney general and US senator; Bruce Thompson, a US District Court judge; Cliff Young, who served as a congressman, state senator, and Supreme Court justice; and Walter Baring, who served as Nevada's lone representative in the US Congress for many years. Twenty-five years later, Griffin was still the debate coach when Jim Santini and I joined the team. We traveled by car to debates throughout the region from the University of Arizona to the College of the Pacific and Pepperdine, among other destinations. Those descriptions he provided of the areas' flora and fauna were nonstop.

Griffin influenced my life in other ways as well. He helped me better appreciate the beauty and historical significance of Nevada's great outdoors and especially the High Rock Canyon country. He wanted to ensure it was protected for future generations to enjoy. The Black Rock High Rock is in western Humboldt County and northern Washoe County and was part of the Applegate-Lassen Trail, which early pioneers used to travel to northern California and Oregon. Griffin elicited a commitment from me to join him at the Black Rock High Rock Canyon after the election. In the summer 1983, I honored my commitment to him. Roland Westergard of the Department of Conservation and Natural Resources was assigned to organize the trip. I flew to Gerlach, a small town in northern Washoe County. Gerlach is perhaps best known for Bruno's Country Club, a popular Italian restaurant owned by Bruno Selmi that is a favorite with hunters. In addition to Westergard, the group included Andy

Grose, Larry Struve, and Susan Lynn, a member of the Black Rock High Rock advocacy group. We met Griffin and his wife at the site.

The next day we made our way to the High Rock Canyon country, as unchanged as the time when John C. Frémont led an expedition through the region in 1843. In 1846, Jesse Applegate discovered the passage was a safer way to reach Oregon's lush Willamette Valley.

I was captivated. Ruts carved into the canyon floor by emigrant wagon trains were still visible. On the canyon wall, the early pioneers had written in axle grease the name of their party and the date of passage. Those, too, were still legible. It was as pristine the day that I visited as it had been more than one hundred years before, and I understood and appreciated Griffin's concern that posterity would be able to enjoy it as we did.

Several years later as a member of the US Senate, I had an opportunity to do something about it.

Before leaving the Black Rock country, I wanted to pay my respects to Selmi and his regionally famous Bruno's Country Club. I walked in and introduced myself as Governor Bryan. I asked if Bruno was available. A few moments later, he came down the stairs. He was surprised to see me.

"This is the first time a governor has ever come to visit me other than when he was campaigning for office," Bruno said.

Over the years I've found the company of straight-talking Nevadans such as Bruno Selmi far more preferable than listening to the false flattery of any number of out-of-state billionaires.

CHAPTER 22

Life in the Governor's Mansion

The Governor's Mansion is a few blocks from the Capitol at 606 Mountain Street in a west Carson City neighborhood surrounded by other residents. Designed by Reno architect George Ferris in a classical revival, Georgian, and Jeffersonian motif, it was completed in 1909.

I knew from my own legislative experience how valuable the mansion could be in advancing a governor's legislative agenda. I decided the first week of the session to invite individual legislators to dinner, and if available to have their spouses join them. Bonnie was my biggest asset. When receiving the invitation, the initial reaction from many was, "What was the agenda?" They anticipated that dinner might be an arm-twisting session used by me to pressure them to support my legislative program. They were surprised to learn I really just wanted an opportunity to get to know them better. There would be ample time later for arm-twisting.

Lawrence Jacobsen, the Douglas County Republican who would serve in the Assembly and Senate for more than three decades, was already a longtime senior legislative leader in 1983. Jacobsen, accompanied by his wife, Betty, was the first legislator Bonnie and I invited to join us for dinner at the mansion. "Jake," as he was known, confided in me that he had never been invited to the mansion for a private dinner with the governor even though he had been a Republican leader in the legislature for two decades.

Legislators claim to be blasé about getting a personal invitation to the mansion. I also knew the next day they would be quick to tell their colleagues they'd dined with the governor the night before. Bonnie and I enjoyed the dinner meetings, and there were always some pleasant surprises. One of them was Bob Fay, a newly elected assemblyman from Clark County. He sounded like a character from a Damon Runyon short story and looked the part with a lightweight's frame and boxer's pug nose. He hailed from the Lower East Side of Manhattan and had the thick Bowery accent to prove it.

During our dinner conversation, he began to complain about the weather and how it was as cold as the Yukon in Carson City. Mention of the Yukon sparked a conversation. Fay offered that he was fond of the poet of the Yukon, Robert W. Service. I could not have been more surprised. What's more, he knew about Service's work, including my all-time favorite, "The Cremation of Sam McGee," which I had memorized as a high school freshman. Later, during the session, he presented me with a special gift, an early edition of Service's poems. It may be trite, it may be hackneyed, but it did make the point, "Don't judge a book by its cover." I continued the legislative dinners throughout the session.

Those dinners became a tradition during each legislative session throughout my time as governor. I invited the legislative leadership, Democrat and Republican, to the mansion on Monday mornings each week for breakfast to discuss the week's agenda.

One of the unique aspects of life in the Governor's Mansion, which always struck my gubernatorial colleagues around the nation as a bit surreal: mansion help, except for the cook and the mansion coordinator, were all inmates in the state penitentiary. Some who were assigned to the mansion had been convicted of serious felony offenses ranging from murder to grand larceny. From time to time, Bonnie met with the warden and reviewed the prison files of any new inmates scheduled to be assigned to the mansion. She had one rule, hard and fast, she did not want any inmate with a record of sexual offenses to be sent to the mansion. She was always concerned about our daughters, Leslie and Blair.

She cherished her life as Nevada's First Lady. We both agreed the mansion belonged to the people of Nevada, and we made the mansion available on many nights to community organizations to hold meetings. It was a politically ecumenical invitation. On some Saturdays, the Republican Women's Club of Carson City met at the mansion.

Today the mansion features a separate annex to host events, but during my years there the only place available was in the living room.

This did have some impact on our privacy, particularly for our children, who were in high school. On any given evening, I couldn't be sure who might be in the living room having a meeting when I came home. In the back of the mansion was a small family room where we would gather on those evenings when the living room was being used as a meeting venue.

One of the other features that my fellow governors found hard to believe is that we had no security at the mansion. There was no gate to secure access to the property. It was not uncommon for the local paperboy to ring the doorbell and collect from Bonnie or me. One of my favorite stories occurred early one spring evening when Bonnie and I were dining alone. The doorbell rang. At the door was an old friend of mine from my John S. Park and Las Vegas High School days, Howard Leavitt. I hadn't seen him in years.

"Howard," I said, "what are you doing here in Carson City?"

Glancing out of the corner of my eye, I saw a bus in the circular driveway in front of the mansion. Howard explained that he was the coach of the Cheyenne High School baseball team, which was in Carson City participating in a tournament. He told his players that he knew the governor of Nevada.

Howard said to me, "They didn't believe me. So, I came over to prove it to them."

I replied, "Great! Have them come on in!"

The team entered, and I had a nice conversation with each of the players. Howard was beaming, and we all had a good laugh. One of the delights of a Nevada governor in those days, at least for me, was the lack of separation between the person in the mansion and his constituents.

In summertime, many events were held in the backyard of the mansion. It was a place shared by all, and Bonnie and I enjoyed that part of our years in Carson City.

The drop-in visit from a high school baseball team wasn't the only knock at the door that brought a smile. During my campaign, as a Shriner, I promised if elected to invite the entire Reno Shrine Temple to join me at the mansion for breakfast on Nevada Day. I honored my commitment, and each Nevada Day while I served as governor more than one hundred Shriners would arrive for breakfast at the mansion. They started arriving at six o'clock in the morning honking their horns and knocking at the front door, ready for breakfast and raring to go.

We had sold our Las Vegas home and moved to Carson City after my election as attorney general. As governor, I needed to be in Las Vegas frequently. I would need a place to stay.

Initially, Bonnie and I often stayed with our friends, the Peccoles or the Powells, at their home. Recognizing the burden that this created for them, I asked some of my real estate friends who had empty apartment units if I could stay in one of the units when I was in Las Vegas. This worked well for a while, and Bonnie and I frequently moved from one vacant apartment to another. Our migratory residency in Las Vegas ended after Bonnie heard gunshots one evening and became frightened.

A solution was on the horizon. A developer supporter offered us a model home in one of his developments. The only request he made was that I tidied the place up a bit each morning and vacated the model home during the day so that he could show it to prospective purchasers. It was conveniently located near the airport. We kept a change of clothes and our toiletries there, and it really made our commute between Carson City and Las Vegas much easier.

The arrangement went well with one exception. After oversleeping one morning, I was awakened by a real estate salesman showing the house to a prospective buyer. "This is our governor," the salesman said.

When the gubernatorial campaign ended, I thought I would no longer need it. But I decided I did not want to stay at a hotel-casino, and I'd grown accustomed to the model home and its proximity to the airport. A few months later, I noticed that the maintenance at the model home was deteriorating. I didn't pay much attention to it until one day I received a call at the office indicating that I would have to vacate the place. It was a good run, and I had no complaints.

That afternoon, I received a call from Parry Thomas, Southern Nevada's most prominent banker and a man whose name appears atop the Thomas & Mack Center where the UNLV Runnin' Rebels play their home games. Parry was effusive with apologies. Initially I didn't know what he was talking about. And then he said, "Governor, I had no idea we had evicted you."

I said, "Parry, if you needed to foreclose on the property, I understand. No problem with me."

I believe I was the only governor in America who could say, "I was evicted by the local banker." Through the years Parry and I had a good chuckle about it many times.

One of America's fighting men in World War II. As a boy, I proudly wore my Navy lieutenant's uniform for every occasion, including elementary school. Courtesy of the author.

Here I am after being commissioned as a Second Lieutenant in the Army Adjutant General Corps in December 1959 at Fort Benjamin Harrison. Courtesy of the author.

During a tour of China with a contingent of state lawmakers, my Nevada legislative pals Bill Raggio and Mel Close surprised me by taping a campaign sign to the Great Wall. The heavily armed Chinese guards were not amused, but an international incident was averted. Courtesy of the author.

Filing for office was a family affair in 1970 with Bonnie, Richard Jr., Leslie, and Blair and Registrar of Voters Stan Colton doing the swearing in. Courtesy of the author.

As Nevada Attorney General, I met President Jimmy Carter in an event arranged by Vice President Walter Mondale, a former Minnesota AG. Courtesy of the author.

One of our favorite parades traveling in a classic Auburn and wending our way through bucolic Boulder City with our friend Gene Sharratt behind the wheel. Courtesy of the author.

Opening Day in 1983 at the new Cashman Field found me throwing out the first pitch before a capacity crowd and Las Vegas Stars general manager Larry Koentopp looking on. I wish I could say I threw a strike that day, but I can say with certainty that I never stopped pitching for Nevada. Courtesy of the author.

I was honored to bring 30 Nevada military veterans to Arlington National Cemetery to lay a wreath at the Tomb of the Unknown Soldier and pay tribute to the Silver State's many sacrifices for the nation. Courtesy of the author.

Although I normally flew American Airlines during my time in the US Senate, this trip from Washington, DC, to Las Vegas on Air Force One courtesy of President Bill Clinton with my friends and fellow Senators Harry Reid and Montana's Max Baucus on board was a special moment. Courtesy of the author.

When it came to the conservation of Nevada's public lands, the state's Democratic Congressional delegation made a formidable team with Harry Reid in the Senate, Jim Bilbray in the House, and President Clinton as our ally. Courtesy of the author.

The Bryan family during my second term in the Senate. Courtesy of the author.

Here I am with the students of Richard H. Bryan Elementary School and its mascot, a friendly bulldog named Hudson. Courtesy of the author.

At the dedication of a state building named in my honor, I was reminded of the importance of government in the everyday lives of citizens. The Richard H. Bryan Building houses Nevada's Department of Conservation & Natural Resources. That's my friend, Nevada Governor Kenny Guinn, on the left. Courtesy of the author.

Bonnie and I loved a parade no matter the size. This one traveled through downtown Reno and was captured by my old University of Nevada chum and photographer Don Dondero. Courtesy of the author.

RICHARD H. BRYAN

This bronze sculpture by acclaimed artist Benjamin Victor anchors Richard H. Bryan Plaza at my alma mater, the University of Nevada, Reno. As usual, the artist caught me reading *The Sagebrush*, the university's newspaper. Victor's sculpture of Sarah Winnemucca graces the National Statuary Hall in the US Capitol. Courtesy of the author.

CHAPTER 23

Building a Stronger State

Diversification of Nevada's economy had been a centerpiece of my gubernatorial campaign, and restructuring the state's economic diversification programs was my top legislative priority.

Once the legislature adjourned, I scheduled meetings with members of the business community to let them know that my commitment to economic diversification was more than a campaign talking point. I told them I was prepared to go the extra mile with my personal support and to commit all the state's resources available to me as governor to assist them in diversifying Nevada's economy.

The reaction could be summed up in two words: "You will?" As a Democrat who had championed consumer causes as a state legislator, I understood there was a concern from the business community of what they could expect from me. I honestly felt the bar had been set pretty low.

That December, I caught lightning in a jug. I received a call from Pat Fitzgibbons, whom I had known as a Las Vegas insurance adjustor and more recently as an attorney. Fitzgibbons informed me that the financial services giant Citibank was again searching for a new site for a major credit card processing center in the West after the New Mexico Legislature had rejected legislation that would have enabled Citibank to locate there.

Modern technology at the dawn of the computer age made it possible for businesses to operate any place they chose. Financial service businesses, which historically had to be in major centers of commerce, were no longer tethered to Wall Street. Citibank was among the first to recognize that there would be opportunities to operate in states where the costs would be less. Citibank had located a credit card processing center in Sioux Falls, South Dakota, and was pleased with its decision.

When Citibank began casting about for a location in the West, New Mexico was their preferred choice. Legislation, however, would be required with respect to interest caps. New Mexico banks and financial businesses became alarmed at the prospect of having one of the largest financial institutions in the world—as they saw it, an eight-hundred-pound gorilla—enter the market and compete against them. They launched a full-court press and defeated the required legislation.

I quickly concluded that New Mexico's loss might be Nevada's gain. If we could get Citibank to come to Nevada, it would be a game changer for our economic diversification efforts. It also would be immensely helpful in rebutting the perception held by many that Las Vegas was a great place to visit, but no place to locate a business.

As a follow-up to my phone call from Fitzgibbons, I contacted Citibank to see if there indeed was an appetite to consider Nevada. The answer was yes. One thing I had going for me was timing. Scarred by the 1981–82 recession, the business community had embraced as an article of faith the need to diversify Nevada's economy.

My first meeting was with the leadership of the Nevada Development Authority, the organization committed to attracting new business to Southern Nevada. They were receptive. I then arranged a series of meetings with other members of the business community. By coincidence, the legislature had created an interim committee to study the state's banking laws and regulations. I asked the interim committee to review the proposed legislation and get its feedback. As in New Mexico, there were concerns about inviting a financial Goliath to come into the state and compete against them. At a pivotal meeting in Las Vegas with local business leaders, I laid out my case. Citibank was prepared to invest millions of dollars on a facility that would ultimately house a thousand employees. I emphasized that this was an unprecedented opportunity for us to bring not only a new business, but a new kind of business, financial services, that could pave the way for others to follow. I further indicated that I was prepared to call a special session of the state legislature so that Citibank could get legislative changes it needed.

Kenny Guinn rose to speak. He had been a highly respected Clark County School District superintendent and had developed close ties to the business community. He was now the president of Nevada

Savings & Loan. He argued that this was an extraordinary opportunity that should not be missed. Competitive concerns that had doomed Citibank's efforts to locate in New Mexico could be alleviated. The meeting went well. Not all bankers were rhapsodic about the proposal, but a broad consensus of support existed.

The next step was to arrange a meeting with Citibank in New York City. I was scheduled to attend the National Governors Association midwinter meeting in Washington, DC, and I indicated that afterward I could meet with the Citibank team. I invited Nevada Development Authority leaders to join my chief of staff Andy Grose and me. We met in Walter Wriston's office with his team. Wriston was no casual corporate observer. As chairman of Citibank, he had revolutionized the banking industry and grown the company into a $120 billion colossus. The man *The New York Times* called "an unabashed apostle of laissez-faire capitalism" had done his homework. His team had many questions, most of which the Nevada Development Authority members easily answered. Then Wriston raised a question about the availability of electricity that would be needed. For what seemed like an eternity, there was an awkward silence. Then James Cashman III, who was on the board of Nevada Power, answered Wriston's question. At the end, Wriston ushered me into his private office. He'd made his decision.

"Governor," he said, "if you are prepared to call a special session so that we can get legislative changes we need, it's a go."

My response was, "You've got it."

As we left that meeting, a sense of euphoria swept over us. Citibank in Las Vegas—that could usher in a new day for us.

But Citibank had another issue. It did not want to have "Las Vegas" as the mailing address for its Nevada operation. People didn't want to address their credit card payments to "Las Vegas." I understood that and wasn't troubled by it. Mayor Bill Briare of Las Vegas, however, was quite perturbed and was strongly opposed to the use of any other mailing address. For me, the goal was to get Citibank to come to Nevada. This would give us, so to speak, the Good Housekeeping seal of approval we could point to in soliciting other businesses to come to Nevada.

Before issuing a call for a special session of the legislature, I wanted to know what kind of corporate citizen Citibank was in South Dakota.

I called Bill Janklow, the Republican governor of South Dakota. He was one of my more colorful gubernatorial colleagues. During his remarkable sixteen years in office, he gained a reputation for being a straight shooter and telling it as it is. His response: "They did everything we asked them to do." That was the green light that I needed.

Calling a special session of the legislature is not something a governor takes lightly. In the 120 years since Nevada's statehood, only fourteen special sessions had been called. If something goes wrong, it would be politically embarrassing and damaging to a governor. To prevent that, I met with key legislators to get them to sign off. There was some apprehension when it came to interest caps that had to be raised, but they recognized this as a game changer for Nevada. I issued the call for the special session on March 26, and it seemed like smooth sailing ahead.

Then the night before, at a meeting in my office, Charlie Long, Citibank's representative, announced that the company would also require the right to engage in the insurance business in Nevada. That was a deal-breaker. A special session was scheduled for the next morning. I was firm. That was not a part of the deal. My heart pounded as the moments passed. And then Long realized I was immovable. He folded his hand.

The session was on. What Long was trying to do was to squeeze me for an additional potentially lucrative concession for the bank. In 1984, banks were generally prohibited from getting into the insurance and real estate business. To include insurance at that time would have almost certainly caused the legislation to fail.

The next morning, I appeared before the legislature and outlined my proposal. I said in part, "I believe a historic opportunity now exists to strengthen the economy of Nevada. It also sends a clear signal to all companies seeking new locations that Nevada is deeply committed to diversifying its economy and promoting a more favorable business climate."

Once again Larry Struve was on point together with Scott Walshaw, who headed up the financial services division. Struve skillfully navigated the concerns of some legislators and worked out the changes necessary to get doubters to sign on board. The legislation was unanimously passed in the Senate and Assembly. We had done our homework.

Initially, Citibank would construct an $8 million, 125,000-square-foot building on West Sahara Avenue. It would employ about one thousand people. The company also provided several amenities for its employees, including a fitness center, cafeteria, and on-site child-care facility. Citibank ultimately selected "The Lakes," the master-planned community in Las Vegas in which the facility was built, for its mailing address. Under postal regulations, a company with a large enough volume of mail could select any name for its mailing address. On my way to the groundbreaking a few months later, we traveled along an unpaved road on West Sahara. No buildings surrounded it. It was open desert at the farthest end of the city of Las Vegas. Today, although Citibank is gone, The Lakes is no longer at the outer edge of the city. It's surrounded by condos, gated communities, shopping centers, and businesses large and small. It's now in the heart of a metropolitan area that has quadrupled in population.

Momentum was building. Porsche, the German automobile manufacturer, was persuaded to locate its finishing plant and North American headquarters in Reno. As the director of the Department of Commerce, Struve was authorized to issue Industrial Development Revenue Bonds (IDRB), which were tax exempt under federal law. The availability of tax-exempt bonds enabled Porsche to recover much of its costs in relocating to Northern Nevada. That made the move to Reno economically viable.

Other companies would follow. The R. R. Donnelley & Sons Company, one of the nation's largest catalog printing companies, joined other businesses moving to Nevada.

To recognize companies that moved their business operations to Nevada and those Nevada companies that had expanded their operations, I established an annual business appreciation luncheon. Grose organized the event in conjunction with development authorities in Northern and Southern Nevada. Individual companies were spotlighted during the luncheon. Nationally renowned speakers were brought in to address attendees, including Donald Kendall, the president of Pepsi Cola, and Bobby Inman, a retired four-star navy admiral who had generated a lot of excitement as a high-tech guru. The response was overwhelming. Those attending represented a "Who's Who" of Nevada business leaders.

We had made progress, but what was needed was a comprehensive economic development plan. It would be a first for Nevada. Under the leadership of Economic Development Commission director Grose, a comprehensive report was prepared in fourteen months in time to be presented to the 1985 legislature. It included 111 specific recommendations.

I convened two governor's conferences to discuss the economic diversification strategy. More than 375 attendees gathered for the Las Vegas conference to hear from fifty experts and panelists.

In one of my visits to Washington, DC, to attend the midwinter Governors' Conference, I stopped by to visit with Senator Paul Laxalt. He suggested that Nevada consider establishing an office in DC. Other states had done so, and he added that they had benefited from a presence in the nation's capital. Hundreds of billions of dollars in federal contracts are awarded each year to state and local governments and private businesses, but Nevada's absence placed the state at a disadvantage when it came to competing for those contracts. I followed his advice and recommended funding for an office in DC. The legislature approved my request.

Under the newly restructured Economic Development Division, a film office was created. It was a natural fit and long overdue. Nevada with its geographical proximity to Hollywood has had a long history as a film location. In the silent movie era, Las Vegas was used as a location. After World War II, the dazzling neon of Nevada's gambling halls held fascination for tourists and film producers alike. A location outside Reno was used as the backdrop of the 1961 movie *The Misfits*, which starred Clark Gable, Marilyn Monroe, and Montgomery Clift.

In the 1950s, the University of Nevada, with its red brick buildings and mature trees, was sometimes used as a film location when producers were searching for an Ivy League campus setting. In my freshman year, director Philip Dunne and producer Herbert Swope chose the campus for part of their filming of *Hilda Crane*, a romantic drama starring Jean Simmons as a multiple divorcee. The campus was abuzz with the news. Coincidentally, Las Vegan Barbara Knudson played a supporting role in the film. Her father, K. O. Knudson, had been my principal at Fifth Street School, and her younger sister, Karen, had been a kindergarten classmate and was now a classmate at the university.

When the call came out for extras at $25 a day, I was among the first to accept. Unfortunately, my performance ended up on the cutting room floor. Bob Faiss, a fellow student and later a law partner at the Lionel Sawyer & Collins firm, had a speaking part. Bob's memorable words as Jean Simmons and Jean-Pierre Aumont stared lovingly at each other were, "Go ahead and kiss her." I think Bob got $75.

The year before my election as governor, film production in Nevada generated about $5.8 million a year. I was convinced we could do better. I traveled to Hollywood and met with film executives and told them we were open for business and would do everything we could to accommodate their needs.

Shortly after returning from Hollywood, I received a call. A director needed a chase scene on a major highway as part of the film *Starman*, featuring Jeff Bridges. Would I be able to block a highway to facilitate the scene?

"Would I-15 do?" I replied.

"You can block traffic on I-15," came the incredulous response.

"I think so," I said.

With Representative Harry Reid's help in DC, we got the interstate briefly blocked for the scene. Little did I know, my action in assisting a Hollywood studio would lead to my only official visit from the FBI. I received a call from federal agents who requested an interview. They were investigating Chris Karamanos, a university regent who among other business interests operated a catering business that regularly served movie crews on location. He had done the catering for the film crew that had done the chase scene. The FBI wanted to know what kind of a business relationship I had with Karamanos.

"None," I responded. The inference was clear that the investigation of Karamanos involved some of his financial dealings.

I was asked, "Why would you close off an interstate if you had no financial interest with Karamanos?"

I explained that I would have done it for anyone given a similar set of facts. In Nevada, we were trying to bring additional revenue to the state by growing our film industry.

One of my more enjoyable experiences involved Sylvester Stallone, who was in Nevada to shoot the 1987 arm-wrestling-themed movie *Over the Top*. I was asked to arm-wrestle Sylvester for a promotion for the movie. I readily agreed.

Meeting Sylvester, I was shocked by his size and physique. His upper body looked like the original Man Mountain Dean. By comparison, his lower body looked like the ninety-eight-pound weakling depicted in the old Charles Atlas ads. He was quite short as well.

We both had a good time, and when I related my arm-wrestling experience with Sylvester in later years I was invariably asked, who won? My standard reply, with a twinkle in my eye, was that I can't answer that question. Sylvester insisted that I sign a nondisclosure agreement.

Our efforts to promote Nevada as a film location bore fruit. In my last year as governor, the state generated more than $40 million from film production.

Japan emerged as an economic powerhouse in Asia in the 1980s. China was still reeling from the effects of the disastrous Cultural Revolution. Japan's rise on the world stage seemed nothing short of miraculous considering how far it had come. In the immediate aftermath of World War II, Japan flooded the American market with cheap and poorly made consumer goods. "Made in Japan" was the antithesis of quality. That would soon change. A Harvard professor by the name of W. Edwards Deming developed a management model that emphasized quality control. The Japanese embraced it. The United States did not.

For the Japanese, the results were stunning. A second wave of exports to America from Japan set new standards of quality. The Japanese were able to achieve significant market share in industries which had long been dominated by the US: automobiles and consumer products. With their newly found affluence, they made major investments in American real estate from Times Square to Pebble Beach and the Las Vegas Strip. They were largely unsuccessful with their real estate acquisitions primarily because they had paid too much.

Japan had become a major player in the global marketplace. At a meeting of the National Governors Association in Boise, Idaho, I listened to a presentation on the potential benefits of placing a state trade office in Japan and came away impressed. Grose accompanied me on the trip, and at one point I turned to him and said, "Andy, develop an international economic development program including a trade office in Japan that I can submit it to the next session of the legislature." This would be a first for Nevada.

Bob Cashell as lieutenant governor chaired the Economic Development Commission. We had had our differences during my campaign for governor and after we both took office. But his support would be helpful, and he readily agreed. The 1985 legislature approved the budget for a state trade office in Japan.

The purpose of the Japanese trade mission was twofold. It was primarily to encourage Japanese investment in Nevada. Secondarily, it enabled us to pursue and promote export opportunities from Nevada businesses to the Japanese market. Grose, working with the local development authorities throughout the state, organized a delegation of business leaders and scheduled meetings with Japanese businesses who might be interested in locating to Nevada.

Our first stop was Tokyo, where we had several meetings. Following our Tokyo visit, we traveled to Osaka aboard Japan's famous Shinkansen, more commonly known as the bullet train. It was impressive. As we streaked across the country at speeds exceeding 200 miles per hour, I was reminded that at one time the US dominated the world in railroad technology and had more miles of track than the rest of the world combined. It was obvious the Japanese had taken the lead.

After arriving in Osaka, we were headed for a dinner hosted by a Japanese business executive. The dinner was served by geishas in their traditional dress. My personal culinary tastes are pretty simple. You might say I'm a meat-and-potatoes guy. On this night, it was clear we weren't in Nevada anymore.

We were seated for dinner around a large grill. As I glanced to my left, I saw small fish swimming around in clear glass bowls full of water. At that point I knew it would be a night to remember. What I was looking at was the evening's main course. I knew the dreaded moment would soon arrive when I would have to eat the fish or risk offending our gracious hosts and embarrassing the delegation.

The presentation was superb. Each fish was dramatically placed on the grill. In no time, they began to sizzle. Their eyes bulged. I tried to turn away, but as I did I had the sense that those pleading eyes were following me. I was immediately reminded of my experience in Washington, DC, at the Lincoln Memorial, where you look at Lincoln and everywhere you turn his piercing eyes seem to follow you.

My discomfort amused the Nevada delegation. When the time finally arrived, I knew I had no choice. I had to eat the fish, or our hosts would be offended. Fortunately, the fish were small, and I had selected beer when offered a beverage of choice. I swallowed each fish whole and washed it down with large quantities of cold Japanese lager. I survived the meal.

No sooner had dinner ended than someone suggested that tomorrow night we would have the pièce de résistance reserved for visiting dignitaries: the superb Japanese dinner, the Emperors Eel. They described it with great relish and in sickening detail. After I was suitably nauseated, they laughed and let me know they were pulling my leg. Relieved, I laughed along with them.

The following day we headed back to Tokyo, a metropolitan area of thirty million people, and I searched every nook and cranny for a restaurant where I could eat something I recognized. Suddenly, there it was. Up ahead loomed the golden arches. I rushed inside and placed my order. It was the best Big Mac I've ever had.

Our meetings were cordial and positive. Business cards were exchanged, and contacts were made that led to future business development.

After departing Japan we traveled to South Korea, where similar meetings ensued. They also proved productive. We were making inroads that would pay dividends in the years ahead for Nevada.

The newly created Economic Development Commission recommended that a state agency be authorized to issue revenue bonds to support the financing of exports from Nevada. Working with state Senator "Spike" Wilson, Struve was successful in persuading the legislature to establish an export guarantee program. At Struve's request, the legislature also authorized the department to form nonprofit corporations to assist businesses in supporting export programs.

Struve continued a theme that I had sounded early in my administration: forming public and private-sector efforts to enhance Nevada's economic development. He founded the Nevada World Trade Council at the request of private sector groups. More than 350 Nevada firms were involved in exporting.

With the commission and new economic development tools authorized for the Department of Commerce in place, a foundation for the state's economic development programs was laid that would serve Nevada for more than twenty-five years.

Jean Ford, a former state legislator, was engaged in the business of promoting tourism, especially in rural Nevada. She was part of our 1982 campaign team and advised us on potential tourism opportunities for the state. On the day of the primary election, she urged me to attend the annual International Pow Wow trade show at the Las Vegas Convention Center. I was aware that the Las Vegas Convention and Visitors Authority and others in the private sector had been urging the state to play a more active role in promoting tourism in Nevada. The International Pow Wow is the country's largest inbound tourism-generating event, sponsored by the US Travel Association, and brings together government and private-sector tourism leaders from around the world. This event rotates between major destinations. It was an outstanding opportunity to promote our state by having it in Las Vegas. I decided to attend.

Walking down the rows of American destination and travel product exhibits, Jean pointed out Nevada's offering. To be charitable, it was pathetic. In a state whose economy was dependent on tourism, Nevada was annually spending less on promotion than Guam, just $40,000. Jean emphasized that Nevada had many historical and recreational destinations that had never been effectively promoted. That was the genesis of my campaign position paper, "Gaming and So Much More."

To carry out the state's expanded role in promoting tourism, I had asked the legislature to create a state commission appointed by the governor with individuals who had expertise in different aspects of tourism. A director would be responsible for managing the day-to-day activities and coordinating with local governments and private sector initiatives. I appointed Steve Richer, former New Jersey tourism director, to head up the new tourism commission as director.

Nevada was given an opportunity to elevate its profile in the national arena in 1986 by hosting the National Tour Association, which brought America's leading tour operators to the state. These tour companies visited the entire state, and major events were conducted in Reno and Virginia City. The Virginia City event was at the historic Piper's Opera House. In the late 1980s, Louise Zimmer Driggs, great-granddaughter of founder John Piper, and her daughter Carol Piper Marshall, reopened the restored Piper's Opera House. Tennessee Ernie Ford provided the entertainment for our event. During the golden age of the Comstock Lode, Jenny Lind, "the Swedish Nightingale," had performed on the same stage. Bonnie served as the unofficial hostess for that event.

Bonnie continued her engagement in our state tourism efforts. She also traveled to Alice Springs, Australia, to participate in an international camel race. The Aussies reciprocated and brought their dromedaries to a Virginia City camel race.

Despite its many natural wonders, Nevada did not have a national park. A national park in the Great Basin centered on White Pine County's Lehman Caves had been proposed in the 1950s. With support from Senators Alan Bible and Howard Cannon, everything seemed in place for it to happen. But Nevada's lone representative, Walter Baring, at the last minute changed his mind, opposing the national park designation at the request of mining interests.

Three decades later, a new effort was launched. The gestation period had ended, and Nevada's only national park was born. The timing couldn't have been better because the newly created tourism commission had initiated a "Visit USA West" campaign with neighboring states, including Alaska and Hawaii. Bonnie was a founding member of the Great Basin National Park Foundation. Parenthetically, it was the only new national park created during Ronald Reagan's presidency.

As the Japanese economy surged, more and more Japanese tourists were visiting the American West, primarily the Grand Canyon and Hollywood. Las Vegas served only as a day-trip stopover with visitors spending as little as fifteen hours in the city. That was soon to change under Richer's leadership. Nevada was about to be the first state to establish a tourism office in Japan. With collaborative funding from Las Vegas, Reno, and the state, the Japan Center Company, headed by Michio Endo, was contracted to promote Nevada from an office in Tokyo. This effort resulted in an increase in annual visitors from Japan from approximately 50,000 to more than 500,000 with almost all staying multiple nights.

The balance of trade with Japan had become a major political issue. There was a large trade imbalance. Tourism assumed a new role as an export industry. Thousands of Japanese and others from around the world came to America spending freely. That was not only a boost to the local economy, but it eased the widening trade deficit with Japan. The biggest impediment to even more Japanese and other international visitors to both Nevada and the United States was the cumbersome American visa process.

Securing visa waivers was the solution to grow inbound tourism. As chairman of the National Governors Association Subcommittee on Tourism, I was joined by other governors whose states depended heavily on tourism to hold a hearing on this issue with the State Department, which had never been tasked with issuing visa waivers to accommodate tourists. With a little work, we were successful in eliminating that obstacle. Today, the Visa Waiver Program enables the vast majority of visitors to the United States to travel here from those countries which have qualified for the program.

In the previous decade, Nevada had the highest growth rate of senior citizens in the nation. Seniors were an important constituency in my campaigns for governor. I asked my friend from university days Suzanne Ernst and her colleague Myla Florence to prepare a white paper on senior issues. Both Suzanne and Myla had extensive experience in that area.

Once elected, I asked Myla to move to Carson City and become the administrator for the state's Division of Aging Services. Myla was reluctant at first. It would be a big move for her. She had made her home in Las Vegas and would be required to live in Carson City, and she knew no one in Northern Nevada. My response: "Myla, you and Suzanne were the architects of the white paper. I'll be asking the legislature to enact many of the recommendations that you made. Who better than you to be the advocate for these measures? This will be your baby. You'll literally be present at the creation." The opportunity and the challenge proved to be irresistible, and she accepted the appointment.

In my first State of the State message, I outlined my view of the responsibility we had to our seniors. I said in part, "A society is judged by the concern it shows for its older citizens. Our seniors are entitled to dignity, personal safety, and financial security. How we treat our seniors today is our own course for the future. I urge the establishment of a Nevada Commission on Aging."

The legislature approved my request and created the commission.

I was aware that seniors wanted to remain in their homes as long as possible. The current bias in state government favored long-term care delivered at nursing homes. I wanted to change that, and that would be the thrust of my recommendations to the legislature.

I had a series of townhall meetings throughout the state to hear directly from seniors regarding what proposals they needed, what proposals were working, and more importantly, which proposals were not working. I loved the town hall format. It was an energizing experience for me. These were the people whom I was trying to help. They were our jury. Every meeting was a personal reminder of what public service was all about.

Seniors needed support services that would enable them to live at home. Because their issues varied, they needed options: in-home attendant care, respite care, adult day care, homemaker services, and meals on wheels. Some seniors would be unable to live at home and would require institutional care. The private sector needed to join the public sector in providing quality care.

The legislature approved a new category of financial institution, a "thrift company," in 1975. Sid Stern was the driving force for its enactment, and he had wisely enlisted the aid of lobbyist Jim Joyce.

As a member of the State Senate Commerce Committee in 1975, I had supported the legislation. Stern had made a persuasive argument that many of Nevada's smaller communities did not have access to banking services. A thrift company would fill that void by enabling customers to deposit money, earn interest on those deposits, secure loans, and participate in other business ventures. We required a thrift company to post a bond to protect the depositors from any loss. That would eventually prove to be the major flaw in the legislation.

Thrift companies performed well for a decade. They provided financial services to long-neglected communities in Nevada. The companies paid higher interest rates on deposits, and depositors were pleased with their returns.

In the early part of 1985, All-State Thrift, operating in Las Vegas, was in trouble. It had been hit hard by the recession of 1981–82 and had made some questionable investments.

In a desperate attempt to stay afloat, All-State Thrift began paying extraordinary interest—more than 20 percent on customer deposits. The Department of Commerce Financial Institutions Division was forced to take over as operator of All-State Thrift because of its insolvency. More than one thousand depositors, many of them elderly, were at risk. The bond that was required was insufficient to protect depositors. Unfortunately, no depository insurance was required at that time.

Larry Struve and his team at the Department of Commerce went to work searching for solutions. Struve made me aware of the dire situation. We were faced with a dilemma and an anguishing decision. If we made a public announcement of the insolvency of All-State Thrift, we would in all probability ignite a run on all other state-chartered thrifts and many more depositors would be placed at risk. If we didn't go public, unsuspecting depositors would continue to make deposits to an insolvent thrift. It was an agonizing decision as we were grappling for a solution. Struve contacted Stern, the president of the Nevada Association of Thrift Companies, and inquired whether any other companies might be willing to buy All-State Thrift and bail them out. The answer was no.

It was now painfully obvious that a mistake had been made by the 1975 legislature not to require depository insurance. When the financial difficulties at All-State Thrift hit the press, other thrift companies experienced withdrawals. Fortunately, the legislature was in session. At my direction, we sought legislation requiring all thrift companies in Nevada to have depository insurance.

Another failure of the 1975 legislation had to do with insolvency: the only option available was to have the Department of Commerce liquidate the assets of the thrift, guaranteeing that depositors would only get a fraction of their money back. The emergency legislation we requested also provided for additional options to be made available to the Department of Commerce. The legislation allowed the department to seek other financial institutions within the state or outside the state to acquire the distressed institution. By allowing other financial institutions outside the state to acquire the failing institution, the state was opening the door to a limited form of interstate banking—generally prohibited at that time.

No offer to acquire All-State Thrift was received by any other Nevada financial institution. The only bid came from Citibank, which had just entered the Nevada market after the 1984 special session approved its credit card processing center. The new legislation would allow an out-of-state bank to acquire All-State Thrift. The initial reaction to the legislation was negative, resurrecting the concerns of allowing a global banking power such as Citibank to enter the Nevada market and compete with existing financial institutions.

The day after Struve testified, an elderly depositor who had placed his life savings in All-State Thrift, committed suicide. The chairman of the committee who a day before had strongly opposed the proposal withdrew his objection. The bill passed, and Citibank acquired All-State Thrift. The depositors of All-State Thrift, ultimately over a five-year period, got all their money back. Prompt action by Struve and the Department of Commerce team, with help from the legislature, had averted what could have been a financial catastrophe.

CHAPTER 24

With Friends Like These:
The "Screw Nevada Bill"

On March 30, 1983, the US Department of Energy (DOE) conducted a hearing at UNLV's Moyer Student Union to promote the recent passage of the Nuclear Waste Policy Act. I had been Nevada governor for less than three months. At that hearing, I was the first official elected to statewide office to express strong opposition to locating the nuclear waste dump in Nevada.

It was potentially disastrous for the state, and even the slightest accident could be ruinous to the state's tourism-dependent economy. I told the members of DOE's glorified road show that I was "unalterably opposed" to the multibillion-dollar project. It wasn't right for Nevada, a state that doesn't benefit from nuclear energy, to become the nation's radioactive waste dumping ground. "It is unfair in my view for the rest of the nation to ask Nevada in light of its past and present commitment in the nuclear field to assume this new burden," I said.

Many of my fellow elected officials weren't present that day. In time, some of us would combine and make our voice heard. Some, no doubt, were mindful that powerful supporters in organized labor and the business community favored the project, which was being touted as a job creator. In my view, it was and remains a fight for nothing less than Nevada's future. During the 1985 session, the legislature established the Commission on Nuclear Projects and the Agency for Nuclear Projects in reaction to the federal government's interest in placing a high-level radioactive waste facility at Yucca Mountain, about eighty miles northwest of Las Vegas.

Nuclear weapons testing at the Nevada Test Site had been part of the state's history for decades. I had worked there briefly myself and over the years had come to understand the test site's importance to national security and to the development of the state itself. But what the DOE and its allies in the nuclear power industry were planning at Yucca Mountain was something very different.

I was fortunate to have Bob Loux on our team as the head of the Nevada Agency for Nuclear Projects. He was familiar with the technical issues, and his dedication proved invaluable in the fight in the years ahead.

It was clear the DOE was focused on Yucca Mountain even as its officials claimed otherwise. Beyond the health and safety concerns, the dump's potential impact on the state's essential tourism industry was uncertain at best. As I observed in my State of the State address on January 23, 1985, "it could prove disastrous" and made little sense to devote millions to promoting tourism and also stand by while the federal government turned Nevada into a nuclear wasteland.

"If Nevada is to avoid this nuclear stigma we must be united in our opposition to it," I said. "Tonight, I reaffirm my opposition to a nuclear dump in our state and call upon those in positions of leadership who have taken a contrary view to reconsider their position in the best interest of the health, safety, and economic well-being of all Nevadans. The position we take today has the potential to affect Nevadans for centuries."

That session I called for the establishment of a seven-member Commission on Nuclear Projects and placed the governor in the breach to appoint commission members who would embrace the requirement that they be informed on issues and developments involving the disposal of radioactive waste. The commission would also be in charge of formulating the administrative policies of the nuclear agency and its divisions. If we were going to have to go to war to block the Yucca Mountain project, we had to be factually informed and strategically prepared.

It was a tense session with much at stake, and partisanship was on the rise. The 1984 general election returned control of the Assembly to the Republicans. They elected Bill Bilyeu as their Speaker. Early in the '85 legislative session, Bilyeu was fulminating that my administrators would not answer the questions he had posed to them. He was quite vocal about it, and we heard his refrain many times. Bill Bible thought a little humor might ease the tension between the governor's office and the Speaker. It was decided that a member of my staff, Susie Coombs, would dress as a clown and deliver a message to him. Susie found a clown costume with all the regalia. She looked like a professional clown straight from Barnum & Bailey.

And with balloons in one hand and a message for the Speaker in the other, she wended her way over to the legislative building and went to his office. It was quite a scene. Legislators, staffers, and lobbyists followed her to the Speaker's office wondering what this was all about. Susie informed Bilyeu's receptionist that she was there to deliver a message from the governor.

Bilyeu emerged from his office a bit startled. Susie read the following ditty:

> Roses are red,
> *Violets are blue,*
> *I will have my administrators*
> Speak to you.

Laughter echoed down the hallway. Bilyeu was not amused and retreated into his office. But it broke the ice, and we never heard Bilyeu again complain that my administrators would not answer his questions.

Other critics were unlikely to be moved by playful poetry.

My firm opposition to Yucca Mountain started receiving political pushback. Not as expected, from DOE administrators and nuclear industry leaders, but from Republican members of Nevada's congressional delegation. Those of us who feared Nevada's Republican congressional leadership had already fallen under the spell of the DOE's rhetoric and the nuclear power industry's lobbying influence only increased our suspicions after hearing from Senator Paul Laxalt, first-term Senator Chic Hecht, and Representative Barbara Vucanovich in their traditional addresses to the joint session of the legislature in the 1985 session.

Although they pledged unyielding loyalty to Nevadans about the possible placement of high-level nuclear waste in the state, they expressed a surprising comfort with the political process playing out before them and conveyed a message of remaining calm and keeping an open mind while suggesting there could be benefits for Nevada.

It became clear that the target of their speeches wasn't really the debate over Yucca Mountain but my public opposition to the waste dump itself. Whether direct or veiled, they took their shots.

Vucanovich led off on February 11 and admitted to lawmakers that, although she hadn't made up her mind, "the governor and I have a fundamental difference of opinion on this subject. . . . I know the governor and many others in our state do not share my interest in assessing the views of Nevada citizens." She talked about the jobs that would be created and the potential economic benefits of becoming the nation's nuclear waste dumping ground. In her eyes the benefits were great, the dangers negligible.

Then it was Laxalt's turn, and on Valentine's Day he was his usual charming self—until it came time to discuss the proposed waste dump.

"You know, this kind of emotional issue lends itself too often to political posturing and 'knee jerk' reaction. . . . No one can tell me that tourists in Nevada are not going to come to Las Vegas because we're depositing and storing nuclear waste at Yucca Mountain or anywhere else. . . . There are all kinds of work that has to be done before a final determination can be made. I say stay cool."

Last came Hecht, who on April 11 blamed my "anti-nuclear letter" to Secretary of Energy Donald Hodel for a loss of government contracts at the Nevada Test Site. He reminded lawmakers of the longstanding economic relationship Nevada had enjoyed with the military industrial complex. "Every time the governor proclaims 'we've already done enough' his words are a slap in the face in efforts to expand the economic base of this state," Hecht said.

I had been reading the political tea leaves most of my adult life. I was convinced that the Nevada Republican delegation had reached a tacit understanding with the Reagan administration. Laxalt and President Reagan were very close. In my opinion, the Republican delegation had agreed to not forcefully oppose Yucca Mountain, and their comments echoed the position of the Department of Energy.

Hecht's comments opened a new avenue of attack on my forceful opposition to the dump. Nevada's opposition could cost the state existing federal benefits, he claimed. The most sought-after scientific project that the federal government was contemplating at that time was the Superconducting Super Collider, which would require a significant capital construction budget. Although they were a distinct minority, the Nevada proponents of the nuclear dump pressured me to reverse my position because it could cost the state an opportunity to get the super conductor project. The DOE in February dangled the prospect of siting the project in several states. (The project would never be built in the United States.) What the quid pro quo was for Nevada's willingness to accept nuclear waste may never be known, but it was clear Hecht would not be a warrior in the fight against Yucca Mountain.

In the meantime, the DOE had reduced the number of sites to be considered for the repository to three: Deaf Smith County in Texas; Hanford, in Washington; and Yucca Mountain. Representative Jim Bilbray, a freshman Democrat representing Southern Nevada, was summoned to a meeting by House Speaker Jim Wright of Texas and the House majority leader Tom Foley of Washington. As the old-time politicians would describe it, it was a "come to Jesus" meeting. Bilbray was told the dump would not be going to Texas or Washington state and was destined for Yucca Mountain. Bilbray emerged from the meeting lamenting, "We've been screwed."

By the end of the year, Congress had passed legislation that targeted Yucca Mountain exclusively. Their rationale was that it would reduce the costs. Legislation was introduced, which in Nevada would be forever referred to as the "Screw Nevada Bill."

CHAPTER 25

A New Term and New Challenges

The year 1986 meant another election for me. The political landscape had dramatically changed in four years. The economy had come
roaring back from the 1981–82 recession. My economic diversification strategy was working. Citibank in Las Vegas and the headquarters of Porsche in Northern Nevada were the jewels in our economic
crown. Nevada had opened a Washington, DC, office charged with
assisting the state's businesses to get their fair share of government
contracts. We had expanded our horizons, looking to opportunities
in Asia with a trade mission to Japan that led to the opening of a
trade office in Tokyo. The growing number of Japanese tourists visiting the United States presented another opportunity. My industry appreciation luncheons brought hundreds of business leaders
together to celebrate their successes and ours in bringing new businesses to the state. A once-skeptical business community had come
to realize that I was their ally and an advocate for their efforts to
bring new business to Nevada.

Debates are a traditional part of politics, and I felt I'd acquitted myself pretty well over the years, but I was no match for Johnny
Carson. When it came to topical humor, the king of late-night television had few peers.

When outspoken Colorado governor Richard Lamm, during
one of his anti-gambling rants, impugned the morals of Las Vegas's
women by suggesting that one of every eight under age forty-five
was a prostitute, I fired back a strong defense. Carson couldn't resist
using the dust-up between two governors as grist for his nightly
monologue. "What's the difference between a girl in Nevada and a
parrot?" Carson asked his audience of millions. "You can teach a
parrot to say 'no.'"

Then it was Carson's turn to feel the heat. I sent him a letter to
set the record straight. Instead of learning a lesson in sensitivity,

Johnny decided to teach me a lesson by reading my letter on the air and playing it for laughs. I have to admit, he was on his game. And he reminded me not to take on a man who hosts the top late-night television show in the country.

The title of the segment was "Lighten Up, Governor Richard H. Bryan," and it included a flashing marquee. From behind a lectern adorned with the official seal of the State of Nevada, Johnny had more than a little fun at my expense. A sample:

> If it weren't for the state of Nevada, the passengers in a vacationer's car would get six hours less sleep on the drive to Utah.
>
> "Nevada was first settled by early Indian tribes: the Engelberts, the Humperdincks, the Jerrys, the Vales, the Siegfrieds and the Roys. . . . Nevada is a rich state with 38 percent of the nation's gold. Most of that in the teeth of six cocktail waitresses in Reno. . . . Kid Nevada, Dick? Your state flower's the sagebrush." Then, holding up a sample: "What woman wouldn't be thrilled to receive a beautiful bouquet of sagebrush. . . . Nevada is the seventh largest state with the sixth smallest population. Does that tell you anything? . . . Need any more clues? Then what about this? If Nevada is not a great state, then how come it's the only one out of all fifty states that the federal government chose to explode atomic bombs on?

By the end of his seven-minute segment the crowd was in hysterics, and thanks to Johnny Carson I finally had my name in lights. With that I returned to the campaign trail.

In the primary that year I faced Herb Tobman, still bitter after losing his casino license at the Stardust. Suffice to say that primary election night was not a nail-biter.

Lieutenant Governor Bob Cashell had changed his political party to become a Republican, and I saw him as my most likely opponent in the general election. He was well known and well liked in Northern Nevada and as a former university regent had many friends in the education community.

The all-important numbers for a candidate contemplating a challenge to an incumbent are the incumbent's reelection numbers.

Mine were very good. I was no longer viewed as a candidate from Las Vegas but a statewide officeholder. The time I had spent in rural Nevada was now paying dividends. Cashell bowed out.

Secretary of State Patty Cafferata became the Republican standard-bearer for governor. She had an impressive family résumé. Her mother was Representative Barbara Vucanovich, a longtime aide to former senator Paul Laxalt. Vucanovich had become the first woman in Nevada elected to Congress after the 1982 reapportionment created a Northern Nevada congressional district. Her husband, Treat Cafferata, was a prominent Reno physician who had deep roots with the large Italian American community in Northern Nevada.

As the returns came in on election night, I received 72 percent of the votes cast for governor and carried every county. It was an auspicious beginning for a new term. Events in the future would change my political trajectory, but on that night my dream lived on.

I had promised during the 1982 campaign that, if elected, I would by executive order make Martin Luther King Jr's birthday a holiday. It was the first executive order I issued. I had urged the legislature in 1983 to make Martin Luther King Jr's birthday a state holiday by statute. There was considerable resistance, but the legislature that session did approve a bill calling for recognition of King and his accomplishments and encouraged public schools to recognize his importance. I tried again in the 1985 legislative session, but the legislature failed to act on my proposal.

The breakthrough came a session later in 1987 after I proposed a compromise with legislative leaders. I agreed to eliminate one of the two days governors at that time had at their discretion to declare state holidays in exchange for their support in making King's birthday a state holiday. At last King's memory attained the honor it richly deserved.

With state Senator Joe Neal and other leaders in the African American community by my side, I proudly signed the bill in the historic West Las Vegas neighborhood.

As I assumed the office of governor in 1983, Nevada had the highest hospital costs in the nation and the highest percentage of people without health insurance. I instructed Jerry Griepentrog, my director of the Nevada Department of Health and Human Services, to develop more cost-effective proposals to control hospital costs. I was also concerned about the lack of transparency in hospital billing practices, and I proposed legislation in my first State of the State to require clearer billing language. (More than thirty years later, hospital billing costs remain a mystery to many of us.)

Two years later, Nevada still had the highest hospital costs in the nation. I renewed my call for legislative action and asserted in my State of the State message that "every Nevadan, young and old, rich or poor, should have access to quality health care at a reasonable cost." My proposal to the legislature was designed to rely on competitive forces in the marketplace in the hope that it would contain costs. I also urged lawmakers to expand the responsibilities of the State Coordinating Council to include the authority to establish a hospital rate commission no later than July 1, 1987, to review and approve hospital charges.

Unlike most states, private for-profit hospitals dominate the marketplace in Nevada's metropolitan areas. The hospital lobby was one of the most powerful in Carson City, and it was successful in blocking my proposed legislation. Under my unrelenting pressure, I did secure a commitment from the lobbyists that they would hold costs down. In fact, by the time the legislature convened in 1987, not only had hospital profits not declined, but they had also increased to obscene levels. Average daily hospital rates climbed from $910 to $972. The result was Nevada's hospital costs were 70 percent higher than the national average. One chain's 1985 annual report boasted that more profit was made from its Las Vegas hospitals than from its forty-one other hospitals combined.

It was time to take the gloves off.

My 1987 proposals to the legislature included a cap on the maximum amount billed to any person hospitalized in facilities exceeding two hundred beds, limiting per-patient revenues, establishing a hospital rate control commission, and finally a requirement that private for-profit facilities had to accept indigent patients so that the entire burden of medical care for the poor and uninsured didn't fall entirely on the shoulders of the taxpayer-funded Southern Nevada Memorial Hospital (now University Medical Center). Among the more egregious actions of private for-profit hospitals was the dumping of indigent patients on University Medical Center. In the first seven months of 1986, 288 poor people were sent from private hospitals in Las Vegas to the taxpayer-funded UMC.

The legislature scheduled a hearing in a joint session of the Senate and Assembly committees. I was the leadoff witness. I called on Griepentrog to take the lead in working with the legislature, which was under tremendous pressure from lobbyists for private for-profit hospitals. Griepentrog enjoyed the respect of the legislature as an able and experienced public administrator. He assembled a mass of data that supported our contentions about the exorbitant hospital costs. In the complicated and convoluted world of hospital costs, Griepentrog also was able to effectively communicate with lawmakers.

Under the capable leadership of Speaker Joe Dini and Jack Jeffrey, the bill easily passed the Assembly. The state Senate would be more challenging. The hospital lobby was none too subtle, telling legislators that there could be political repercussions for them in the next election if they supported the bill. At the outset, only Joe Neal in the state Senate had agreed to support my proposals. I personally lobbied every senator and made it clear that this was personal for me. I said my support for them in the next election would be based on their support of the hospital legislation. I asked Don Williams, who had produced the very effective commercial during my 1982 gubernatorial campaign calling out Nevada Power for its rate increases, "If it makes you mad, honk." I had Williams bring a film crew to Carson City to record individual senators' votes as they were tallied. The Southern Nevada lawmakers who knew Williams got the message. I didn't get the rate commission I sought, but many of my proposals were included in the bill that was passed.

In 1988, the Legislative Counsel Bureau published a report on the effectiveness of the 1987 legislation to control health-care costs. Revenues for private for-profit hospitals had declined by $25 million. The for-profit hospitals had finally started treating indigent patients, saving taxpayers millions of dollars. It was not a total victory, but we made real progress. In my view, that's what public service is all about.

There were missteps along the way as well. In the 1987 legislative session, Paul May, an assemblyman representing North Las Vegas, authored a bill creating a new Nevada county, Bullfrog County, named for a historic Nevada mining district in the area. It was no coincidence that its boundaries included the site of the proposed high-level nuclear waste dump at Yucca Mountain. Its official purpose was to generate additional state revenue by imposing a tax on all industries, occupations, and professions involved with the transportation and storage of high-level nuclear waste within the county's boundaries. It was of questionable constitutionality. Nevertheless, I signed the bill and appointed three persons to its county commission as required by statute. They were Dave Powell, Mike Melner, and Dorothy Eisenberg.

Before the newly appointed commissioners could meet, a legal challenge was filed and the statute creating Bullfrog County was declared unconstitutional. The names of the commissioners appointed to Nevada's short-lived eighteenth county would stump even the most sophisticated Silver State historian. But for me the creation of the county became an issue in my 1988 campaign for the US Senate against Chic Hecht. He attempted to use my signing of the Bullfrog County legislation to assert that I really wasn't adamantly opposed to the storage of high-level nuclear waste at Yucca Mountain if Nevada could secure benefits.

On May 4, 1988, I was in my Carson City office talking on the phone with Lieutenant Governor Bob Miller, who was at the Bradley Building in Las Vegas. Suddenly, and somewhat abruptly, he interrupted our conversation to tell me he was looking out the window and saw a huge plume of smoke. He added, "It looks like it may be coming from the airport. Something may have happened at the airport."

A short time later he called back to inform me there had been a massive explosion at the Pacific Engineering and Production Company (PEPCON) in Henderson. After hanging up from Miller, I directed Marlene Lockard to get the state plane ready. We immediately flew to Las Vegas to get a first-hand look.

The PEPCON plant manufactured ammonium perchlorate, which is used by the National Aeronautics and Space Administration (NASA) in the space program and the military as an oxidizing agent for solid rocket fuel propulsion. Following the 1986 disaster with the space shuttle *Challenger*, NASA had placed a moratorium on shuttle flights. About 4,500 metric tons of ammonium perchlorate were stored at the Henderson plant. We learned that a fire had started in one of the adjacent buildings where chemicals were being processed, causing an initial explosion, which ignited about 4,000 pounds of ammonium perchlorate. The estimated force of that explosion was between 17 and 41 kilograms of TNT, approximately the impact of a small nuclear device. Other explosions followed, and a fire fueled in part by ammonium perchlorate raged.

The PEPCON plant was leveled, and a marshmallow plant about five hundred feet away was destroyed. Houses two miles from ground zero were knocked off their foundations. The radius of the damage extended up to ten miles. Miraculously, only two employees were killed. It could have been much worse.

Landing in Las Vegas, we were met by my Nevada Highway Patrol driver and immediately proceeded to the blast site. As we approached the PEPCON site, we passed heavily damaged cars along the roadside with their windows blown out as if the explosion had occurred inside the vehicles. I was briefed on the extent of the damage and decided on the spot to active the National Guard to prevent any looting that might occur.

Henderson was established in 1941 to produce magnesium for the war effort. After the war, it continued to grow and was incorporated in 1953. Since that time, it has blossomed into the second-largest city in Nevada. A proud and prosperous community has grown up around those manufacturing plants.

The magnitude of what had happened caused me to ponder: Were there other buildings where highly combustible materials were stored near inhabited areas? Several days later, I created a blue-ribbon commission to be chaired by Lieutenant Governor Miller and to include a panel of distinguished citizens to examine existing safety regulations on the manufacture, storage, and transportation of highly combustible material. I directed the Henderson Commission, as it came to be known, to report back to me within ninety days.

Those appointed to the commission included Clark County Commissioner Bruce Woodbury, who represented the Henderson area; Danny Evans, the president of the local steelworkers union that represented PEPCON employees; the Reverend Caesar Caviglia,

a popular Catholic priest who had served the Henderson community for many years; Gerald Hiatt, a representative of the US Environmental Protection Agency; Mark Fine, the president of a major
land development company in the area; Rex Jordan, the state fire
marshal; and representatives of local government who had knowledge of fire codes and public safety.

The commission had a report on my desk by August 10. It made
several recommendations. Among them, adopting of the latest version of the uniform fire and building codes; requiring regular safety
inspections; increasing penalties for violations of health and safety
codes; labeling of hazardous materials being stored at specific sites
so the emergency responders and public can take appropriate action;
increasing transparency when hazardous materials are transported
on the state's highways and railways. And, finally, there was a recommendation to impose financial responsibility for those who manufacture and store and transport extremely hazardous materials.

The commission's response was favorably received. Miller and
the commission had done a good job. It reinforced my view that it
was important for me to be available whenever a crisis arose that
required my immediate attention. Because of this, I was always ill
at ease whenever I traveled outside the state. My travels were limited to meetings of the National Governors Association, or in pursuit of new business with a state trade mission.

As I took office in 1983, women had been entering the fields of business, government, and other professions in increasing numbers. When
I graduated from law school in 1963, there was only one woman
in our class. Thirty years later, when my daughter Leslie graduated
from law school, dozens of women were in her graduating class. But
many glass ceilings remained to be shattered. Bonnie was active in
several women's organizations, including Junior Mesquite and Junior
League. She met many talented women, not all of whom had a college degree. She had urged me to include them in my campaign for
governor. I heeded her advice and was the beneficiary of their good
work. They joined Jenny DesVaux, Lou Gamage, and Marlene Lockard —the first woman chief of staff in the history of the Nevada Governor's Office—as integral members of our team.

Patty Becker was another one of many outstanding women in my administration. She paved the way for many others, first as my chief deputy in the gaming division when I served as attorney general. Upon my election as governor, I asked her to serve as one of three members of the Nevada Gaming Control Board, the first woman ever to serve in that capacity. It would be another twenty-five years before another woman would be appointed to the board.

Myla Florence, whom I had persuaded to move from Las Vegas to Reno, headed up the Aging Services Division and on senior issues she was the go-to person. Linda Ryan, who had considerable experience in state government, served as the director of the state Office of Community Services.

By the end of my first term as governor, I had appointed more than thirty-five women to major policy positions and dozens more to boards and commissions.

Although there had been a Nevada Women's Conference in 1977, it was not sponsored by any agency of state government. In 1987, that would change. I sponsored the first Governor's Conference for Women. It was a forum for women to discuss the issues, opportunities, and challenges they faced. Among the prominent female speakers was Geraldine Ferraro, the 1984 Democratic nominee for vice president.

Before leaving the Nevada Governor's Office, I had signed into law legislation protecting children from abuse and neglect, family preservation and reunification programs, emergency assistance for families who were unable to provide food and medical care for their children, screening and training programs for foster parents, and establishing grandparent visitation rights. I was proud of what we had accomplished.

Governors often propose major legislative changes that take years to reach fruition. But some things can't wait. I am reminded of the time Marlene came to me and informed me of a fatal accident that had occurred on the Pyramid Highway north of Reno. It was a largely undeveloped stretch of the highway with a residential subdivision on one side and a convenience store on the other. The store represented what lawyers call "an attractive nuisance." Children would rush across the busy highway to buy a soft drink, and one day a youngster was killed. Learning of the tragic event, I went out to the scene of the accident and met with neighborhood families. It was unbelievably sad. I assured them I would do something about it.

I called the Nevada Department of Transportation and was told that there wasn't the requisite number of vehicles traveling on the highway to qualify that stretch of road for a traffic control device. That wasn't good enough. As governor, I was chairman of the state transportation board and directed the department to construct a flashing light that would warn drivers to use caution because pedestrians were present. Within two weeks, it was installed. I couldn't bring back that lost child, but over the years I have thought that maybe my decision had saved another family from enduring that unimaginable heartache.

CHAPTER 26

On the Road

Bonnie loved her life as Nevada's First Lady. She was my not-so-secret weapon. And I must say that when we went on the road together, we were a hard pair to beat.

She adopted several projects as First Lady. One was called "the Bonnie Bryan Brown Bag" program. Accompanied by a pharmacist, she would visit senior living facilities all over the state. The purpose was to advise seniors to discard prescriptions that were out of date and to help them understand the importance of taking their prescriptions at the proper time and in the proper amount. At the time, I didn't think much about that. Now, as an octogenarian, I understand the importance of taking medications at the proper time and in the proper amount. She also initiated a Safe Ride program, which encouraged teenagers who had been drinking to call and get a safe ride home. She also brought the Susan G. Komen Breast Cancer Foundation march to Reno.

I enjoyed the daily policy work of the governor's office, but getting out from behind the desk and into the field generated some of my most cherished memories. From a trip with Bonnie on a Rose Parade float in Pasadena, California, to economic development efforts that took me from Colorado Springs, Colorado, to Tokyo and Seoul, I kept pretty busy.

As a student of military history and former captain in the army reserve, I had made the solemn journey to Arlington National Cemetery several times in my life. While visiting there once, I had noticed that Nevada had no presence in the historic cemetery's Memorial Display Room. As governor, I decided to remedy that.

I invited forty-eight veterans to join me at Arlington to present the Nevada Medal of Valor, the highest honor that can be conferred upon a Nevadan based on his or her heroic military service. Remembering those who had served and those who made the ultimate sacrifice for their country was a stirring experience. I was proud to be joined that day by most of Nevada's congressional delegation, including Senators Paul Laxalt and Chic Hecht, Representative Barbara Vucanovich, and former representative Jim Santini. Former senator Howard Cannon was also there.

Early in my first term, I received a call from Harry Wald, Caesars Palace president, who was part of a group of locals attempting to bring the National Finals Rodeo to Las Vegas. Wald wanted me to throw the weight of the governor's office behind the economic development pitch. It was a way to end the Strip's notorious December doldrums, but it was something of a long shot. The NFR had been in Oklahoma City, Oklahoma, for more than two decades, but nobody parties like Las Vegas. I decided to saddle up for the cause. Braving a snowstorm in Denver, I joined a Nevada delegation consisting of Mayor Bill Briare of Las Vegas and members of the Nevada Development Authority and business community. We prevailed by a single vote of the NFR's leadership.

By 1985, the Strip was transformed in December into a cowboy paradise. December was a dead month no more. Over the next three decades, Las Vegas would generate hundreds of millions of dollars from the event.

But I have to admit my most memorable experiences happened in the Silver State, where Bonnie and I rarely missed a small-town parade. And I do mean small. The annual Hazen Days Parade can't quite match the Rose Parade for grandeur. Back then it averaged only four or five entries. The good people of the town in Churchill County a dozen miles southeast of Fernley made up for it by circling the parade route several times.

Many Nevada politicians hit the rural circuit in an election year. Bonnie and I attended all the traditional events whether I was on the ticket or not. That's how we wound up at the first Treasure Days. It's now called Goldfield Days, and it's a must-see event in central Nevada.

Another favorite of ours was the Virginia City Firemen's Muster with its old-fashioned contest featuring firehouse pumpers operated by units from all over the West Coast and rigs dating back to 1849. During the competition, contestants jumped on their firetrucks, raced down the street against the clock, pulled their hoses, attached them to a hydrant, and aimed streams of water at a cone until it was knocked over. The women went head-to-head in the "hose cart" competition doing the same thing. Asked to judge parade entries at the event one chilly morning, I was handed a shot of brandy as a brace against the cold. Bonnie was there every minute and loved it as much as I did.

One unique event I attended during my tenure as governor didn't draw the largest crowd. It was a high school graduation in Jackpot in northern Elko County. I received many requests to speak at graduations and tried to honor as many as I could, but when I received a request from the school's only graduate, I had to say yes. She'd had her choice to graduate in Wells with a larger contingent of seniors but chose to graduate from the newly created high school in Jackpot. It was a ceremony of one. I couldn't say no.

The event took place at a gambling hall, and the room was jammed with perhaps one hundred family members and citizens. "Pomp and Circumstance" was played, and she entered the room carrying a bouquet of flowers and dressed to the nines in a white gown, white mortarboard, and white high heels. With the poise of a Hollywood actress, confident beyond her years, she gave a wonderful talk. She was proud to be from Jackpot, Nevada, and it showed.

Her graduation was covered by reporters and recorded by television crews from Reno; Idaho Falls, Idaho; and Salt Lake City, Utah. I hope she went on to do great things, but I know she had her day in the sun.

Bonnie and I were proud to be there to witness it. Our days on the road in Nevada were some of the best times of my life.

We didn't know it at the time, but by 1988 our road trips were about to get much longer.

CHAPTER 27

A New Race to Run

The 1987 legislature had been good to me. After my two unsuccessful attempts in the 1983 and 1985 sessions, it approved my proposal to make Martin Luther King Jr's birthday a state holiday and enacted a cooling-off period for members of the Nevada Gaming Control Board, Nevada Gaming Commission, and the Nevada Public Service Commission.

I had carried every county in the 1986 general election. I had the job that I had long sought, and I loved it. Life at 606 Mountain Street was good.

But there were ominous developments in Washington, DC, in the fight to oppose Yucca Mountain. By the end of the year Congress had passed the "Screw Nevada Bill." The nuclear dagger had been plunged into Nevada's heart.

Senator Chic Hecht and I had served together in the Nevada Legislature. We had traveled together to Carson City for legislative sessions. I liked him. As a small businessman, owning a women's apparel store in downtown Las Vegas, he was on the phone constantly trying to manage his business affairs from Carson City. As a sole law practitioner, I could relate to that. I was doing the same thing.

Chic was absolutely enthralled with Paul Laxalt and expressed to me on more than one occasion that he hoped Paul would be the next president of the United States. It was clear that Chic had drunk the nuclear waste Kool-Aid. As Chic's 1988 reelection loomed, he was identified as the most vulnerable United States senator seeking reelection. His 1982 defeat of Howard Cannon, a four-term incumbent, was one of the major political upsets in Nevada history.

Following adjournment of the 1987 legislative session, Senator Harry Reid urged me to run against Chic. Harry was beginning the first of what would be five terms in the US Senate after beating

Santini, who had switched parties, in the 1986 general election. The
seat was previously held by Laxalt, who did not seek re-election. I
told Reid I would take a pass. Serving as a United States senator had
never been on my political agenda. But those who know Reid know
he's persistent. There is no doubt in my mind that he was the catalyst
for several phone calls that followed urging me to get into the race.
John Kerry of Massachusetts headed up the Democratic Senatorial
Campaign Committee (DSCC), and I received several calls from him
urging me to run. Bob Graham, a former governor of Florida and
now a United States senator and someone with whom I enjoyed a
close relationship, was also part of the full-court press to get me to
throw my hat into the ring.

Candidates that the DSCC were trying to recruit were invited to
attend a meeting at Piney Point, Maryland. I reluctantly agreed to
attend. Bonnie joined me. I had run statewide four times, twice for
governor and twice for attorney general, but the Piney Point meeting was an eye-opener for me. Under state law, contributions could
be made by corporations. At the federal level, corporate contributions were prohibited. As a candidate for attorney general and governor, most of my campaign contributions came from Nevadans and
Nevada businesses. As a candidate for the US Senate, I would need
to develop a national donor base. I had none.

At Piney Point, I renewed friendships with former gubernatorial
colleagues Chuck Robb of Virginia and Bob Kerrey of Nebraska, who
were also being recruited by the committee to run for the Senate. I
also met Joe Lieberman, then attorney general of Connecticut, who
was considering a run against incumbent Senator Lowell Weicker.
In that highly charged political environment, my competitive juices
began to flow. I began to waver. The prospect of serving in the US
Senate with former gubernatorial colleagues appealed to me. It was
a long way from home, but all of a sudden I began to think, you
know, this might be an exciting opportunity.

There was an undeniably good reason to run. Nevada's future
was at stake. Harry, in his first year in the US Senate, led the opposition to Yucca Mountain but received little help from Hecht. We
had two senators from Nevada, but only one was prepared to take
up the fight to oppose Yucca Mountain as the site of the nation's
nuclear waste repository.

I was persuaded to have a poll taken. I asked Peter Hart, who had conducted my 1982 gubernatorial poll and knew the state well, to conduct the survey. Hart's polling data were very encouraging, showing I had a comfortable lead over Hecht. With that, I was hooked and reeled into the Senate campaign boat.

In March 1988 with Bonnie, Richard Jr., Leslie, and Blair by my side and four hundred supporters in attendance, I made my official announcement at UNLV. The race was on.

My first move was to assemble my old campaign team. Marlene Lockard would continue to serve as chief of staff in the governor's office, but as in previous campaigns she would be one of my closest strategists. Jenny DesVaux would continue to run the Southern Nevada office. Lou Gamage would take a leave of absence from the governor's office and organize my state fundraising efforts, ably assisted by Jan Nitz. Frank Schreck chaired my finance committee as he had in my gubernatorial campaigns. Jim Nave, whom I had appointed to the Nevada State Athletic Commission, had expanded his range of contacts and played a major role in my fundraising efforts.

Bill Bible agreed to take a leave of absence from the state budget director's office and serve as my campaign manager. Having worked with Bill for six years, I knew how invaluable he would be as my campaign chairman. He proved to be a superb choice.

At Piney Point it was made clear that I would need a fulltime fundraiser in Washington, DC, to connect me with the political action committees that were disposed to contribute to Democratic candidates and individuals within the Beltway who supported Democratic candidates.

As governor I had become acquainted with Wright Andrews, a Washington, DC, lawyer with whom I had worked in assisting one of his clients in opening a credit card processing center in Nevada much like Citibank had done a few years before. I asked Andrews if he knew anyone who could help me with my DC fundraising operation. He urged me to consider Jean Marie Neal, with whom he had worked. Neal knew the Washington players, he said, and had worked on the Hill as a member of South Carolina representative John Spratt's staff. Andrews's suggestion turned into a perfect addition to my campaign heading up my DC fundraising efforts. Daughter Leslie graduated from Arizona State University in December, and she was eager to go to Washington to work with Neal in the fund-raising operation.

Sam Singer was another new addition to our team. He served as our press secretary, and he would be invaluable in the coming months as the campaign turned increasingly nasty. The firm I hired to run my media campaign came highly recommended but did not know Nevada—and that would present several problems as the campaign heated up. In all, it was an impressive campaign team and I felt confident that its members would serve me well in the coming months.

When the campaign began, the polling data had me running far ahead. The campaign recognized, as did I, that these numbers would move only in one direction, showing the race was tightening.

With Neal and Leslie heading up the Washington effort, I had a delicate balancing act. Running the state was a full-time job, but I had to spend time in DC and around the country raising money. I was constantly under pressure from the DSCC to attend more fund-raisers in DC and around the country. Graham was very helpful running interference for me. As a former governor, he understood that my job as governor was both my biggest asset and biggest potential liability. Running the state demanded most of my time. Every time I left the state for fundraising events, I was always fearful that a crisis in the state would require my immediate attention. My absence from the state during a crisis would be very damaging politically. In that regard, I was fortunate to be in the state when the PEPCON explosion occurred on May 4, 1988. My handling of the emergency was well-received.

Leading up to the primary, Senator Hecht was consolidating his Republican base of support. He engaged Ken Reitz, a hard-hitting, no-holds-barred GOP campaign operative. Reitz was tough and creative, as I would soon learn. A poll taken in August for the gaming industry showed me with a fourteen-point lead, which gave me little comfort. I sensed the race was tightening by the day.

On primary election night, I received 80 percent of the vote, a comfortable margin over my opponents Pat M. Fitzpatrick, "Cave Rock" Manny Beals, and former undercard boxer Larry Kepler. Hecht's numbers were strong as well with 82 percent of the Republican vote followed by Larry Scheffler with 8 percent. The low-key primary battle was over.

I accused Hecht of being ineffective in representing Nevada's interests in Washington. Hecht accused me of being out of touch with the state because I was beholden to the big labor bosses. It was pretty tame stuff.

Hecht then attempted to make my signing of the Bullfrog County legislation an issue. He asserted that I wasn't deeply committed to opposing Yucca Mountain if there were benefits that Nevada would receive. The hypocrisy of the charge was evident, as Hecht played virtually no role in opposing the nuclear waste dump.

In September, the campaign reached the boiling point. I hit Hecht on his meek opposition to Yucca Mountain. Hecht tried to link me to the liberal views of Democratic presidential nominee, Massachusetts governor Michael Dukakis. I was placed in an awkward position. I had endorsed Dukakis for president, and my rationale for doing so in part was that he opposed the placement of the high-level nuclear waste dump at Yucca Mountain. He stood with Nevadans, I argued. Then in mid-October, with his hopes of winning Nevada fading, Dukakis pulled the rug out from under me by reversing his position in announcing he supported Congress's decision to locate the nuclear waste dump in Nevada. Jon Ralston, a leading political columnist in Nevada, described it best: "The brutal and expedient political maneuver" had the effect of removing my political safety net.

The Hecht campaign pulled out all the stops with appearances in Nevada by President Reagan and six Republican senators. I was helped when a poll taken by the administrative assistants in each of the US Senate offices was leaked, and Chic was rated that body's "least effective" member.

The campaign had taken on a personal and nasty tone. Personal innuendos were directed at me, and all kinds of spurious allegations were made. Singer attributed these below-the-belt tactics to Reitz, and he released a stack of newsclips linking Reitz to political espionage during the Watergate era. Singer included a quote from Vice President George H. W. Bush, the Republican National Committee chairman in 1973 and now the Republican nominee for president: "I want none of the people involved in that activity ever working on a GOP campaign again." Singer added, "There are dirty fingerprints everywhere. Nevada's gaming industry has a Black Book of unsavory types excluded from gaming establishments. And if Nevada politics had a Black Book, Senator Hecht's campaign would be in it."

Hecht's personal gaffes played into the scenario of how ineffective he was in Washington. He described the nuclear waste dump at Yucca Mountain as the "nuclear suppository." You know, he may have been right, but he hadn't been making an attempt at humor. And when asked who his closest Senate colleague was, he named Oklahoma senator Don Nickles, whom he called "Bob Nickles."

Hecht gained traction with his charge that I was abandoning the state of Nevada by pursuing a run for the US Senate. A clever and effective ad made the point. It depicted firefighters arriving at the scene of a blazing building suddenly laying down their firehoses and abandoning the scene. Hecht had raised a legitimate issue that was potentially very damaging. Fortunately for me, the Hecht campaign shifted its focus to other issues.

But the issue that almost cost me the election was one that had not been on my radar screen. Credit Reitz for his creativity.

The state plane is owned by Nevada Department of Transportation and is used by state highway department personnel to visit road projects throughout Nevada. As governor, I had used the plane for state business, most recently when Marlene and I flew to the site of the PEPCON explosion. NDOT Director Garth Dull and chief pilot John Kielty came to me and said they no longer felt safe flying in the state plane, which was used virtually every week for official business. Their argument for a replacement was compelling and persuasive. I could have never lived with myself if I had not heeded their warning and the plane crashed. The legislature was not in session, and I would need to seek approval of the Interim Finance Committee (IFC) to purchase the aircraft. The IFC is composed of all members, Republican and Democrat, of the Senate Finance and Assembly Ways and Means committees. After listening to the pilot's concerns, the IFC swiftly and unanimously approved the purchase. The process was transparent and above board.

But that didn't prevent Reitz from getting creative. In the closing weeks of the campaign, he produced a television ad that claimed I had used state funds to purchase a plane for my personal use. The claim was so patently false and so preposterous that I thought no one would believe it. Hecht's team then produced a campaign mailer featuring a paper cutout of a plane with a tag line, "You too can have your own plane."

Sara Besser was the first to sound the alarm, reporting to the campaign team that as our volunteers went door to door all everyone was talking about was my purchase of a plane for personal use at state expense. Our campaign consultant said not to worry. But the drumbeat continued, and the campaign offices were flooded with outraged constituents demanding an answer. Our consultants were confident and professional in many ways, but I had frequently during the campaign found we were not on the same page.

That could be attributed to the fact they didn't know Nevada. As an example, as governor I received many invitations to speak at high school graduations throughout the state. The consultants urged me to use those occasions as an opportunity to advance my candidacy. I refused, pointing out that family and friends attending a high school graduation didn't want to hear a political speech. Indeed, I believe they would have been greatly offended.

My numbers went into a free fall. At the next strategy meeting, I demanded that the campaign produce an ad rebutting Hecht's specious commercial and setting the record straight. What I needed, however, in addition was a Republican member of the IFC who had voted to approve the plane's purchase to rebut the ad's falsity.

As she had so many times during my career, in rode Marlene Lockard to the rescue. Lawrence Jacobsen, a Republican who had been Speaker of the Nevada Assembly in 1971 when I served there, was a member of the IFC and had voted to approve the plane's purchase. Jacobsen and I had long enjoyed a close personal relationship since my days at the legislature. When I became governor, he was one of the first legislators I invited to the mansion for a private dinner. Lockard said Jacobsen might be prepared to make a public statement to set the record straight if asked by a member of the press. Jake, as everybody called him, was a staunch Republican, but also an eminently fair man who was clearly bothered by Hecht's false claim. When Marlene asked him, he agreed. And when asked by the press to set the record straight, Jake was true to his word.

Armed with an ad refuting Hecht's misleading commercial and with Jake's statement rebutting his claim, I hoped that the hemorrhaging had stopped. I knew the race would be very close.

In the closing weeks, Bonnie and I and our campaign volunteers were whirling dervishes of activity. We worked day and night. One last debate was scheduled for November 1. Bob Maxson, president of UNLV, was the moderator. Hecht came out swinging and took a cheap shot at Lieutenant Governor Bob Miller, who would become governor if I was elected to the US Senate. Hecht pointed out that Miller, as governor, would appoint members of the gaming control board and the gaming commission and asserted that because of Miller's family history he probably couldn't get approved for a gaming license in his own right.

That did it. It was the proverbial last straw. I exploded. Maxson struggled to keep me under control. Miller had been legal advisor to the Las Vegas Metropolitan Police Department, a justice of the peace, and a two-term district attorney. There had never been the slightest hint of impropriety or unsavory connections on Miller's part.

Tension filled the air on election night at my campaign headquarters in both the north and south. The unanswered question: had we been able to stop Hecht's momentum? We knew it would be close.

Bible was on the phone getting the returns from around the state. And, equally important, he was discovering which precincts had yet to report. There were anxious moments. I was leading early on, but I had been in that position before. Fourteen years earlier in my race for attorney general against Bob List, early returns had favored me. But the late results from the rural counties put List over the top by a few hundred votes.

It seemed like an eternity waiting for the final tally. My early lead held. Bryan: 175,548 votes, 50.21 percent. Hecht: 161,336 votes, 46.14 percent. None of the above: 7,246.

Bonnie and I would be heading East in the new year.

CHAPTER 28

A New Day—and New Challenges

The day after my election, my schedule was clear. Every day I had my schedule printed on a card that I kept in my pocket to remind me of the day's activities. There was nothing on the card on the day following my election. I felt like the proverbial Maytag repairman waiting for a call. Although it would be almost two months before I would officially resign as governor with Bob Miller assuming the office, it was clear that a change of the guard had already taken place. Miller was receiving the calls that I used to get.

My focus had changed as well. My top priority was assembling my US Senate staff. For most members of my Las Vegas and Carson City offices, it was essentially a change of address. Marlene Lockard would become my state director, and most of the people in my Carson City office would move to my Northern Nevada senate office in Reno. The exception was Tim Hay, who wanted to work in the DC office. Newly added to my team was Tom Baker, who would serve as my rural representative based in Carson City. In Southern Nevada, Jenny DesVaux and Sara Besser would head up the office with most of those from the gubernatorial office joining them in the federal building.

Staffing the Senate office in Washington was a different ballgame. My choice as chief of staff was obvious: Jean Marie Neal. We had worked well together during the campaign, and her knowledge of the Washington scene was essential. She had worked in two congressional offices in the House, and she knew the political players and the lay of the land. At the end of each election cycle, because of retirements of members and incumbents losing their bid for reelection, there would be an opportunity to pick up staff members with considerable experience on the Hill. Thanks to her experience in the House, Neal knew many of those people and made several valuable recommendations for my consideration. I traveled to DC, interviewed those she'd recommended, and accepted all of them. Many of those chosen would remain on my staff for my entire twelve-year tenure.

There would be an adjustment as well for Bonnie and me as well. From a family perspective, the timing of my election to the US Senate could not have been better. Richard Jr. was a medical student at the University of Nevada, Reno, and about to begin his residency at the University of Utah. Armed with a degree from Arizona State University and the experience she gained working with Neal during the campaign, Leslie decided to remain in Washington, DC, and work in the office of Herb Kohl, the newly elected Democratic senator from Wisconsin. Blair was a student at the University of Nevada, Reno. Unlike so many members who had to make critical decisions on where they would live based upon the availability of good schools for their children, Bonnie and I were effectively empty nesters. I knew that I wanted to be as close to the US Senate office as possible. We searched the Capitol Hill area and found an apartment within easy walking distance.

I had been informed that I would be appointed to the Commerce Committee and the Banking Committee. Commerce was my first choice, and I had hoped to get on the Armed Services Committee, but no slot was available. I did not fully appreciate at the time how much of my work in my twelve years in the US Senate would occur in the Banking Committee.

On the road to DC with Bonnie, I would stop from time to time and call Neal for updates on any events that may be occurring. In the era before cell phones, I made my calls from a telephone booth. At a stop in West Memphis, Arkansas, I learned from her that Senator Hollings of South Carolina, chairman of the Senate Commerce Committee, had offered me the chairmanship of the consumer subcommittee. Neal was ecstatic, and I quickly accepted his offer. Chairing a major standing subcommittee as a freshman was a real opportunity for me. I knew that seniority was important in the US Senate. What I did not comprehend was just how pervasive seniority is on almost every issue a new member confronts. Seniority would determine where I would sit on the Senate floor, what office space I would occupy, and whether I would get a "hideaway," an office located close to the Senate chamber.

Where I would sit on the Senate floor was the most interesting and amusing theater. Because of the retirement of senators, and incumbents having lost reelection, more senior members had opportunities to select new seats. Popes have been chosen faster than some senators picked their seats. It was a process that took weeks before my turn came to select. There was even a model of the Senate floor maintained in the cloakroom indicating the floor seats available. As incumbent senators came in to look at the model to see if they would like to move to a new position, they would sit in that seat and review the available TV camera angles. Where the House of Representatives makes its decision on member seating in one day, it would be several weeks before it would be my time to select my seat.

It was an auspicious beginning for me, and I was excited to get started.

Two stories dominated the national headlines in my first year. One was the multibillion-dollar collapse of the savings and loan industry closely associated with flamboyant developer Charles Keating Jr.'s Lincoln Savings and Loan. The other was the disastrous grounding of the *Exxon Valdez* oil tanker. Both were political quagmires that would test the mettle of the US Senate. My assignments to the Banking and Commerce Committees placed me in the middle of the action as the Senate tried to craft solutions to two very complex problems.

When the *Exxon Valdez* oil tanker ran aground on March 24, 1989, on Bligh Reef in Alaska's Prince Edward Sound, spilling about eleven million gallons, it was recognized as the largest oil spill in the nation's history and had a devastating environmental impact that was felt all the way to the halls of Congress. In response, legislation that became the Oil Pollution Act of 1990 was drafted and debated, and eventually passed by unanimous vote. It reminded me just how far the nation had come in its response to pollution and environmental issues, and the fact the bill emerged with unanimous consent seems all the more remarkable.

The Lincoln Savings and Loan scandal was another kind of disaster. Keating was the tip of the iceberg, and he emerged as the most notorious figure in the $200 billion savings and loan scandal. Lincoln owed the federal government $3.4 billion when it collapsed in 1989. The bigger story was Keating's attempt to subvert the actions of federal regulators with the assistance of five senators whose careers had benefited substantially from his political largesse. Four were Democrats: Alan Cranston of California, Dennis DeConcini of Arizona, John Glenn of Ohio, and Donald Riegle Jr. of Michigan. The lone Republican was John McCain of Arizona, who like the others had known Keating as a generous political benefactor.

As Federal Savings and Loan Insurance Corporation deputy director William Black put it, "The Senate is a really small club, like the cliché goes. And you really did have one-twentieth of the Senate in one room, called by one guy, who was the biggest crook in the S&L debacle."

After an investigation by the Senate Ethics Committee, Cranston, DeConcini, and Riegle were found to have "substantially and improperly" acted on Keating's behalf. Cranston was formally reprimanded. The Democrats were playing a little politics by keeping McCain as the only Republican on the list of senators under investigation. Ultimately, it was determined that McCain and Glenn were minimally involved and had only used "poor judgment." They stayed the course, running and winning reelection.

Fallout from the savings and loan failures led to hearings and the eventual drafting of legislation that resulted in the Financial Institutions Reform, Recovery, and Enforcement Act of 1989 (FIRREA). It established the Resolution Trust Corporation, which closed hundreds of insolvent thrifts, distributed insurance funds to depositors, and added substantial new regulation and oversight. After much negotiation, and after a multibillion-dollar bailout, FIRREA set the new regulatory standard for the savings and loan industry. Keating's name would live in infamy.

My first year in the Senate would be riddled with reminders that even the mightiest of public players have feet of clay. Senators fended off the Keating scandal, but it was a challenging year in the House, too. Powerful House Speaker Jim Wright had been under investigation since the previous year by the House Ethics Committee over compensation his wife received in association with bulk purchases of his own political memoir. Despite his thirty-four-year tenure and all his congressional clout, Wright's fall from grace was precipitous. He submitted his resignation as Speaker on May 31 and resigned his seat in Congress on June 30.

Later that same year, I was part of an ad hoc committee that reviewed the evidence of perjury and conspiracy to obtain a bribe against US District Judge Alcee Hastings of Florida. Although he was acquitted of criminal charges, in October the Senate voted to impeach him and remove him from office. He'd later return as a member of the House of Representatives and served multiple terms. Less than a month later, the Senate voted to convict US District Judge Walter Nixon of Mississippi of lying under oath before a grand jury. He was removed from office.

As chairman of the Consumer Affairs Subcommittee, I was able to drive the agenda. I focused on auto safety through oversight of the National Transportation and Safety Board (NTSB) and improving fuel economy standards. My lifelong passion for automobiles, still very much alive, manifested itself during my advocacy for improving safety through mandatory airbags and side-impact standards. I also worked to increase automobile gas mileage through the implementation of the Corporate Average Fuel Economy (CAFE) standards. Challenging the auto industry lobby also gave me an introduction to real political pushback.

It didn't take long to separate allies from adversaries. One of my first hearings as chairman was with Secretary of Transportation Samuel Skinner of Illinois, who testified before the committee on the issue of fuel economy standards. Suffice to say we were not on the same page. I made it clear to him the importance of substantially increasing the fuel efficiency standards for the auto industry. It would have been considered bold at any time given the industry's undeniable clout, but it was audacious for a freshman senator to be looking for a fight with the nation's car manufacturing giants.

I hadn't invented CAFE. Congress enacted the first CAFE standards in 1975 following the 1973 Arab oil embargo and the quadrupling of gasoline prices by the Organization of Petroleum Exporting Countries (OPEC). Americans waited in lines stretching around the block to fill their gas tanks. Unlike Japan, American car manufacturers had no fuel-efficient vehicles and wanted none. Ford officials in testimony claimed without evidence that the proposed standards would require everyone in America to drive a car smaller than the company's Pinto, its smallest vehicle that year. By 1978, average miles per gallon (mpg) for new automobiles was set at 18 with graduated increases by the end of the decade before a freeze during the Reagan years.

I proposed to raise the 27-mpg standard then in place with gradual increases going forward.

My critics howled like scalded dogs.

I was hit from every side. The Bush administration hated it. The automobile manufacturers pronounced me a danger to the industry. Leaders of the United Auto Workers Union were also incensed, asserting I was trying to kill thousands of American jobs.

Actually, the failure of the American auto industry to produce fuel-efficient vehicles left the door open for Japanese automakers who had fuel-efficient vehicles to enter the US market and capture a significant share of that market, which they continue to enjoy today.

The petroleum industry weighed in, in part through the conservative think tank The Heritage Foundation. The foundation's business analyst William Laffer III asserted my Motor Vehicle Fuel Efficiency Act of 1990, co-authored with Washington Republican Slade Gorton, "would force Americans truly to pay in blood" by forcing them to make automobiles lighter to comply with increased fuel economy standards. Among the falsehoods floated was the idea that a lighter vehicle was necessarily more unsafe than a heavier one. The facts weren't well served by the government's own grim illustration of a crash test between a heavy vehicle and a light one.

The opposition's estimates of additional highway deaths ranged wildly from 3,900 more per year to a whopping 8,600. It was dramatic and misleading, but their media megaphone was deafening. I couldn't expect to receive much help from the National Highway Traffic Safety Administration, whose bureaucracy-laden rule-making process "has a longer gestation period than anything known in the laws of nature."

At one point, a front group took the attack to my constituents with a television ad targeting ranchers and farmers claiming that increasing CAFE standards would deprive them of the equipment they needed to operate. It was absurd, but I had learned over the years that there was real danger in leaving those seemingly wild allegations go unanswered.

Ford Motor Company executive "Red" Foley was among my chief critics, charging before the Commerce Committee that the future of the auto industry was at stake should my bill see the light of day. It was nonsense, but he carried a big stick, had the full support of senators in key states, and for a change had support from the United Autoworkers Union. Opening a line of communication would not be easy.

As luck would have it, Foley also played tennis.

That's where Andy Vermilye came in. In addition to his very effective staff work, Andy also played a more than competitive game of tennis. Foley, an avid player, wasn't about to accept a serve from me. Andy was our only hope.

"Go play tennis with him," I said. He did, and it helped melt the ice.

So did my visit to Detroit, the proverbial lion's den of the auto industry. The reception and factory tour with industry executives and union officials did not change anyone's mind, but by the end of the tour they knew that I knew what I was talking about. To that extent, it was a productive exchange.

I then met with the Automotive Press Association at the Detroit Press Club. The reception was only slightly warmer. I tried to keep my sense of humor, quipping, "This will be the last free meal I ever get in Detroit." I was later described by a *Detroit Free Press* reporter as "the industry's walking anxiety attack."

What I had not expected was a real cheap shot from one of the journalists covering the meeting. In a later column, he excoriated me for having arrived at the meeting in one of Detroit's gas guzzlers. In effect, he accused me of being a hypocrite. I did not select the vehicle that brought me to the meeting, of course, and the reporter knew that.

I was not a shrinking violet and had done my homework. I came to every hearing prepared to do battle and was seldom disappointed. In one hearing, after yet another hand-wringing soliloquy about the burden increased fuel efficiency would have on the industry, I replied, "The most striking thing about these claims is their similarity to claims made in the 1970s, when the industry opposed the current law. History has demonstrated that the fears were misplaced."

The auto and petroleum industries had no shortage of friends in Washington. Chief among them was Senator J. Bennett Johnston of Louisiana, chairman of the Energy Committee. Nevadans would long remember the Democrat as a driving force behind the "Screw Nevada Bill" that limited the search for the location of the nation's high-level nuclear waste dump to Yucca Mountain. While my CAFE proposal was an aggressive, expert-driven attempt to make a difference in fuel efficiency at a time American automakers were lagging behind foreign manufacturers, Johnston's version could have been written by the publicity departments at General Motors, Exxon, and the Bush administration. It proposed a slight increase in fuel efficiency standards, but also opened Alaska's Arctic National Wildlife Refuge to oil and gas exploration. Johnston made it clear he was trying to block my bill. What he really wanted was to hand the petroleum industry a key to the 19-million-acre, 30,000-square-mile wildlife refuge.

The showdown came on Johnston's home court on May 15, 1991, in a hearing before the Energy Committee. After much debate both legislative versions were defeated, but I stood on the right side of history and progress. Energy policy in America was continuing to evolve, and the rejection of the Johnston bill with its attempt to permit oil drilling in the Arctic National Wildlife Refuge was a nonstarter.

Environmental lobbyists were heartened by their victory, which dashed the Bush administration's plan to greatly expand oil and gas exploration on public lands. When Johnston's version failed 13–7, Sierra Club lobbyist Daniel Becker called it a "train wreck."

As I feared, my bill lost 15–5. Looking back, I have to smile with a sense of nostalgia: Those votes were bipartisan. There wasn't the rabid political polarization that exists in today's Senate.

To my disappointment, the bill didn't make it to the floor in 1991. But taking on the big car companies put me in the thick of things about automobile safety and fuel economy. It helped introduce me to the national press, which paid dividends when it came to getting out my message and informing the public. I continued to push for greater auto industry fuel efficiency standards throughout my time in the US Senate. Gradually, others came to share my appreciation that automobiles could achieve better mileage without sacrificing safety.

The debate is still alive today. With the threat of global warming and the role that exhaust emissions play in it, the industry finds itself gradually transitioning toward even greater fuel efficiency and electric vehicles.

When it came to automobile safety, few innovations rivaled seatbelts and front and side airbags for effectiveness. As early as 1966, the year Congress passed the National Traffic and Motor Vehicle Safety Act, it was estimated that seatbelts would save many thousands of lives—as long as you could get people to wear them. Change came only gradually over the next decade, and I take pride in my strong advocacy on this issue.

Airbags were another innovation that was a long time coming. The technology was available in the early 1970s, and the ensuing years saw them increasingly installed by car companies. It wasn't until 1991 that federal law mandated them, and the actual implementation didn't go into effect until 1997 to give the companies time to convert their factories. But the changes undoubtedly saved many lives.

Tenacity has its rewards.

CHAPTER 29

Operation Desert Storm

After much saber rattling, Iraq invaded Kuwait on August 2, 1990. The tiny emirate nation was oil-rich and possessed a deep-water port, but it was no match for the military might of Iraq and President Saddam Hussein's forces.

President George H. W. Bush's response to the invasion was patient and skillful. He let the wheels of the United Nations turn as he prepared for a military response. The ensuing weeks would see the massive Operation Desert Shield, the US troop buildup of more than 500,000 in the Persian Gulf and Saudi Arabia as the United Nations condemned Iraq's brazen act of aggression. Bush effectively assembled a coalition of Arab leaders to join the United States.

Congressional backing of Bush was no slam dunk. Democrats were very uneasy about giving Bush a resolution of support to take military action. A United Nations resolution condemning the invasion set a deadline for Saddam to retreat by January 15, 1991, or face military action by a building coalition.

At one point late in the year, Senate Majority Leader George Mitchell asked a small delegation to go to the Middle East and meet with King Fahd of Saudi Arabia, President Hosni Mubarak of Egypt, and Prime Minister Yitzhak Shamir of Israel. I was a member of the delegation that included Bob Graham, Chuck Robb, Joe Lieberman, and Herb Kohl. Except for Graham, we were all newly elected. We were all viewed as more moderate Democrats. I also suspect Mitchell thought that by going over there we would better understand just how complicated things were and would be disinclined to support the president's intervention.

We arrived at Riyadh late in the evening at King Fahd's private airport. We were the only people in the terminal. The king received us at almost midnight. He was very supportive of the intervention to repel Saddam Hussein's aggression.

Next, we traveled to Israel, where we met Prime Minister Shamir, who was also supportive of the coalition effort. Under pressure from President Bush, who was working to keep together the Arab coalition, Shamir did not respond militarily against Saddam's Scud missile attacks.

Our last meeting was with President Mubarak, and it was the most interesting of the three. During our discussion with the Egyptian president, I asked Mubarak: After our forces push Iraqi troops out of Kuwait, should we go all the way to Baghdad and take out Saddam?

It was clear from his answer that the coalition was limited to support repelling Iraqi aggression, not regime change.

We were transported to a massive forward supply base the following day. As far as the eye could see, men and materiel were everywhere. It looked like a giant outdoor warehouse: row after row of ammunition and supplies were stacked ten feet high. Cargo planes were landing one after another with more supplies, more troops in staggering numbers.

Like a modern-day Lawrence of Arabia, we went off across the desert in Humvees leading out to where army General Norman Schwarzkopf had his headquarters. As the head of the United States Central Command, he led all coalition forces in the Gulf War. We were ushered into a tent where the general had arranged several large maps that laid out his battle plan day by day. As they used to say when I was in the army, the general had real command presence. His briefing was persuasive, and we were impressed with the strategy that he'd outlined.

As the days passed and the end of the year approached, it became clear that Bush was willing to act on his own. After the new year, Senator Tom Harkin, a Democrat of Iowa, upset the apple cart and forced the US Senate to vote on a resolution that supported US intervention. A marathon debate on the floor on January 11 ensued with Harkin speaking at great length against the resolution. There were strong feelings on both sides. Decorated Vietnam War veterans John McCain of Arizona and John Kerry of Massachusetts offered experienced but opposing views.

Republican John Warner led the group of cosponsors that included twenty-nine Republicans and five Democrats. Senate Joint Resolution

2, the Iraq Resolution, was approved on January 12, 1991, by a narrow vote, 52–47.

Although all but two Republicans voted for it, only a handful of Democrats supported it—just ten of the fifty-six seated. Many Democrats refused to stand with the president, some believing that economic and political sanctions against Iraq hadn't been given enough time to work.

We could not know what military action would bring, but I believed we could not stand by and let a despot go unchecked. I reminded my colleagues that the armies of Saddam Hussein had marched twice in the previous decade across international borders and invaded peaceful neighboring nations. The invasion of Iran had cost thousands of lives. And now he had rolled into Kuwait.

"We have seen such lawless conduct before in this century," I said. "In the stormy decade of the Great Depression, Americans watched as Nazi Germany occupied the Rhineland. The world looked the other way, believing that this would satisfy Adolf Hitler."

But there's no appeasing a despot.

I also noted the reality of America's dependence on foreign oil and reminded all present that those long gas lines of the mid-1970s were not so long ago. In my estimation, we had to stand with President Bush.

"We can wish for a utopian world . . . but as Saddam Hussein has cruelly reminded us, it is a wish as yet unfulfilled," I said. "As President Bush moves into this critical phase, we should stand united. The signal to Baghdad from Washington should be firm, and our thoughts should be of our troops in the desert."

I was in my office when the war started. A staff member bolted in and shouted, "It's begun!" Like most Americans at that moment, I turned on the television in the office and watched as explosions filled the screen. The voices of anxious anchors tried to explain what we all were seeing: the American response to Iraqi aggression. In all, forty-eight nations joined the coalition with the United States, United Kingdom, Australia, and Poland contributing troops to the invasion force. Coalition aircraft neutralized Iraqi jet fighters and pummeled targets in and around Baghdad.

Success of Operation Desert Storm was immediate. Iraq paid a terrible price for Saddam's aggression. By the end of February, the

Iraq army had been swept out of Kuwait. Thousands of Iraqi troops surrendered. All the coalition's preparation had paid off.

President Bush declared a ceasefire on February 28. By April 6, after suffering one of the most one-sided defeats in military history, Iraq agreed to the terms set forth by the United Nations Security Council.

Bush was a class act. He directed three-star General Brent Scowcroft, his national security advisor, to invite the Democrats who had voted for the resolution to the White House for a private dinner with him and First Lady Barbara Bush. "You gentlemen are real patriots," Scowcroft said. "And the President appreciates your support."

The invitation was to each of us and our spouses. I expected that we would have dinner with the president and Mrs. Bush in one of the dining rooms downstairs. I was surprised when the president led us upstairs to the family's private quarters. The president's style was low-key and casual, as was Mrs. Bush's. At one point in the evening, Bonnie needed to excuse herself to use the bathroom. The president said, gesturing, "Use Barbara's bathroom."

Bush was more moderate than Ronald Reagan, but the tide was clearly running to the right in the Republican Party. Bush couldn't announce that he was pro-choice, although I believe he was, and Barbara certainly was. He had to tone down several of his views, but that's politics.

In the Senate, Democrats who had voted against the resolution tried to walk a political tightrope, offering a measure that put them on record supporting the president and the troops after they'd failed to support the resolution authorizing military action. It was an extremely thin line.

Senator Sam Nunn of Georgia, the chairman of the Committee on Armed Services and a conservative Democrat and defense expert, was one of the Democrats who voted against the resolution. Nunn came to greatly regret his vote. As he neared retirement in 1996, Nunn told the *Washington Post*, "I think I was wrong on that. I think I was wrong because if I had voted that way, it would have given a more solid vote for the authorization of the war, which I thought was justified." I suspect others felt the same way.

History tells us that the trouble with Saddam Hussein didn't end there, and many still speculate what might have happened had we chosen to remove him from power. Bush received much criticism for not moving on to Baghdad and taking Saddam out. The Iraq army was in full retreat. From a military perspective, it would not have been difficult. Bush, to his credit, recognized that the coalition he had put together was premised only on repelling Saddam's aggression. He did not want to do anything that would jeopardize Arab leaders' participation in the coalition. I believe the verdict of history will be supportive of Bush's decision.

CHAPTER 30

The Clarence Thomas Hearing

I certainly didn't agree with every move the first President Bush made. Far from it. His decision to nominate Clarence Thomas to the United States Supreme Court is a prime example.

President George H. W. Bush's July 1, 1991, nomination of Clarence Thomas, a US Court of Appeals judge for the District of Columbia Circuit, to replace retiring US Supreme Court justice Thurgood Marshall sent shockwaves through the nation's civil rights organizations. If confirmed by the Senate, Thomas would become just the second Black justice to serve on the highest court in the land, but his staunchly conservative legal views were thought to be anathema to the long struggle for racial equality in the United States.

Thomas was a forty-three-year-old darling of the Federalist Society with barely more than a year on the federal bench. Elections have consequences, and the previous year Bush had nominated David Souter to replace retiring Justice William Brennan. Now it was the legendary Marshall's time to hang up his robe, and Thomas was headed for the confirmation process.

Souter was a legal scholar, but his balanced philosophy from the bench was a disappointment to conservatives. The Federalist Society led the effort to ensure a true conservative was selected to replace Marshall, and Thomas was their man despite his unremarkable legal scholarship. His personal story was another matter. Born in Pin Point, Georgia, Thomas overcame poverty and prejudice to reach the threshold of the Supreme Court. Now all he had to do was cross the finish line.

His libertarian views of the role of government alarmed many. He was considered an extreme idealogue by some legal authorities. Environmentalists noticed his former representation of Monsanto Corporation. Liberals were disturbed by his opposition to affirmative action, his record as assistant secretary for civil rights at the US

Department of Education, and his tenure as head of the federal Equal Employment Opportunity Commission.

Thomas enjoyed the distinct advantage of having his mentor and advocate, the highly respected Republican Senator John "Jack" Danforth of Missouri in his corner, guiding the nomination and defending his record. That became especially important after law professor Anita Hill, who had been supervised by Thomas at the Education Department and Equal Employment Opportunity Commission, stepped forward to accuse Thomas of multiple instances of sexual harassment and unwanted advances. Thomas denied Hill's claims and later called the grilling he experienced a "high-tech lynching."

Republicans aggressively supported the Thomas nomination to the point of harassing Hill under the heat of a nationally televised spotlight. The Democrats, meanwhile, appeared to be playing from an obsolete political playbook. Where they ought to have defended Hill's highly credible story, they were content to remain in the traditional role of objective jurors while the Republicans had a field day as all-out advocates. Hill simply did not receive the protection she deserved, and if the confirmation hearing were held today her treatment would be very different. That's little solace to her, but I believe history will remember the Thomas hearing as another important turning point in the increasingly partisan politics in Congress.

I was greatly troubled by Hill's allegations. I thought she was a credible witness. Long before the vote, I had made up my mind against the Thomas confirmation.

On the morning of the confirmation vote, Senator Reid called and wanted to meet with me. He had not yet made up his mind on how to vote on the Thomas confirmation. During our discussion he shared with me that Landra, his wife, had urged him to vote against the Thomas confirmation. By the end of our discussion, Reid concluded he would also vote against Thomas.

After further investigation of Hill's allegations and almost one hundred days later, Thomas was narrowly confirmed by the Senate, 52–48. I voted against him and have never regretted it.

CHAPTER 31

Preserving Galena

The Galena Creek basin seven miles northwest of Incline Village on the edge of Lake Tahoe's North Shore had tempted developers for decades as a prime site for a ski resort. By the early 1980s, a plan began to take shape to turn the forest and meadows of Galena into yet another of the region's popular winter destinations. Top planners and professionals from the skiing industry came together with developers who assembled more than 6,000 acres with dreams of three villages, 1,460 multifamily residential units, 720 hotel rooms, conference areas, and 265,000 square feet of commercial space. Add to that a championship golf course, employee housing, and of course the ski slopes, and it added up to a nearly two-decade-long vision capable of accommodating many thousands of skiers on a given day. Potential economic impact on the Reno-Tahoe area: $140 million.

For the better part of seven years, the developers of the proposed ski resort had successfully navigated each of the federal requirements and were prepared to break ground in late 1990. The environmental community in Northern Nevada was strongly opposed to the project. In their view, Galena was an idyllic setting that should be preserved for future recreational purposes.

In May 1990, the Sierra Club, Citizens First, and the Friends of Mount Rose organized "Save Galena Day." More than two hundred people attended, and one thousand signatures were affixed to a petition opposing the project.

Inexorably the federal process for approval of the development continued to move forward. In October 1990, the US Corps of Engineers issued a final permit allowing the ski resort to be built.

The environmental community was caught behind the power curve and was greatly dismayed. At their request I met with them and listened to their arguments in support of preserving Galena. I thought they made a persuasive case, and I agreed to support them, but I also told them that there were no guarantees. Like so many other worthwhile public policy issues in my career, saving Galena would be a long uphill struggle.

The problem was simple: The developers had had several years head start and the train was leaving the station. The developers were in the catbird seat. We had to devise a strategy to get them to change course, and we had to move swiftly.

Marlene Lockard would be on point for me. Anyone who knows Marlene understands that when she enlists for a cause she would be indefatigable. A longtime resident of Truckee Meadows, Marlene was familiar with the Galena area. And when she met with the environmentalists, she was fired up and ready to pursue the cause. The immediate challenge we faced was getting the developers to the bargaining table for negotiation. From their perspective, they felt they were home free. It was decided that I would introduce legislation that would get the developers' attention.

In February I introduced the Galena Regional Recreational Development Act of 1991, which authorized the Secretary of Agriculture and Secretary of Interior to acquire Galena for recreation, either through a like-value land exchange or a purchase.

When the developers became aware of my legislation, they went ballistic. From their perspective, they had done all they needed to do. Bob Weiss, one of the developers, charged into my Reno Senate office and confronted Marlene. As Marlene later described the meeting, "It was ugly." That was an understatement.

What we did not know at that time is that we had a strong ally on our side: Mother Nature. Little snow had fallen on Galena in the previous three winters. In fact, so little that even if the ski resort had been completed there would be insufficient snow for the resort to become operational.

We opened a dialogue with the developers. For the next three years we experienced every register on the scale of human emotions from exultation to despair. There were many obstacles that we had to overcome on this roller-coaster ride. In the first of many setbacks, the Trust for Public Land, which had joined the buyout effort, dropped out.

One of the initial challenges was getting an appraisal on the Galena property on which the Bureau of Land Management (BLM),

Forest Service, and the developers would agree. After much back and forth, in December 1992 negotiations collapsed and the developers walked out of the meeting with the BLM. With much help from Marlene and others, in January the developers were brought back to the table and an agreement was reached that the Forest Service would conduct the appraisal. In June, all parties agreed to an appraised value of $19.4 million.

In July 1993, Secretary of Interior Bruce Babbitt weighed in by directing the BLM to work with Harriet Burgess of the America Land Conservancy. Burgess was well known to all of us, and she had considerable expertise in land exchanges. She was highly respected. Her addition to the team provided additional momentum to the buyout.

Trouble soon reappeared. Washoe County in September was prepared to file a lien in the amount of $1.3 million for a sewer bond payment that the Galena developers would owe. We were facing a timeline given to us by the developer, but the developer agreed to an extension. In January 1994, a $1.3 million loan was secured from the Packard Foundation. The project was alive again.

A month later, another issue threatened the project. The 7,500 acres of property in Clark County, which had been identified to be sold to private developers to generate the $19.4 million to be used as the funding source to buy out the Galena developers, reached an impasse. The parties involved were unable to agree on a price. Negotiations collapsed. Enter Burgess. She located another parcel of land in Clark County that was suitable.

Our roller-coaster ride continued in May. Mining claims were filed on the property that was identified for the exchange. To further complicate the process, the Clark County Flood Control District and the Nevada Department of Transportation filed protests. The following month, those objections were resolved.

In the middle of August, yet another problem arose at the last minute. The deeds that were to be executed to transfer the parcels had to be redone.

On August 12, the earth cleaved and the sky burned. The final closing took place. An odyssey that had begun a decade before ended in a win-win. Galena had been saved, the developers had been fairly compensated, and some claims by the Paiute tribe had also been resolved. It was a public policy victory, and for Marlene it was a personal victory. She had worked tirelessly on the project for three years.

All the parties attended a celebration at Galena later in the month. Marlene and I joined the developers, the environmental groups, and the federal agencies involved. I thanked everyone for their patience, and I wanted to do something special for Marlene. I proposed that a tree be named in Marlene's honor. Although that didn't happen, one of the developers who attended, Nick Badami, beamed from ear to ear and presented Marlene and me with a logger's crosscut saw.

The symbolism was obvious. The saw would no longer be needed. Galena had been saved.

CHAPTER 32

The Packwood Affair

Oregon's Bob Packwood was a moderate Republican, an increasingly rare species in the US Senate in the early 1990s. After sweeping into office in an upset in 1968, he immediately showed a willingness to part with his own party when he felt it necessary. As the first Senate Republican to support President Nixon's impeachment, Packwood was considered a reformer who was more than willing to cross the aisle when he believed the issue justified it. During his 1992 reelection campaign, scattered reports began to surface about his unacceptable conduct with women on his staff and lobbyists. He successfully fended off those allegations and was reelected.

Shortly afterward, a devastating article in the *Washington Post* reported allegations of sexual abuse and assault by Packwood on ten women, most of whom had been staffers or lobbyists. Packwood denied the allegations even as more women came forward.

The Senate Ethics Committee is composed of three Democrats and three Republicans. At the time the Packwood scandal broke, I was one of three Democrats. Democrat Terry Sanford of North Carolina was the chairman, and New Mexico's Jeff Bingaman served as the second Democrat. I was the junior member of the committee and was content to remain so. Then the committee turned upside down. Sanford lost his reelection bid in 1992, and Bingaman persuaded the majority leader George Mitchell to let him leave the committee so that he could prepare for his 1994 reelection campaign. That suddenly thrust me, the junior senator, into the chairmanship of a committee that's not exactly coveted by members of the Senate. And I had my own campaign for reelection to consider. I did not want to be chairman. I was essentially instructed by Mitchell to take one for the team.

Meanwhile, the Packwood scandal was a ticking time bomb.

The allegations in the news accounts were ugly, and they continued to mount. By Senate practice the Ethics Committee didn't open an official investigation until it received a written complaint, and no written complaint had been received. But the calls for action were increasing.

As the complaints against Packwood grew, Jean Marie Neal made the point that a failure to act would reflect terribly on the Senate, the committee, not to mention its chairman. It would appear the Senate was using a technicality as an excuse to do nothing. She was right. The public would think the Senate was sitting on its hands, even covering up for a colleague. My ambivalence about the chairmanship aside, Neal made her point with characteristic clarity. I moved to begin a preliminary inquiry based on the available facts, and thereafter we moved methodically toward a full investigation as Packwood continued to profess his innocence.

It was clear from the start that not everyone was thrilled with the investigation, especially some of Packwood's fellow Republicans. Senator Mitch McConnell of Kentucky, the ranking Republican on the Ethics Committee, did everything possible to delay the process, slow-walking subpoenas and making it obvious he was interested in wrapping up the matter as soon as possible. I refused to go along.

Despite Senator McConnell's lack of enthusiasm, I pressed forward. After learning about allegations of potential witness intimidation and attempts to discredit witnesses who appeared willing to come forward, we expanded the scope of the inquiry. We had begun a marathon. According to the rules of the Senate, all proceedings would be conducted behind closed doors.

We took the deposition of every woman who would agree to come forward to either corroborate the allegations or exonerate Packwood. In all, more than two hundred witnesses were interviewed or offered statements. The pages of documentation approached ten thousand, and we had yet to hear from Packwood himself.

We took his deposition in early October 1993. During his deposition he was questioned about an alleged transgression that occurred in Oregon at a time Packwood insisted he was not in the state. It was then his own counsel stepped forward to say the proof could be found in Packwood's voluminous personal diary, which he had been dictating to his secretary daily since 1969. It included not only his official activities, but his most personal and intimate interactions with women.

The deposition was put on hold while attorneys for both sides reviewed his diary entries, some six thousand pages in all, from the years 1969 to 1989. Some passages appeared to be missing. Packwood's troubles mounted when diary entries revealed that he had contacted lobbyists whom he had helped and asked them to put his estranged wife on their payroll to reduce his own alimony payment. The potential misconduct was impossible to ignore, and later we referred the matter to the FBI for its review.

Suddenly Packwood was no longer willing to cooperate. By October 20, the committee voted unanimously to subpoena Packwood's diary tapes. He refused to comply, and after two days of debate by the Senate on November 2, 1993, a resolution was passed with a 94-6 vote supporting the issuance of the subpoena.

As the pressure mounted, Packwood made more mistakes. Our deposition of his secretary discovered that he had withdrawn several diary tapes from her possession, admitting he was concerned about a possible subpoena. She later confirmed that he had edited the tapes. That information was provided to US District Judge Thomas Penfield Jackson in mid-December, and he approved the subpoena request. The judge's order provided for a review of the diaries and designated former federal judge and legal scholar Kenneth Starr as special master for the court. In that role, Starr would review the content of the diaries and determine whether the information we were requesting was relevant for the purposes of our investigation. Starr granted every committee request for information in the Packwood diary. This is the same Ken Starr who later led the impeachment proceedings against President Clinton.

Packwood bought time by appealing every step. After Judge Jackson approved the subpoena, Packwood appealed to the Court of Appeals and ultimately to the US Supreme Court, where Chief Justice William Rehnquist declined to intervene.

As the months ground on and the committee's deliberation continued, it came under considerable criticism. It was called a rogue committee that was out of control. I was terribly frustrated. I was getting criticized even by my fellow Democrats about the length of time it was taking. My hands were tied, and I was unable to indicate to my colleagues the gravity of the allegations against Packwood that we were investigating.

Working closely with Starr, I found him to be professional. The November election would be good to me, but 1994 was a disaster for Democrats. Republicans gained the majority in the Senate and the House. When we convened in 1995, my role on the Ethics Committee was that of vice chairman with McConnell assuming the chairman's role in the middle of an investigation of a member of his own caucus.

By May the gravity of Packwood's transgressions was undeniable after seventeen former staffers and lobbyists came forward on the record to report the senator's improper sexual advances. The evidence was overwhelming.

By May 16, 1995, after a full review of the evidence and the production of staff counsel's preliminary inquiry report, the committee voted unanimously that substantial evidence existed that Packwood had abused his power through improper and discrediting conduct, had engaged in improper conduct and possibly violated federal law, and had traded on his position for financial gain. Behind the scenes, the calls for his resignation were beginning.

Packwood's Republican colleagues had protected him throughout the process, and he had every opportunity to exit the political stage with a little dignity.

Tired of waiting for Packwood to resign, Senator Barbara Boxer, a freshman Democrat of California, spoke up in July and called for public hearings. Boxer was part of a group of female lawmakers elected following the Anita Hill debacle. It was clear many were still stinging from the treatment Hill had received. The partisan lines were drawn, and McConnell at one point threatened to retaliate by holding hearings into the drowning of a woman in a car driven by Senator Ted Kennedy at Chappaquiddick in 1969. McConnell threatened to stall the committee's process unless Boxer ceased her call for public hearings.

On August 2, the verge of the summer recess, Boxer again pressed for a floor vote. I learned that Senator Larry Craig, an Idaho Republican on the Ethics Committee, was ready to withdraw his support of Packwood's expulsion. In other words, he was about to cave in and desert us. In the end, he did. When the smoke finally cleared,

Boxer's spirited push for public hearings lost, 52–48, along hardening party lines.

The hits kept coming—and they were getting uglier. On August 3, the Ethics Committee announced two new sexual misconduct allegations against Packwood that would be immediately investigated.

All that saved Packwood was the August recess, during which time he told reporters that he wanted public hearings after all. "The entire process is so unfair," he said, presumably with a straight face. "I've never had a chance to cross-examine my accusers."

Packwood's ill-considered quotes incensed McConnell and his Republican Senate colleagues. He claimed that he had no objection to a floor vote. The effect of Packwood's statement left the Republicans hanging out there.

When the Senate reconvened following its summer recess, McConnell made a mad dash to the press gallery. Jean Marie Neal advised me that I had better get over to the press gallery to see what McConnell was up to. When I got there McConnell expressed his opinion that Packwood should resign.

The committee unanimously approved a resolution on September 7 calling for Packwood to be expelled from the Senate. Even at that moment Packwood outwardly remained confident. But the game was over. In private, McConnell and I met with Packwood and told him he would have to resign. His disgrace was undeniable, and the pressure he faced was immense, but I remember him being as cool as a cucumber.

The next morning, Packwood resigned from the Senate.

An ugly chapter in the history of the US Senate was over, but we hadn't heard the last of Ken Starr.

CHAPTER 33

Running against a Rising Tide

The Packwood affair wasn't the only frontline battle in which I found myself. By the time 1994 arrived, I was also in the middle of a fight for reelection at a time that was not exactly a high-water mark for the Democrats. Bill Clinton's first two years as president had gotten off to an inauspicious beginning. He was hounded by the growing scandals involving the Whitewater Development Corporation and Madison Guaranty Savings and Loan Association of Arkansas, and Republican strategists decided to make the president the issue in the midterm elections. In the House of Representatives, new Republican leadership mounted an aggressive campaign centered on their "Contract with America." Developed by Newt Gingrich and Dick Armey, much of the so-called contract had been lifted from President Reagan's 1985 State of the Union speech and reflected the talking points of the conservative Heritage Foundation. Among its many promises to the American people was term limits. The anti-incumbent tone of the contract resonated with the voters. As a political strategy it was brilliant, and the Republicans executed it flawlessly.

In the Republican tidal wave of 1994, the GOP would gain eight new seats in the Senate and a stunning fifty-four seats in the House to gain control of both chambers. But 1994 was also an election year for me, and I recognized early on it would be a tough campaign season for Democrats.

Gearing up for my reelection campaign, I wanted a campaign team that functioned well working together. The Washington, DC, consulting firm Squier Knapp et al. seemed to fit that bill. Bob Squier had represented top Democrats ranging from Hubert Humphrey to Clinton, and he was known for his inspired campaign spots and consulting insight in tandem with partner Bill Knapp. They were highly regarded and did not disappoint. After a meeting with them and discussing my view of the campaign strategy we needed to pursue, I was convinced they'd be a good choice. From the outset I had a comfort level with them as my campaign consultants that I lacked in the 1988 Senate race. Knapp was assigned to my race. Jim Mulhall, my press secretary for several years, took a leave of absence from my Senate office to head up the campaign's link to the media. Jim and I had worked closely together, and I was convinced he was the right person to serve as a campaign strategist. He was on board with my choice of Squier Knapp. When the campaign began, we were all on the same page.

Hal Furman emerged as my Republican challenger after defeating four other contenders in the primary. I was unopposed in my primary. Furman was well known in Republican circles but largely unknown to Nevada voters.

Furman would be a formidable adversary. He was bright, articulate, and an effective presence on the stump. We had our work cut out for us. In a big year for Republicans, he was a dangerous opponent who positioned himself as part of the new generation of political outsiders in the GOP.

As the campaign heated up, I caught a break. In a year when being a "Washington insider" was toxic, Furman was himself a registered Washington lobbyist. Not only that, he also lobbied for a foreign country—Thailand. Voters believed that lobbyists exercised an undue influence on members of Congress. Unpopular as incumbent members of Congress may be, lobbyists were considered even worse.

Here is where being a fresh face in politics can be a disadvantage. Because Furman was largely unknown to voters, our campaign decided to define him. We made him the ultimate insider. As Furman was certain to describe me as a tax-and-spend Democrat aligned with an unpopular president in the White House, we would remind voters of his history as a lobbyist in a series of campaign ads.

One ad in particular helped to make our case. The ad featured emergency responders on their knees with an ambulance in the background studying a large map. Suddenly, one exclaims in an incredulous voice, "Thailand?"

Then the punchline, "Don't we need someone to represent us?"

The ad caught on.

To make matters worse for Furman, the Thai Embassy objected to the commercial and demanded a retraction. Their intervention helped to drive home the point that my Republican challenger represented a foreign country. The implication was damning: did Nevadans really want their next US senator, who had represented Thailand as a registered foreign agent, to represent them?

Furman made a rookie mistake during the campaign. Joe Dini, Speaker of the Nevada Assembly, represented several rural counties at the legislature. He was well known and well liked in Northern Nevada. He had also been my friend from the time I was first elected to the Assembly in 1968. Joe's wife, Jeanne, had passed away, and Joe asked me to speak at her funeral in Yerington. I readily agreed. I would miss a couple of votes, but some things transcend politics.

Furman made an issue of my missing a couple of votes during my brief absence from the Senate to speak at Jeanne's funeral. His comments were ill-advised and utterly tone deaf. The backlash in Lyon County's *Mason Valley News,* Dini's hometown newspaper and an important editorial voice in Northern Nevada, was swift. Furman was eviscerated for what was perceived to be a cheap shot at me. I do not know whether the blowback from Furman's attack made the difference, but I carried Lyon County in the general election.

Furman and I debated on one occasion. As anticipated, he was an effective debater, but I held my own.

Clark County was my political base, and I expected to do well there. Washoe County, the second most populous county in the state, was long a Republican stronghold, but by 1994 was beginning to lean Democratic. I thought there was a reasonable chance I might carry Washoe County as well. In the 1960s, when I began my elective career, several rural counties continued to elect conservative Democrats to the legislature and statewide office. There had been a seismic shift in rural Nevada, and by 1994 the state's rural counties were Republican strongholds where Democrats generally fared poorly. I yielded no ground.

I was no stranger to rural Nevada. Since my election as attorney general in 1978, I spent most of my summer traveling through the rural counties and continuing my tradition of attending annual small-town events such as Jim Butler Days in Tonopah, Carson Valley Days in Minden, and the Firemen's Muster in Virginia City, to name but a few.

On election night as polls were closing, the extent of the Democratic disaster started to unfold. It was ugly. Tennessee, home to Al Gore, the vice president and former senator, was among the states the Republicans took from the Democrats in the Senate. Big-name Democrats were dispatched into retirement as the party fell into the minority. To make matters even worse, after the smoke cleared Democrats Richard Shelby and Ben Nighthorse Campbell switched parties. Most political pundits predicted a Republican surge, but few thought the GOP would control the House of Representatives.

In Nevada, my friend Jim Bilbray, who had represented the state's First Congressional District for eight years, was defeated by newcomer John Ensign.

The news was better for me. I defeated Furman with 193,804 votes, 50.9 percent of the total. Furman received 156,020, or 41 percent. I carried Clark and Washoe Counties, and to the surprise of many I also won White Pine, Mineral, Lyon, Carson, Pershing, and Humboldt and lost several of the remaining rural counties by single digits.

Many of my fellow Democrats were surprised by my strong showing in rural Nevada. "How did you do it?" they asked.

In addition to attending traditional events and holding townhall meetings in rural Nevada since I was elected to statewide office, I had Tom Baker as my rural representative. Baker loved traveling out to the "Cow Counties" and making the rounds. Whenever there was a request for help with an issue with a federal agency, Tom viewed it as another opportunity. During my first term in the Senate, he was instrumental in getting Bureau of Land Management property for a school site in Storey County, assisting Yerington with a flood-control issue, and Fallon with an irrigation issue. Baker was always eager to find a solution. He developed a close relationship with local government officials. It was apparent when I made my annual swing through the rurals during the Senate summer recess that they saw Baker as the go-to guy when they needed help.

CHAPTER 34

Protecting Consumers

Congress enacted the Fair Credit Reporting Act (FCRA) in 1970 to enhance the accuracy of the credit reporting system. Consumer reports are reports of information compiled on individual consumers to determine, among other things, their eligibility for credit, insurance, employment, even applications for student loans. The credit reporting industry maintains files on more than 190 million Americans and each month adds two billion new bits of information to those credit histories. The extension of credit is a significant part of consumer spending each year in the United States.

The 1970 FCRA gave consumers the right to challenge inaccuracies in their credit histories. The fatal flaw, however, was that the burden was on the consumer to prove the information in his or her credit report was inaccurate. Frequently, this resulted in protracted and frustrating negotiations with a credit provider to remove the inaccurate information from the report.

Although most of the erroneous entries were unintentional, they could be devastating to a consumer trying to qualify for a loan to finance the purchase of a home, an automobile, or even to get a job. The FTC reported that errors in a consumer's credit history, and the difficulty in fixing those errors, was the No. 1 consumer complaint. A study conducted by Consumers Union revealed that 48 percent of all credit histories contained erroneous information. Of those, about 28 percent were serious enough that the consumer was denied credit.

As consumer frustration with the credit reporting system mounted, my Republican Banking Committee colleague, Senator Kit Bond of Missouri, and I began an effort to reform the law. The focus of our efforts was to correct the problems consumers all too often experienced in getting inaccurate information removed from their credit histories. Once a consumer notified a credit reporting agency of inaccurate information, our proposal gave the agency thirty days to verify the information or they had to delete it. In effect, the burden of proof shifted from the consumer to the credit reporting agency.

As observers of the congressional legislative process could attest, enacting major legislation is a marathon. Otto von Bismarck, the great German chancellor, once venting his frustration on the matter, commented that there were two things that people ought not to see made: "One of those is sausages, and the other laws."

When the 103rd session of Congress convened, our reform legislation began to gain traction. We worked tirelessly to get support from both sides of the aisle, and we thought enactment was close at hand. It had cleared both the House and the Senate and was now before the Senate again for final action. Despite having almost unanimous support, on the final day of the 103rd Congress, Senator Phil Gramm, a Republican from Texas, put a hold on our bill, effectively killing it for that session. I was furious. Gramm had never previously articulated any concerns with the bill. There was considerable speculation that he was flexing his muscles as he was set to assume the Banking Committee chairmanship in the next Congress. Gramm was known to use the expression: "Don't take a hostage unless you're prepared to kill it."

Undaunted by our setback, we reintroduced the credit reporting reform legislation when the next Congress convened. In September 1996, the bill was again on the Senate floor for final action. In my comments from the floor that day, I characterized the Consumer Credit Reporting Reform Act of 1996 as the most significant consumer legislation enacted in that session of the Congress.

I cited the case of a couple from McDermitt on the Nevada-Oregon border. They thought they had been successful in removing an inaccurate entry on their credit history. However, three years later when they sought to finance the installation of a satellite dish at their home, they were shocked to find the inaccurate entry had reappeared and prevented them from qualifying for a loan. Another part of our legislation prohibited the reintroduction of erroneous information, once deleted, without giving the consumer prior notice.

The Nevada couple was not alone. We heard from a young woman about her experience in attempting to secure a student loan. She was initially turned down for a loan and almost had to drop out of graduate school because of an erroneous entry on her credit report. The entry on her credit report asserted that she was married, and her husband had a long history of troubled credit. In fact, she had never been married. She endured many frustrating experiences to get the false entry removed. Ultimately, she got the student loan—but at a higher interest rate because of the inaccurate information in her file. "Under the new legislation we act upon today," I commented, "the burden of proof has been changed from the consumer to the institution extending the line of credit."

The process of getting legislation enacted is often long and arduous, entailing the efforts and teamwork of many congressional members and staffers. Having a colleague from the other side of the aisle as an ally is invaluable. Without Bond's efforts, it's uncertain if we could have gotten these significant consumer protections over the goal line. Kit was known for his love of cigars, and you always knew you were getting near his office when you picked up the aroma. That brought back fond memories of my father, who also had a love of cigars. He and I had our political differences, but we shared common experiences as former governors.

There was a special bond among former governors during my service, including Senators Bob Graham of Florida, Bob Kerrey of Nebraska, Dale Bumpers and David Pryor of Arkansas, and David Boren of Oklahoma. I don't know if the working relationships we had would be possible in today's Senate. The Senate was far less polarized in the 1990s, and there was room to find common ground. The ability to reach across the aisle for the common good made possible the enactment of legislation that affected millions of Americans in dealing with their credit history.

The effort of staff is often overlooked in the congressional process. Andy Vermilye was another of the outstanding members of my staff recruited by my chief of staff Jean Marie Neal. Vermilye was a perfect fit for us because he had experience in the House on issues that were before my two major committees: Banking and Commerce. He had the ability to work effectively with Republican and Democratic staffers and developed relationships with members of the Senate, particularly those who enjoyed a good tennis match. He was a consummate professional, and I relied on him on many occasions. He played a major role in securing the passage of the Consumer Credit Reporting Reform Act of 1996.

CHAPTER 35

Defending Nevada, a Pariah State

In 1931 Nevada became the first state to legalize casino gaming. In the years that followed, the state was largely viewed as a pariah and Las Vegas as a modern-day Sodom and Gomorrah. Under the common law, gambling debts were unenforceable. Enforcing such debts was contrary to public policy, and that was the law in Nevada as well until the 1970s.

To say the least, gambling was not a favored industry in the Congress. Unfavorable national publicity about the influence of organized crime in Nevada's gaming industry placed casino operations at considerable risk. As the only state with legalized gambling, for decades Nevada had no natural allies. The only procedural weapon available to Nevada to protect its largest industry was the filibuster. Southern states had effectively used it to prevent votes on civil rights legislation. Nevadans elected Pat McCarran to the US Senate in 1932. McCarran was well known to Nevadans. He had been a state Supreme Court justice and had gained national headlines as the attorney who represented Mary Pickford, "America's Sweetheart" in the silent film era, when she came to Nevada to get a divorce so she could marry another Hollywood icon, Douglas Fairbanks Sr.

McCarran's shortcomings have been well documented. But, fortunately for Nevada, McCarran had amassed considerable seniority in the US Senate. He was a force to be reckoned with and wasn't shy about wielding his power.

Nevada and the southern states, for very different reasons, saw the filibuster as a useful procedure to protect their interests. Only a majority of votes were required to pass legislation, but sixty votes are required to invoke cloture, the process employed to end a filibuster. Nevada and southern senators entered an unholy alliance to protect their political interests. Nevada senators agreed to oppose cloture on civil rights legislation, and southern senators would do the same on legislation that would have a negative impact on Nevada's gaming industry. Ever the dealmaker, McCarran had found a way to effectively block federal intervention in the casino industry. No Nevada senator had ever voted for a cloture petition until the 1960s, when Senator Howard Cannon broke ranks to support cloture on the civil rights bill.

As an industry, and despite setbacks, gaming continued to evolve through the 1960s with the arrival of eccentric business titan Howard Hughes in Las Vegas and the dawn of the corporate gaming era in 1967 under Governor Paul Laxalt.

When I arrived in the state legislature two years later, some leftover business from the '67 legislature required our attention. When Laxalt took office as governor, no corporation could hold a gaming license. And, indeed, every individual owner regardless of the size of their investment had to be licensed. Laxalt's proposal would be a seismic shift for Nevada gaming regulators. Some of the old-timers felt that the state would lose effective regulatory control. George Dickerson, chairman of the Nevada Gaming Commission, resigned over the issue feeling that Nevada's regulatory control of gaming would be compromised.

It fell to us in the 1969 legislature to add the finishing touches, and we did.

More than fifty years later, the impact of Laxalt's proposal has transformed the Las Vegas Strip into a world-renowned corridor of mega-resorts. Those palaces could not have been built before corporate licensing. The new resorts require billions of dollars to construct. In the pre-corporate gaming era, it would have been impossible to amass that amount of investment capital.

When I came to the Senate in 1989, Nevada was no longer the only state to have legalized casino gambling: New Jersey and Mississippi had joined the club. In Nevada, where gaming is our largest industry, Senator Reid and I viewed it as our responsibility to defend the industry from unwarranted federal intrusion. Gaming wasn't the largest industry in those other states, and elected public officials' support of the industry was tepid at best. As governor, I got a preview of that attitude when New Jersey governor Tom Kean refused to attend an Atlantic City gaming conference to make opening remarks. When I received a call requesting that I give the opening remarks, I was happy to attend.

Senator Bill Bradley of New Jersey, who had been an All-America basketball player at Princeton and later starred with the New York Knicks in the NBA, was a critic of gambling and supportive of a ban on sports betting. And Frank Lautenberg of New Jersey generally followed Bradley's lead.

It was a different time, but much like in McCarran's era it was Nevada's Senate delegation, Harry and I, who did the heavy lifting to protect the state's economic best interests.

The first challenge I faced came with the introduction of the Professional and Amateur Sports Protection Act (PASPA). Its avowed purpose was to essentially outlaw sports betting nationally. The fact that professional sports betting and bookmaking were already against the law in most states, and that Nevada was the only state in which the activities were licensed and regulated, the legislation seemed to target Nevada's sports betting industry.

Working with Senator Dennis DeConcini of Arizona, who chaired the subcommittee which had jurisdiction of the bill, we were successful in carving out an exemption for Nevada. Oregon, Montana, and Delaware, which offered nominal sports gambling options, also secured exemptions. New Jersey was given a one-year window to request its own exemption but failed to exercise its option. PASPA became law in 1992 and went on to accomplish little to counter illegal bookmaking or protect sporting events. Ironically, it was New Jersey's effort to legalize sports betting years later that led to the US Supreme Court's decision to overturn PASPA in 2018. Since then, state after state has joined the parade of legalization of sports betting.

Four years after PASPA's passage, gaming was once again on the congressional front burner with the creation of the National Gambling Impact Study Commission. The enabling language of the commission authorized a comprehensive study of the societal and economic impact of gambling in the United States. It was obvious from the beginning that opponents of gambling would seek to stack the deck against Nevada. The appointments of gaming critics Kay James as the chair and James Dobson, founder of Focus on the Family, confirmed our worst fears.

The act provided for the appointment of nine members to the commission. Harry and I were successful in making the case for a more balanced commission and secured the appointment of Bill

Bible, Nevada Gaming Control Board chairman; John Wilhelm, Hotel Employees and Restaurant Employees Union president; and Terry Lanni, MGM Grand chairman.

James and other anti-gaming commissioners attempted to circumvent the protections of the opening meeting law and employed other tactics which were a cause for continuing concern. Ultimately, the final report recommended only two areas for an appropriate federal regulatory role—Indian gaming and the internet. Regulation of gambling was left to the states.

In 2000 I was in my final year in the Senate. The Amateur Sports Integrity Act was proposed. The purpose of the legislation was to close the so-called "Las Vegas loophole" that allowed legalized gambling in Nevada on amateur sports. The forces arrayed against us included not only the moral critics of gambling, but also the major league sports organizations, university presidents, coaches, and the NCAA. Twenty years later, major league sports teams openly embrace partnerships with gaming companies. Today Las Vegas has its own major league franchises, including the NFL's Raiders, the NHL's Golden Knights, and the WNBA's Aces.

On March 29, the Senate Commerce Committee convened under the chairmanship of Senator John McCain of Arizona, who was a strong supporter of the bill. An impressive list of witnesses was called, including a college coach, a university president, and university academics who studied gaming. The committee was told there was a crisis in America with sports wagering on amateur athletics. Despite his opposition, McCain was generous in giving me considerable time to examine witnesses. In my view, the NCAA and college presidents who supported the legislation were hypocritical: all talk but little action.

I focused my line of questioning on Charles Wethington, president of the University of Kentucky and chairman of the NCAA's executive committee. It was no secret that Kentuckians love to bet on sports and horse races, and I began by noting that my daughter-in-law was from Lexington.

"Let me ask you," I began, "are there any illegal bookies on the University of Kentucky's campus?"

He responded in the affirmative.

"And how many have been prosecuted since you have been president of the University?"

"I am not aware of any that have been prosecuted since I have been president," he replied.

"And what efforts do you as a university—I am asking just to you, sir, because you are here. I am not suggesting the University of Kentucky is probably different from any other university in America, but what efforts, what kind of commitment do you have in terms of your own enforcement efforts to locate these bookies?"

Wethington spoke of the "considerable commitment" made by the university to "avoid the pitfalls that we believe that are there both for legal and illegal gambling." He bragged about bringing in NCAA officials and the FBI, along with sports fixers to discuss the slippery slope of sports betting.

I was compelled to remind him that the NCAA had recently signed a $6 billion television rights deal with CBS. What else had the NCAA done to irradicate this evil?

He responded that the governing body had produced a video on the evils of sports wagering. I asked him how much it cost. His response: $25,000. Wethington then digressed about funding priorities and other challenges, but the hypocrisy was on display.

At one point I asked him, "How many staff members at the NCAA national level are assigned as their primary responsibility dealing with the issue of illegal gambling on college campuses?"

Wethington replied, "I believe at this point there are three."

"And how many member institutions do we have?"

"One thousand, seventy-four, I believe at last count."

The facts: Nevada wasn't responsible for illegal sports wagering, game fixing, or crooked ballplayers. The truth told, it was Nevada's licensed sports book operators who were the canaries in the coal mine when it came to sensing suspicious irregularities in games, and the FBI knew it. After all, for years agents had relied on those same sports book managers' insights to help investigate illegal gambling cases.

Brian Sandoval, then the chairman of the Nevada Gaming Commission; Bobby Siller, chairman of the Nevada Gaming Control Board; and the American Gaming Association's Frank Fahrenkopf offered effective rebuttals. The bill did not become law.

Another experience in my Senate career demonstrates how Nevada senators would be required to take the lead on any legislation that would damage the gaming industry. Senator Conrad Burns, a Republican of Montana, had introduced legislation to assist his state's agriculture industry, but it added a cost to the federal treasury. Under the "pay-go rules" then in effect, legislation that added to the federal budget had to be offset by new revenue. For that offset Burns had chosen an additional tax on gaming, which was generally considered an easy target.

I met with Senate majority leader Trent Lott from Mississippi to discuss Burns's proposed actions. He summoned Burns to his office and said, "We can't have that—get a new offset." Burns quickly shifted directions. I appreciated Lott's assistance and thanked him. His response: "Don't tell anyone I was helpful." Apparently, in Mississippi supporting the gaming industry was not universally appreciated.

Gaming legislation was not my only concern. The casino industry is potentially affected by a plethora of federal regulations. The US Treasury, for example, proposed a regulation which would have severely limited casino play by imposing an ill-timed withholding requirement that would have interrupted patron play. I was able to explain the impact on the industry, and Treasury withdrew its proposal.

Because casinos are included within the federal definition of a bank, when the Treasury proposed reducing the number of currency transaction reports (CTR) that had to be filed, I was successful in making sure that casinos enjoyed the same reduction in CTRs as traditional financial institutions.

It's been almost a century since Assemblyman Phil Tobin and the 1931 Nevada Legislature launched legalized gambling in the state. Nevada was the least populated of the then forty-eight states with just 90,000 residents in 1930. Today, Nevada's population is more than three million. Mining and agriculture, once the state's premier economic drivers, have long been eclipsed by the impact of the gaming and tourism industries. Las Vegas has become the Entertainment Capital of the World. That experiment of legalization, although far from perfect, has served the state well.

Another word about my friend John McCain. We might have sparred when it came to issues involving the gaming industry, but we found ourselves in the same corner when it came time to stand up for the health and safety of professional boxers.

When I was a boy growing up in Las Vegas, my father would regale me with stories of the great boxers. He was an enthusiastic fan of the fight game. He was a special admirer of the heavyweight champion "The Manassa Mauler" Jack Dempsey, who had his own colorful history in the ring in Nevada. My dad could recount in great detail how Dempsey had been knocked out of the ring in the second round of his championship fight against Argentina's Luis Ángel Firpo, "The Wild Bull of the Pampas." Sports writers ringside that night at the Polo Grounds pushed Dempsey back into the ring, and he won by a knockout. I followed boxing but was not the fan my dad was.

As governor, I appointed members to the Nevada Athletic Commission, which regulated boxing in the state and was considered the gold standard in the sport. In my six years as governor, appointments to that commission were the most sought after. My friend Jim Nave was a key appointment for me and brought to the commission a wealth of badly needed business experience. He was a real boxing aficionado who understood its economic benefits to the state. After I entered the Senate, I continued to rely on Jim on all boxing issues. He gave me insight into some of the abuses of the fighters, and he was not a big fan of some of the promoters.

Although I wasn't a regular at ringside, McCain qualified as a super fan. When McCain introduced the Professional Boxing Safety Act of 1996, better known as the Muhammad Ali Boxing Reform Act, I knew it was a fight I wanted a piece of and became a cosponsor. When I was governor, boxing was such an important part of the Las Vegas tourism economy that a single major prizefight in Las Vegas could cause a noticeable uptick in state revenue for the month. Put simply, it moved the needle.

The sport suffered from many challenges, not the least of which were unstable sanctioning bodies, notoriously deceptive contracts, unethical promoters and managers, and inconsistent fighter safety enforcement from state to state.

The act, introduced during the 104th session of Congress, addressed a long litany of issues and concerns.

Without an organization to represent their interests and rights in the sport, professional boxers were particularly vulnerable to exploitation by unscrupulous promoters, managers, and sanctioning bodies. Because regulations varied widely from state to state, it was common for unethical promoters to simply pick up and move to avoid sanctions and scrutiny.

Among its many achievements, our legislation discontinued what had long been the essentially unlimited power of promoters over the fighters' careers. It banned promoters from having a direct or indirect financial interest in the management of a boxer. It prevented a manager from playing the role of promoter, and it enabled boxers to act as their own promoter or manager. It improved the uniformity of the ranking system by establishing objective and consistent criteria for ratings.

It improved transparency in a traditionally shadowed sport, and it set penalties for violating its anti-exploitation provisions. It required license revocations to be treated as suspensions. And, importantly, it required state commissions to honor the suspensions of boxers ordered by other state commissions for unsportsmanlike conduct or other inappropriate or unprofessional behavior.

Some of its critics fretted that it was an example of federal overreach, but what the act really accomplished was setting a baseline of standards that in many ways helped save the sport from its darker impulses. The health and safety of the fighters improved because they had us in their corner in Congress.

CHAPTER 36

When Everyone Wins:
The Public Land Management Act

If there was a silver lining with the defeat of Jim Bilbray, it was that I was able to persuade his public lands expert Brent Heberlee to join our DC office. Eighty-six percent of the land in Nevada—and in some counties more than 90 percent—is owned by the federal government. His expertise would be very helpful.

Heberlee was from Las Vegas. I had known his mother from my days at Las Vegas High School. She was a class behind me and lived across the street. I had followed Heberlee's career from afar and was aware that he had graduated from the University of California at Berkeley. He joined Bilbray's Washington, DC, staff shortly after graduation and, like my daughter Leslie, he discovered that having a law degree would be very helpful in advancing his career. He left Washington for the University of Iowa, where he obtained a law degree before returning to Bilbray's staff.

I was unaware that Bilbray was working on a comprehensive public lands bill for Clark County and that Heberlee was on point for that effort. I learned later it was a bill that contemplated a ring around the Las Vegas Valley. Everything outside the ring would remain under the purview of the Bureau of Land Management (BLM) or US Forest Service. Inside the ring were parcels of property too small for the BLM or the forest service to manage for recreational purposes. These parcels would be available at no cost to local governments as sites for schools, fire departments, and police stations. If local government did not have a need, the development community would have an opportunity to acquire them at fair-market value.

Under the law at that time, developers could apply to secure BLM-owned parcels through a land exchange process. Developers could exchange parcels that they owned for parcels the BLM owned if the government wanted to acquire those parcels. Each parcel would be appraised. This was a cumbersome, time-consuming process. Between the time of the appraisal and the completion of the exchange, the value of the federal land often appreciated considerably. There was a hue and cry that, in effect, the developer had gotten a sweetheart deal, and the taxpayer was on the short end of the exchange. Bilbray, with Heberlee taking the lead, was developing a public auction process in which the developers would bid openly on a BLM property, obviating the criticism that the developers had not paid fair-market value.

Many interests were competing: environmentalists, developers, local and state governments, and federal land agencies. To have all sides be heard, Bilbray and Heberlee created the Southern Nevada Public Lands Task Force. With all the parties at the table, a determined effort was made to reach a compromise that would satisfy the concerns of all. That was the state of play when John Ensign defeated Bilbray in the 1994 general election.

A member of Bilbray's staff who wanted me to head up the negotiations contacted Sara Besser on my staff. When Sara approached me, I was less than enthusiastic. I told her that it had all the trappings of a children's crusade. Fashioning a compromise with people who seldom could agree on anything seemed like an impossible dream to me. Sara was an environmentalist at heart, and she was eager to have me take the lead.

With Heberlee joining my DC office, additional pressure mounted. He convinced me that there was a path forward. He thought legislation could be crafted that would enjoy wide support. The most challenging issue was determining precisely where to draw the line around the Las Vegas Valley.

Heberlee continued to push forward, and I must say that I was pleasantly surprised. Progress was being made. Local governments liked the proposal because it gave them a process to acquire parcels needed for their purposes. Smaller developers especially liked the auction process because it was simple and enabled them to get into the ballgame. Under the old system of land exchanges, only the bigger developers such as Howard Hughes and the Olympic Group had the expertise, contacts, and resources to participate.

The environmentalists, specifically the Friends of Nevada

Wilderness, liked the bill because the proceeds generated from the sales went largely to projects that they favored: improvements to local trail systems, the Great Basin National Park, the Lake Tahoe Basin, the Red Rock Canyon National Conservation Area, and the Spring Mountains National Recreation Area.

The Santini-Burton legislation of 1980 to protect Lake Tahoe was the template we followed. My old friend Jim Santini joined Phil Burton in drafting the legislation. All money from the sales of BLM property in the Las Vegas Valley was retained and used only for protection of Lake Tahoe. Our legislation would propose to do the same for public purposes in Nevada.

The proposed bill provided that all the money generated from the public land sales would remain in Nevada, not diverted to the federal treasury where members of the House and Senate Appropriations Committee would wrangle for control of the funds.

In DC, the Senate Appropriations Committee took a dim view of diverting money from its jurisdiction. Heberlee allayed the committee's concerns by downplaying the amount of money involved and sending the message that this was really not a hill to die for. In actuality, over the next twenty years billions would be generated.

With the House and Senate now controlled by the Republicans after their sweeping victories in the 1994 election, I would need the support of the newly elected Ensign. Heberlee had already done the heavy lifting. Although Ensign was not involved in any of the negotiations, without his support in the House, the bill was unlikely to pass. Ensign signed on to the cause.

With the BLM under the umbrella of the Department of the Interior, we would also need the support of Secretary of the Interior Bruce Babbitt. I had a personal relationship with Bruce. He had been attorney general and governor of neighboring Arizona, and our paths had crossed many times.

I called him to arrange an appointment. Heberlee and I met in his office. The corridors leading to Babbitt's office were like a history of the department's more than century of activity in developing the West. When Heberlee and I showed him the proposed fifty-fifty division of money expected to be generated by the land sales, I thought he might have a cardiac arrest. Local governments had pulled out all the stops to get as much money as they could. Both Heberlee and I realized that it was a stretch too far. There would never be an agreement to share the money equally.

After Babbitt composed himself, he said those revenues were all generated by the sale of federal properties. He asked why shouldn't 100 percent of the revenues generated go to the Department of the Interior? Our rejoinder was that those properties would not be worth much without water and other infrastructure improvements that would be done at the expense of local governments. Ultimately, we agreed to a division that sent 85 percent of the proceeds back to Interior with local governments receiving 10 percent and state government receiving 5 percent for educational purposes. But none of the money would be subject to the control of the appropriations committees of the Congress.

Although Senator Reid was a cosponsor of the bill I introduced, his staff was not supportive of adding it to the omnibus public lands bill that would be acted upon before the Congress adjourned. I suspected that their concerns were magnified by the defeat of Bilbray in the 1994 election and the possibility that Ensign could emerge as a future challenger to Reid. We had to wait for the next session of Congress. In January 1997, we reintroduced the legislation. This time the road to success was smoother. Our bill was signed into law in 1998 as the Southern Nevada Public Land Management Act.

JFK once opined, "Victory has a thousand fathers, but defeat is an orphan." So it was with the enactment of the Southern Nevada Public Land Management Act. In the intervening two decades, more than $3.5 billion was generated for Nevada-based projects. In a long career filled with many long fights, this was a pardonably proud moment.

Although many have claimed credit, the people who need to be recognized are Jim Bilbray, who began the process; Brent Heberlee, who skillfully navigated through all the obstacles and political landmines, and Sara Besser, who was an invaluable liaison with all the local government and environmental and development interests, and members of the Southern Nevada Public Lands Task Force.

CHAPTER 37

Intelligence Committee
in a Time of Crisis

Majority Leader Tom Daschle appointed me to the Senate Intelligence Committee. I had not sought the appointment, but I believe Daschle was grateful for my service on the Ethics Committee, a thankless assignment where no one wanted to serve. The Intelligence Committee deals with highly sensitive national security information.

The nation's intelligence operations are housed with several federal agencies. The National Security Agency collects "signals intelligence" and controls certain satellites that aid in deriving intelligence from electronic signals emanating from communications systems, radars, and weapons systems. The Defense Intelligence Agency provides intelligence to the military, and the FBI and CIA also play major roles in intelligence gathering and evaluation. The National Reconnaissance Office oversees satellite operations.

In the mid-1970s, the congressional armed services committees in the House and Senate had nominal oversight over the intelligence community. Congress created a new intelligence oversight committee because of congressional investigations of US intelligence operations and concerns over alleged CIA abuses, including potentially illegal domestic surveillance of the anti–Vietnam War movement, and CIA's activities relating to national elections in Chile. Chaired by Frank Church, a Democrat of Idaho, the Senate's investigative committee issued a series of recommendations, including one that would create a Senate Select Committee on Intelligence.

The recommendation did not sit well with the Senate Committee on Armed Services when first proposed because the committee would lose a significant part of its jurisdiction. A compromise was struck giving the Senate Select Committee on Intelligence exclusive CIA oversight authorization of annual appropriations for all "intelligence activities," but preserving the Senate Committee on Armed Services' authority over "tactical foreign military intelligence activities serving no national policymaking function." Eight-year terms were adopted for the new intelligence committee so that member rotation would provide a greater number of members with exposure to intel matters.

Finally, eight members of the committees were to be selected from standing committees with related jurisdictions. To keep the new committee as bipartisan as possible, unlike other Senate standing committees, the majority party would have only a one-vote majority on the committee.

In a rapidly changing world, the committee was about to be tested.

On August 7, 1998, bombs exploded almost simultaneously outside the American embassies in Nairobi, Kenya, and Dar es Salaam, Tanzania. The carnage was devastating—224 dead, including twelve Americans, and more than 4,500 wounded. Before the smoke cleared the FBI had begun to dispatch dozens of agents into a new field. The attacks were quickly linked to a previously little-known terrorist organization called al Qaeda and headed by Usama bin Laden. The embassy bombings were a bloody warning to the nation, one punctuated by the October 12, 2000, terrorist attack on the USS *Cole* in the Yemeni port of Aden, a bomb blast that killed seventeen Americans. The events suddenly brought Africa into focus.

When I joined the committee, Democrat Dennis DeConcini of Arizona was the chairman, and Arlen Specter was the ranking member. After the 1994 election placed the Senate in Republican control, in my last year on the committee I became the vice chairman and ranking member. Richard Shelby, a Republican from Alabama, had assumed the chairmanship.

Before the 1994 Republican tidal wave, Shelby had been a Democrat and had chaired a major subcommittee of the Armed Services Committee. After being hospitalized for surgery, he had asked me as a member of the committee to serve as acting chairman. We had established a bond. Under Senators DeConcini and Specter, the staffs did not have a good working relationship. I met with Shelby and indicated I wanted two things: first, to retain the vice chairman's prerogative to appoint certain senior staff positions, and second, to appoint my own legal counsel. Shelby agreed. In return, I promised him that my appointees would work constructively with his staff. There would be no games played. We may not always agree, but I would always make him aware of any difference of opinion that I had with his recommendations.

Fortunately, as had been the case throughout my thirty-six years of public service, I had able staff assisting me. Al Cumming was cut out of the same bolt of cloth as so many of my staffers over the many years. He and I agreed on strategy and approach. He was excellent.

As the vice chairman of the Senate Intelligence Committee, I was automatically made a member of the so-called "Gang of Eight," which consisted of the House Speaker and minority leader, the chairman and vice chairman of its Intelligence Committee, and the Senate majority leader and minority leader, and chairman and vice chairman of its Intelligence Committee. Only eight people in the Congress would be privy to this highly sensitive information.

On the day I became a ranking member of the committee, a red "scramble" phone was installed in my office and home. Later that first afternoon, the phone rang in my congressional office. I assumed it was a test call to ensure I was properly connected. Following the appropriate protocol when the red phone rang, I cleared everyone out of my office. I was informed the nation's satellite system was down, but it was believed the problem was the result of a mechanical malfunction and temporary, and not related to a security breach or act of espionage.

With Africa now very much on the Intelligence Committee radar, chairman Shelby organized a fact-finding tour beginning with Egypt and including Kenya and Tanzania, Mozambique, the Island of Madagascar, South Africa, and Namibia. Much has been written about these kinds of trips called congressional delegations, or codels for short.

Unquestionably, some codels are thinly veiled boondoggles. This was a legitimate trip. The committee was focused on learning from our embassy staff with first-hand knowledge and experience. Another benefit of codels is that they provide opportunities for committee members to get to know each other personally away from the demands of constituent visits, committee hearings, and floor votes. While spending many hours in small planes, Shelby and I talked a great deal about our respective interests. Both of us had an interest in history.

At each of the embassies we visited, a "country team" meeting was held in a secure location with necessary counterintelligence measures taken to prevent any interception. The country team consists of foreign service officers with expertise in political, economic, intelligence, and other issues, and it advises the ambassador on such matters. We were briefed by the country team, which shared with us critical information on the economic conditions, the current political playing field, and other issues that would be relevant to the United States. In the larger embassies there are CIA operatives who operate with a different cover, such as political analyst or agriculture consultant.

Egypt was our first stop. For many years it had been a nation that played a precarious but pivotal role as our partner in fighting terrorism. Although no terrorist-related deaths were reported in Egypt in 1999, that September an assailant attacked and wounded President Hosni Mubarak. Hostilities from members of Egyptian Islamic Jihad and al-Gama'a al-Islamiyya were very real. And, of course, the assassination of Egyptian president Anwar Sadat on October 6, 1981, by Islamic fundamentalist army officers had shaken the foundation of a precarious Middle East peace.

Our first meeting was with President Mubarak. It was not my first meeting with him. In 1989 before the Gulf War, I had met with him as part of the delegation that George Mitchell appointed to meet with leaders in the Middle East. On this trip, it was a cordial exchange in every way. As the meeting was about to conclude, Mubarak turned to us and said, "Have you ever been to Abu Simbel?" None of us had.

Then, with tongue in cheek, he said, "I won't give you clearance to leave Egypt until you visit Abu Simbel."

There was no resistance.

For more than two thousand years the desert sands had covered an extraordinary massive temple structure carved into a solid rock cliff on the Nile River. Two temples had been constructed during the reign of Egyptian pharaoh Ramses II more than 1,200 years before Christ. It might have been lost to the sands of time had a Swiss explorer Johann Ludwig Burckhardt in 1813 not noticed a suspicious outcrop of rock that led to the rediscovery of four colossal statues of the pharaoh himself and queen Nefertari. By the time of our visit, Abu Simbel was a UNESCO World Heritage site and equally remarkable because they had been relocated from their original site on the Nile in 1964 ahead of the construction of the Aswan High Dam.

Abu Simbel was where the people and culture of sub-Saharan Africa met those of the north. Even to the untrained eye, carvings on the temple wall vividly depicted the difference in their appearance. Standing at Abu Simbel, I couldn't help but be impressed by the civilizations that had come before us.

We traveled farther into Africa, landing in Tanzania. It's the country Dr. David Livingstone set out from on his nineteenth-century search for the source of the Nile River in central Africa. His disappearance generated worldwide interest. Reporter Henry Morton Stanley secured support from James Gordon Bennett of the *New York Herald* to conduct a search for the lost explorer. After eight months, Stanley's long sojourn ended when he approached the shore of Lake Tanganyika and encountered the only white man he had seen in central Africa. He inquired, "Doctor Livingstone, I presume?"

Tanzania is rich in resources but wracked by poverty. With a per capita annual income of less than $300 in 1999, it was one of the poorest nations on the planet. In addition to creating a humanitarian crisis, it made the country a breeding ground for extremist idealogues and terrorists. Our group couldn't help but realize that America's ongoing fight against terrorism would have to transcend military might to be successful.

In Kenya, where our embassy had been bombed, similar challenges presented themselves. The country team gave us a briefing of the security measures that had been taken since that event. Severe poverty and political corruption had made recruitment for extremist causes easier. Transnational terrorist organizations, many of them Islamic, exploited the poverty and corruption.

In Kenya, we were also introduced to a member of the Leakey family, the world-famous paleontologists who for decades had argued that the origin of the human species was in Africa. Initially resisted by the scientific community, ultimately, the Leakeys persuaded the scientific skeptics that they were correct. Between briefings, a member of the embassy staff pointed out the site of the famous scene from *Out of Africa* where Meryl Streep in her role of the coffee farmer Karen Blixen (pen name Isak Dinesen), finally received the respect of her male peers at an exclusive safari club.

From Kenya we traveled to Mozambique and Madagascar before reaching South Africa. Arriving late in Cape Town, most of the group was tired after a long day. I was not. I wanted to see as much as I could.

A member of the South African secret service team that had been chosen to provide security for us had been imprisoned at wind-swept Robben Island when Nelson Mandela was there serving what would be a twenty-seven-year prison term before the collapse of apartheid. The security officer described in detail the outpouring of tens of thousands upon Mandela's release and triumphant return to Cape Town.

During our conversation, the secret service agent asked, "Would you be interested in seeing where Cecil Rhodes lived? It is now where the president of South Africa lives when he comes to Cape Town." The South African legislature meets in Cape Town. "Yes," I responded.

I knew Rhodes was the British mining baron who also had served as prime minister of the Cape Colony when it was under English rule. An imperialist explorer, Rhodes was part of a group that claimed for Britain the southern African territory named North and South Rhodesia in Rhodes' honor and later renamed Zambia and Zimbabwe, respectively.

Arriving at the old Rhodes compound, I saw a single palm perhaps thirty feet high. The security officer assigned to us asked, "Do you have any idea what that hook at the top is?"

I hadn't a clue.

"More than a hundred years ago, that's where Cecil Rhodes tethered his horse."

Rhodes was a key architect of Britain's colonial experience in Africa. Most Americans know the name Cecil Rhodes only because his legacy included endowing the Rhodes Scholarship at the University of Oxford. We headed to the Cape. To the east was the Indian Ocean. To the west was the Atlantic Ocean. The two oceans have a discernible difference in color, easily visible to the naked eye.

At the capital of South Africa, Pretoria, we received a briefing from the country team. The embassy staff joined us for a reception that night. As a student of history, I knew something about the Boer War. And I knew Winston Churchill, future prime minister of Great Britain, had been confined as a prisoner somewhere in Pretoria. I asked the staff if anyone knew about it. The initial reaction was that nobody did. Finally, a young man approached me and said, "I know what you're talking about."

"Does the building still exist?" I asked.

"It does," he replied. "It's used as a library."

Would it be possible, I asked, to visit it before our first meeting the next morning? He promised to arrange it.

When we arrived at the library early the next morning, a woman right out of central casting greeted us. She would have been identified as a librarian in any country in the world. She smiled warmly, and I tried to be gracious and thanked her for arriving early so I could see it. Then I committed a faux pas.

"I know a bit about the Boer War," I began.

And the librarian reflexively corrected me: "You mean the Anglo-Boer War."

"Oh, I do, indeed," I said, chastened despite her polite manner. I realized she was descended from the Afrikans, who were primarily Dutch settlers who arrived at the Cape of Good Hope beginning in the seventeenth century. The Afrikans and the British were the protagonists in the Boer War.

Moving through the building she showed us a large room, where, she explained, was the place captured British officers were confined. In the Victorian era, British officers were often from aristocratic families, people with money and political influence. Despite their incarceration, they had the ability to hire servants to bring fresh produce from the marketplace to the prison. They gleaned the latest war developments from those trips to the market, and upon their return they provided information to the imprisoned officers.

On one wall was a large painted map of South Africa perhaps ten feet high and thirty feet wide. Certain events were depicted. The colors were as vibrant as they had been the day that they were painted a century before.

The librarian, keeping me on my toes, inquired, "Do you know what this map depicts?"

"I do," I replied, carefully. "Those were the main battles of the Anglo-Boer War."

She smiled, just a little, at her improving student. Then she showed us where Churchill, then just twenty-five years old, jumped over the

340 Intelligence Committee in a Time of Crisis

wall and escaped on his way to the east coast of the continent and a celebrated return to England.

After a briefing in Namibia, a former German colony, we headed home. I reflected on my experience. Virtually every country had sought to erase evidence of its colonial heritage. What surprised me was that the names of principal cities and geographical regions in South Africa had not been changed. In front of the South African Parliament was a statue of Queen Victoria.

As we prepared to leave, there were several takeaways. I was impressed with members of our foreign service. Several of the countries we visited were poor, without extensive medical care. Some of our young diplomatic service personnel had families with young children. Not all these assignments could by any measure be considered coveted. They lacked the comfort and glamor of those posted in France or the Court of St. James in London. But they were dedicated and impressive young men and women.

I also benefited from getting to know Shelby and his staff on a personal basis. Unlike today, I think that camaraderie helped in making our approach to intelligence issues more collegial. We had our differences, but partisanship rarely surfaced. Oh, how we could use more of that today.

CHAPTER 38

The Clinton Impeachment

Bill Clinton's presidency had been tumultuous from the start, but by September 1998 it threatened to collapse under the weight of the growing scandal stemming from his sexual relationship with twenty-two-year-old White House intern Monica Lewinsky. Clinton initially denied the existence of the affair. Who can forget "I did not have sexual relations with that woman, Ms. Lewinsky"? Then he reluctantly admitted under oath, and later to the American people, that he had engaged in an inappropriate relationship. His greater trouble was that he had given conflicting answers in separate sworn testimony, lying about the affair in a sexual-harassment lawsuit but telling the truth before an August 17, 1998, federal grand jury.

Was that mistake in judgment enough to impeach a president and remove him from office?

The scandal erupted at a time House Republicans presiding in the majority had called upon a special prosecutor to investigate the Clintons' business dealings years earlier with an Arkansas savings and loan in what became commonly known as the Whitewater affair. The special prosecutor in that investigation, Ken Starr, was well known to me. As chairman of the Senate Ethics Committee, I had worked closely with him as a special master to review information contained in Bob Packwood's diary. Starr had given the committee everything we requested.

But the atmosphere in Washington was changing. Led by House Speaker Newt Gingrich, a new breed of Republican was sensing blood in the water, and an era of partisanship was dawning that was more extreme than I'd experienced in any time in my public life.

By September 9 Starr submitted to the House his voluminous official report of the investigation along with eighteen boxes of supporting documents. *The Starr Report* would become a bestseller and be called a "literary bodice ripper" by the *Washington Post*. It made an argument for the impeachment of Clinton on eleven grounds, including obstruction of justice, perjury, witness tampering, and an abuse of power. With their hands on the report the Republicans believed they had everything they needed. Four articles of impeachment were considered by the House on December 19. Two were rejected. When the House voted to adopt the charges of perjury and obstruction of justice, Clinton became just the second US president to be impeached.

By the next morning, negotiations began between Republicans and Democrats in the Senate that stretched through the holidays and into the new year. At one point, it appeared the two sides, with cooler heads prevailing, would negotiate a settlement and agree to forgo a full trial.

Among the House managers was Lindsey Graham, a Republican from South Carolina. The leader of the House managers, Representative Henry Hyde of Illinois, appeared to sense the fire fading. "Everything is under negotiation," he told a reporter. "All kinds of rumors are going around. Time is wasting. We need to agree on a format." When the censure negotiations failed in the stoked heat of the moment, only one course of action remained.

The Republicans had overplayed their hand, and public opinion was shifting in Clinton's favor. The real issue was whether the Senate would call witnesses.

At one point, the entire Senate met in the Old Senate Chamber to discuss how to proceed and whether witnesses would be called to appear in person. It was then that Republican Phil Gramm of Texas, a firebrand in his own right, stood and proposed a course of action for us to follow. Democrat Ted Kennedy of Massachusetts then stood and responded, as I recall, "I think we're getting to third base." The two men had precious little in common politically, but they had found a way forward. The decision was eventually made for the impeachment trial to rely on depositions and prior statements under oath rather than call witnesses.

The historic gravity of those days is difficult to overstate. On January 7, 1999, with the ghost of the 1868 impeachment trial of President Andrew Johnson haunting the Senate Chamber and Chief

Justice William Rehnquist presiding over the proceedings, we senators were sworn in as jurors in the Clinton impeachment trial.

Given two articles of impeachment to consider, it would take a two-thirds vote of the Senate to convict the president. The withering allegations contained in *The Starr Report* had been narrowed to two areas—perjury and obstruction of justice. That begged the ultimate question: is this enough to remove an elected president?

Jean Marie Neal produced a daily record of the impeachment for distribution to my staff, which was inundated with calls from constituents expressing their opinions and seeking coveted tickets to sit in the gallery for the historic event.

The trial ground on through its procedural paces the first week, after which thirteen House managers spent three days detailing their opening statement. Then it was the Clinton team's turn. Memorably, wheelchair-bound White House counsel Charles Ruff methodically responded to the House prosecutors with a finely detailed rebuttal on behalf of the president. Dale Bumpers, Arkansas's senior senator, was at his eloquent best in arguing against the conviction.

As the trial began, senators submitted questions to Rehnquist, who read them to the defense or prosecution team members.

By January 24, a judge ordered Lewinsky to cooperate with House prosecutors. Following a private, two-hour interview with House managers, her moment on the infamous stage was nearly over. She was deposed again behind closed doors. Clinton's defense team asked her no questions and expressed the president's regret in the matter.

The pressure she endured in those difficult times is hard to imagine. When I reviewed her depositions in private, one thing was clear to me. She was given many opportunities to further damage the president. It was clear she didn't want to bury him.

The impeachment commanded the full focus of the Senate. My schedule, normally overflowing with meetings, appointments, and phone calls, narrowed to that of the duties of juror. A vote to dismiss the case generated a lively debate, but I don't think anyone really expected it to succeed. The trial would continue, past the president's State of the Union address and on toward the end of January. By January 27, two motions to dismiss failed, essentially along party lines.

Then something happened that set me off. Senator Mitch McConnell, a Republican from Kentucky, went before the press and called for public hearings with witness testimony in the Clinton impeachment and compared the president's affair to the Packwood sexual misconduct investigation that had gone before the Senate Ethics Committee just a few years earlier. McConnell's statement was hypocritical and misleading, and I was compelled to call him on it.

"Senator McConnell made some statements with respect to the Packwood matter," I began as reporters settled into their seats in the gallery during a break in the hearing. "In my judgment, I'm somewhat perplexed because I do not believe that the two cases can be compared in any way."

I reminded those assembled that as a ranking member of the Ethics Committee throughout the Packwood investigation, a laborious effort resulted in a unanimous finding of facts against the embattled Oregon senator. Among the distinctions between it and the Clinton impeachment, we found that Packwood withheld, altered, and destroyed relevant evidence; many hostile witnesses volunteered to testify in public against him; and the conduct alleged against Packwood by seventeen witnesses was not consensual. The committee also found that Packwood had attempted to reduce his alimony payment, and thus enhance his personal wealth, with a scheme to get several lobbyists to hire his estranged wife.

Although the Packwood investigation operated in private for months without a leak – a rarity in Washington—the Clinton investigation had been a public spectacle from the start. Unlike the secretive Packwood investigation, the Clinton investigation had long since spilled into the public with a 60,000-page investigative file and *The Starr Report*, which went up on the internet immediately after it was handed to members of Congress.

"I believe that those distinctions make it clear that there's a very different situation that we were dealing with in Packwood, where our colleagues knew none of the information that we had," I said.

McConnell's call to arms went nowhere. By the second week of February, the time to vote approached. In all that time, I was never lobbied by the administration, not once. The protracted Starr investigation and relentless pursuit of the president had done something no lobbyist could accomplish: it had the effect of wearing down the public's interest in the case. I was not alone in concluding that even those who were opposed to the president had grown tired of hearing all the criticism.

When it came my turn to speak to my colleagues on February 12, 1999, I recognized we were writing a new page in presidential history. Like my fellow senators, I knew what we said and did would be studied as long as the republic remained.

"We are about to embark upon a roll call vote that only one other Senate in the history of our Republic has been called upon to cast," I began. "It is a weighty decision. We have taken an oath that requires us to render 'impartial justice according to the Constitution and the laws.' By doing so each of us has undertaken a solemn obligation to be fair to the president, fair to the American people, and faithful to our constitutional responsibility."

After reviewing the historical precedents, I was convinced that neither the perjury charge nor the alleged obstruction of justice rose to the legal standard that I believed was necessary to take the grave step of removing a president from office.

"The president's conduct is boorish, indefensible, even reprehensible," I said. "It does not threaten the Republic. It does not impact our national security. It does not undermine or compromise our position of unchallenged leadership in international affairs."

I then strongly suggested that after the impeachment vote, which I predicted would fail, the Senate should seriously consider voting to censure the president's conduct and send a strong message that it was a moral dereliction of his duty.

The prosecution needed a two-thirds majority and didn't come close. After five weeks, the Senate rejected the perjury charge, 55–45 with ten Republicans joining the Democrats. The obstruction charge was closer, 50–50, but still failed.

Clinton later said he was "profoundly sorry" to the American people for the suffering his behavior had caused.

CHAPTER 39

Going Home to Nevada

In the aftermath of the 1994 general election, when the Republicans gained control of both the House and the Senate, the Senate became much more partisan and polarized. It was not the institution I had joined in January 1989. Moreover, the amount of money required to seek election to the Senate had increased exponentially. Each member of the Democratic caucus was expected to spend some time each week at the Democratic Senatorial Campaign Committee headquarters to solicit contributions. It was referred to as "dialing for dollars."

I began to think that this may be the time for me to step down. Several thoughts raced through my mind. I was losing contact with longtime friends, some of whom I had known since childhood. Even though Bonnie and I came back to Nevada almost every weekend, our weekends were filled with constituent appointments and attending community events. Our friends and their lives moved on without us.

Another event in my life was that my children had married, and grandchildren were on the way. Although I was not a neglectful father, I missed much of their childhood because of my nonstop public life schedule. From evening meetings to long absences during legislative sessions, I was absent from home a lot. With grandkids on the way, I thought, perhaps I could get a mulligan. I recognized that having grandchildren would give me a last opportunity to experience some of the joys that I had missed with my own children.

Another factor played into my mind. Although I was in good health and remain in good health, my father had died at the age of fifty-two from prostate cancer. I was sixty-two, and I was aware of the passage of time.

I discussed this with Bonnie, of course. She loved her life in DC, and her preference was for me to run for reelection. As always, she was supportive of my decision. I understood where she was coming from. I thought my prospects for reelection were good, but for me the time was right to step down.

Like Alan Bible and Paul Laxalt before me, I wanted to make my announcement early so that those who sought my seat would have plenty of opportunity to make their own Senate runs. The Clinton impeachment hearings delayed that timetable.

So, within a few days after the impeachment hearings had concluded, with a tearful Bonnie at my side and joined by my brother and sister and daughter Leslie, I announced on the steps of my alma mater, Las Vegas High School, my decision not to seek reelection. The reaction was one of complete surprise. I think some of my staff must have gotten an inkling of my intention because I had postponed various campaign initiatives such as setting up a campaign headquarters and organizing the campaign structure and team. But the media was caught flatfooted. I remember calling reporter Jane Ann Morrison of the *Las Vegas Review-Journal* and telling her that she might want to get down to Las Vegas High School because I would be making a newsworthy announcement. She later told me that she could not have been more surprised.

The front-page headline in the *Review-Journal* the following day said it all: "Bryan Coming Home."

I had eleven months left in office, and there was work left to do. How many times over the years I had heard many constituents comment, "You guys come around only at election time." In my case, that was not true. After announcing my decision, I maintained the same pace, scheduling weekend appointments and spending most of the summer recess holding townhall meetings and attending traditional events in rural Nevada.

I got a measure of satisfaction when people approached me, quizzically wondering aloud, "Why are you here? You're not running for reelection."

My response was always the same: "I'm still your senator, and there's still much that remains to be done."

Even after I had announced my retirement, the constituent requests kept coming. Some were personal. One day my office received a call from a Nevada family whose son was in his fourth year at the Naval Academy but had recently been informed that he would not be able to graduate with his class due to a medical issue.

John Gibson and I were grade school friends, and I recalled him telling me about his older brother, Jim, who was in his last year at the Naval Academy. Because of Jim's failing eyesight, Naval Academy officials weren't going to allow him to graduate. The family called Pat McCarran, Nevada's senior senator at the time, requesting his help. Upon learning of the situation, McCarran informed the Naval Academy that its budget appropriation was going to be placed on hold until Midshipman Gibson's graduation was approved. In a short time, the academy relented. Gibson graduated with his class. After leaving the service, Jim Gibson served in the Nevada Legislature for four decades. By the time I was elected to the legislature in 1968, Gibson was acknowledged as the foremost legislative expert on budget issues.

Much like McCarran had done fifty years before, I placed a call to the Naval Academy. I made it clear this was an important issue for me. I was no Pat McCarran, but I was able to persuade the Naval Academy to change its position and allow the midshipman to graduate with his class.

One tradition I truly enjoyed during my twelve years in the US Senate was Academy Night. Each year one was scheduled in Northern Nevada and in Southern Nevada. Every member of the Nevada congressional delegation participated, and the responsibility for organizing the event rotated each year. Every high school student in the state who had an interest in attending a service academy was extended a letter of invitation to attend Academy Night. What made it so very special is that each of the academies was represented by a midshipman or cadet who shared their personal experiences. One of the underlying messages that each student gave was the importance of really wanting to be there. Don't go because your dad was an army colonel or your parents would think that it was a prestigious thing for the family. You have to go because you want it. Because it's not easy.

Each member of the Nevada delegation had a committee that screened academy applicants. I received many calls from parents saying, "We're Republicans. Is that going to make a difference?" My reply never varied. "Not at all," I told them. I never failed to forward a recommendation from my academy committee and had no idea of the political affiliation of the family of the applicant.

It was always a thrill to visit one of the academies and have lunch with one of my appointees. It was so impressive to see all those young men and women marching to lunch or participating in activities. Even after many years, I continue to receive calls from former midshipmen and cadets whom I had appointed. Many had successful careers in the private sector after they left the service.

More than twenty years later, Caleb Cage, one of my academy nominees, attended a meeting where I was a speaker. He brought with him my letter to him congratulating him on his appointment.

Call it a good day at Black Rock. My final legislative accomplishment in the Senate was the creation of the Black Rock Desert–High Rock Canyon National Conservation Area. It remains an accomplishment of which I have always been very proud.

Bob Griffin would have been proud, too. It was at his insistence that I see the rugged beauty and historical significance of the place for myself during my time as governor. Joining the Senate put me in position to give the area the protected designation it richly deserved. He would have loved the creation of the Black Rock Desert–High Rock Canyon as a national conservation area.

Not everyone was thrilled by the prospect. The legislation was opposed by Nevada's rural counties, and none more vociferous than the city council of Winnemucca in Humboldt County. The only support that I had for the proposed national conservation area was from Clark and Washoe Counties. It would be my swan song, and the legislation was enacted in my last year as a member of the Senate.

The legislation protected a significant part of the Applegate-Lassen Trail in the High Rock country. At the time, it was the largest national conservation area in the country. Brent Heberlee, my legislative director, made sure my bill was included in the omnibus public lands bill that was certain to be enacted. Without his skillful navigation, it is highly doubtful that my Black Rock legislation would have been included in the omnibus bill.

An irony lay ahead. The year after I had left the Senate, I received a call from one of the loudest critics of the conservation area plan, a Winnemucca city councilman whom I'd known from my university days. He had been adamantly opposed to the federal designation, but he now noticed it was boosting the economy by attracting more visitors to the area. He began by requesting, although I was no longer in the Senate, my assistance in helping to get the City of Winnemucca designated as the "Eastern Gateway to the Black Rock Desert–High Rock Canyon Conservation Area." A Winnemucca bed-and-breakfast owner who had been one of the plan's most vocal detractors revised her business brochure to include a passage that promoted her business "in the heart of Nevada's newest conservation area." As comedian Jackie Gleason used to say, "How sweet it is!"

As I reflect on my long career in public office, I am reminded of all those who came before me and of those intrepid characters who went West through the Black Rock Desert and during a pause along the way to their destiny took time to make their mark on a timeless wall in an all but nameless place. In my own way, I'd like to think that I, too, made my mark in my own life's journey.

CHAPTER 40

My Civic Rent and a Rainy Day

I was a winner of the ovarian lottery, blessed with a mother and father who taught me the values that would guide me in my journey through life. From them, I learned the importance of hard work.

As a young boy I often heard my father say, "Each of us is obligated to pay our civic rent." By that he meant finding a way to contribute to your community. I chose public service. My dream was to serve as Nevada's governor. I hope he would agree that I have paid my civic rent.

I benefited greatly from the sacrifices of the generation that preceded me. They were tested by the Great Depression and a world war that threatened democracies everywhere. Tom Brokaw called them "the Greatest Generation," and I believe they are. My generation is "the luckiest generation," coming of age at a time of American prosperity unequaled in human history.

Thomas Jefferson, near the end of his life, reportedly was asked how he would like to be remembered. And he replied, "as the author of the Declaration of Independence, the author of the Statute of Religious Freedom for Virginia, and the founder of the University of Virginia."

"What about serving as president of the United States, as governor of Virginia, and as America's first secretary of state?" he was asked. His response, "I'd rather be remembered for what I gave others rather than for what others gave to me."

I am often asked, "How would you like to be remembered?" I hope it may be said that I was an honest man who worked hard in each of the public positions I held. Although I wasn't always successful, I always tried to do the right thing.

Among those things of which I am most proud is my effort to provide opportunities for women to serve in top-level positions that they had never occupied before; enacting consumer protections at the state and federal levels; protecting Nevada's public lands for future generations; and leading the fight against Yucca Mountain.

Following my retirement announcement, I received several calls from DC law firms expressing interest in talking to me about my future. I thanked them for their interest, but I told them I meant what I had said in my retirement announcement. I was going home.

On the long drive west from Washington, I received a call from a federal agency indicating the matter on which I had requested their help had been approved. Former Senator Paul Laxalt had asked for my help on behalf of a client he represented. I called Laxalt and shared the good news. The book on my Senate career had been closed.

Home again, I interviewed with several prominent Nevada law firms. Daughter Leslie had joined the Reno office of Lionel Sawyer & Collins, then the largest law firm in the state. Sam Lionel, the lead partner in the firm, was highly respected among members of the legal profession. Bob Faiss had joined the firm and was my contact there. Salary had never been a big issue with me, and it was never mentioned with any of the firms I interviewed with. Faiss assured me that I would have the ability to select the cases I would work on. When I met with the firm's executive committee, I was informed I would be a partner and serve on the executive committee. I accepted their offer.

The siren call of public service remained deeply imbedded in my DNA. I joined several boards with the understanding that I not be asked to fundraise. Among them: the Great Basin National Park Foundation, the Las Vegas Chamber of Commerce, the Commission for the Las Vegas Centennial, the National Museum of Organized Crime and Law Enforcement (better known as the Mob Museum), Preserve Nevada, and The Smith Center for the Performing Arts. My experience as a child begging for eleven more cents to gain admission to the Huntridge Theater matinee continued to cast its spell. I also was proud to serve as an adjunct professor at UNLV and to work for many years with UNLV history professor Michael Green on Nevada Public Radio station KNPR's *Nevada Yesterdays* series.

Decades after I began my fight against burying high-level nuclear waste at Yucca Mountain, I kept my hand in the battle as chairman of the Commission on Nuclear Projects.

Bonnie and I were able to spend more time with our children and six grandchildren. Reconnecting with old friends and visiting several world-famous destinations were other pluses. Life was good for Bonnie and me.

Henry Wadsworth Longfellow's poem "The Rainy Day" contains a well-known passage, "Into each life some rain must fall / Some days must be dark and dreary." That day came for me in July 2014. As part of a routine medical exam, Bonnie was diagnosed with an incurable form of cancer and given approximately two years to live. Dr. Ed Kingsley, Bonnie's oncologist, was compassionate but candid.

With the help of the medication she was prescribed, for more than a year after her diagnosis her daily routine did not change, and we made the best of that time.

In the summer of 2016, the disease began to take its toll and she was hospitalized. Two days before our fifty-fourth anniversary, she left us. Nevada lost a great First Lady, and I lost the partner of a lifetime. She was with me every step of the journey, and I couldn't have done it without her.

During that same time, my professional life was upended. Lionel Sawyer & Collins closed its doors. Many of the partners, including my daughter Leslie, joined Fennemore Craig, and I joined them.

In April 2022, I retired from the practice of law, ending a journey that began November 20, 1963, when I was admitted to the State Bar of Nevada.

When I look back over these pages, it occurs to me that those who were anticipating a "tell-all" memoir might not have found what they were looking for. Astute readers will notice that I have declined to revisit the failings of even my political adversaries. Public life offers many benefits, but for those who enter the arena the pitfalls are also great. I'll leave it to others to take their critical measure.

Acknowledgments

As you have no doubt read by now, many people contributed to my success throughout my long political career. To name one hundred is to leave out one thousand, and I appreciate them all more than I can express. Among the many, some are obvious: my parents, my many teachers and professors, Bonnie, and my wonderful children.

District Attorney Ted Marshall of Clark County gave me my start on my political journey by appointing me as one of his deputy district attorneys. Almost thirty years earlier, then district attorney V. Gray Gubler gave my father his start by appointing him as one of his deputy district attorneys.

When the legislature authorized a public defender system, District Judge John Mowbray was my unrelenting advocate. Without his support, it would have been highly unlikely that the county commissioners would have appointed a twenty-eight-year-old lawyer just three years out of law school as Clark County's first public defender.

Where would I have been in my early political career without Bob Peccole and Dave Powell? They had no personal political agenda but only wanted to help a good friend. Jim Joyce was always there with his political advice. And I'll always cherish Jim Santini's friendship and encouragement.

In elected office and on the campaign trail, there were no better teammates and allies than Tom Baker, Joe Barry, Patty Becker, Sara Besser, Bill Bible, Paul Bible, Tracey Buckman, David Chairez, Al Cumming, Kevin Curtin, Andy Cutler, Jenny DesVaux, Jeff Eskin, Linda Faiss, Andy Grose, Tim Hay, Brent Heberlee, Bart Jacka, Kari Karwoski, Kathy Kelly, Joan Kovacs, Laurie Welch Leavitt, Marlene Lockard, Rita Meir, Jim Mulhall, Jean Marie Neal, Jan Nitz, Ray Pike, Crystal Jackson Reynolds, Steve Richer, Danelle Snodgrass, Tod Story, Larry Struve, Terry Sullivan, Andy Vermilye, Roland Westergard, Brenda Williams, Opal Winebrenner, and Kay Zunino. No list of this kind would be complete without mentioning Keith Lee.

As coordinator for several of my statewide campaigns, Keith was always available when I needed advice.

Jean Marie Neal was the glue that held my Washington office together. She was fiercely loyal and her vast experience on Capitol Hill was invaluable. Whenever a crisis confronted us, she was always there to help us resolve it.

Fortunately for me, many of these friends were able to share their own memories for this project.

During my two campaigns for attorney general, I was a sole practitioner. I would be out of my law office on the campaign trail for extended periods of time. I needed someone to cover for me. John O'Reilly, an able attorney whom I trusted, volunteered. He did a superb job and later was actively involved in my governor and senate races.

Statewide campaigns require an enormous amount of money, and by now readers surely know of my aversion to fundraising. I was fortunate to have Frank Schreck and Jim Nave leading the charge, ably assisted by Jan Nitz and Lou Gamage.

Every candidate relies on hundreds of volunteers for their success, and I was blessed to have had hundreds of tireless supporters. Amy Ayoub, Cathaerina Costa, Butch Snider, and Dave Rice gave countless hours of their time to my campaigns.

Writing a book has been a memorable and challenging experience, and I benefited from help along the way. At the Legislative Counsel Bureau, Teresa Wilt provided her professional insight into my legislative years, for which I am truly grateful. Thanks also to dedicated Las Vegas historian and longtime journalist Bob Stoldal for his friendship and insight.

Many thanks are due to my friend, UNLV history professor Michael Green. With help from the Henry L. Schuck Scholarship, he assembled a group of energetic students to assist with research for this book. They include Martha Amaya, Chase Avecilla, Khadija Bhatti, Kyleigh Brigman, Maribel Estrada Calderón, Aimee Clouse, Ariadna Perez Mendez, Brandon Monson, Mina Nguyen, Ashley Schobert, and Jenni Tifft-Ochoa.

John L. Smith would like to thank his wife, Sally Denton, family, and friends for their love, inspiration, support, and patience.

Thanks also to University of Nevada Press director JoAnne Banducci, acquisitions editor Curtis Vickers, and staffers Caddie Dufurrena and Jinni Fontana for their hard work and professionalism. A special thanks to copy editor Paul Szydelko for his sharp eye and insight.

Finally, without John L. Smith this book would not have been possible. Writing a book is not easy, as I soon found out. John helped guide me through each step of the process. He was a skillful writer and superb researcher, and as a native Nevadan brought a strong understanding of the state's history. Most of all, I appreciate his patience during our journey.

Index

Unnumbered pages after p. 246 contain illustrated matter.

About the Authors

RICHARD H. BRYAN was born in Washington, DC. He is a graduate of the University of Nevada, Reno, and served in the US Army and army reserve. Bryan earned his law degree from the University of California, Hastings College of Law. He was admitted to the Nevada Bar in 1963 and was appointed deputy district attorney in Clark County in 1964. He served as prosecutor for two years and in 1966 became Nevada's first public defender and the youngest public defender in the nation. In 1968, he became legal counsel for the Clark County Juvenile Court. The same year, he was elected to the Nevada Assembly from District 4 in Clark County and went on to serve a second term. He won election to the Nevada Senate in 1972, was reelected in 1976, serving as chair of the Taxation Committee and the Education Committee. He was elected Nevada attorney general in 1978. He was elected governor of Nevada in 1982 and reelected in 1986. During his tenure, he served as president of the Council of State Governments. He resigned as governor in 1989 after winning election to the US Senate.

JOHN L. SMITH is a freelance writer, journalist, and author of more than a dozen books, including *Saints, Sinners, and Sovereign Citizens: The Endless War over the West's Public Lands* and *The Westside Slugger: Joe Neal's Lifelong Fight for Social Justice,* both with the University of Nevada Press. A native Nevadan, he writes a weekly column for *The Nevada Independent* and is a contributor to a wide range of publications. An award-winning columnist, he was inducted into the Nevada Press Association Hall of Fame in 2016. In the same year, Smith and his colleagues were honored with the James Foley Medill Medal for Courage in Journalism, the Ancil Payne Award for Ethics in Journalism from the University of Oregon, and the Society of Professional Journalists Award for Ethics.